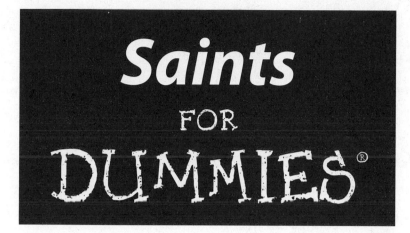

Saints

FOR

DUMMIES®

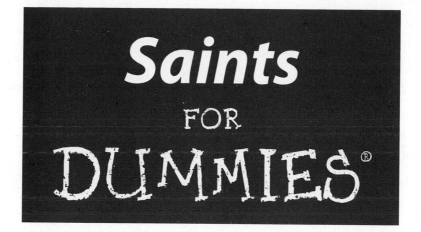

Saints
FOR
DUMMIES®

by Rev. John Trigilio, PhD, ThD,
and Rev. Kenneth Brighenti, PhD

WILEY

Wiley Publishing, Inc.

Saints For Dummies®

Published by
Wiley Publishing, Inc.
111 River St.
Hoboken, NJ 07030-5774
www.wiley.com

For general information on our other products and services, please contact our Customer Care Department within the U.S. at 877-762-2974, outside the U.S. at 317-572-3993, or fax 317-572-4002.

For technical support, please visit www.wiley.com/techsupport.

Wiley also publishes its books in a variety of electronic formats. Some content that appears in print may not be available in electronic books.

Library of Congress Control Number: 2009942435

ISBN: 978-0-470-53358-1

Manufactured in the United States of America

10 9 8 7 6 5 4 3 2 1

WILEY

About the Authors

Rev. John Trigilio, PhD, ThD: A native of Erie, Pennsylvania, Father Trigilio serves as the pastor of Our Lady of Good Counsel (Marysville, Pennsylvania) and St. Bernadette Catholic Churches (Duncannon, Pennsylvania). He is the President of the Confraternity of Catholic Clergy and Executive Editor of its quarterly journal, *Sapientia* magazine. Father Trigilio co-hosted several weekly TV series on the Eternal Word Television Network (EWTN): *Web of Faith, Council of Faith, Crash Course in Catholicism,* and *Crash Course in Pope John Paul II.* He also serves as a theological consultant and online spiritual advisor for EWTN. He has been listed in *Who's Who in America* and *Who's Who in Religion* and is a member of the Fellowship of Catholic Scholars. He was ordained a priest for the Diocese of Harrisburg (Pennsylvania) in 1988.

Rev. Kenneth Brighenti, PhD: A native of New Britain, Connecticut, Father Brighenti is an Assistant Professor and Spiritual Director at Mount Saint Mary University and Seminary in Emmitsburg, Maryland. He is the Managing Editor of *Sapientia* magazine and a member of the Board of Directors for the Confraternity of Catholic Clergy. He has co-hosted three weekly TV series on the Eternal Word Television Network (EWTN). Father Brighenti also served as a U.S. Naval Reserve Chaplain for ten years and was ordained a priest for the Diocese of Metuchen (New Jersey) in 1988. He is the author of *Marriage as Covenant* (CreateSpace), and he and Father Trigilio coauthored *The Everything Bible Book* (Adams Media), *Catholicism For Dummies, Women in the Bible For Dummies,* and *John Paul II For Dummies* (all by Wiley). Fathers Brighenti and Trigilio are also Knights of Columbus and members of the Order Sons of Italy in America (OSIA) and the National Italian American Foundation (NIAF).

Dedication

This book is dedicated:

In honor of the Blessed Virgin Mary, Queen of all saints, whose maternal intercession and guidance helped us throughout the research, writing, and editing of this project.

In honor of St. Joseph, spouse of the Virgin Mary, head of the Holy Family, and patron of the Universal Church, for his paternal protection of ourselves, our families, and our friends.

In honor of St. John Vianney, patron saint of all priests, and St. Padre Pio of Pietrelcina, whose examples of personal piety, sacerdotal sanctity, and zeal for souls constantly inspires us in our vocation.

To his holiness Pope Benedict XVI, for his saintly leadership as chief shepherd and supreme pastor of the Universal Church.

To the members of the Confraternity of Catholic Clergy, a national association of priests and deacons that seeks to foster ongoing spiritual, theological, and pastoral formation of the ordained in a fraternal environment so as to be better prepared and equipped to serve the needs of the souls entrusted to our care.

To the priests, deacons, seminarians, and faculty of Mount St. Mary Seminary in Emmitsburg, Maryland, for their dedication to forming competent, orthodox, pastoral, and reverent men to serve Holy Mother Church and the people of God.

Acknowledgments

Fathers Brighenti and Trigilio would like to express their deep appreciation and gratitude to the following persons:

Percy and Norma Brighenti (parents); Elizabeth Trigilio (mother); Priscilla Brighenti Collin (sister); Mark Trigilio (brother); Lou and Sandy Falconeri (friends); Keith and Christina Burkhart (friends); Thomas and Bridgette McKenna; Michael Drake; Rev. Fr. Robert Levis, PhD; Rev. Msgr. James Cafone; Rev. Msgr. Steven Rohlfs; Archbishop Edwin O'Brien (Baltimore); Bishop Kevin Rhoades (Harrisburg); and Bishop Paul Bootkoski (Metuchen).

We are also very grateful to Molly Rossiter, Meg Schneider, and Barb Doyen for their invaluable assistance in formatting and editing this book.

And special mention to Mother Angelica of the Poor Clare Nuns in Hanceville, Alabama, and founder of EWTN (Eternal Word Television Network), who often said on her weekly programs, "God calls us all to become great saints. Don't miss the opportunity."

Publisher's Acknowledgments

We're proud of this book; please send us your comments at http://dummies.custhelp.com. For other comments, please contact our Customer Care Department within the U.S. at 877-762-2974, outside the U.S. at 317-572-3993, or fax 317-572-4002.

Some of the people who helped bring this book to market include the following:

Acquisitions, Editorial, and Media Development

Senior Project Editor: Christina Guthrie

Acquisitions Editor: Tracy Boggier

Copy Editor: Todd Lothery

Assistant Editor: Erin Calligan Mooney

Editorial Program Coordinator: Joe Niesen

Technical Editor: Rev. Msgr. James M. Cafone

Editorial Manager: Christine Meloy Beck

Editorial Assistants: David Lutton and Jennette ElNaggar

Art Coordinator: Alicia B. South

Cover Photos: SambaPhoto/Izan Petterle

Cartoons: Rich Tennant (www.the5thwave.com)

Composition Services

Project Coordinator: Patrick Redmond

Layout and Graphics: Samantha K. Cherolis, Joyce Haughey

Proofreaders: Rebecca Denoncour, Bonnie Mikkelson

Indexer: Cheryl Duksta

Publishing and Editorial for Consumer Dummies

   Diane Graves Steele, Vice President and Publisher, Consumer Dummies

   Kristin Ferguson-Wagstaffe, Product Development Director, Consumer Dummies

   Ensley Eikenburg, Associate Publisher, Travel

   Kelly Regan, Editorial Director, Travel

Publishing for Technology Dummies

   Andy Cummings, Vice President and Publisher, Dummies Technology/General User

Composition Services

   Debbie Stailey, Director of Composition Services

Contents at a Glance

Table of Contents

Part VI: The Part of Tens..................... 257

Introduction

· ·

*A*lthough people view them with reverence and even awe, saints are simply ordinary men and women who, through their faith, overcome common weaknesses, failures, and shortcomings. And even though they're often portrayed as perfect examples of holiness, saints are sinners, just like everyone else. Mother Teresa of Calcutta — likely to be made a saint sometime soon — often said that the only difference between a saint and someone who isn't a saint is that the saint never gives up. Perseverance is the key to sainthood.

Real saints are real people. They have real struggles, real temptations, and real problems. Those who are granted sainthood become role models for the rest of us, showing that holiness and sanctity aren't for the few but are available to anyone and everyone. Saints are spiritual heroes who show us that if they can overcome their personal foibles, so can we. This book is about these real people who weren't perfect but who never quit and never gave up trying to do and to be better.

About This Book

Everyone who's in heaven is a saint, so there are far too many to count, let alone name in one book. This book doesn't try to give an exhaustive list of every saint known to man; rather, it provides brief histories of the men and women who lived faith-filled lives worthy of admiration and emulation. We're limited by the data that's available, so most of the saints we examine here are those recognized by the Catholic Church, which has the oldest, most extensive resources on this topic. Other faith traditions — Greek or Russian Orthodox, Anglican, Lutheran, and other churches — have holy men and women who are considered saints or considered to have lived saintly lives, but unlike the Catholic religion, those churches have no systematic and complete documentation on them. It's merely a matter of better record keeping, as well as the theology and doctrine of the Communion of Saints.

You don't have to be Catholic to appreciate or to be interested in the lives of the saints. Human nature is the same, regardless of what creed one professes. The stories of these brave men and women who fought temptation and persevered in their struggle to become better children of God are something anyone can appreciate.

In this book, we look at most of the popular saints and those whose existence has been verified. Saints who are missing from this book may very well exist and be in heaven, but some may have been only part of the imagination.

Part of the problem is that in the ancient church, there was no real, formal process by which one was named a saint. Some people were declared saints by unanimous consent, or acclamation, while others were named so by the local bishop or council of bishops. It wasn't until the pope took the responsibility for the process that beatification and canonization came to be properly documented.

We cover sainthood both before and after the formal process developed. Because of translation and historical inaccuracies, there may be variant spellings of certain saints' names, or dates and places of birth and death. Remember, before and even well after the invention of the printing press, a lot of church records were completed by hand — without the luxury of spell check!

Conventions Used in This Book

Following are some conventions we use that you'll want to keep in mind when reading this book:

- ✔ We use the traditional dating system of AD (*anno domini,* Latin for the "year of the Lord") instead of the more recent usage of CE (common era), because of consistency. In the original records, the AD and BC (before Christ) designations of linear time are the only ones used. This convention isn't meant to be insensitive to non-Christian readers but to be consistent with the setting in which the documents were made.

- ✔ The saints we look at in this book are those whose existence has been verified and documented. The abbreviation of the word "saint" is St. for the singular and SS. for the plural.

- ✔ Most saints of the early church, before the East-West Schism of 1054, are recognized by both Catholic and Orthodox Christians, while many of the post-Reformation (16th century) saints are typically only venerated by Catholics.

- ✔ We use *italics* for emphasis and to highlight new words or terms that we define.

- ✔ When known, we list the saint's town or country of origin on the first line below the saint's name.

- ✔ If the dates of the person's beatification and canonization are known, we include that information on the next two lines.

- ✔ We list patron information on the next line for those saints who are designated patrons of certain countries, occupations, or human conditions.

- ✔ Lastly, if the saint has a date on the Roman calendar (the liturgical celebrations for the Catholic Church around the world), we include that date on the next line before we look at his or her life in more detail.

What You're Not to Read

This book is a reference book, so you don't have to read everything. Sidebars — text enclosed in a shaded gray box — give you information that's interesting but not necessarily critical to your understanding of the chapter or section topic. You can skip them if you're pressed for time and still get the most important information. You can also skip any text marked by a Technical Stuff icon (see "Icons Used in This Book" later in this introduction for more information).

Foolish Assumptions

In writing this book, we made some assumptions about you, the reader:

- ✔ You aren't yet a saint yourself — that is, you're still among the living — but you want to know something about those men and women of faith who lived before you and who are honored for their holy lives.

- ✔ You may not be a Catholic Christian (you may be a Protestant or Evangelical Christian), but you're curious about the lives of those particular men and women who are honored and venerated as being loyal friends and servants of God.

- ✔ You may be a Catholic who remembers reading or hearing about the lives of the saints, and you want to refresh your memory or clarify some details.

- ✔ You may have no religious affiliation but you have respect and admiration for the men and women who showed courage during trial, tribulation, suffering, and persecution in defending their faith.

- ✔ You're just curious and want to know the patron saint of your occupation or homeland, or you want to know more about those saintly people who overcame the same obstacles you're battling each day.

How This Book Is Organized

This book comes in 7 parts, consisting of 22 chapters and 3 appendixes. Throughout the book, we refer you to other parts of the book to make it easy for you to get a better appreciation and understanding of a certain subject, but each part and chapter stands on its own, so you can read them in any order you like.

Part 1: In the Beginning

In this part, we look at sainthood in general, the process involved, and how it's applied specifically to certain individuals. We also examine the very first to be called saints — the apostles and disciples whom Jesus chose to start and to preach in his church.

The Catholic Church has the most saints because it's the oldest religion venerating the saints and is one of the few faith traditions to have an elaborate system to publicly declare someone a saint. This part looks at that procedure, which has been streamlined by recent popes.

Part 11: Put to the Test

Saints are holy men and women who more often than not had to endure many trials and tribulations. This part looks at those brave souls who overcame their own personal weaknesses and temptations and never gave up in their struggle for sanctity.

We also look at those who battled religious persecution and opposition, not to mention prejudice and discrimination, because of their faith, as well as those who had to contend with the natural desire to marry and have children but who, for a higher love of God, embraced a celibate life of virginity and service to the Church. Finally, we look at those exceptional and rare saints who overcame even the ravages of time and whose dead bodies remain incorrupt (undecayed).

Part 111: Living the Faith

From popes to pioneers, founding fathers to founding mothers, and noble kings to noble queens, this part looks at those pivotal saints who influenced and shaped Church history and Church life because of their position in the world or in the Church. These saints put their faith into practice and were instrumental in spreading and sustaining that same faith.

Part IV: Explaining the Faith

The learned wise men and women of this part are the saints whose love of truth and ability to defend and teach the faith preserved and promoted their beloved religion. Though not all held academic degrees, their titles of honor are based on the success they had explaining Christian theology.

Fathers, Doctors, and Pastors of the Church are looked at for their vital contribution to the establishment of Christianity — not just as a religion but also as the means to sow the seeds of faith.

Part V: Living with the Saints

In this part, you meet some of the saints-to-be — those men and women currently beatified who are awaiting the final decree of canonization from the pope, whereby they become official saints of the Catholic Church.

We also examine things associated with saints, like their relics and shrines. Relics are either parts of the saint's body or things that he or she owned, touched, wore, and so on. These artifacts are honored not for any magical reason but because that's all that's left of these holy men and women.

Part VI: The Part of Tens

If you like lists, the Part of Tens is for you. We give you ten of the most popular litanies and novenas of saints. We also give you ten places of saintly pilgrimage (shrines) and ten famous families of saints.

Part VII: Appendixes

Here we list the feast day for each saint as found on the current Roman calendar (the Catholic Church liturgical observance), as well as a list of patron saints and their particular patronage (place, occupation, or condition).

Icons Used in This Book

Icons are the fancy little pictures in the margins of this book. Here's a guide to what they look like and signify:

This icon marks interesting information that makes it easier for you to get the inside scoop on saints and saintly facts.

This icon points out ideas that sum up and reinforce the concepts we discuss. In fact, if you're short on time and can't read an entire section, go straight to this icon. Also, if you need a refresher in a chapter for any reason, you can skim through and read these to reinforce the main points.

Think of this icon as bonus material — the info it flags gives you some background about the subject that's not critical. In some cases, this information gives you the brief history of a point, or more detail than is absolutely necessary. We think the information is interesting, so we include it — but if you're in a time crunch, you can skip over it.

Where to Go from Here

You can start right in with Chapter 1 and read to the end, or you can use the table of contents and index to find just the bit of information you're looking for. If you're curious about the Apostles, turn to Chapter 3. For information on the Virgin Mary and the archangels, go to Chapter 2. Or, if you're interested in people like Mother Teresa — people who've been beatified but aren't yet official saints — check out Chapter 18.

The great thing about this book is that order doesn't matter. In most chapters, the saints are listed alphabetically (in a few chapters, chronological listing makes more sense, and we clarify that in each of the chapters), and the chapters are arranged by broad categories. You can read any chapter or any part of a chapter that interests you, or you can read the entire book from cover to cover.

For more in-depth study, we recommend Fr. Alban Butler's *Lives of the Saints* in multi-volume and single-volume editions. He did a tremendous amount of research and study on almost every saint the Church recognizes.

Part I
In the Beginning

The 5th Wave   By Rich Tennant

@RICHTENNANT

"Her devotion, faith, and miracles all qualify
her for consideration to sainthood. Still, one
wonders how she'd react to a long weekend
babysitting the Fitzgibbon boys and their
Irish wolfhound."

In this part . . .

We can't really expect you to understand the saints until we explain what sainthood is and how it all comes together. In this part, we discuss the idea of sainthood, its qualities and characteristics, and the criteria the Church uses to determine whether someone is qualified to be named a saint. Anyone who makes it to heaven is a saint, but the true "official" saints are those of whom the Church has said: That man or woman lived a holy life worth imitating.

Saints are considered friends of God who were his faithful servants while alive on earth. This part looks at some of the first Christian saints of history — the Apostles and the Evangelists. We also include the most famous and beloved of all the saints, the Virgin Mary, and we briefly examine the mysterious spiritual beings who live with the saints in heaven — the angels.

Chapter 1

Understanding Sainthood

*I*n this chapter, we discuss the idea of sainthood in general, especially how the Catholic Church understands the notion of holiness in its members. We take you through the canonization process and explain how it has evolved over the centuries. We explain how saints are venerated, and we discuss the unique role patron saints can play in your spiritual life. Finally, we examine the reasons for pursuing a saintly life and the means to achieve it.

Ordinary Saints versus Official Saints

In the Catholic Church, anyone who goes to heaven is considered a *saint.* Those who make it to heaven but are never canonized are still as saintly as those named so by the pope; in fact, the unnamed and unnumbered saints in heaven are in the majority, and God alone knows who they are and how numerous. These ordinary saints lived normal lives but did so with faith in and love for the Lord. Official *saints,* on the other hand, are men and women who lived lives worthy of recognition, honor, and imitation.

The Catholic Church has never taught that a person has to be perfect or sinless to get to heaven. In fact, it teaches that every man and woman who has been born since Adam and Eve (except for the Virgin Mary, by a special divine grace from God) suffers from the effects of original sin. This means that all of us are sinners and need forgiveness. The saints were all human, with their own vulnerabilities, but by the grace of God they were able to overcome their shortcomings. They lived holy lives, even with their quirks and weaknesses, proving that others can do it, too. To be named a saint (a decision reserved for the pope), candidates are *canonized,* or formally authenticated through an intense study of the person's life. Everything that's known about a candidate — his words, deeds, and writings — comes under close scrutiny. If the details of the candidate's life are determined worthy of formal sainthood, the facts and evidence are presented to the pope for approval. No one becomes a saint until the pope says it's so.

Official sainthood isn't merely an honor for the saints themselves. The saints serve as examples for the faithful who struggle to reconcile their human natures with their spiritual aspirations.

The following sections explore the making of a saint, from the initial nomination process and early examinations, to everything the Church must consider and the events that must take place after the candidate's death.

The Canonization Process Then and Now

As we mention in the previous section, any declaration of sainthood must come from the pope. That's true now, but it wasn't always so. Before the 12th century, the local bishop was the one who canonized saints — either on his own or in a council or synod of bishops. In very early and ancient times, saints were declared by *acclamation,* or unanimous consent of the people. If a popular holy person died, usually a martyr, the diocese where he or she lived and died eagerly pushed for sainthood.

But dying for the faith wasn't the only way of sanctity and holiness. Living a good and holy life — even if it didn't end in martyrdom — meant something, too.

The question arose, then: Who gets to be declared a saint? In this section, we look at the development of the formal process by which someone is declared (canonized) a saint.

Centralizing the process with Pope Alexander III

Pope Alexander III was the first to rein in the canonization process. In the late 12th century, he made canonization the exclusive province of the papacy, and he and his successors established elaborate processes and regulations to make sure that every candidate met uniform eligibility guidelines. The result was something very much like a trial. Each investigation involved a promoter for the saint-to-be (sort of a defense attorney) and an opposing side (the equivalent of a prosecuting attorney), called the *devil's advocate,* whose job was to expose any heresies in the candidate's writings or sermons, and/ or any immoral behavior in the candidate's life.

For the next 800 years, those who wanted to advocate a particular person for sainthood had to follow a time-consuming path. First was *beatification,* a formal decision that a person can be called "Blessed." Beatification involved a canonical trial with advocates and judges. Those who knew the candidate or witnessed postmortem miracles testified, and the candidate's writings and teachings were examined and entered into evidence. All this took place in Rome, because one of the regulations that came from Alexander's centralization policies was that all such trials be held at the Vatican.

Oh, yes, there was also a 50-year waiting period between a person's death and the earliest date he or she could be considered for sainthood. The purpose of the waiting period was to allow time for emotions to settle, thus reducing the number of grief-induced petitions for sainthood. Fifty years was considered the length of time for one generation to disappear.

Revamping the process with Pope John Paul II

In 1983, Pope John Paul II made major changes to the canonization process. For one thing, he reduced the waiting period from 50 years to 5 years, in large part because, after 50 years, finding witnesses who knew the candidate personally can be difficult.

The pope has the authority to reduce or waive this waiting period; in fact, John Paul waived it himself in the case of Mother Teresa (see Chapter 18).

John Paul II also replaced the trial process with a more scholarly, document-oriented approach. Officials still gather the candidate's writings and facts about the candidate's life, but the contentious roles of the devil's advocate and the trial setting are gone (see the upcoming section "Examining lives and allowing for human nature"). And he returned much of the process to the authority of the local diocese; local bishops and dioceses now do much of the preparatory work and the first phase of research, as they're the ones on location where the proposed saint lived and worked.

When a bishop accepts a case for review, the candidate is called a "Servant of God," until a decision is made to send the case on. When that occurs, the proposed saint is considered Venerable, and research focuses on proof of a miracle connected with the candidate (see the "Confirming miracles" section later in this chapter). After a bona fide miracle is established, Rome decides whether the person can be called "Blessed" and formally beatified.

The next phase is one of waiting for another miracle and the documentation on it. Not all beatifications continue to canonization, but as long as a verifiable second miracle exists, there is hope.

Pope John Paul II reserved all beatification ceremonies to himself, but Pope Benedict XVI has restored the ancient practice of allowing other bishops to beatify their local candidates for sainthood. Benedict still has final say on elevating a "Blessed" to "Saint."

If sufficient evidence exists, and if the pope decides to canonize someone, the feast day is typically the day he or she died. This is considered the saint's "heavenly birthday." Some saints die on a day already taken in the universal calendar, so their feast day is designated on the closest open day to their actual date of death.

Examining lives and allowing for human nature

When people are proposed as possible saints, their lives — their actions and words — are closely examined. No one looks for perfection — just for reassurance that the person in question didn't lead a notorious or scandalous life. Catholic authorities scrutinize the candidate's speeches, sermons, books, and other writings to make sure that they contain nothing contradicting defined doctrines or dogmas.

Still saints, just no feast days

Some saints, like St. Christopher and St. Valentine, have been removed from the Roman calendar, but that doesn't mean that they were defrocked of their sainthood. Saints for whom there isn't enough evidence to establish the date and place of death are considered saints, but their traditional feast days may be given officially to someone whose departure from this world can be verified.

So, for example, February 14 was traditionally St. Valentine's Day and still is. However, there are no records unequivocally establishing the actual day of his death, and even the precise year is unknown. (We don't even know what century some saints lived in.) On the other hand, we have proof that SS. Cyril and Methodius died on February 14. So Valentine's Day is the official feast day for St. Cyril and St. Methodius.

What happened to St. Valentine and St. Christopher? They're still in heaven; they're just not on the liturgical calendar, that's all. Other saints went from the universal calendar to the local or regional feast calendar.

If the candidate's words and deeds pass muster, examiners then search for _heroic virtue_ — the desire and effort to seriously pursue a life of holiness.

Saints are human, and as such, they make mistakes. They're not angels, they don't have wings or halos, and they don't glow in the dark. Saints are simply sinners who never gave up trying to do and to be better.

Confirming miracles

The definition of an _accepted miracle_ varies almost as widely as those proposed for sainthood. Traditional miracles involve unexpected healing that's immediate and complete, as well as inexplicable to modern science.

Other miracles can be used as corroborative evidence, such as

- **Incorruptibility:** A phenomenon in which the dead person's body doesn't decay, no matter how many years have elapsed since death. Only non-embalmed bodies are considered for evidence of incorruptibility.

- **The odor of sanctity:** A sweet smell of roses exuding from the dead body, despite rigor mortis and the number of years since death. Again, only non-embalmed bodies are considered for this miracle.

- **Signs of stigmata:** Marks resembling one or more of the five wounds Christ suffered upon crucifixion, present only while the person was alive.

- **Bilocation:** Being in two places at the same time. Because this only happens before death, while the saint candidate is still alive, only the most reliable testimony from unimpeachable witnesses can be used. _Levitation_ also can be used as evidence.

Intercession (Patron Saints)

You have mediators and intercessors in your lives every day; you just don't call them "mediator" and "intercessor." Sometimes you call them "doctor" and "nurse," or "store manager" and "clerk." The intercessor is the person you turn to in order to seek help from someone higher up: The nurse relays your information to the doctor; the clerk relays requests or concerns to the store manager.

That's how it is with God and saints. Jesus is the mediator in our lives, the one who can speak on behalf of an entire group and who has the authority to negotiate, make agreements or treaties, and represent both parties. The saints are those who make requests to the one and only mediator on behalf of someone else. Their role is optional — not everyone turns to an intercessor, or saint, to address God.

Patron saints serve as intercessors for particular areas. For example, St. Lucy was a martyr in the ancient Church who died a horrible death when her Roman persecutors gouged out her eyeballs (see Chapter 6). She is invoked as the patron saint for ailments of the eye.

Just as the living on earth can and do pray for others (intercession), the saints in heaven can and do pray for the living here on earth. In both cases, the intercessor prays to the one mediator on behalf of someone else. The Catholic Church sees the intercession of the saints as one big prayer chain in the sky.

Venerating the Saints

Just because saints have their own days on the Church calendar doesn't mean they're to be worshipped — that's held for God alone. Rather, saints are worthy of public honor or veneration, called *dulia* in Latin. Holy men and women in heaven deserve honor just as our nation honors those who died defending our country.

Statues, icons, and images of the saints are not to be considered idols (a claim some have used to criticize Catholicism, citing one of the Ten Commandments warning against worshipping false idols). Again, the proper analogy is not worship but honor. Memorials such as statues of George Washington, Thomas Jefferson, and Abraham Lincoln are public and government-supported ways to honor brave heroes who either died in service of their nation or who spent a good portion of their lives in service to it. The same type of honor exists within the Church. Statues, icons, and images of the saints are memorials meant to remind us of the courage and piety of these holy men and women.

Do you have a picture of a deceased loved one in your wallet or hanging on the wall at home? Those images aren't idols. The pictures of saints displayed in church or in homes are the same thing: a visible reminder of someone you honor and appreciate.

Canonized saints not only have a feast day but also can have churches named after them, such as St. Bernadette's Church or the Church of St. Ann. The building is still a house of God and place of divine worship, yet the place is dedicated to the intercession (see the next section) of this particular saint. Schools (elementary, high school, college, and university), too, can be named after canonized saints to honor their legacy of faith.

Following the Saints' Examples

By canonizing many new saints, Pope John Paul showed the world that sanctity and holiness don't belong to a clerical minority. Heaven is open to anyone who wants it and is willing to live a good and holy life.

Sainthood is a multi-step process, both in life and after death. In life, achieving holiness may involve a one-time decision to accept God, but that decision must be followed by a lifetime of living according to that decision. Martyrdom — dying in the name of faith — is a one-time act, but making such a strong commitment requires a lifetime of working toward being a true and faithful servant of God.

Sainthood is a reminder that perseverance and dedication to one's faith can bring us to our goals. As Blessed Mother Teresa of Calcutta often said, "God does not call us to be successful; he calls us to be faithful." We know we aren't perfect and, save for the grace of God, won't be; as such, we should stop trying to reach for that which is out of our grasp. Instead of trying to be perfect, we are called to be faithful in our efforts to do and be better.

Sainthood is also a reminder that even the most hardened sinner isn't without help or hope. Through God's grace, anyone can turn his life around and return to the faithful.

In this section, we look at the moral, everyday life of the hopeful saint-to-be. Because the saints are normal human beings, they have the same wounded human nature all men and women are born with, thanks to original sin. And because they have the same moral weaknesses we all do, their ability to overcome them by God's grace is also available to everyone else.

Setting a moral and ethical foundation with the four cardinal virtues

St. Thomas Aquinas, a brilliant theologian of the 13th century, taught that "grace builds upon nature." This means that before anyone can hope to live a holy life worthy of sainthood (being in heaven), he or she must have a solid moral and ethical foundation upon which the life of grace is built. Being a holy or saintly person is no accident. You must intend and want to be holy. One must first pursue goodness before holiness. The former lays the groundwork for the latter.

The moral or cardinal virtues have been known and discussed since antiquity. Socrates, Plato, Aristotle, Cicero, and the Stoics, just to name a few, were philosophers who lived centuries before Christ and who were Greek or

Roman pagans. They had no revealed religion like the Jews and Christians. But they had the use of human reason and saw that there were four cardinal (from the Latin word *cardo,* meaning "hinge" — that is, the hinges to a good moral life) virtues. The ancient philosophers realized that prudence, justice, fortitude, and temperance were the underpinnings of an ethical life and would bring peace and happiness to the individual person and to the community and society at large. Faith complements reason, so religion continues the process by adding to the cardinal or moral virtues the three theological virtues of faith, hope, and love.

The moral (cardinal) virtues can and ought to be practiced by anyone and everyone. They're good for you and help you to be and to do good, as each one is considered a habit you must acquire through effort and practice. The theological virtues come via divine grace through the sacraments, especially Baptism, which is the gateway to the other sacraments (Penance, Eucharist, Confirmation, Matrimony, Holy Orders, and Anointing of the Sick).

To be considered holy, one must first seek a life of virtue — a life guided by the four cardinal virtues of prudence, justice, fortitude, and temperance. As with any life change, each of these virtues must be practiced often before it becomes an ingrained habit.

The following sections give a closer look at each of the cardinal virtues.

Prudence

The premiere of all virtues, prudence is the ability to make good decisions and to have the ability to practice tact — knowing when, where, and how something is appropriate. You wouldn't ask a friend to repay a debt at the friend's mother's funeral. In the same vein, prudence is knowing how to approach a delicate situation with sensitivity and charity.

St. Thomas More (16th century) was a most prudent man. As Lord Chancellor of England and a wealthy nobleman, Thomas always weighed his words and deeds before he said or did them. Some may have called him cautious, but prudent best summarizes his life as a Catholic layman. During his conflict with King Henry VIII, Thomas prudently kept quiet when needed and spoke eloquently and boldly when needed as well. Never rash or impetuous, Thomas prayed and gave deliberation to every aspect of his political, social, and private life. Being wise in knowing the right time and place and the right word and action is what prudence is about.

Justice

Justice is doing the right thing for the right reason; *quid pro quo* (this for that), the Romans used to say. There are three kinds of justice: commutative, distributive, and social, each defined by the people involved.

✔ Commutative justice involves just two parties: the buyer and seller, teacher and student, neighbor and neighbor. It involves equity and fairness between the two parties.

✔ Distributive justice is the balance between the individual and the group, such as between a resident and a government, or a union member and the union. A resident pays taxes and votes in elections; in return, the government provides for safety and well-being.

✔ Social justice is the responsibility everyone has to preserve natural resources for future generations and look out for one another. When one government oppresses its people, for example, social justice drives other governments and citizens to stand up in defense of the oppressed.

St. Joseph (first century) is literally called a "just" man in the Gospel, and he epitomizes the virtue of justice. He knew what was the right thing to do, and he sought to be fair at all times. His protection of his wife Mary and her son Jesus was motivated out of love, to be sure, but it was his practice of justice that enabled him to be the husband and foster father he needed to be for his family. Being fair to everyone and doing the right thing — and not for reward or recognition — is what justice is all about.

Fortitude

Everyone has been in the position of wanting or needing to do or say something that's necessary, although not easy. Fortitude is having the courage to do or say it anyway.

Blessed Teresa of Calcutta (20th century) is certainly the poster child for fortitude and courage. She was unflinching in her determination to do what had to be done and to say what had to be said, no matter how powerful her opponents. Whether it was helping the poorest of the poor or defending the lives of the unborn in the womb, this little Albanian nun became very familiar with the virtue of fortitude, and hence, she never gave up and never quit. She spoke with charity and kindness but also with firmness of conviction — to leaders of the First, Second, and Third Worlds; the UN; Congress and the White House. Having the guts to do the job (God's will, that is) and not be influenced by ambition or fear is what fortitude is about.

Temperance

Temperance is knowing when enough is enough. Temperate people set limits on their own legitimate pleasures and activities. You may allow yourself a glass of wine, for example, but temperance keeps you from overindulging.

St. Josemaria Escriva (20th century) was a very temperate man. He practiced moderation in his work and in his play (leisure and recreation). No party pooper, Josemaria would enjoy parties and responsibly partake of alcoholic beverages, such as wine. But he knew there had to be limits, and he didn't overindulge. He balanced work with rest. Temperance taught him the value of moderation in pleasures so as not to abuse himself or others. Josemaria also practiced some self-denial called mortification, but again in moderate ways so as not to incur injury or harm. A healthy balance is what temperance is about.

Building on moral virtues with the theological virtues

The road to sainthood involves not only the moral virtues but also the *theological* virtues. These virtues are bestowed at Baptism but can be enhanced throughout one's lifetime. Baptism remits original sin and makes a person an adopted "child of God." Sanctifying grace is given at Baptism, which makes a person holy and thus able to enter the holiness of heaven. Along with sanctifying grace, Baptism also makes the soul pliable and ready for actual grace, which is the supernatural gift from God that enables you to do holy things (like pray, forgive your enemies, endure hardships, make sacrifices for others, have courage in the midst of difficulties, and so on).

Following are the theological virtues:

- **Faith** is believing what God says simply because it comes from God.

- **Hope** is trusting in promises that God has yet to fulfill, knowing that those promises one day will come to fruition, at a time and place that is right for God.

- **Love**, theologically, is a spiritual love, wanting what is best for someone else, putting others above one's self. It's not a sexual love or a biological love; it's seeking to love God and to love your neighbor.

The theological virtues build on what the moral, cardinal virtues hopefully establish as a foundation. Faith, hope, and love empower you to believe what God has revealed, to trust in his mercy and providence, to love God with your whole heart and soul, and to love your neighbor as yourself. The daily struggle to live a holy life is made possible by the theological virtues. Hence, people want and need more faith, more hope, and more love every day of their lives until they finally get to heaven, where there is the fullness of grace and the total joy without end.

Sainthood begins with virtue and ends in holiness. It's a lifelong process — there's never a time when a person can stop being prudent, just, temperate, or courageous. In the same way, faith, hope, and love are never fully realized until we get to heaven, but God gives us little morsels to savor along the way.

Chapter 2

Angels and the Blessed Virgin

. . . .

. . . .

Saints are human souls living in heaven. They're considered friends of God and deserve respect and honor because of their fidelity. Of all the saints in heaven, the highest honor is given to the Virgin Mary, the Mother of Jesus Christ. She's not only the biological Mother of the Savior but also his most faithful disciple. Mary always put the will of God before her own, and she even says in the Gospel of John, "Do whatever [my son] tells you."

As saints warrant honor and veneration (but never adoration or worship), Catholics and the Eastern Orthodox Church give the Blessed Mother the highest type of honor, though they stop short of crossing the line into adoration (because worshiping Mary would be idolatry). She is given the utmost respect because of her special relationship with Jesus.

The angels are second only to Mary in terms of their dignity. Both are creatures made by God. Though angels are far superior to human beings in terms of intelligence and power, the Virgin Mary outranks them because of her unique position as the Mother of Christ.

Three angelic beings are named in the Bible and a few more in the apocryphal Scriptures. In this chapter, we examine them and the special woman chosen to be the Mother of the Messiah, the Virgin Mary.

Understanding Angels (And Why Some Angels Are Considered Saints)

Contrary to popular belief, angels aren't people who've died and gone to heaven and then earned their wings. *Angels* are spirits that God created before he made human beings; they were the first creatures ever created and were the most powerful, most intelligent, and most beautiful. Angels are pure spirits in that they have no bodies — only intellect and will. Men and women — from Adam and Eve to today — are body *and* soul, both material and spiritual.

People who die and go to heaven don't become angels — they become saints. Angels and saints are two separate beings, separate species. Confusion arises when, on occasion, some angels are given the title *saint,* which is typically reserved for humans. The overlap is merely a matter of semantics: The Latin word for saint is *sancta,* which means holy. Once in heaven — saint or angel — one is automatically holy.

It can be confusing, but look at it this way: Angels are spirits in heaven, and saints are human beings in heaven. Angels can be called "saint" (as in the case of St. Michael the Archangel) as a sign of respect and honor. A human being is called "saint" only after death and once in heaven.

Christianity believes that angels and demons (fallen angels) are separated according to their loyalty and obedience to God. The first angels were tested on their loyalty and obedience, and those who failed, like Lucifer, were cast into hell. In hell, the angels became demons with Lucifer (whose name means *bearer of light*), who later became known as the devil (also called the *prince of darkness*).

Kicked out of heaven?

Many talk about the devil and his fellow fallen angels being kicked out of heaven and thrown into hell by St. Michael the Archangel, but that theory goes against the Christian belief, "Once in heaven, always in heaven." The Bible speaks about a war in heaven (Revelation 12:7) where St. Michael defeats the dragon and one-third of the angels fall with him (Revelation 12:4), but this book of the Bible is *apocalyptic,* meaning that the sacred author used lots of allegory and metaphor in writing it.

Theologians explain that the angels were created and tested before they entered heaven, because entry into the kingdom was the reward for passing the test. After you're inside heaven, you can't leave because you can't be tempted. Heaven is seeing God face to face, and after you see pure truth and experience pure love and goodness, you want nothing else. Outside of heaven, however, angels and men can be tempted. Therefore, just as Adam and Eve were tested in the Garden of Eden (but not yet in heaven), so, too, the angels were somehow tested and the good ones (about two-thirds) were allowed into heaven, while the bad ones who failed were cast into hell.

The Bible names only three specific angels — Michael, Gabriel, and Raphael. *Apocryphal* books (texts that aren't considered authoritative on Sacred Scripture) mention others, such as Uriel and Ramiel. Because these others aren't named in the canonical books of the Bible, their identities aren't considered reliable or above reproach. The three biblical archangels are treated as true angelic beings.

Scholars have speculated for centuries on the number of angels. St. Thomas Aquinas — often called the *angelic doctor* (see Chapter 13) — believed that the precise number of angels was beyond human comprehension. Some things, however, are known, such as the fact that angels are separated into nine subdivisions, or choirs.

The nine subdivisions, from greatest to least, are

- Seraphim
- Cherubim
- Thrones
- Dominions
- Virtues
- Powers
- Principalities
- Archangels
- Angels

St. Michael the Archangel

Patron: police officers, the military

Feast day: September 29

Michael means "who is like God?" — a fitting name for one whose mission is to battle the egos of others and remind them that no one is like God. St. Michael is the only angel mentioned in both the Old Testament (Hebrew Scriptures) and New Testament. Daniel 10:13, 21 describes him as the prince of the angels and a protector of Israel. The Epistle of Jude and the Book of Revelation also mention Michael as the one who victoriously battles the devil. He is invoked anytime there is suspicion of demonic or diabolical activity. The prayer to St. Michael is used on such occasions and also was prayed after every Mass in the Catholic rite from 1886 (by Pope Leo XIII) to 1964, when Pope Paul VI dropped it. The prayer to St. Michael is:

St. Michael, Archangel, defend us in battle. Be our protection against the wickedness and snares of the devil. May God rebuke him, we humbly pray. And do thou, prince of the heavenly host, by the power of God, thrust into hell Satan and all the other evil spirits who prowl about the world for the ruin of souls. Amen.

St. Michael is typically depicted in military armor (see Figure 2-1), thrusting a sword or spear into a dragon. The Sanctuary of Monte Sant'Angelo sul Gargano in Apulia, Italy, is the oldest shrine in Western Europe dedicated to St. Michael. Pious tradition holds that the archangel appeared there four times in a 1,000-year period. Pilgrims of St. Padre Pio of Pietrelcina often visit, as St. Pio had a strong devotion to the place and to St. Michael. Also, St. Joan of Arc had visions of St. Michael (accompanied by St. Catherine of Alexandria and St. Margaret) in the 15th century.

Figure 2-1:
St. Michael
the
Archangel.

© National Gallery, London/Art
Resource, NY

Although he's called *archangel,* St. Michael is most likely a member of the seraphim, the highest rank of angels, whose mission is to praise God day and night. Any angel above the rank angel can be called archangel out of respect.

St. Gabriel the Archangel

Patron: messengers, journalists, and communications

Feast day: September 29

St. Gabriel is probably most widely recognized as the angel who comes to Mary and tells her she's carrying the Christ child. He also appears to Zachariah to inform him that his wife Elizabeth — the Virgin Mary's cousin — will give birth to a son, John (the Baptist).

The name *Gabriel* means *strength of God.* Images of St. Gabriel often depict him with a herald's trumpet, as he was the divine messenger to the Virgin Mary.

St. Raphael the Archangel

Patron: travelers

Feast day: September 29

Raphael means *healing of God.* This angel appears in the Book of Tobit, where he is sent by God to help three people: Tobit, his son Tobiah, and his future daughter-in-law Sarah. Sarah had been cursed by the demon Asmodeus so that her husband died on their wedding night before they consummated the marriage, leaving her without offspring.

Widows without children were considered the most desperate and pathetic of society, because in ancient times, women literally depended on their husbands and sons to care for and protect them. Without either husband or children, a widow was as vulnerable as an orphan. For Sarah, the situation was even more tragic: Before she married Tobiah, she had had seven previous husbands, and all of them died on their wedding night.

Tobit, a wealthy and devout Jew, lived among the captives being deported to Nineveh from the northern kingdom of Israel in 721 BC. According to Jewish tradition, Jews are required to bury their dead, especially the Hebrew victims of King Sennacherib of Assyria. The burial rite was against the law, however, as Hebrew captives had no civil rights whatsoever.

One night, after burying a fellow Israelite, Tobit slept outside his bedroom and was blinded by droppings left by birds. In those times, blindness was as much a tragedy as being a widow or orphan. Raphael was sent to help restore sight to Tobit, to end the curse of Sarah, and to unite Sarah and Tobiah as husband and wife. During his visit, he appeared in human form, and only when he was about to return to heaven did Raphael reveal his true identity. Because of his time accompanying young Tobiah on a journey, St. Raphael is invoked as the patron of travelers, especially those on a pilgrimage.

Knowing other angels

While Catholicism only publicly acknowledges St. Michael, St. Gabriel, and St. Raphael, Eastern Orthodox Christians (like the Russian Orthodox and Greek Orthodox churches) also recognize the following angels:

✔ *Uriel,* whose name means *Fire of God* (III Esdras 3:1, 5:20)

✔ *Shealtiel,* whose name means *Intercessor of God* (III Esdras 5:16)

✔ *Jehudiel,* whose name means *Glorifier of God*

✔ *Barachiel,* whose name means *Blessing of God*

✔ *Jeremiel,* whose name means *God's exaltation* (III Ezra 4:36)

Tobit is one of the seven books of the Old Testament that are in the Catholic and Eastern Orthodox Bibles but are missing in the Protestant Bibles, or sometimes placed at the back of the book in a section called *Apocrypha* (other writings). Catholicism calls these books *deuterocanonical,* which means from a second (*deutero* in Greek) *canon* (authorized list). The first 39 books are from the first canon and were written originally in Hebrew before the Babylonian Captivity (586 BC), when two-thirds of the Jews were exiled from the southern kingdom of Judah. (The northern kingdom of Israel had been conquered by Assyria in 720 BC.) The seven books of the Deuterocanon (or Apocrypha in Protestant theology) are Baruch, Maccabees I and II, Tobit, Judith, Ecclesiasticus (Sirach), and Wisdom. They were written in Greek during the captivity and were included in the Septuagint (the first Greek translation of the entire Hebrew Bible/Christian Old Testament), written in 250–150 BC.

The Blessed Virgin Mary

As the Mother of the Son of God, the Virgin Mary is the highest of all saints and deserving of the highest praise possible.

None of the saints can be *worshiped* — that's an honor reserved for God alone. Theologians call the honor given to saints *dulia* to distinguish it from *latria,* the worship of God. The honor given to Mary is called *hyperdulia* because it's the highest form allowed and required.

Beatified or canonized?

The Virgin Mary is called the *Blessed Virgin Mary* or the *Blessed Mother,* yet she's considered queen of all the saints. Deceased people get the title *Blessed* when they're officially beatified, and the last step is to be formally canonized, at which time the title *Saint* precedes their proper name. Does this mean that Jesus's mother is only beatified and not yet a saint? No. The title *Blessed* in Mary's case is unique because of what is said in the Gospel of St. Luke, when Mary says, "All generations shall call me 'blessed'" (1:48), just as St. Bede of England is still referred to as *Venerable Bede.* He has been beatified and canonized, so he is a saint, but people became accustomed to always calling him Venerable Bede, and so the name stuck. Likewise, to differentiate Mary from the other saints, outside the Anglican use of St. Mary, Catholicism normally refers to her as Blessed Virgin Mary, or *BVM* for short. So, no need to worry that Our Lady got busted down a rank or something like that.

Mary, Joseph, and baby Jesus

The story of Mary is one of the most repeated stories of the Bible. She had been engaged to be married to Joseph of Nazareth for some time as a young girl. Before the wedding, however, the angel Gabriel appeared to her and announced that she was to give birth to the *Messiah* (Hebrew word for anointed one), also called the *Christ* (from the Greek word for anointed one, *Kristos*).

Mary, a virgin and engaged to be married, was confused — how could she become the Mother of the Savior? Gabriel tells her that through the power of the Holy Spirit, she'll become pregnant with Jesus without the biological cooperation of any human male. It will literally be a virgin birth. This miraculous beginning of Jesus is foretold in the Old Testament prophecy of Isaiah 7:14 that a virgin shall conceive and bear a son.

Joseph, knowing he isn't the biological father but initially ignorant of the divine origin of Mary's pregnancy, plans to divorce her quietly. Gabriel then appears to him in a dream and tells him that Mary has indeed been faithful but is with child by the power of the Holy Spirit. Joseph awakes and takes Mary into his home. When she is about to give birth, the Roman Emperor Caesar Augustus issues a decree for a universal census, making Mary and Joseph travel to their ancestral hometown of Bethlehem, where her baby, Jesus, is born.

The family is forced to flee to Egypt after Jesus's birth, when King Herod tries to kill the baby Jesus in an attempt to thwart the prophecy. Herod orders all firstborn males age 2 and under to be slaughtered; Jesus only escaped because his mother and her husband hid in Egypt until the death of their enemy.

Back in Nazareth, Mary and Joseph raised Jesus in a normal home setting, and Jesus became known as a carpenter's son. (See Figure 2-2 for a depiction of the Holy Family.) Jesus lived with Mary and Joseph for 30 years before he began his public ministry. That ministry continued for three years until his Crucifixion, death, and Resurrection in AD 33.

Figure 2-2:
The Holy
Family
of Mary,
Joseph, and
Jesus.

Réunion des Musées Nationaux/Art Resource, NY

Other key references to Mary in the Bible

Mary is mentioned in the Gospel in the beginning of Jesus's life, from his conception at the Annunciation (when Gabriel tells Mary she's to become the mother of the Messiah) to the Nativity (Christmas Day, when Jesus is born) of Christ, and also at other key moments.

Meeting the Magi

Shortly after Jesus's birth and before the family flees into Egypt, Mary encounters the Magi, or three wise men, who bring gifts to the Christ child (this event is called the Epiphany). One brings a gift of gold, to represent the kingship of Christ; one brings frankincense, to represent the divinity of Christ; and the third brings myrrh, to represent the human mortality of Christ (Matthew 2:1–11).

Seeing the future

On the eighth day after his birth, Jesus was to be circumcised according to Mosaic law, and Mary and Joseph take the child to the Temple in Jerusalem, where he is also presented for a blessing. While there, the family meets Simeon, an old holy man who has been promised by God that he won't die until his eyes see the Messiah. Simeon prophesies that Mary will be pierced by a sword of sorrow as her son will be the rise and fall of many in Israel (Luke 2:22–35). After Jesus's death on the cross on Good Friday, a Roman soldier thrusts a spear into his heart, whereupon blood and water flow out. Mary's maternal heart also must have been wounded, emotionally speaking, as she helplessly watches the horrible ordeal her only son endures for our salvation (John 19:34).

Fearing for a lost child

When Jesus was 12 years old he was thought to be missing for three days (Luke 2:41–52) during the Feast of Passover. It's a mother's nightmare: Your only child is gone, and you have no idea where he is. Mary and Joseph look frantically for three days after leaving Jerusalem, only to find Jesus among the religious teachers, not only listening to them but teaching them, as well. Confronting the adolescent Savior, Mary asks Jesus why he put his parents through all this anxiety and worry. Jesus replies, "Why were you looking for me? Did you not know that I must be in my Father's house?" Like the prophecy of Simeon and the gifts of the Magi, Christ's response to his mother stays with Mary, as Scripture says she "pondered these things in her heart" (Luke 2:51).

After the incident in the Temple, the Bible says nothing more of Jesus until he turned 30 and began his public ministry. Most likely, Jesus lived with his mom and worked in the carpenter's shop with Joseph, because in several places in the Bible, he's called not only the carpenter's son but also a carpenter himself.

Jesus's first miracle

Jesus's first miracle came at the request of his mother. Jesus was in the early days of his ministry after 40 days of fasting and praying in the desert. Mary comes to him as an intercessor for the Church, seeking his mediation. Jesus is the one and only mediator between God and man because he is both human and divine (see Chapter 1 for more on intercessors and mediators).

Mary and Jesus attend a wedding reception, and Mary notices that the wine has run out. Weddings then were much like weddings today: As long as the food and wine kept coming, the guests were happy. When either ran out, the guests left. So Mary tells Jesus the situation ("they have no more wine") in John 2:3, and he replies mysteriously: "Woman, what does this have to do with me?" (John 2:4).

If the story ended there, it would be logical to conclude that Jesus rebuked his mother. When looked at more closely and in context, it's a totally different matter. The original Greek text of John's Gospel says: *gynai, ti emoi kai soi,* which literally translates to "woman, what [is] to me [is] to you," and the Latin of St. Jerome's Vulgate is the same *(quid mihi et tibi est mulier).* Immediately after he responds to his mother, she tells the waiters, "Do whatever he tells you." Then Jesus orders them to take six stone water jars (each holding 20 to 30 gallons), fill them to the brim with water, and then pour some to the wine steward. What he tastes is not water, but the best wine he's ever had.

Standing at the foot of the cross

After all his disciples abandon him during his Crucifixion and death at Calvary, save for St. John the Evangelist, Jesus's mother, the Virgin Mary, stands at the foot of the cross. Her presence gives him comfort, but at the same time, it's a cause of great suffering. It's a comfort because, in his sacred humanity, Jesus has the same human love any son would have for his mother. He also sees that his pain and suffering cause her emotional pain and suffering. What son wants to see his own mother in such agony? Yet it's his physical agony that causes her emotional agony. Knowing that his death is weighing heavily on his mother, Jesus gives his only possession not stolen from him by his persecutors: his mother. He gives her to St. John when he says, "behold, your mother" (John 19:27).

Silent according to Scripture, Mary says nothing — just remains a disciple with Jesus to the very end. After his death, she takes his lifeless body when it comes off the cross and holds it lovingly in her arms (as depicted in Michelangelo's *Pieta*).

Mary's final appearance in the Bible takes place at Pentecost, 50 days after Jesus's Resurrection on Easter Sunday. The Acts of the Apostles tells us that Mary was present in the same Upper Room that Christ had used before on Holy Thursday, when he celebrated the Last Supper with his 12 Apostles. Now, each of those same men, along with the Mother of Jesus, will experience the coming of the Holy Spirit upon them. Her presence at what is considered the birthday of the Church convinced the bishops at Vatican II to call Mary the Mother of the Church.

Mary's perpetual virginity (before, during, and after the birth of Christ her son) is a doctrine of the Catholic faith, as are her Immaculate Conception and her Assumption. These dogmas flow from the same central dogma that any and all privileges and honors given to Mary are based solely on her unique relationship to Christ, her son.

Celebrating Mary's feast days

Mary has several feast days. Being the human Mother of Jesus, her maternal relationship is real and permanent. Therefore, just as any son or daughter would honor special occasions in the life of his or her mother, so, too, the Church observes the unique events in the life of the Mother of the Savior. Following is a quick rundown:

- Her birth is celebrated on September 8 in the Latin Church. The Church only celebrates three earthly birthdays: Jesus Christ on December 25; St. John the Baptist on June 24; and the Virgin Mary's. The feast days for the other saints usually mark their heavenly birthdays — that is, the day they died. Mary's earthly birthday is important because Jesus would have honored his mother's birthday.

- The Church celebrates Mary's conception just as it celebrates Jesus's. December 8 is the Solemnity of the Immaculate Conception, flowing from the dogma of the Immaculate Conception defined by Pope Pius IX in 1854. This dogma teaches that by a special grace from God, the Virgin Mary was preserved from all sin, even original sin, from the moment of her conception so that when she grew up, she could become the Mother of the Messiah. As such, she would need to be free from sin so she could give Jesus an untainted human nature.

- Mary's *Assumption* into heaven is celebrated on August 15. This day marks the taking up of Mary's body and soul by Jesus. (The *Ascension* is when Jesus himself took his body and soul into heaven 40 days after Easter. The Assumption is when he took his mother's body and soul to the same place.)

- The *Motherhood* of Jesus is celebrated on January 1. It was formerly the Feast of the Circumcision, but the Second Vatican Council wanted to begin the civil new year by honoring Mary, the Mother of God.

- Mary's *Queenship* is celebrated August 22. This feast is relatively new on the calendar, but the title is ancient. It's an extension of the honor due to Christ the King and by extension to Mary, who is the Mother of the King. As Queen Mother, she is honored, venerated, and highly respected above all other humans and angels.

- Numerous other Marian feasts honor various *apparitions* (appearances of Mary) such as Lourdes, Fatima, Guadalupe, Knock Ireland, and so on. Other feasts associated with Mary, such as Our Lady of Mount Carmel (July 16) and Our Lady of Seven Sorrows (September 15), are secondary to the major ones listed here.

Did Mary die?

The Church has never defined the death of Mary as doctrine. The Orthodox and Byzantine churches celebrate the Feast of the Holy *Dormition* of Mary, which basically means *falling asleep.* Because the Immaculate Conception preserved her from original sin, Mary also would have been spared the consequence of sin, namely death. But because she freely chose to share her son's sufferings by staying with him at the cross, theologians believe that she would have freely chosen to share in death as well.

This is why Pope John Paul the Great speculated that it would be theologically sound to hold that Mary died before her Assumption into heaven. But he didn't formally endorse that teaching as official doctrine. Hence, the question is still open for reasonable debate among theologians. Her body being taken up to heaven, however, is not open for debate.

Why take her body into heaven anyway? Jesus took his body when he ascended, and the Church solemnly teaches the resurrection of the body at the end of the world. Each human person is a unique union of one body and one soul, temporarily separated at death and reunited at the end of time, when the Second Coming of Christ takes place. To reward his mother and to give the faithful hope in their own resurrection, Jesus took his mother's body and soul into heaven — just as believers hope he will do with them on the last day.

Chapter 3

Starting at the Beginning:
Apostles and Evangelists

In This Chapter

▶ Jesus's followers as the first saints

▶ Early saints who spread the Gospel

he early saints are those who witnessed firsthand (or who personally knew actual eyewitnesses of) the teachings and miracles of Jesus Christ and who helped spread the word of God. In this chapter, we introduce you to the Apostles and Evangelists who walked alongside Christ and documented the journey. We discuss the struggles they faced, the battles they fought, and the way each one met his demise.

An *Apostle* is one of the original 12 men chosen by Jesus to be his follower. *Evangelists* are the four men inspired by the Holy Spirit to write a Gospel account of Jesus.

St. Peter

Galilee (first century BC–AD 64)

Patron: diocese of Rome, fishermen

Feast day: June 29

Peter, a fisherman, was given the honor of leading the disciples after Jesus ascended into heaven 40 days after his Resurrection from the dead. Born Simon bar Jona (*son of John* in Hebrew), Jesus later called him Peter (from the Greek word *petra,* meaning "rock") to designate that he would be the "rock" on which Christ would establish the Church (Matthew 16:18).

St. Peter's keys

One of the most ancient symbols of the papacy are the two keys, one gold and the other silver, symbolic of the keys Jesus mentions in the Gospel when he says

> Blessed are you, Simon Bar-Jonah! For flesh and blood has not revealed this to you, but my Father who is in heaven. And I tell you, you are Peter, and on this rock I will build my church, and the gates of hell shall not prevail against it. I will give you the **keys** of the kingdom of heaven, and whatever you bind on earth shall be bound in heaven, and whatever you loose on earth shall be loosed in heaven.

Bible scholars see the keys as a symbol of authority. Traditionally, kings had prime ministers who were given two keys: a gold one to the royal treasury to protect the collected taxes, and a silver one to the royal prison where the king's enemies were incarcerated. With these keys, a prime minister could, at his own discretion, release prisoners to show the mercy of the crown or levy more taxes to replenish a depleted treasury. Statues and icons of St. Peter typically portray him holding two keys in his hand.

When Jesus gave Peter the "keys of the kingdom of heaven," he symbolically gave Peter full authority to loose and to bind, just as a trusted prime minister would in service to his king. This passage is invoked to support the Catholic teaching on papal infallibility and papal primacy. The first refers to the pope's teaching authority (limited to faith and morals), assuring that the Holy Spirit prevents him from imposing an erroneous doctrine on the faithful. The second refers to the pope's jurisdiction as supreme head of the Catholic Church in terms of internal organization; in other words, he possesses executive, legislative, and judicial authority on Church matters.

The Gospel mentions Peter's mother-in-law, so he must have had a wife at some time. However, her name is never revealed, and she isn't even mentioned in the telling of Jesus's miraculous cure of her mother (Mark 1:29–31). This anonymity, combined with Peter's travels spreading the Good News, indicates that his wife may have passed away before Jesus called him to be an Apostle.

Of the 12 Apostles handpicked by Jesus, Peter was chosen to be in charge after Christ's Ascension to heaven. The other Apostles recognized Peter's authority and didn't challenge him as the head of the Church on earth. This is evidenced when John ran to the tomb ahead of Peter on Easter Sunday. He was younger and faster, but, although he got there first, he didn't go in; rather, he waited for Peter out of respect for his position as chief Apostle (John 20:4–5).

The Acts of the Apostles (the book following the Gospel of John) discusses several examples of Peter's leadership of the early Church, especially after Pentecost, when the Holy Spirit came upon the Apostles and the Virgin Mary, 50 days after Easter and 10 days after Jesus ascended to heaven.

St. Peter's Cross

Traditionally, the inverted cross is known as the Cross of St. Peter or St. Peter's Cross because, according to pious tradition, Peter felt himself unworthy to be martyred the same way Christ was, and the Roman soldiers crucified him *upside down*. Unfortunately, the advent of Satanism and the occult brought its perversion of an upside-down crucifix of Jesus. Thus, today you rarely see St. Peter's Cross on any contemporary piece of church art or vestment.

Peter's authority also is shown when he presides over the election of Matthias to replace Judas (Acts 1:26) and when he leads the Council of Jerusalem (Acts 15). Even St. Paul (after his conversion and change of name from Saul) "goes to see Peter" out of respect for his position (Galatians 1:18).

Peter was martyred in Rome during the reign of Emperor Nero, who ruled from AD 54 to AD 68. It's believed that Peter was arrested and imprisoned not far from where the Roman Coliseum now stands. Today, the St. Peter in Chains Church marks the spot of Peter's arrest. It's a minor basilica with a great treasure: a statue of Moses that Michelangelo carved out of Carrara marble.

According to pious tradition, Peter didn't consider himself worthy of Christ-like crucifixion because he had denied his association with Jesus three times on Good Friday. Roman soldiers instead crucified him upside down (see the nearby sidebar on "St. Peter's Cross").

Peter is buried on Vatican Hill, the present-day site of the Basilica of St. Peter, where the pope most often celebrates Mass.

Three churches have been built over this site through the centuries. The first was built in the fourth century by Constantine, who first proclaimed the joint feast of Peter and Paul. The second was built in the ninth century directly on top of the earlier edifice. Pope Julius II laid the cornerstone in 1506 and Pope St. Pius V finished the present-day basilica in 1615, again directly over the ninth-century church.

In 1938, Pope Pius XII permitted archaeologists to excavate under the basilicas, all the way to the first-century cemetery, which led to the discovery of the famous "Red Wall." The wall of one of the tombs is marked in red graffiti, noting the final resting spot of Peter and Paul. The first-century tomb lies directly under Bernini's magnificent 16th-century canopy over the high altar.

SS. Peter and Paul are shown together in Figure 3-1. Paul is depicted on the left holding a sword, the means of his martyrdom, while Peter is on the right holding keys, referencing the authority Jesus gave him as head of the Church in the Gospel of Matthew (16:19).

Figure 3-1:
SS. Paul
(left) and
Peter.

St. Andrew

Bethsaida (first century AD–AD 69)

Patron: fishermen, Scotland, Greece, Constantinople

Feast day: November 30

Brother to the man who would become their leader, Andrew was the first of Jesus's Apostles.

Andrew was born in Bethsaida in Galilee, the same area in which St. John the Baptist, a cousin to Jesus, first preached that Jesus was the Messiah. Andrew was so impressed that he sought out Jesus for further instruction. Inspired, uplifted, and overjoyed, Andrew recruited his brother (Simon, whom Jesus renamed Peter — see the preceding section), who also became a disciple.

The Sea of Galilee and fishing played an important role in the brothers' lives. Fishing was their livelihood, and the Lord used the sea and fishing many times as points of reference. The Lord used their fishing boat as a pulpit to preach to those gathered along the shore, right before the miracle of the loaves. Andrew and Peter witnessed Jesus walking on the water from their boat. Finally, after a bad night of fishing, Jesus encouraged them to go out once again in their fishing boat, and the brothers came back with their boat overflowing with fish. When they returned, the Lord bid them to become "fishers of men" and to follow him (Matthew 4:18–19).

St. Andrew is believed to have taken the message of the Gospel to Greece and even as far as Constantinople. He was martyred by crucifixion, tied to the cross in the form of an X. To this day, the 24th letter of the alphabet is a symbol of St. Andrew. The Scottish flag is blue with a white X representing its patron.

During the Middle Ages, the relics of St. Andrew were transferred to the Republic of Amalfi on the southwest coast of Italy, where the Basilica of St. Andrew still houses some of his remains; other relics are in Rome. In a gesture of ecumenism, Pope John Paul II returned the relic of St. Andrew's head to the patriarch of the Greek Orthodox Church. Customarily, a 30-day Christmas novena commences on his feast day and continues to the feast of Christmas.

St. James the Greater

Galilee (first century AD–AD 44)

Patron: Spain, arthritis, hat makers

Feast day: July 25

James is one of a three-man privileged inner circle of Jesus's Apostles, joining St. Peter and St. John the Evangelist. These three were allowed to witness miracles that the other Apostles only heard about. James witnessed the cure of Peter's mother-in-law and the raising of Jarius's daughter from the dead, among other miracles.

James the Greater was the brother of St. John the Evangelist and one of Zebedee's sons. (Two Apostles are named James; this one is known as "the Greater" because he was the older of the two.) Like Peter and Andrew, James earned his living as a fisherman. He and his brother, John, were called by the Lord at the same time he called Peter and Andrew.

Peter, John, and James were the fortunate witnesses to Jesus's Transfiguration on Mount Tabor. This event was most important, for the Lord dazzled the Apostles with his divinity right before his pending passion. As members of the inner circle, their testimony and faithfulness would be needed after the Lord's crucifixion.

Pious tradition holds that, after the Ascension of the Lord, James brought the message of Jesus to Spain and evangelized that country. In fact, there's a magnificent basilica of Santiago (Spanish and Portuguese for *St. James*) in Compostela, in Spain's northwest corner. Compostela lies at the center of the most famous pilgrimage trails throughout all of Europe; since the early Middle Ages, pilgrims have traveled roads from Rome, France, and Spain to this shrine, where relics of St. James are believed to lie in repose. (Other relics of the saint are housed in Rome.)

As he was led outside Jerusalem for martyrdom, James walked by a man crippled with arthritis, who begged James for a cure. James prayed over him and commanded him to stand up, and the man was miraculously cured. Today, despite all the advances in medicine, arthritis has no cure. Those suffering from it may seek relief through prayers to James the Greater.

St. John the Evangelist

Galilee (first century AD–AD 100)

Patron: editors, writers, burn victims, poison victims

Feast day: December 27

St. John the Evangelist, the Beloved Disciple, was the youngest of the Apostles and the third to be admitted to Jesus's privileged inner circle, alongside St. James the Greater and St. Peter. He wrote the fourth Gospel and is also known as John the Divine for his lofty theology.

John was one of the three Apostles (along with his brother, James the Greater, and Peter) privileged to witness Jesus's Transfiguration on Mt. Tabor (Matthew 17:1–6). On Easter Sunday, John raced to the tomb after hearing that Mary Magdalene discovered it empty. Out of respect for Peter's position as the leader of the Apostles, John waited outside the tomb until Peter entered (John 20:1–9).

Before the Savior died, he entrusted his mother, the Virgin Mary, to the care of John, the Beloved Disciple (John 19:27). Pious tradition holds that she lived with John in Ephesus until her Assumption in Jerusalem.

Pious tradition also asserts that after Mary's Assumption, John began his missionary expeditions throughout Asia Minor. He was arrested under the reign of the Emperor Domitian, who tried to boil him in oil. John was miraculously preserved, not only from death but also from any harm.

He was then banished to the island of Patmos in the Aegean Sea. On this island, John received personal revelations that formed the Book of Revelation or the Apocalypse, the last book of the New Testament and of the Christian

Bible. He received these revelations in a cave located under the present-day monastery dedicated to his honor. John later traveled to Ephesus, where, inspired by the Holy Spirit and aided by his devoted friends, he wrote the Gospel According to St. John and the three Letters of St. John. In his letters, he addresses the Christian community as *catholic,* meaning "for all."

Figure 3-2 shows an artist's rendering of John on the island of Patmos. The eagle (sitting on the book to the right) is the most ancient symbol for John the Evangelist, just as the lion is for Mark, the ox is for Luke, and the man is for Matthew.

Figure 3-2:
A depiction of St. John on the island of Patmos.

© National Gallery, London/Art Resource, NY

Compared to the Gospels of Matthew, Mark, and Luke, John's is much more theological and philosophical. He writes for a Christian audience and gives more substance in some areas, such as the Holy Eucharist (John 6). His symbol as Evangelist is the eagle, because he opens his Gospel with lofty ideas of preexistence: "In the beginning was the Word, and the Word was with God and the Word was God." His symbol as Apostle is a cup, with a serpent representing a failed attempt to poison him.

Because John was the youngest of the 12 Apostles, he's often depicted in sacred art as beardless, unlike the other 11. This is why, in Leonardo da Vinci's painting of the Last Supper, John, seated to Jesus's right, looks very young. John is also the only Apostle who wasn't martyred. He lived into his 90s and died of natural causes, probably in Ephesus in present-day Turkey.

St. James the Less

(first century AD–AD 62)

Patron: fullers, pharmacists

Feast day: May 3

St. James was named the first Bishop of Jerusalem, and because of his location, he became a champion for Jewish converts to Christianity.

REMEMBER

James is the author of the New Testament epistle in his name. He is called "the Less" to distinguish him from the older James (see the section on St. James the Greater, earlier in this chapter).

St. James the Less was the son of Alpheus, brother to Joseph (often written as "Joses") and cousin to Simon and Jude. Although he was sometimes referred to as the "brother of the Lord" or the "brother of Jesus," in reality he was a cousin, although we don't know whether the relationship was through the Virgin Mary or her husband Joseph. (Ancient Greeks used the word *adelphos* to refer to any male relative, be it brother, cousin, uncle, or nephew, so precise relationships are often difficult to determine.)

Unlike Paul, St. James the Less favored following the Mosaic laws of circumcision and diet. This debate led to the First Ecumenical Council of Jerusalem. Historic in nature, the council showed the workings of the Church after the Ascension of the Lord. James had been a strong proponent of requiring Gentiles to first convert to Judaism before converting to Christianity. After listening to Peter say in Jerusalem that there was a direct, fast-track conversion from paganism to Christianity, James deferred to that decision.

There are many stories concerning the death of James the Less, but the most credible one comes from the Jewish historian Josephus. He wrote that James was martyred in AD 62 by being thrown from a pinnacle off the Temple and then stoned and beaten with clubs.

St. Bartholomew

Palestine (first century AD)

Patron: shoemakers, cobblers, butchers, tanners

Feast day: August 24

St. Bartholomew is believed to have carried the Gospel to several countries, resulting in a martyrdom of being flayed, or skinned, alive.

Nathaniel Bar-Tholmai is known just by his first name or by the common rendering of his surname, which literally means *son of Tolomai.*

Philip introduced Bartholomew to the Lord. When told that the Messiah had arrived and that he was Jesus of Nazareth, Bartholomew's response was, "Can anything good come from Nazareth?" which prompted Jesus to say, "This man has no guile" (John 1:47); in other words, he speaks his mind.

John's Gospel mentions Bartholomew as one of the Apostles to whom the risen Christ appeared at the Sea of Galilee after his Resurrection. Bartholomew is believed to have carried the Gospel to India, Mesopotamia, Persia, Egypt, and Armenia.

The remains of St. Bartholomew were transferred to two churches in Italy: Benevento and the Church of St. Bartholomew-in-the-Tiber in Rome. This saint's main symbol consists of three knives representing his gruesome death.

Because of the manner in which he died, St. Bartholomew became the patron saint of butchers, tanners, and leather workers, who peel the hide off animals before the carcasses are sent to the butcher.

St. Thomas

Galilee (first century AD–AD 72)

Patron: India, Pakistan, doubters

Feast day: December 21

St. Thomas is perhaps best known for his post-Resurrection confession to the risen Savior.

After the Crucifixion, most of the Apostles were devastated; they didn't quite grasp the fact that Jesus was the Messiah. When the Lord appeared to them on that first Easter Sunday, Thomas was missing. When the other Apostles told Thomas about seeing the risen Lord, Thomas said he wouldn't believe it was Jesus until he had seen and felt the Lord's wounds for himself — thereby becoming known as Doubting Thomas (and thus the namesake of skeptics who demand proof before being convinced).

A week later, the risen Lord once again appeared to the Apostles, and this time Thomas was present. He had Thomas probe his wounds, and Thomas made his solemn confession of faith in the risen Savior. Thomas's doubt has become the certitude of faith for all those who weren't eyewitnesses to the Resurrection. His famous confession is a classic for all those preparing to receive Holy Communion at Holy Mass: "My Lord and my God!"

There are many folkloric tales concerning Thomas, but most historians agree that he evangelized India, where he was martyred. Christians belonging to the Syro-Malabar Rite attribute their group's foundation to Thomas.

Legend has it that King Gundafor commissioned Thomas to build a palace. He gave Thomas the money and then left on a long journey. When he returned, the monarch asked to see his new home. Thomas had spent all the money to help the poor and told the king that he had built him a heavenly home instead. Gundafor ordered Thomas's death, but the night before the execution, the king dreamt of his dead brother, who told him of the gorgeous home Thomas had built for him in heaven. The next day, the king released Thomas, and his whole family converted to Christianity. King Mazdai, however, didn't convert and was enraged when his wife did. He had Thomas speared to death in AD 72.

The apocryphal Gospel ascribed to Thomas was probably written by Gnostics who sought to vindicate their heretical ideas, and thus it isn't part of the *Canon* (approved lists of inspired books) of the Bible.

St. Jude Thaddeus

Galilee (first century AD)

Patron: lost causes, hopeless cases, impossible burdens

Feast day: October 28

Jude is Aramaic for *support of God*. Jude Thaddeus was the brother of James the Less and author of the New Testament epistle named after him. The epistle isn't addressed to any particular Christian community; rather, it's a general exhortation concerning the scandalous behavior of some converts who have no intention of following the Lord.

After the commissioning of the 12 Apostles, Jude aligned with Simon and went to preach the Gospel in Persia. There he was martyred by being clubbed to death. He's often pictured holding or resting on this instrument of torture.

St. Jude became the patron saint of lost causes partially because he was often mistaken for Christ's betrayer, Judas (Jude) Iscariot, as they had the same first name.

This devotion as patron of desperate cases has two celebrated shrines in the United States. The first, in Chicago, was built as a place of hope for people hit hard by the Great Depression. The other is in Baltimore, the famous St. Jude Shrine on Paca Street, founded by Italians in 1873. The devotion to St. Jude at this church expanded during World War II, and many prayed for the safe return of the nation's armed service men and women. Today, St. Jude's Shrine in Baltimore is still a popular pilgrim destination for East Coast Catholics.

Another famous place is St. Jude Children's Hospital in Memphis, Tennessee. Actor Danny Thomas prayed to St. Jude Thaddeus in the early 1950s when he was a young, unknown, and struggling entertainer with a baby on the way. Penniless, he promised St. Jude he would build a shrine if the saint would intercede on his behalf before the Lord. Soon his career in television took off, but he never forgot his promise and helped build the now-famous children's hospital in honor of St. Jude, who had helped him many years before.

St. Matthew

Galilee (first century AD)

Patron: tax collectors, accountants, bookkeepers

Feast day: September 21

Matthew, originally known as Levi, may have been the last person Jesus's followers would have chosen as an Apostle. He was a tax collector, a profession loathed as being traitorous and collaborating with the occupying Romans. So despised were these "civil servants" of the Roman Empire that Jews were forbidden to marry or even associate with them.

Because of Matthew's profession, there was something of a scandal when Jesus approached him. Yet, as Jesus himself often said, he came not for the healthy but for the sick, to seek the lost that they may be found. While not physically ill, Matthew was spiritually in need of healing. The invitation to become a follower of Christ was too great to resist, so he became a disciple when asked.

Author of the first Gospel in the New Testament, Matthew wrote for a predominantly Hebrew audience — that is, to Jews who were curious about or interested in Jesus but didn't know the story. This is seen in his meticulous attention to biblical references in the Old Testament prophesying the Messiah. His genealogy of Christ in the first chapter begins with Abraham and ends with Joseph, the husband of Mary. (Although Jesus wasn't the biological son of Joseph, he was the adopted and legal heir in Mosaic law, so Jesus was properly known as the "son" of Joseph.)

Matthew also accentuates the connection between Jesus and Moses, the hero of the Old Testament, particularly through his comparison of Jesus's Sermon on the Mount (Matthew 5:1) to Moses receiving the Ten Commandments from God (Exodus 19).

How St. Matthew was martyred isn't known. His symbol is the figure of a man with wings, because he begins his Gospel with the genealogy of Jesus that shows the humanity of the Lord united to his divinity in one divine person.

St. Matthias

Judaea (first century AD–AD 80)

Patron: reformed alcoholics, tailors

Feast day: May 14

St. Matthias, whose name in Hebrew means *gift of the Lord,* was appointed an Apostle following the betrayal and suicide of Judas Iscariot, one of the original 12 Apostles. Matthias was one of the original 72 disciples of the Lord from the time of Jesus's baptism in the Jordan River.

 After the Ascension of Jesus to heaven and the descent of the Holy Spirit at Pentecost, Peter and the other Apostles met to decide what to do about the vacancy left by Judas. The choice was between Matthias and Barsabas, and the Apostles chose Matthias by casting lots (Acts 1:26).

St. Clement of Alexandria explains how Matthias preached throughout Judea, Greece, and Cappadocia (in present-day Turkey), as well as the great discipline Matthias practiced. Based on his experiences with the Lord, he was able to abstain from legitimate pleasures in order to control the lower passions. Subsequently, he became one of the patron saints for alcoholics.

He was martyred in Jerusalem, stoned to death. In the fourth century, St. Helena transferred his relics to Rome.

St. Philip

Galilee (first century AD–AD 80)

Patron: pastry chefs, jockeys and horsemen, Uruguay, Luxembourg

Feast day: May 3

Little is known about St. Philip, other than he was with the other 11 Apostles for the Last Supper, for the Ascension, and for Pentecost.

A Galilean from Bethsaida, Philip was probably a disciple of John the Baptist before being called to follow Jesus. He introduced Nathaniel (also known as Bartholomew) to Jesus and is the one who said to Christ, "Show us the

Father," to which he responded, "Philip, whoever has seen me has seen the Father" (John 14:8–9).

He was present at the miracle of the loaves and fishes as Jesus directly asks him, "Where are we to buy bread so as to feed them [the five thousand]?" Philip replies, "Two hundred denarii would not buy enough" (John 6:5,7).

Philip is believed to have traveled to Ephesus in present-day Turkey and to Phrygia and Hierapolis in present-day Greece, where he was martyred and buried. He was crucified upside down under the reign of Emperor Domitian. In the seventh century, his relics were transferred to the Basilica of the Apostles in Rome, where they are venerated today. His name means *lover of horses,* and so he is the patron saint of jockeys, horse breeders, and horse-back riders.

St. Simon the Zealot

Cana (first century AD)

Patron: lumberjacks, woodcutters

Feast day: October 28

In Hebrew, Simon's name means *God has answered.* He is also known as the zealot because of his religious zeal for the Hebrew religion. Not much more is known about Simon except the fact that he is listed as one of the 12 Apostles in the Gospels.

Pious tradition maintains that he preached in Egypt and Mesopotamia and was martyred in Persia in the first century by being sawed in half. He's often pictured holding a lumberjack's saw as his symbol.

St. Mark

Palestine or Libya (first century AD–AD 68)

Patron: Venice, lion trainers

Feast day: April 25

St. Mark, one of the original 72 disciples, was never appointed an Apostle. He was the youngest follower of Christ; when Jesus was arrested prior to his Crucifixion, Mark fled from the Temple guards so quickly that he left his tunic behind.

Author of the second Gospel, Mark wrote for a Roman audience. His Greek (the language used by all four Evangelists to write the Gospels) was so good that scholars believe he was a Greek convert to Judaism before becoming a follower of Jesus. His mother was the sister of St. Barnabas, companion to St. Paul.

Mark used the same kind of literary tools as Matthew in that he reported what he knew a Roman would want to hear — no more and no less. Mark is the shortest of the four Gospels and is very active with short sentences.

Mark eventually preached the Gospel all the way to Alexandria, Egypt, where he was martyred. Arrested for his faith, Mark was bound and gagged and then dragged by horses through the streets of the city.

His symbol is the lion with wings, as his Gospel opens describing John the Baptist as a "voice crying in the wilderness," much like a lion would do (Mark 1:3). The relics of St. Mark were transferred to Venice more than a thousand years ago, and even today, there are lions all over the city. Even the great basilica, originally the Doge's Chapel, was renamed St. Mark.

St. Luke

Antioch, Syria (first century AD–AD 84)

Patron: physicians, healthcare workers, painters

Feast day: October 18

St. Luke, a Greek physician and convert to Christianity, wrote the third Gospel and the Acts of the Apostles in his native language. After his conversion, he belonged to the Christian community in Antioch and met St. Paul. Eventually, Luke accompanied Paul on some of his missionary journeys. St. Paul was physically not very healthy, and it's widely believed that Luke took care of him.

Besides being a physician, Luke was also a historian and documented happenings of the day. His attention to detail is reflected in his writing. Only in St. Luke's Gospel are there such details as the Annunciation of Mary, the Visitation, 6 miracles, and 18 parables. The miracles are especially poignant, because Luke was a doctor and naturally concerned with physical illness. In Acts, Luke shares wonderful insights into the workings of the first-century Church.

Luke's Gospel accentuates Jesus in his universal call to holiness to save all men and women, not just the chosen people of Abraham. He mentions the conspicuous times Jesus speaks and interacts with non-Jewish persons, like Samaritans, Greeks, and Romans. The Gospel of Luke has been called the "gospel of mercy" for all the miraculous healings it describes, and the "gospel of women" for the prominent role women play, in contrast to the other Gospels.

Legend relays that Luke was also an artist. The first icon of Mary and the baby Jesus is attributed to him.

Luke eventually met up with the Virgin Mary in Ephesus. This is where he learned about the infancy of Christ and everything that surrounds the Lord's birth.

Not much is known about Luke's death. Some early Church Fathers declare he died at the age of 84; others say he was martyred. In any event, his relics were transferred to Constantinople, the new capital of the empire in the fourth century. Before the fall of the Byzantine Empire, his relics were moved to Rome.

St. Paul

Tarsus (first century AD–AD 65)

Patron: preachers, writers, tent makers

Feast day: January 25 (Conversion of St. Paul)

Known before his conversion to Christianity as Saul of Tarsus, Paul is probably the most mentioned in all of the New Testament Scriptures — 14 of the 27 books of the New Testament are ascribed to his name. While he wrote no Gospel, he did write pastoral letters to early Christian communities with a message that transcends time and space and which the Church considers divinely inspired.

He was born in Tarsus and was thus a Roman citizen. A member of the Pharisees, Saul was a militant persecutor of the new-found sect of Christianity. He saw Christians as disloyal to their Hebrew religion and considered Christianity a perversion, not a valid expression of Judaism. He was present at the stoning of St. Stephen, the first Christian martyr and deacon of the Church (Acts 7:58).

Saul's outlook irrevocably changed while he was on the way to Damascus to round up Christians (men, women, and children). He was knocked to the ground and heard the voice of Jesus say, "Saul, Saul, why do you persecute me?" (Acts 9:4). He realized that he was persecuting Jesus by persecuting his followers. Christ had already died, risen, and ascended when Saul had this encounter. From that moment onward, he was known as Paul. Temporarily blinded after hearing the voice, Paul fully recovered his sight when Ananais laid hands on him and baptized him (Acts 9:18).

After his conversion, Paul went on three missionary journeys. On the first journey, he wrote his Epistle to the Galatians. On his second journey, he wrote his Epistles 1 and 2 Thessalonians. On his third journey, he wrote his Epistles 1 and 2 Corinthians and Romans.

Paul had to use his Roman citizenship to escape the death penalty in Jerusalem by his former colleagues, the Pharisees and Sadducees. During his imprisonment he wrote letters (epistles) to Christian communities, encouraging whenever possible but also chastising when necessary. These epistles include Colossians, Ephesians, Philemon, Philippians, 1 Timothy, Titus, and 2 Timothy. His whole journey on foot and at sea is seen as a living symbol of the spiritual journey every Christian must make to get from this world to the next.

Because of his Roman citizenship, he couldn't be crucified and could only be executed by the sword (beheading); he also appealed his case to Emperor Nero. This assured him safe passage to Rome, and at imperial expense. He was shipwrecked for a while in Malta, but eventually was sent on to Rome, where he was martyred in the same place as St. Peter before him.

Today, a magnificent basilica marks the spot of Paul's martyrdom, known as St. Paul Outside the Walls because it's literally located outside the Aurelian Walls of the city of Rome.

Part II
Put to the Test

The 5th Wave   By Rich Tennant

"Incorruptible saints were people whose lives were so pious that when their bodies were exhumed from their graves they showed no signs of decay. Of course, today we don't need piety, we have moisturizers."

In this part . . .

The lives of would-be saints weren't without trials; many were persecuted and even killed for standing up for their faith, while many more faced battles with their own individual weaknesses. Whether living a life of total celibacy and chastity (consecrated virgins) in service to the Church or dealing with unpleasant, unhappy, difficult, painful, and almost unbearable obstacles, these saintly men and women are equally honored.

In this part, we look at how some of the saints overcame obstacles and their own weaknesses, and we also look at the peculiar phenomenon of the *incorruptibles* — those saints whose bodies stayed wholly or partly undecayed, regardless of how long they'd been dead. Other saints we examine are the brave men and women who suffered a martyr's death, as well as the holy virgins and religious women who faithfully served their God with every fiber of their being.

Chapter 4

Overcoming Weakness

● ●

In This Chapter

▶ Persevering over personal character flaws

▶ Dealing with bad influences

● ●

*T*he saints we profile in this book weren't perfect or sinless by any stretch of the imagination; they were normal human beings with the same temptations and foibles as anyone else. Some were weaker or more flawed than others, and they overcame their disadvantages through God's grace.

In this chapter, we focus on some of these saints who had to vanquish various weaknesses in order to have a closer relationship with God.

St. Augustine (Playboy to Puritan)

Northern Africa (AD 354–AD 430)

Patron: theologians, reckless youth

Feast day: August 28

Augustine was the eldest of three children born to a pagan, Patricius, and his devout Christian wife, Monica (see the entry on St. Monica later in the chapter). He spent his youth living a wild and immodest life filled with indulgence and sin. In his autobiography *(Confessions),* Augustine told of sinning with gusto and breaking every one of the Ten Commandments, except the prohibition against murder. To make up for that one, he said, he broke the others even more often.

It wasn't until he reached middle age and was accompanied by his illegitimate son, Adeodatus, that Augustine began to see the error of his ways. He abandoned the playboy culture and gravitated to the opposite pole of the heretical Manichaeans. Theirs was a dualistic philosophy holding that the physical, material world was evil. Only the spiritual, immaterial world was important and had value to Augustine at this time, so he embraced a life of sacrifice and denial.

The Manichaeans disdained marriage and children, as children were the fruit of sexual intercourse, and anything so physical had to be evil. Christianity bridged and healed the gap between Augustine's two lives, and Bishop Ambrose in Milan convinced Augustine and his son to embrace Catholicism.

Augustine became a priest and, finally, Bishop of Hippo. He also synthesized the philosophy of Plato with Christian theology and was pivotal in establishing monastic life in the Western Church.

St. Camillus de Lellis (Compulsive Gambler)

Italy (1550–1614)

Beatified: 1742

Canonized: 1746

Patron: nurses, addicted gamblers

Feast day: July 14

Camillus was the son of a successful military officer and a mother who died when he was very young. He followed in his father's footsteps and entered the military when he was of age. His father kept him busy, hiring out his services whenever someone needed a soldier.

Camillus didn't have a stable or wholesome upbringing and thus lived a rebellious adolescence. Following once again in his father's footsteps, he acquired a taste for heavy gambling and wagering, which often led to barroom brawls.

Once, when he and his father were traveling on foot to join the army in Venice, which was being raised to fight the Turks, both men fell terribly ill. Camillus's father's illness was the worse of the two, and he eventually succumbed to the illness. On his deathbed, seeing his disillusioned life pass before him, Camillus's father asked for a priest and made a good confession, was anointed, and received the last rites. He died a repentant man.

Camillus, however, took a bit longer to see the error of his ways, joining a Franciscan monastery only after becoming totally destitute from gambling debts. At the monastery, he found that old habits truly do die hard. He often snuck out of the monastery to meet with old friends and engage in old habits, such as drinking to excess and gambling. His superiors at the monastery dismissed him, believing he wasn't ready to commit to the monastic life.

Returning to his mercenary career, Camillus found little or no happiness. Remembering the peace his father had found, Camillus tried to reenter the Franciscan monastery, but his previous track record tarnished his reputation enough that he soon had to leave.

Camillus eventually founded his own religious community, the Fathers of a Good Death, in 1584. He bound himself and the members by a vow to devote themselves to the plague stricken, but their work wasn't restricted to hospitals — they also cared for the sick in their homes. Pope Sixtus V confirmed the congregation in 1586.

St. Dismas (Thief)

(first century AD)

Patron: reformed thieves/criminals

Feast day: March 25

Dismas is believed to be one of the two thieves between whom Jesus was crucified. He was the "good" or "repentant" thief who appeared remorseful of his sins and asked Jesus to "remember me when you come into your kingdom." Jesus replied, "This very day you will be with me in paradise."

Folklore surrounding St. Dismas in the Middle Ages alleges that both Dismas and Gestas, the unrepentant thief to Jesus's left, first met the Holy Family (Jesus, Mary, and her husband Joseph) while they were fleeing from King Herod in Egypt during Christ's infancy. Something about the three prompted Dismas to bribe Gestas not to rob them, and it's believed that the thieves left them alone. This story is based on apocryphal, or noninspired, text, and no evidence exists to corroborate the information.

Evidence does exist, however, of the devotion to St. Dismas: Many reformatories have been named in his honor as an homage to the belief that it's possible to turn a new leaf and live a better life.

St. Jerome (Bad Temper)

Dalmatia (AD 340–AD 420)

Patron: anger management, Bible scholars, and translators

Feast day: September 30

Jerome was a brilliant scholar and linguist who was commissioned by Pope Damasus I to translate the Bible into one language (see Chapter 13). The Old Testament was written mostly in Hebrew, with several books in Greek, and the New Testament was written in Aramaic and Greek. Other than the academicians, the general populace of the Western Roman Empire was literate only in Latin.

Jerome finished his Latin translation of the Bible, known as the *Latin Vulgate,* in AD 400; it took almost 30 years to complete.

Prior to being tasked with this monumental project, Jerome had spent a good part of his life battling his own demons. His Achilles' heel was his quick temper; if verbal arguments didn't get him into trouble, his writings did. A genius in his own right, Jerome got so absorbed in his research and work that he became detached from the social world. That's where most of the contretemps began: He hated distractions while working on an important project, like translating the Bible into Latin.

The archetype of curmudgeons, Jerome didn't take well to criticism or opposition and wasn't anyone to tangle with. He responded to comments that he deemed unfair with tirades that would demean any notable adversary. Even St. Augustine, who admired Jerome's high intellect, feared his vitriolic temper.

Knowing his own weakness and wanting to remove himself from temptation, Jerome found refuge living like a hermit away from people and avoiding people who annoyed him. He didn't make excuses for his short temper, but he tried to adapt himself so that others wouldn't become collateral victims of his wrath. Like an alcoholic who must avoid the bars, Jerome saw the benefit of retreating to his own oasis, where he wouldn't be tempted to lose his patience or temper.

St. Mary Magdalene (Former Prostitute)

(first century AD)

Patron: wayward women

Feast day: July 22

The Scriptures identify Mary Magdalene by name only three times: as the woman from whom Jesus exorcized seven demons, as one of the women at the foot of Christ on the cross, and as the first to discover the risen Jesus at the tomb on the day of the Resurrection.

Pious tradition (common belief on a nondoctrinal matter) extended beyond Sacred Scripture and identified Mary Magdalene as the adulterous woman whom Jesus saved from being stoned to death when he said to her accusers, "Let he who is without sin cast the first stone." Some also believed her to be the woman who washed Jesus's feet with her tears, wiped them with her hair, and then anointed them with perfumed oil.

Some people allege that the male, patriarchal Church is responsible for imposing the image of a former prostitute on Mary Magdalene to keep her "under control." Many spiritual writers and theologians, however, believe that there was truly a Christian motive behind the identification. Jesus's life and trials epitomized mercy and love, and what better example of those traits than showing forgiveness to a woman whose life was marred by sin?

Jesus went beyond showing mercy and may have intervened on Mary Magdalene's behalf, preventing her from being murdered because of her sinful lifestyle. Rather than being an insult, the "former prostitute" label demonstrates that a woman at the lowest social and spiritual realm — a woman who committed the very public sin of prostitution — could rise to the highest heights, serving as "apostle to the apostles" by announcing Christ's Resurrection.

Biblical scholars still debate the issue — some insist that Mary wasn't a prostitute or adulteress, and others contend that the circumstantial evidence says she was. The Church has never formally declared her occupation, but the late Archbishop Fulton Sheen, who had a popular TV show in the 1950s, thought that Mary's dubious past was a romantic example of how much divine love can forgive: anyone and anything.

Mary also had the honor and privilege of being at the foot of the cross when Christ died on Good Friday. So far from being dismissed by the Church Fathers, Mary Magdalene became the premiere example of a sinner being redeemed and rising to great levels of holiness, thanks to the divine mercy of God.

Over the centuries, many "Magdalene" houses have been established to help save women from the abuse and exploitation of prostitution. The belief has always been that if someone as notorious as Mary Magdalene can turn her life around and become a devout disciple of the Lord, then, by God's grace, anyone can follow in her footsteps.

St. Monica (Mother of a No-Good Son)

Northern Africa (AD 331–AD 387)

Patron: abused or neglected wives, mothers of wayward children

Feast day: August 27

St. Monica was the quintessence of patience. She was the wife of an abusive, cheating man, Patricius, who had a short fuse and a violent temper, in addition to a wandering eye. When he wasn't arguing with Monica, he was cheating on her.

Monica also had to endure her horrible mother-in-law who lived with them — a stereotypical busybody who thrived on criticizing her son's wife. Making matters worse was Monica's lazy, irresponsible, reckless, and amoral son, Augustine. The eldest of three children, Augustine eventually moved in with his girlfriend without being married to her.

Despite their problems, Monica loved her family very much and wanted nothing less than their conversion to Christianity and lives of holiness and moral living.

After almost 30 years of perseverance and prayer, Monica saw her dreams realized: Augustine and his illegitimate son were baptized.

She followed Augustine when he left northern Africa for Rome, foiling an attempt he made to lose her by altering his route and going to Milan instead. In Milan, Augustine met St. Ambrose, who was the one to finally baptize Augustine and his son. (See his section earlier in the chapter for more on Augustine.)

St. Padre Pio (False Accusations)

Pietrelcina, Italy (1887–1968)

Beatified: 1999

Canonized: 2002

Patron: those falsely accused

Feast day: September 23

Although St. Pio (see Figure 4-1) became famous for having the *stigmata* — the miraculous appearance of the five wounds of Christ — on his hands and feet, he also gained notoriety by surviving the stigma of false accusations leveled against him. Though revered today as a holy man of God, St. Pio had enemies who at one point so twisted and distorted the facts that he was considered a devious fake.

Figure 4-1: St. Padre Pio ultimately triumphed over false accusations and the animosity of those who doubted his piety.

© GAUDENTI SERGIO/CORBIS KIPA

Born Francesco Forgione, St. Pio wanted to become a Capuchin monk — a branch of the Franciscan friars — which persuaded his father to emigrate to the United States to raise money for the seminary education of his son.

Ordained in 1910, he began going into trances while celebrating Mass, and he was often in a trance for nearly an hour. Although many, such as St. Catherine of Siena, considered this a sign of great sanctity, others complained that Pio's masses took too long, and he was consequently ordered to keep the daily celebration to just 30 minutes.

The stigmata appeared eight years later, and Pio's hands often bled while he conducted Mass. His parishioners witnessed the phenomenon and word spread quickly; large crowds came from all over Italy to attend a Mass celebrated by this saintly man.

Pio often spent 18 hours in the confessional and had the gift of discernment, which allowed him to read souls and tell penitents when they forgot (or intentionally omitted) a sin during confession. The number of pilgrims to visit him at San Giovanni Rotondo escalated dramatically.

The local bishop was suspicious of the Capuchin Franciscans and doubted the authenticity of Pio's gifts. He thought that the religious community was profiting from the sales of religious goods to the pilgrims that visited. The bishop complained to what was then called the Holy Office, now known as the Sacred Congregation for the Doctrine of the Faith (run by Joseph Cardinal Ratzinger before he was elected Pope Benedict XVI in 2005).

Both Pope Benedict XV and Pope Pius XI started Vatican investigations into Pio's activities in the 1920s, and one papal physician, Franciscan Fr. Agostino Gemelli, accused Padre Pio of fabricating his stigmata by using carbonic acid. The mere allegation of fraud — despite the lack of due process or adjudication — led Church authorities to forbid Pio from receiving visitors, hearing confessions, or celebrating Mass in public.

The censures were lifted in 1933, but the suspicion remained, and many didn't believe that Pio was an authentic stigmatist. Others, a large majority of the faithful, never doubted his sincerity. Area Communists tried to implicate him in financial malfeasance, but again, nothing was ever proved.

Another investigation by Pope John XXIII in the 1960s was also inconclusive, but some influential Vatican bureaucrats kept the scrutiny going. More accusations were cast against Pio, this time alleging sexual misconduct with some of his female devotees. Not only was no credible evidence discovered, but a thorough investigation exonerated Pio of all allegations. It took some time for his name to be cleared; Pio remained obedient through it all and quietly obeyed his supervisors, even when being unjustly punished.

When Pope Paul VI was seated in 1963, a Polish bishop, Karol Wojtyla, visited Pio. This bishop later became Pope John Paul II, who beatified Pio in 1999 and canonized him in 2002.

Padre Pio is the patron saint of those falsely accused and/or those whose reputations are destroyed by slander and calumny. Instead of retaliating or seeking revenge, Pio prayed for his persecutors and forgave his enemies.

Chapter 5

Looking at Undecayed Saints (Incorruptibles)

In This Chapter

▶ Looking good after death

▶ Showing God's favor

Asmall handful of saints have the extraordinary holiness of having been *incorruptible,* meaning that their bodies didn't decay or decompose the way a body normally does after death. Their bodies weren't embalmed or otherwise preserved, yet they remained intact long after decomposition normally would set in. In this chapter, we introduce some of these saints, sharing details of their lives and experiences as well as the circumstances in which their bodies were unearthed and examined.

St. Bernadette Soubirous

Lourdes, France (1844–1879)

Beatified: 1925

Canonized: 1933

Patron: those suffering from poverty

Feast day: April 16

The Virgin Mary made 18 visits to a poor, uneducated girl in France at a time when Catholicism was still viewed with suspicion. Although she was born into a prosperous wheat-milling family, Bernadette Soubirous's fate changed at an early age. Her parents fell on hard times when she was 13 and eventually made their home in a one-room building that was once the town jail but had been deemed unfit for housing prisoners.

Because of her impoverished upbringing as a teen, Bernadette didn't receive Holy Communion at the appropriate age and was quite a bit older than those with whom she served in preparation. She was often ridiculed for her lack of knowledge and understanding in both the spiritual and secular disciplines.

Bernadette's first apparition came on a trip to the town dump with her sisters to collect firewood. She didn't know the woman who came to her until after her first few apparitions, when she came to know the woman dressed in white with a blue sash as "The Immaculate Conception," a term that meant little to a girl of low intellect living in a remote Pyrenees village.

At this time in France there remained a residue of anti-Catholicism from the French Revolution. Processions, religious devotions, and especially shrines marking apparitions weren't approved by the extremely secular government. For years, Bernadette underwent examinations, tests, and observations from both government leaders and the Church. Eventually, authorities determined that her apparitions were authentic.

Bernadette entered the Sisters of Notre Dame of Nevers, the same order that staffed her parish. She died from complications due to chronic asthma and tuberculosis of the bone, a horribly painful disease.

Bernadette was buried at the motherhouse chapel in Nevers on April 16, 1879. Her body was first exhumed in 1909 in front of doctors, representatives for the cause of her canonization, and the sisters of the order. Upon exhumation, they found no decay on Bernadette's body; only the clothing, the wood around the casket, and the rosary she held had perished. The casket was opened again in 1919, and the body of the future saint was found in the same condition as it was in 1909. Today, you can visit the motherhouse of the Sisters of Notre Dame of Nevers and venerate the saint in a beautiful glass retainer located in the chapel.

St. Catherine Laboure

Fain-les-Moutiers, France (1806–1876)

Beatified: 1933

Canonized: 1947

Feast day: November 25

Zoe Laboure was a French farmer's daughter whose mother died when she was 8. Zoe entered the Sisters of Charity on the Rue du Bac in Paris on the same day a celebration was being held as the relics of St. Vincent de Paul were transferred to the convent chapel. (As you can read in his section later in this chapter, St. Vincent de Paul had influenced Sister Louise de Marillac to establish the Sisters of Charity.) Upon entrance to the Sisters of Charity, Zoe took the name of Catherine.

The same evening that she entered the order, Sister Catherine began receiving apparitions. The first was the Lord bidding her to chapel; then came the Blessed Virgin Mary. Mary gave Catherine a task that was quite challenging for a young postulant, particularly at a time when France and the French Catholic Church were recovering from the devastating effects of the French Revolution and weren't inclined to be impressed with a nun receiving miraculous visits from heaven.

The Blessed Virgin instructed Catherine to create a medal with the image of Our Lady of Grace stomping on a serpent and the words, "O Mary, conceived without sin, pray for us who have recourse to thee." On the back of the medal, two hearts were to represent the Sacred Heart of Jesus and the Immaculate Heart of Mary. Those who wore the medal with devotion would receive great graces from God.

Fifteen hundred medals were made in 1832; by 1834, more than 130,000 had been made. Out of humility, Sister Catherine didn't want her name to be attached to the medal or the miraculous information. After the first medals were cast, Sister Catherine returned to normal convent life in obscurity; only her confessor and the Mother Superior knew of Catherine's apparitions. It was only eight months before Catherine's death, under specific instructions from the Mother Superior, that the facts regarding the medal and the miraculous information were revealed for posterity.

Sister Catherine died in 1876 and was buried in the crypt of the chapel. In 1933, Rome announced her beatification and, following routine, the casket was excavated. The outer wooden casket had deteriorated while the inner casket, made of lead, remained intact. The third, wooden casket began to crumble upon opening, but the future saint's body was in good condition and intact. The body of St. Catherine was transferred to the motherhouse chapel on the Rue du Bac, where her religious life had begun.

In this chapel, pilgrims can see St. Catherine Laboure in her blue habit with white coronet at the side altar. To the side of the high altar is the blue chair that the Blessed Virgin sat in when she appeared to St. Catherine.

St. Charbel Makhlouf

Bika'Kafra, Lebanon (1828–1898)

Beatified: 1965

Canonized: 1977

Patron: Lebanese Catholics

Feast day: September 5

Following his ordination into the priesthood at age 31, Father Charbel joined a monastery of strict observances and lived his life in solitude as a hermit.

Hermits generally take a vow of silence and live alone in small buildings known as *hermitages*. They generally come together for work, meals, and prayer, but live alone in an effort to solidify their relationship with God. During Father Charbel's solitude, he practiced extreme penances of fasting and wearing a hair shirt to further discipline his body and make him even freer to love and worship God. His reputation for holiness increased, and people began to seek him out for prayers and blessings.

In 1898, Father Charbel suffered a fatal stroke. His tremendous love of the Holy Eucharist was apparent in that the host had to be physically removed from his hands after the stroke. He was buried in the monastery cemetery without being embalmed. Indeed, he wasn't even placed in a casket because it was customary for the poor order to place their deceased members directly into the earth. When Father Charbel was buried, a bright light shone from his grave for more than 45 days. This marvel necessitated that his body be unearthed and examined. Despite abundant rain and no embalming or hermetically sealed casket, the body was in excellent condition. In addition, oil resembling blood dripped from his pores in such abundance that the monks had to change Father Charbel's habit twice a week.

In 1927, the body was examined again and was still in excellent condition. Father Charbel's body was then laid to rest undisturbed until 1950, when oil exuded from the crack of the tomb. Again, the body was examined, and again it was in perfect condition, pliable and oozing this oil. Father Charbel was beatified in 1965 and canonized in 1977. At the time of his beatification, the Blessed Charbel's body began to deteriorate. Today, only the bones of the saint remain, clothed in the vestiture of a priest with wax hands and face. His body is displayed in the St. Maron Monastery in Ananaya, Lebanon.

St. Francis de Sales

France (1567–1622)

Beatified: 1662

Canonized: 1665

Patron: journalists and writers

Feast day: January 24

Despite his father's discouragement, Francis de Sales pursued the virtuous order of religious life early on. After ordination, he served as a missionary to the Lake Geneva region, an area that had fallen to the radical Calvinist Protestants. With the help of pamphlets explaining the Catholic faith, Father Francis recatechized the region of Chablis.

Upon the death of the Bishop of Geneva, Father Francis was named his successor. He continued to work to reeducate people about the Catholic faith and authored *The Introduction to the Devout Life,* a practical guide for Catholics to give up old sinful habits and bring them in closer union with God. The guide is still used in spiritual direction and read by those who want to advance in the spiritual life.

Along with then-Sister Jane Frances de Chantal (see the next section), Francis founded the Visitation Sisters of Holy Mary. He also established a congregation of men known as the Oblates of St. Francis de Sales, who were devoted to preaching parish missions-retreats, staffing colleges, and working in parishes. His legacy had a powerful influence on other men and women in the centuries that followed, including St. John Bosco, founder of a congregation dedicated to the education of poor boys. This community, the Salesians, follows the spirituality of St. Francis de Sales.

Francis de Sales was canonized in 1665 and was declared a Doctor of the Church in 1877 (see Chapter 13 for more on what this means). His body was laid at rest in the Visitation Convent in Annecy next to St. Jane Frances de Chantal. When his body was exhumed in 1632, it was in perfect condition, but in subsequent years only the bones were found. Today, St. Francis de Sales can be venerated at the Basilica of the Visitation in Annecy, where his bones are placed under bishop's clothing and a wax mask covers his face.

St. Jane Frances de Chantal

Dijon and Moulins, France (1572–1641)

Beatified: 1751

Canonized: 1767

Patron: people who feel abandoned and people with in-law problems

Feast day: August 12

Unlike many saints, Jane Frances didn't immediately turn to a life of religious service. Her mother died when she was quite young, leaving her upbringing to her father. Jane married the Baron de Chantal, and for nine years she lived a peaceful and religious life as a good wife and mother of four children. A hunting accident claimed the life of her husband, leaving Jane Frances to sink into a deep depression.

Upon the urgings of her father, Jane devoted her life to her children as well as to the poor and sick in her area. She also ministered to the dying, to whom she offered much comfort, and continued to practice works of charity, mortifications, and prayer. Following a Lenten retreat and hearing the great

Francis de Sales (see the preceding section), Jane wanted to enter the cloistered Carmelite Nuns. Francis became Jane's spiritual director, regulating her penances and devotional practices and sharing with her his vision of a new community of sisters, the Visitation Sisters of Holy Mary. Jane expressed great interest in helping Francis to establish this new community.

Jane overcame many obstacles in seeing the dream become a reality. She left her son with her father and took her three daughters to the convent. Within a year, one daughter passed away; the other two eventually married. The deaths of her father, son, son-in-law, and many sisters from the plague added to Jane's suffering. In 1641, Jane died at the age of 69 in the state of grace and was buried near St. Francis de Sales in Annecy, France.

In 1722, her tomb was unearthed, and with the exception of some mold on her habit, Jane's body was perfectly intact. During the French Revolution in 1793, the relics of St. Francis de Sales and St. Jane Francis de Chantal were carried by boat and hidden during the night for protection until the restoration of the church in 1806. In the restoration, the relics suffered much, and only the bones remained of the two saints. St. Jane was canonized in 1767 and her relics are on display for veneration at the Basilica of the Visitation. The bones are dressed in the habit of the order and a wax mask covers her face.

St. John Marie Vianney

Dardilly and Ars, France (1786–1859)

Beatified: 1905

Canonized: 1925

Patron: parish priests

Feast day: August 4

John Marie Vianney was born in the South of France just before the French Revolution. A national church was created after the Revolution, and priests or religious persons loyal to the Roman Catholic Church were banned from serving and were often martyred as a result.

By the time John Vianney wanted to enter the priesthood, seminaries and most Catholic institutions were closed. After the restoration of the hierarchy of the Church, instruction of candidates for the priesthood was left to parish priests and later to the bishops of the dioceses. Education of candidates was sporadic and fell short of typical preparation in the great seminaries and institutions of higher education.

John received his religious education under these circumstances. That, and the fact that he was a poor learner, created doubt that he would ever be ordained. Churches and entire parishes were without priests, however, and bishops felt the urgency to ordain men, even if the new priests weren't intellectually equipped. John Vianney was ordained in 1818. He began his ministry under tutelage of a very holy pastor, and upon the death of his pastor, Father Vianney became pastor of a small, abandoned parish in Ars, France.

The town was remote and Catholic only in name and revealed the full effect of the French Revolution. The church building and priest house were in great disrepair, people didn't attend church services, men frequented the bars and brothels to the abandonment of their families, and children weren't properly educated in the Catholic faith. Father Vianney took the challenge and, little by little, began to turn things around in Ars. He repaired, cleaned, and restored the church building. He began catechism classes for the children and wrote a catechetical book easy enough for the children to grasp. Along with a wealthy patron of the village, Father Vianney even founded a school for girls. He went to village bars and dragged husbands back to their families, preached magnificent but down-to-earth homilies, and conducted parish missions — a type of retreat that resulted in a boom of confessions.

All his efforts to restore the Church community came at quite a cost for John Vianney. Clergy in surrounding towns soon became jealous and maliciously maligned him. He was personally attacked by the devil when he tried to sleep. His health deteriorated due to extreme penances and denial of nourishing food. Yet, people from Ars and around the region came to the village to seek the Cure of Ars for confession and spiritual direction. Habitually, Father Vianney would stay in the confessional for eight to ten hours a day.

John Vianney died after receiving the Sacrament of the Sick, commonly known as the last rites, on August 4, 1859. In 1904, his body was unearthed. Though a bit dried and darkened, his body was entirely intact. After his beatification, St. John Vianney was placed in a gold reliquary in a newly constructed shrine. Today, his body lies in a glass casket above the high altar in a newly constructed basilica near the old parish church in Ars.

St. Josaphat

Volodymyr, Poland (Lithuania) (1580–1623)

Beatified: 1643

Canonized: 1867

Patron: Ukraine

Feast day: November 12

Josaphat entered religious life at a time of strife within the Church. He had been baptized in the Ruthenian Orthodox Church, but that branch of the Orthodox Church later reunited with Rome. The reunification was a source of hostility and derision among the Orthodox, who still call the groups that have reunited with Rome the *Uniates*.

It was in this environment that young Josaphat entered the Basilian Order of Religious Men. He was soon ordained a bishop and later an archbishop. Despite the dangers, he labored and preached for the reunification of the Orthodox Church to Rome, which caused him political and personal strife.

Josaphat was killed and thrown into a river, and when his body was retrieved a week later by faithful followers, it was in good condition. It didn't show the normal signs of deterioration that would be evident after a week in water. Twenty-seven years after his death, while the body was being prepared for a new elaborate reliquary, fresh blood flowed from the saint's mortal wound. Because of the many wars in the region, the body was moved to St. Peter's in Rome and can be seen today in this basilica. With the passage of time and many moves, Josaphat's body has seen some deterioration in the face but otherwise remains in good condition. Pope Leo XIII canonized Josaphat in 1867 and, because of his successful proselytizing among the Orthodox Church, he was given the title "the Apostle of Union."

St. Lucy Filippini

Corneto-Tarquinia, Italy (1672–1732)

Beatified: 1926

Canonized: 1930

Patron: schoolteachers

Feast day: March 25

Lucy Filippini dedicated her life to the education of poor girls, establishing a community of sisters further dedicated to that pursuit in the 17th century.

Cardinal Barbarigo, aware of the piety of the young Lucy, was instrumental in bringing her to an institute for teachers, where she excelled in study, devotion, and service. She later founded the Maestre Pie Filippini, or the Religious Teachers Filippini, an organization that helped expand the pontifical community and establishment of schools for girls.

Pope Clement XI summoned Sister Lucy Filippini and her sisters to launch a school in Rome. The number of students far surpassed the available space, and the community soon expanded throughout Italy, offering education to young, poor girls at a time when education wasn't mandatory.

Sister Lucy Filippini died in 1732. Her body was uncovered in 1926 and found to be nearly undamaged, save for minute deterioration on her face. Her body is located under the Baroque Domo of St. Margaret in Montefiascone, in a chapel carved out of an earlier church. Opposite St. Lucy Filippini are the remains of Cardinal Barbarigo.

In 1910, Pope Pius X responded to the needs of Italian immigrants to the U.S. by sending five sisters to America to staff parochial schools with the Maestre Pie Filippini. In 2010, the community will celebrate 100 years in America. The provincialate of the Religious Teachers Filippini is located in Morristown, New Jersey, and they retain the same charisma of St. Lucy. The sisters are now located in Italy, the U.S., Ireland, England, Brazil, and India.

St. Mary Magdalene de Pazzi

Florence, Italy (1566–1607)

Beatified: 1626

Canonized: 1669

Patron: Naples, Italy

Feast day: May 25

Sister Mary practiced an ascetic way of life, often denying herself food other than bread and water. She suffered numerous attacks from the devil in the areas of chastity and gluttony. He would tempt her with impure thoughts, which she immediately rejected, and he would also tempt her to overeat, even when she wasn't hungry. At other times, she experienced extreme dryness in her prayer life that left her with no compensation at all. It wasn't until later in life that Mary Magdalene began to experience the spiritual phenomenon of ecstasy and on several occasions was found to be in an almost comatose state.

As novice mistress and director of the young nuns at the monastery in Florence, Sister Mary Magdalene encouraged the sisters to exercise the penances that she imposed upon herself, but she also cautioned that they strive for a balance in prayer, work, and relaxation. She acknowledged that not everyone was called to the extremes, as she was.

Sister Mary Magdalene died in 1607 and was entombed underneath the high altar in the monastery's chapel. A year after her death, she was exhumed, and her remains were still intact. Her body soon began to emit a fragrant oil, a phenomenon that continued for 12 years. Three additional unearthings took place, the final one in 1663; Sister Mary Magdalene's body remained flexible.

Today, the relic of the saint lies in the chapel of the monastery in a glass casket for all to view. She's clothed in the Carmelite habit *discalced* (without shoes). Although her face is now colored, the flesh, muscle, and bones of her head, feet, and hands (that which is exposed to the public) remain intact.

St. Philip Neri

Florence, Italy (1515–1595)

Beatified: 1615

Canonized: 1622

Patron: Rome

Feast day: May 26

A young man born and raised into wealth, Philip Neri gave it all up at the age of 17 when he left home and chose to serve the Lord rather than pursue a career in business.

Philip went to Rome and found the city in great physical and spiritual deterioration. There were many slums, and children of the city often ran amok. Suffering from the ill effects of the Renaissance, the city of Rome saw a decline in papal authority and in the education and sense of loyalty of the clergy. Philip committed himself to the re-evangelization of the city.

He began with the youth. Philip established pilgrimages for the children during the middle of the day, when they were most likely to get into mischief. He took the children to the seven churches of the city, talking to them all the way. Eventually, the children began to confide in Philip.

The practice of the pilgrimages to the seven churches is still followed today, especially on Holy Thursday, with the visits to seven repositories. (*Repositories* are temporary mini-chapels where a smaller tabernacle is used to keep the Blessed Sacrament after the Mass of the Lord's Supper on Holy Thursday evening until the Easter vigil on Holy Saturday evening, thus leaving the main tabernacle in the church empty.)

Philip also reached out to young businessmen, offering weekly informal talks on theology and religion, which eventually led to the men staying for prayers. The gatherings were moved to a larger facility to accommodate the growing number of attendees.

After his ordination into the priesthood, Philip remained a champion of the Catholic faith, becoming an instrument for many to return to the sacraments and the Church. He instituted the devotion known as *Forty Hours,* in which the Blessed Sacrament is exposed on the altar of a church for 40 hours while continuous prayer is made. This devotion to the Holy Eucharist is based on the 40 hours Jesus spent in the tomb from his death on Good Friday until his Resurrection on Easter Sunday. Some parishes in the diocese are assigned a 3-day (40-hour) time slot on the calendar every year where the Blessed Sacrament is exposed on the altar for public adoration. He also established a group of priests, known as the Oratorians, for which liturgy and youth conferences were a hallmark.

Philip died in 1595. Four years later, his body was exposed and was found to be in good condition despite damp conditions. His body was embalmed in 1602, when it was moved to the new Oratorian Church, or *Chiesa Nuova,* where it still rests today. In 1622, Pope Gregory XV canonized St. Philip Neri and gave him the title "The Apostle of Rome."

St. Rose of Lima

Lima, Peru (1586–1617)

Beatified: 1667

Canonized: 1671

Patron: Latin America and the Philippines; gardeners

Feast day: August 23

After ten years of disagreements with her parents regarding her desire to live as a cloistered nun — and her parents wishing to see her married — Rose of Lima was finally allowed to join the Third Order of Dominicans.

The order was a pious organization designed for laypeople, and it allowed Rose to continue to live at home while following the Rule of St. Dominic and wearing a habit. She eventually moved to an outer house on the property where she could practice her religious virtues.

As their fortunes began to wane, Rose helped support her family. She continued to practice her charity to those less fortunate by opening a small clinic in her family home to provide essential medical treatment to the poor.

From the days when she would disfigure herself by rubbing pepper on her skin, hoping to keep potential suitors at bay, Rose always practiced mortifications on herself. She continued to do so while in the order, but with the permission of her priest-confessor. In addition to the many penances, self-denials, and prayers, she wore a crown of thorns over her veil. Eventually worn out by her penances, charitable work, and long hours of meditation, Rose died in 1617 at the age of 31. She was canonized in 1671 by Pope Clement X as the first saint of the New World.

Eighteen months after her death, her body was unearthed and found to be in excellent condition. Signs of deterioration were present, however, when her body was exhumed again a few decades later. Today, her relics are on display in the Dominican Church of Santo Domingo and in a small shrine church built on the spot where she lived.

St. Veronica Giuliani

Mercatello, Duchy of Urbino, and Citt'di Castello, Italy (1660–1727)

Beatified: 1804

Canonized: 1839

Feast day: July 9

Sister Veronica developed a somewhat mystical devotion to the Passion of Christ in the early years of her religious life. After some disagreement with her father regarding her desire to become a cloister nun rather than marry, she was finally allowed to enter the Capuchin Order of Nuns based on the reform rule of the Poor Clares.

Sister Veronica experienced many mystical phenomena as a cloister nun, most notably the vision of the Lord offering the chalice of suffering to her. The apparitions and the impression of the stigmata of Christ led to a formal investigation by the bishop of the diocese who observed her wounds.

For a time, Sister Veronica was isolated from any outside influences and couldn't even receive Holy Communion. The isolation was a heavy cross for her to bear, yet the young nun endured the trial with patience and obedience, eventually being allowed to return to convent living.

Sister Veronica served for 34 years as a novice-mistress and forbade her young charges from dwelling on or reading any forms of extreme, mystical, theological works. Eventually, she was elected abbess of the order; she took care of the mundane problems of the convent with the same fervor she gave her spiritual life, thus living a well-balanced religious life while keeping her sufferings and stigmata private.

Following her death, Sister Veronica's body remained incorrupt until the Tiber River overflowed its banks in a terrible flood. Now the bones of the saint are preserved with a wax facial mask and the habit of her order. Her heart is kept separately and miraculously remains in very good condition. Her remains are at the Monastery of St. Giuliani (Monastero Santa Veronica Giuliani) in Città di Castello, Italy.

St. Vincent de Paul

Gascony, France (1580–1660)

Beatified: 1729

Canonized: 1737

Patron: charitable societies

Feast day: September 27

Immediately upon ordination, Vincent's life was dedicated to the corporal and spiritual works of mercy, notably among the sick, the poor, and the galley prisoners in France. To better meet those needs, he founded the Congregation of Missions, more commonly known as the Vincentians. The priests worked among the poor in missions and helped establish seminaries to provide proper education for future clergy.

Vincent's work inspired St. Louise de Marillac, who cofounded the Daughters of Charity (also known as the Sisters of Charity). These sisters worked in hospitals and among the destitute. In the U.S., the Sisters of Charity are known through St. Elizabeth Ann Seton, who established an American branch of that community. The Daughters of Charity is what the worldwide religious community of women is known by today. It includes both the American and French sisters as well as those all over the world.

Vincent died at the age of 80 and was buried in the St. Lazare Church in Paris. In 1712, his body was exposed and found to be in good condition except for some decay in the face. However, when the body was exhumed again, there was additional damage because of a flood. His bones are now encased in wax in the provincial headquarters of the Congregation of the Missions in Paris. His perfectly preserved heart is at the motherhouse of the Sisters of Charity on the Rue du Bac in Paris.

Frederic Ozanam was inspired by Vincent's work and in 1832 created the St. Vincent de Paul Society. This society, made up of laymen and women, quietly performs the corporal works of mercy among the destitute in local parishes.

St. Zita

Monte Sagrati and Lucca, Italy (1218–1271)

Canonized: 1696

Patron: servants

Feast day: April 27

Born to devout Catholic parents, Zita was a pious girl at a very young age. When she was 12, she moved into the home of a wealthy wool merchant in Lucca, Italy, as part of the cleaning staff. She considered her work part of her prayer life. She attended daily Mass, recited morning and evening prayers, and slept on the bare floor for penance.

Zita's colleagues didn't initially understand her devotions; some were jealous, and others felt guilty for not practicing their own faith. She was persecuted for her piety, to the point that a male colleague made advances toward her and she was forced to physically defend herself. Her employers at first refused to believe her side of the story that she was an innocent victim and object of lustful and indecent intentions. They and many of her fellow servants preferred to believe the worst and presumed she had led the man on or had wanted to seduce him. She was totally chaste and pure but refused to answer their lewd interrogations because they had already decided she was guilty. Her innocence was later established and she was vindicated.

Zita's reputation for charity soon spread throughout Lucca. During a famine, people lined up for food, and Zita gave away almost all of the family's dry beans. She'd intended to restock the pantry but didn't get the chance before the master of the house decided to take stock of the beans and sell them at market. Fearful that she would be fired or thrown into jail because of the missing food, Zita prayed, and, miraculously, the dry beans were restored.

Zita died at age 60 and lies in state at the local parish of San Frediano in Lucca. Her casket was opened three times, the last time being in 1652. Each time, the body remained perfectly incorrupt. Today, the saint's body remains the same except for a bit of dryness and darkness to the skin.

Chapter 6

Holy Martyrs

· ·

In This Chapter

▶ John the Baptist and other famous martyrs

▶ Lesser-known martyrs

· ·

Martyrs are people who believe in their faith so strongly that they're willing to die for it. The original Greek word means "witness," and these people are witness to their love of Jesus Christ and the Church in that they'd rather die than betray their God. Martyrs don't murder anyone — suicide bombers aren't martyrs, they're homicide bombers. Martyrs don't cause the death of innocent victims — martyrs are victims themselves. The martyrs we mention in this chapter were in love with the Lord and heaven more than with this world.

St. Agatha

Sicily (birthdate unknown–AD 251)

Patron: Sicily and Malta, women at risk of sexual assault, bell makers, and against breast cancer

Feast day: February 5

Agatha lived during the persecution of Emperor Decius. She decided very early to dedicate her life to Christ and to live in a pure and chaste manner. She forsook all advances from men, even Roman dignitaries.

One dignitary Agatha spurned was Quintian, a Roman official. Angered by her rejection and knowing she was a Christian, he reported her to the emperor. She was arrested and brought before a judge, but even threats of torture and death didn't influence Agatha's loyalty to God.

Quintian subjected Agatha to many forms of torture and abuse. He placed her in a house of ill repute and ordered her stretched on the rack and burned with iron hooks. Her breasts were tortured and then cut off, and she was then returned to prison without medication. Through it all, Agatha became more cheerful in her love for Christ.

St. Peter came to Agatha in prison and healed her wounds. Quintian was a witness to the miracle, but instead of converting to a life of faith, he increased his torturous efforts, ordering that Agatha be rolled naked over hot coals. It was after this last event, when she was returned to prison, that Agatha died.

The early Christians so revered Agatha that her name is in the Roman Canon of the Mass, also known as Eucharistic Prayer I. Devotion to St. Agatha soon spread throughout the empire and especially in Rome, where Pope Symmachus built a church in her honor in AD 500 on the Aurelian Way.

St. Agnes

Rome, Italy (AD 291–AD 304)

Patron: chastity, gardeners, girls, engaged couples, rape victims, and virgins

Feast day: January 21

Agnes consecrated her life to Christ at a young age and considered herself his spiritual bride. Like Agatha, Agnes came from a noble family and was much sought after by Rome's noblemen. She thwarted their affections, however, and stood by her vows of purity and chastity. Her determination didn't sit well with her prospective suitors, and they accused her of being a Christian, which was outlawed by Emperor Diocletian.

The Roman governor first tried simple things to influence Agnes and move her away from her consecration to the Lord. Seeing he was having no effect, he turned to threats. Agnes remained courageous, even while being dragged before Roman pagan idols and ordered to make an offering and worship. She refused, vowing to worship only the one true God. She was sent to a house of prostitution with orders that her virginity be violated.

A series of miracles kept Agnes pure. She was ordered to participate naked in a processional through the streets, but once outside, her hair grew from her head to cover her. At the house of ill repute, the governor allowed everyone to have his way with Agnes, yet when people approached her, they were instantly blinded. One of the attackers was carried back to her room; Agnes prayed over him, and his sight was restored.

This final act so infuriated the governor that he ordered that Agnes be beheaded, and she went to the gallows cheerfully.

Agnes was buried in a cemetery on the Via Nomentana, and Emperor Constantine built a basilica in her honor over the cemetery. Pope Innocent X built a second church in Rome on the site where her chastity was threatened.

On her feast day, it's customary to bring lambs into St. Agnes Basilica in Rome for a special blessing; afterward, the lambs are raised in a local monastery until shearing. The wool is spun into strips of cloth, known as *pallia*. The pallia are blessed by the pope and given out to all the new archbishops on the feast of St. Peter and Paul.

St. Agnes is commemorated in the Roman Canon of the Mass. She is always pictured with a fern and a lamb. John Keats wrote the poem "The Eve of St. Agnes" in 1819, which is based on folkloric romanticism of a girl and a dream on the day before the saint's feast day.

St. Blasé (Blaise)

Armenia (third century AD–AD 316)

Patron: the city of Dubrovnik, the wool industry, wild animals; and against ailments, diseases, and throat cancer

Feast day: February 3

Blasé was born in Armenia at the end of the third century. He was a pious young man who had a Christian education and became both a physician and an ordained bishop of the diocese of Sebaste in Armenia. He suffered persecution under the reign of Emperor Diocletian. When harassment reached his see, Blasé retreated to the forests and lived in a cave, where many wild animals would gather around him peacefully.

While Blasé was in the cave, the Roman governor of Cappadocia, Agricola, came to Sebaste to continue mistreating the Christians. He sent men into the nearby forests to capture animals for their games in the amphitheater. The men found Blasé, deep in prayer and surrounded by wild animals. Agricola had him arrested and tried him for being a Christian, but Blasé wouldn't give up his faith. Exasperated, the governor sent him to prison.

While on his way to prison, Blasé was approached by a mother whose son was choking on a fish bone. Blasé prayed over the child, and the bone was dislodged.

It's customary on his feast day to receive the traditional blessing of the throats in honor of St. Blasé. Two candles placed in the shape of a cross are used in the blessing. The prayer that's invoked for the special blessing reads: "Through the intercession of St. Blasé, bishop and martyred, may the Lord deliver you from all sicknesses of the throat and every other evil."

One of the most beautiful shrines in his honor is in the port city of Dubrovnik, part of old Yugoslavia. In the 11th century, he became its special patron, and through his intercessions, he warned the people of the city about an imminent attack of the Venetian Republic, which ruled the Adriatic.

St. Boniface

Crediton (Devon, England) (AD 673–AD 754)

Patron: Germany, brewers, file cutters, and tailors

Feast day: June 5

Boniface was educated in a Benedictine monastery in Exeter, England, and was instrumental in reorganizing the Church in France. King Charles, the last Merovingian (the French dynasty that preceded the Carolingian, made famous by Charlemagne) king, was a tyrant and left the Church in decay. Although it was customary for the kings to appoint bishops, Charles often left positions empty or sold them to the highest bidder. And many of the bishops of the time were uneducated and lived lives of decadence.

After Charles's death, his sons Pepin and Carloman ascended to the throne, and Boniface had much greater influence with these men. He was able to convene a synod, or church council, that approved decrees calling for improved education and discipline among the clergy.

The relationship between the papacy and the Frankish king, Pepin, improved greatly. The Carolingian dynasty became a great supporter of the Holy See, and the seeds that Boniface sowed helped make the Church in France the Holy See's eldest daughter.

Boniface was sent to Germany to establish the first diocese there in Fulda in AD 722. The Lord granted him great gifts of preaching and teaching as well as strong discipline to learn the many dialects of language in the region.

Boniface is often depicted with an axe, an image that dates back to a legend in which he is thought to have chopped an oak tree that was a sacred part of pagan ceremonies in Germany. After chopping the tree, he is said to have built a chapel in honor of St. Peter the Apostle on that very site.

The new chapel marked a turning point for Christianity in Germany. Boniface then established abbeys — schools staffed by Anglo-Saxon nuns. The monasteries served as a basis for the beginning of missionary work, while the schools helped to further Christianity.

When he returned to Germany after visiting the pope in Rome, Boniface encountered a common problem: The newly converted Christian Germanic people, left without a strong structure, reverted to the old pagan religion. This occurred in the area where Boniface first established the Church. In AD 754, he returned to celebrate the Sacrament of Confirmation, but he and his companions were attacked and martyred.

St. Cecilia

Rome, Italy (second century AD)

Patron: musicians

Feast day: November 22

Much of the information available about Cecilia is *pious tradition* (possible legend, or oral history without any other evidence); little about her life has actually been recorded as fact. The dates of her birth and death are unknown. Originally thought to have lived in the third century, later scholarship now dates her 100 years earlier to the second century AD.

Common belief is that Cecilia was given in marriage to a pagan nobleman, Valerian, after she had already vowed to live a life of chastity. On the night of the wedding, Cecilia was able to not only convince her new husband to let her remain a virgin but also to convert him to Christianity. The two also converted Valerian's brother, Tiburtius, and the two men were baptized.

Valerian and Tiburtius were such staunch defenders of the faith that they sought the bodies of martyred Christians and buried them, an act that wasn't looked upon with favor in those times. They were arrested and refused to recant their faith; both were put to death.

Cecilia found their bodies and buried both men. She, too, was captured. When she wouldn't offer sacrifice to pagan idols, she was sentenced to death by suffocation in the bathroom of her home. She survived the suffocation and was ordered beheaded, but somehow remained alive for three days.

When Cecilia died, her hands were beside her confessing in the Trinity — three fingers extended for the three persons in one God, and two clutched to denote the second person's incarnation.

She was originally buried in the Catacombs of St. Callixtus, where a statue of her was erected that depicted her real martyrdom of beheading. In the ninth century, Pope St. Paschal I transferred her body to a basilica in her honor.

Cecilia's body is recorded as incorrupt, or non-decaying (see Chapter 5 for more on incorruptibles). Since the third century, without embalming and after laying at rest at first in the humid, subterranean conditions of the catacombs, her body miraculously remains intact. The last time it was exhumed, in the 17th century, her body remained the same.

St. Denis

Italy (third century AD–AD 258)

Patron: Paris, and against diabolical possession and headaches

Feast day: October 9

Denis was one of seven bishops sent on a missionary expedition to present-day France. He was the first Bishop of Paris and is considered the city's patron. He and the other bishops were quite successful in gathering several conversions on their mission trip, a feat that angered the pagan religious leader. Denis was beheaded on Montmartre — mount of martyrs — and his body was dumped into the Seine River. Some of his faithful followers went to retrieve his body and his head.

According to witnesses, Denis picked up his head and walked two miles, delivering a sermon the entire way, stopping only when it was time to die. A basilica was built in his honor at this site, and today, statues and images of St. Denis portray him holding his head in his hands. A monastery, St. Denis, was built on the site of his martyrdom and today houses his relics.

SS. Felicity and Perpetua

Birthplace unknown (AD 181–AD 203)

Patron: Carthage, mothers, expectant mothers, ranchers, and butchers

Feast day: March 7

Felicity and Perpetua were arrested during the Christian persecutions ordered by Emperor Septimius Severus. Felicity was Perpetua's maid and companion; Perpetua was a married noblewoman who'd just given birth. Perpetua's mother and two of her brothers were Christians; her father was a pagan. Her brothers and her mother were arrested alongside Perpetua and Felicity.

Felicity was eight months pregnant and Perpetua was nursing her newborn when they were arrested and martyred. At the time, many Christians and *catechumens* (pagans who were studying to convert to Christianity) were tortured by being fed to hungry animals. The Romans did this to appease the crowds and to dissuade others from following the new religion of Christianity. The emperor ordered that all citizens and inhabitants worship him and the Roman gods. When Christians like Perpetua and Felicity refused to commit idolatry, they were brutally martyred. Instead of discouraging others, the murder of these holy women actually encouraged more people to sacrifice — even sacrifice their lives — in order to gain heaven.

Perpetua wrote a detailed account of her imprisonment and the murders of her companion Christians. It was known as the *Acta* (account) and was very popular soon after their deaths.

St. Fidelis of Sigmaringen

Sigmaringen, Prussia (1577–1622)

Beatified: 1729

Canonized: 1746

Feast day: April 24

Fidelis was acutely aware of and in service to the poor and the sick, often giving up his own meals and tending to the ill — administering the sacrament as well as praying over them — at various infirmaries. He was recognized very early in life for his piety, wearing hair shirts under his clothes for a penance he knew no one else would see.

He was very successful in bringing people back to the Church during the Counter-Reformation. Because of his knowledge of philosophy and theology and his skill as a preacher, he was sent with a group to Switzerland with hopes to reconvert those who left the Catholic Church to follow Zwibgili and the new Protestant religion.

His success in bringing people back to the Church angered the Calvinist Protestants, and they threatened his life. They made an unsuccessful attempt to kill him on April 24, 1622. A pious Protestant offered to house Fidelis for protection, but Fidelis refused. On his way home to his base at Grusch, Switzerland, he was murdered by 20 Calvinist soldiers.

Fidelis is depicted with a sword to denote his fidelity as a soldier of Christ and a palm branch to denote martyrdom.

St. George

Nicomedia, Mesopotamia (AD 275–AD 303)

Patron: England, Catalonia, The Netherlands, Georgia (the former Soviet country), Bavaria, Aragon, agricultural workers, equestrians, soldiers, and knights

Feast day: April 23

George was a Roman soldier for Emperor Diocletian at a time when being a Christian was a dangerous endeavor — never mind being a Christian in the emperor's army.

Emperor Diocletian issued an edict in AD 302 calling for Christian soldiers to be arrested if they didn't offer sacrifice to the pagan gods. George refused, but, remembering the bravery of George's father as a soldier, Diocletian wasn't prepared to lose him. He tried to bribe George with money, property, and titles if he would renounce Christianity, but George remained steadfast.

The emperor ordered that George be beheaded on April 23, AD 303.

The popularity of St. George soon spread through the East, and during medieval times, a story called the "Golden Legend" brought his popularity to the West as well. It tells of a dragon living in a lake near Silena, Libya. Entire armies tried to defeat the creature and lost their lives. The beast ate two sheep a day, but when they were gone, the local villagers sacrificed their own maiden daughters to spare the entire town. St. George arrived and, hearing the dire fate of a young princess about to be eaten by the fiery dragon, he blessed himself with the sign of the cross and charged off to battle the serpent, killing it with a single blow of his lance. He then preached a moving sermon and converted the local pagans to the Christian faith. He was rewarded with a generous gift from the king whose daughter he rescued. St. George immediately distributed it to the poor and rode off to his next adventure.

St. Hippolytus of Rome

Rome, Italy (AD 170–AD 235)

Patron: Bibbiena (town in Italy), prison guards, and horses

Feast day: August 13

It may seem a bit odd that a man who once established himself as the first rival pope, or anti-pope, would reunite with the Church and become a saint, but that is the life of Hippolytus. He was born in the second half of the second century AD and was ordained a priest of Rome. An astute man and a great preacher and teacher, he was considered a rising star in the ecclesiastical chain. Yet his pride and knowledge got the best of him.

Hippolytus tangled with Pope Zephyrinus and Pope St. Callixtus and was eventually elected as a rival bishop in Rome. Pope St. Pontian had Hippolytus banished to the island of Sardinia under the new Christian persecution initiated by Emperor Maximinus. Life on the island was abysmal and provided Hippolytus ample time to think. He reconciled himself with the Church, made amends for his pride, and confessed his loyalty to the true successor of St. Peter and authentic Bishop of Rome.

He was martyred in a most gruesome manner: Hippolytus was strapped to two wild horses who were then turned loose to drag him to death.

St. Ignatius of Antioch

Antioch (AD 50–AD 107)

Patron: the Church in the eastern Mediterranean and North Africa; throat disease

Feast day: October 17

Ignatius was a convert to Christianity under St. John the Evangelist and was named third Bishop of Antioch, the same diocese that once had St. Peter the Apostle as its bishop. Ignatius remained the bishop until his death.

Emperor Trajan started a fresh wave of persecutions against Christians who wouldn't offer worship to the pagan gods. Although considered a good emperor, Trajan nevertheless was thankful to the gods for his victories, and he persecuted those who didn't worship these gods.

Ignatius was arrested and brought to Rome for trial. On his journey, he stopped at Smyrna and wrote four important letters: one each to the churches in Ephesus, Magnesia, Tralles, and Rome. In the town of Troas, he wrote three more letters, these to the churches in ancient Philadelphia (also called Alaşehir, located in modern-day Turkey), Asia Minor, and Smyrna, as well as a letter to St. Polycarp. In Rome, he was fed to the lions.

His relics are housed at St. Peter's Basilica in Rome, and he is represented as a bishop surrounded by lions.

St. Irenaeus

Smyrna, Asia Minor (AD 125–AD 202)

Patron: archdiocese of Mobile, Alabama

Feast day: June 28

Many of Irenaeus's early writings attacked the Gnostic heresy, holding that only Catholic bishops, those in communion with the pope, could provide correct interpretation of the Sacred Scriptures. He hoped to counter the ill effects of Gnosticism and stress Christianity.

His writings include a famous five-volume series, *On the Detection and Overthrow of the So-Called Gnosis*. He wrote quite extensively about the heresy of Gnosticism, pointing to the fact that it was a sect with very limited reaches in the Church. In other words, these so-called Gnostic Gospels were not universal in nature, like the four authentic Gospels, and were tied to a particular people, message, and time. At the same time, he emphasized the four authentic Gospels of Matthew, Mark, Luke, and John.

He was likely martyred in Lyon, France, in AD 202. Unfortunately, his relics were destroyed as a result of the Protestant revolt in the 16th century.

St. Januarius

Benevento, Italy (AD 275–AD 304)

Patron: Naples, blood banks, and against volcanic eruptions

Feast day: September 19

Januarius was a fourth-century bishop of Benevento, Italy, who lived and died during the reign of Emperor Diocletian. He was among a group of Christians arrested and taken to Pozzouli, a section of modern-day Naples, to be food for wild bears. The beasts wouldn't touch the Christians, so the Christians were all beheaded by Roman authorities.

More interesting than Januarius's life is what happened to him in death. At first, the relic of his head was left in Naples and the rest of his body was taken to Benevento, where he had served as bishop. Eleven hundred years later, in the 15th century, his head and body were reunited and placed in the Cathedral of Naples, and he was made patron of the city.

A phenomenon involving the saint's blood has occurred since the 14th century: When the relics of the saint and vials of his blood are brought in procession and unite, the blood liquefies. The liquefaction of the blood can take many forms: boiling, turning a bright crimson color, or turning sluggish and dull in color.

St. Januarius has specific days set aside in the Church year on which he is celebrated. September 19 is the day of his martyrdom, and the Saturday before the first Sunday of May memorializes the reunification of his relics. December 16 commemorates the aversion of the eruption of the Mt. Vesuvius volcano (he's the patron saint against volcanic eruptions, because Naples exists in the shadow of Mt. Vesuvius, still a very active volcano).

St. John the Baptist

Palestine (5 BC–AD 30)

Patron: Baptism, converts, the Knights of Malta, lambs, and tailors; the dioceses of Charleston (South Carolina), Dodge City (Kansas), Paterson (New Jersey), Portland (Maine), and Savannah (Georgia); invoked against convulsions, epilepsy, spasms, and hail

Feast days: birth, June 24; beheading, August 29

John the Baptist is the cousin of the Lord Jesus and son of Zachary and Elizabeth, who was the cousin of the Blessed Virgin Mary. According to Jewish genealogy, he is from the line of Aaron. Zachary, a Jewish priest, was struck mute when he doubted the veracity of an angel's news that his wife was pregnant. When the infant was born and Zachary was asked the infant's name, his voice returned and he proclaimed the baby "John."

When both Elizabeth and Mary were pregnant, Mary came to visit her cousin (see Figure 6-1 for an artist's rendering of this event). John is said to have leapt inside his mother's womb when he encountered Jesus in Mary's womb. Those in the pro-life movement in the Catholic Church today look to the visitation of Elizabeth and the meeting of John and Jesus in the wombs as an inspiration for the sanctity of life beginning in the womb.

John started his ministry at the age of 27, living a penitential life in the desert. He preached of repentance and baptized many people in the River Jordan — a baptism that was different from that Sacrament of Baptism instituted by the Lord. The Lord's Baptism is a purification of the body; the baptism performed by John was a means of interior repentance.

Figure 6-1: The Virgin Mary visiting her cousin Elizabeth, with Zachary (far left) and Joseph, husband of Mary (far right).

Réunion des Musées Nationaux/Art Resource, NY

John's staunch preaching against vices and evil caught the ear of King Herod, who was living in sin with his brother's wife, Herodias, who also happened to be his niece. John preached rather severely against this particular sin and was arrested. The king both feared and revered John but was not in favor of his preaching. Herod threw a party attended by many guests, and the king got drunk. Herodias's daughter, Salome, performed an exotic dance that pleased the king so much he granted her anything she wanted. Salome conspired with her mother to silence John the Baptist, and so he was beheaded.

Today, the relics of St. John the Baptist are in Rome and Amiens, France. He's often depicted in art clothed in a hair shirt ready to baptize, or with his severed head on a platter.

St. John Fisher

Beverley (Yorkshire, England) (1469–1535)

Beatified: 1886

Canonized: 1935

Patron: diocese of Rochester, New York

Feast day: June 22

John Fisher's defense of the bonds of marriage and his refusal to dissolve that of King Henry VIII to Catherine of Aragon were the ultimate reason he was put to death.

Henry wanted to divorce Catherine because she couldn't produce a male heir, but that wasn't a valid reason for annulment in the Catholic Church. Bishop John Fisher defended the marriage bond, and the case was eventually upheld by the Roman Rota, the highest court in the Church. Henry broke with the Catholic Church and named himself head of a new church. The bishops who were in their positions as a result of nepotism or other royal favors soon swore allegiance to the new church, but not to John Fisher. He swore allegiance to Henry as the king of England but not head of the church.

Bishop John Fisher was arrested and sent to the Tower of London, despite having once been chaplain to the king's mother. He languished in prison for 18 months until Pope Paul III appointed him a cardinal. That was the last straw for King Henry, who ordered Fisher to be beheaded for treason. His body was buried unceremoniously in a churchyard not far from the tower, but his head was placed on a stake on Tower Bridge to be viewed by the populace. It was only removed two weeks later to make room for Thomas More's head (see the Thomas More entry later in this chapter).

St. Lucy

Siracusa, Sicily (AD 283–AD 304)

Patron: Sicily and Syracuse (Siracusa), ailments, injuries, and eye cancer

Feast day: December 13

Lucy had devoted her life to Christ, but after her father's death, her mother betrothed the girl to a rich pagan. She wanted to retain her consecration, but it took three years and an intercession from another Sicilian martyr, Agatha, to convince her mother to let her remain chaste.

Her fiancé was not pleased and accused her of being a Christian, and then turned her over to the Roman governor. The governor sentenced Lucy to a house of prostitution, but the Lord came to protect her. She was then tortured by having her eyes plucked out. She eventually succumbed to the torturous orders from the governor, but not before her eyesight was restored. Lucy's name was added to the Roman Canon of the Mass.

St. Lucy, pictured in Figure 6-2, is often shown with two eyeballs on a plate, or, as in this rendering, two eyeballs on a spike, to indicate the horrible method of her martyrdom.

Lucy's name means "way of light." On the Julian calendar, which predates the Gregorian calendar, Lucy's day of martyrdom, December 13, is the darkest day in the Northern Hemisphere.

Figure 6-2:
St. Lucy.

© DeA Picture Library/Art Resource, NY

St. Maximilian Kolbe

Poland (1894–1941)

Beatified: 1971

Canonized: 1982

Patron: prisoners, drug addicts, journalists

Feast day: August 14

Maximilian's life was filled with strife. He was born in the section of Poland that was under enemy control of the Russians, and he died during the Nazi regime. His parents were industrious workers who faced many hardships: Many of Maximilian's siblings died, and his father was hanged for working for independence. His mother eventually entered a Benedictine convent, and his surviving brother became a priest.

In 1907, Maximilian entered the Conventuals, a reform branch of the Franciscan Order, and he later went to the Pontifical Gregorian College in Rome. In Rome, he founded an organization to promote the Catholic Church, the Army of Mary.

Maximilian received another doctorate, this one in theology, from the Pontifical University of St. Bonaventure, and then returned to Poland to teach in a seminary. He later joined four other men on a missionary trip to Japan, where they founded a monastery and established a Catholic newspaper.

The Nazis were in power when he returned to Poland. Many congregations were shut down, Catholic presses came to a halt, and the infamous prison camps were filling up. Maximilian entered the Auschwitz death camp on May 28, 1941, and ministered as a priest calmly and quietly to other inmates. He was beaten, starved, dehydrated, and eventually given a lethal drug.

St. Polycarp

Birthplace unknown (AD 69–AD 155)

Patron: people who suffer from earaches or dysentery

Feast day: February 23

Polycarp was a disciple of St. John, the Beloved Disciple, and was part of the apostolic fathers, those who were instructed firsthand by the Apostles. Soon after his conversion in AD 80, he became a priest and then Bishop of Smyrna, which is located in present-day Turkey.

Polycarp traveled to Rome to meet with the pope. There, he also met the great *heretic* — a teacher of false doctrines — Marcion, who was quite indignant that Polycarp said anything to him. A new wave of Christian persecution welcomed Polycarp when he returned to Smyrna. He refused to worship the pagan Roman gods, partake in emperor worship, or offer incense to the pagan deities. He was arrested at the age of 86 and was burned to death.

St. Sebastian

Milan, Italy (AD 257–AD 288)

Patron: archers, athletes, bookbinders, gunsmiths, lace makers, police officers, soldiers, stonecutters, victims of arrow wounds, and victims of the plague

Feast day: January 20

Sebastian is commonly known by his means of death. According to pious tradition, he volunteered to become a soldier in Caesar's army, specifically becoming a Praetorian Guard (the elite personal protectors of the emperor). He wanted to be close to the Christians awaiting martyrdom. It's said that he would comfort them, give them courage, and properly bury them after death — an act punishable by his own death under orders of Emperor Diocletian.

Sebastian was brought to his execution site, tied to a stump, and shot with arrows. The soldiers left, believing him dead, but Irene, a pious woman, went to retrieve his body and found he was still alive. She nursed him back to health, and rather than flee, Sebastian returned to his post as a Praetorian Guard, which startled Caesar. Sebastian reproached Diocletian for persecuting Christians and was sentenced to death by beating.

Sebastian was buried in a common catacomb that would later take his name. A magnificent basilica stands over the cemetery in his honor.

St. Thomas Becket

London, England (1118–1170)

Beatified: 1173

Canonized: 1174

Patron: secular (diocesan) clergy, Exeter College, and Portsmouth, England

Feast day: December 29

Thomas Becket was a loyal friend and supporter to King Henry II. As a supporter, he worked tirelessly for the monarch; as a friend, he accompanied the king on hunting expeditions.

At the death of the Archbishop of Canterbury, Henry wanted Thomas to take over. Thomas warned the king that their relationship would change, but Henry was too intent on controlling the Church with his friend to listen.

Conflicts arose, and Thomas sought to halt the king's interference in Church matters, which didn't sit well with Henry. On December 29, 1170, four knights set out for Canterbury seemingly under direction of the king. They tried to bring Thomas back to Winchester but killed him upon his refusal.

St. Thomas More

London, England (1478–1535)

Beatified: 1886

Canonized: 1935

Patron: lawyers and attorneys

Feast day: June 22

Thomas More was a lawyer and writer who became a friend and personal adviser to King Henry VIII. Thomas was elected Speaker of the House of Commons in 1523 and, when the king was still Catholic, assisted him in writing the *Defense of the Seven Sacraments.* Henry made him the Chancellor of England from 1529 to 1532, a position that he ultimately resigned.

The men retained their friendship until Henry challenged the validity of his marriage to Catherine of Aragon. Thomas agreed with the presiding bishop that the bond was valid. When the Church in Rome also ruled that the marriage was valid, Henry left the Church and set himself up as the Supreme Head of the Church of England, which denied the pope's authority. To recognize Henry as head of the church was against Thomas's faith.

Thomas resigned his position and was imprisoned in the Tower of London and martyred for his refusal to take the Oath of Supremacy. On July 6, 1535, he was beheaded and buried at the Tower of London. His head was placed on a lance to be viewed from the Tower Bridge.

Other Notable Martyrs

Not all martyrs' stories are complete; in some cases, very little is known about them other than that they lived — and ultimately died — for their love of neighbor and love of God.

- ✔ **St. Charles Lwanga and companions (1865–1886):** Charles was from Uganda and was abused as a page as a young man. He became head of pages and wanted to protect other young pages, converting them to Catholicism. King Mwanga separated the Christians from the pagans and ordered them killed when they refused to renounce their faith.

- ✔ **St. Cyprian (died AD 258):** Cyprian was an excellent rhetorician before his conversion to Christianity. A highly educated man, he wrote many theological treatises. Christian persecutions were commonplace, and the Emperor Valerian started a new wave in AD 256, making martyrs of Pope Stephen I, Pope Sixtus II, and Pope St. Cornelius. Cyprian prepared the people of his diocese in Carthage, and he was arrested and put to death by the sword for refusing to offer sacrifice to pagan gods.

- ✔ **First martyrs of the Church of Rome (died AD 64):** The city of Rome was a blaze of fire in AD 64. Emperor Nero, seeing the charred remains, needed someone to blame. The emerging Christians, to Nero, were the perfect scapegoat. They were rounded up and put to death.

- ✔ **Holy Innocents:** The Holy Innocents are commemorated in Matthew 2:16–18, in which the Evangelist recounts the anger of King Herod over the Magi not returning to reveal where the baby Jesus, the Messiah, was located. Herod ordered all boys 2 years old and younger to be massacred in Bethlehem and its environs (see the entry on the Blessed Virgin Mary in Chapter 2). The victims of this act of barbarism are considered to be the first martyrs for Christ. In the later part of the 20th century, the Holy Innocents came to be the patron saints of all the aborted babies in the world.

✔ **St. Josaphat (1580–1623):** Josaphat joined the Basilian Fathers (in Lithuania) and was ordained a priest in 1609. In 1617, he was ordained a bishop and was later made archbishop. He worked tirelessly to restore the Byzantine Catholic Church in areas that had gone over to the Orthodox Church, and in doing so, he created enemies. Animosity and jealousy eventually led to his martyrdom in 1623.

✔ **St. Lawrence of Rome (died AD 258):** Lawrence was one of seven deacons to serve the Church in the third century, protecting the goods and property. When a prefect from Rome came looking for the Church's riches, Lawrence presented him with the elderly, needy, and sick, indicating that they were the true riches. The prefect wasn't amused, and Lawrence was sentenced to death by being grilled over a gridiron.

✔ **SS. Marcellinus and Peter the Exorcist (died AD 304):** Marcellinus and Peter were jailed for their positions in the Church — notably, Peter's position as an *exorcist* (one who recites the exorcism prayer at Baptism). They are said to have converted the head jailer and his family, an act that so angered Emperor Diocletian that he ordered them beheaded.

✔ **SS. Nereus and Achilleus (died AD 98):** Nereus and Achilleus were brothers. They served as guards to the noblewoman, Domitilla, a niece to Emperor Domitian. Domitilla converted to Christianity and consecrated herself as a virgin to the Lord, and the brothers were baptized by St. Peter the Apostle. All three were arrested and sent to the island of Ponza in the Mediterranean Sea, near the island of Capri. Nereus and Achilleus were beheaded, and Domitilla was burned for her refusal to offer sacrifice to the pagan idols.

✔ **St. Pancras (AD 290–AD 304):** Pancras and his uncle, Dionysius, were beheaded for not offering worship to the pagan Roman gods and were buried in the catacombs, which later took Pancras's name. In the sixth century, a basilica was built over the site, and the head of St. Pancras was placed in a splendid reliquary in the new basilica.

✔ **SS. Paul Chong Hasang and Andrew Kim Taegon and companions (1793–1839):** Paul and his friends were martyrs from Korea. Paul was a layperson who was very instrumental in getting more clergy into Korea. Andrew Kim was the first Korean-born Catholic priest. Catholics in Korea had to practice their faith secretly because the ruling dynasty persecuted Christians. Andrew was beheaded in 1846, along with hundreds of other Catholics.

✔ **St. Paul Miki and companions (1562–1597):** Paul was born to rich parents in Japan, entered the Jesuit community, and was ordained a priest. Paul and other Catholics marched 600 miles to Nagasaki, where he was crucified.

✔ **St. Peter Chanel (1803–1841):** Peter, a Frenchman, was ordained in 1827 and sent to a parish that fell into decline following the French Revolution. With papal approval, Peter and his companions were sent to the South Pacific. They were the first Catholic missionaries, specifically to the Futuna Islands. To the native king's dismay, most of the island converted to Catholicism. The king ordered Peter to be killed.

✔ **St. Stanislaus (1030–1079):** Stanislaus was ordained a priest and later became Bishop of Krakow, Poland. He was well known for his eloquent preaching, generosity, and penitential living. Because of his strict discipline and defense of morality, he came into conflict with King Boleslaus of Poland. The confrontation eventually led to Stanislaus being hacked to death while celebrating Mass.

Chapter 7

Holy Virgins and Religious Women

• •

In This Chapter

▶ Meeting some remarkable nuns

▶ Discovering some selfless saints

• •

*Y*ou need only look to the Blessed Virgin Mary to begin to see the important role that women have played throughout the formation of the Church. Some of these women didn't necessarily die a martyr's death, but they left a powerful legacy of holiness by setting an example with the way they lived their daily lives and in the influence they had on the faithful.

In this chapter, you discover these special women of faith — wives and mothers, married and single — who served as religious sisters and nuns.

St. Angela Merici

Italy (1474–1540)

Beatified: 1768

Canonized: 1807

Patroness: people with physical disabilities

Feast day: January 27

Despite having a difficult childhood — her parents died when she was 10 and her sister died after the two children had moved in with an uncle — Angela lived a life full of faith. When her sister died before a priest could administer the Anointing of the Sick (also known as the Last Rites), Angela was greatly distressed; that night her sister came to her in a dream, assuring Angela that she was in heaven and all was well. Angela's worry and anxiety dissipated. Angela became a Franciscan Tertiary, or a Third Order Franciscan. In religious life, the First Order is made up of all the priests of a religious community; the Second Order are the cloistered nuns living in a monastery; and the Third Order includes those men and women who live outside, either in convents or separately in their own residence. Members of the Third Order don't take the solemn vows of poverty, chastity, and obedience, but they do follow the spirituality of the whole order and often wear the religious garb. Angela wore the Franciscan habit but lived by herself.

Angela's uncle died when she was 20, and she returned to the town in which she was born. Young women and girls there had little to no education and no religious formation. With the help of other women, namely widows and those who had never married, Angela worked to educate these ladies and teach them the apostolate. She later called her community the Ursulines.

St. Bridget of Sweden

Sweden (1303–1373)

Canonized: 1391

Patroness: Sweden, widows

Feast day: July 23

Bridget became an orphan at age 12 and a wife at age 14. She was married for 27 years and bore eight children, but she embraced a life of simplicity and penance when her husband died in 1344. She started having private visions and revelations from the Lord during her life of solitude. She founded the Brigittine Order (also called the Order of St. Savior) the same year her husband died. The order included monastic women who lived lives of prayer and monks whose primary role was the spiritual care of the sisters.

Bridget was also very outspoken and decried both secular and ecclesiastical corruption. She reprimanded kings and princes, exhorted popes and bishops, and urged Pope Urban V and his successor, Gregory XI, to move back to Rome and abandon the papal exile in Avignon.

St. Catherine of Genoa

Genoa, Italy (1447–1510)

Beatified: 1675

Canonized: 1737

Patroness: brides, childless couples

Feast day: September 15

Denied entry into the convent at the age of 13, Catherine was forced into an arranged marriage three years later. The couple was childless and unhappy, but a revelation of God's love for her made Catherine bring her husband to the Catholic faith.

The couple lived a chaste marriage from then on and worked with the sick and poor until her husband's death in 1497. Catherine then became a Franciscan Tertiary and survived a bout with the plague in 1493.

St. Frances of Rome

Rome, Italy (1384–1440)

Canonized: 1608

Patroness: automobiles and auto drivers

Feast day: March 9

Frances was a young bride and mother, marrying at the age of 12 after her father denounced her desire to become a nun. The early years of her marriage were hard on Frances, as she preferred prayer and penance over her husband's parties and play.

Frances and her sister-in-law snuck away daily to Mass, pledging to God that they would be dutiful wives despite their longing to work with the poor. Frances saw everyone — rich and poor, nobility and peasantry — as her equal, and thus was a positive influence on her peers. Other women of class and privilege turned to Frances for spiritual advice and support and often imitated her generosity to the poor, as well as her devotion to her husband and children. They also came to follow her in her faith and service to God.

St. Frances of Rome is known as the patroness of automobiles and auto drivers because of her love and enjoyment of taking carriage rides, as well as her ability to see her own guardian angel anytime she rode such a vehicle. On her feast day, priests and deacons bless cars.

St. Gertrude the Great

Saxony (1256–1302)

Patroness: travelers, West Indies

Feast day: November 16

Gertrude showed a love of and hunger for her faith at a very early age, becoming well-versed in the Bible and demonstrating a voracious appetite for learning as much as she could as early as age 5. She was orphaned at that age and left at a Benedictine monastery. She started having visions of the Sacred Heart of Jesus at the age of 26 and would continue having these visions for the rest of her life. She also had glimpses of the souls in purgatory and was therefore known to ask for devotion to both.

St. Hedwig

Silesia, Poland (1174–1243)

Canonized: 1267

Patroness: Brandenburg, Germany; Poland

Feast day: October 16

As Duchess of Silesia, Hedwig was very concerned about the establishment of new monasteries. She had been educated in one as a child and so she knew firsthand the intellectual, economic, and spiritual benefit of these institutions. When her husband, the duke, died in 1238, she moved into a monastery in Trebnitz and gave most of her earthly possessions to the poor.

At the monastery, she wore a grey habit but wasn't received into the order as religious so she could spend her revenues in charities. Her love for the poor and needy is her lasting legacy.

St. Jeanne Jugan

Britanny, France (1792–1879)

Beatified: 1982

Canonized: 2009

Feast day: August 30

Foundress of the Little Sisters of the Poor, St. Jeanne Jugan lived a simple, humble, obedient life. She grew up in post-revolutionary France, where anti-clericalism and hatred for the Catholic Church were intense.

Her father was missing at sea and presumed dead when she was only 4 years old. Her mother took odd jobs sewing and knitting. As a teenager, Jeanne worked for wealthy women as a kitchen maid. One of her employers took her along to visit the poor sections of town and give the locals food and clothing. That experience opened the door for Jeanne to see that Christ was calling her to serve the poor.

Jeanne and two other women got together in 1837 to establish a religious community of women, the Little Sisters of the Poor. She and her confreres went begging door-to-door for food and clothes to give to the poor.

As her community began to grow, however, Jeanne went through a trial many call a *dry martyrdom*. Ordinarily, a martyr is an innocent victim who is killed because of her faith. When someone is subjected to nonphysical suffering and persecution, there is no physical death, but the trial and ordeal are just as real. Hence, the term dry martyrdom refers to the absence of shedding blood, as happens with regular martyrs.

Jeanne's dry martyrdom wasn't her difficult childhood but the success of her religious order. An ambitious priest, Father le Pailleur, was giving spiritual direction to Jeanne and the other sisters. When her community had its first official elections in 1842, Jeanne was unanimously elected. Father le Pailleur, however, nullified the election and designated a much younger woman, Sister Marie Jamet, as the mother superior.

Because she took a vow of obedience, Sister Jeanne never revealed the conspiracy that denied her of being the mother superior and also led to the false information that the priest had been the original founder.

Only after her death did Church authorities learn of the skulduggery committed by the ambitious Father le Pailleur. He was removed from office and censured, and the history of the community was amended to show that the real foundress had always been Jeanne Jugan. Jeanne took it all in stride, even to her death. Her community, the Little Sisters of the Poor, is in many places around the world doing the work she first began.

St. Juliana Falconieri

Florence, Italy (1270–1341)

Beatified: 1678

Canonized: 1737

Patroness: people who suffer from violent vomiting

Feast day: June 19

With strong influence from her uncle, Saint Alexis Falconieri, Juliana rejected an arranged marriage to live her life as a bride of Christ — a nun — becoming a Servite Sister at the age of 15. Her uncle was one of the founders of the Servite Order.

Legend has it that, on her deathbed, Juliana was unable to receive the consecrated host because she had been so ill; instead, the priest laid a corporal (square piece of white linen that priests place on altar upon which the chalice is put) on her chest and then placed the Host on top. When she died, the corporal disappeared and left a cross on the cloth where the Host had been.

St. Margaret Mary Alacoque

Burgundy, France (1647–1690)

Beatified: 1864

Canonized: 1920

Patroness: polio victims, devotion to Sacred Heart of Jesus

Feast day: October 17

Margaret learned patient endurance and kept her faith during a five-year struggle with rheumatic fever that left her bedridden. Her love of Christ sustained her through those trying times.

Margaret chose religious life and in 1671 entered the Visitation convent at Paray-le-Monial. In her first two years, Margaret began experiencing divine revelations in which Christ called her his chosen instrument to spread devotion to him. He instructed her to establish what would become known as the Nine Fridays and the Holy Hour and asked that she create the feast of the Sacred Heart.

The Nine Fridays mark Christ's desire to have the faithful voluntarily come to Mass and Holy Communion for nine consecutive first Fridays of the month. The Holy Hour is 60 minutes of prayer from 11 p.m. to midnight on the eve of the first Friday of every month to make reparations for the sadness Jesus endured when he was abandoned by his Apostles in his Agony. (See the nearby sidebar to find more about Jesus's promises for those who followed these rituals.)

12 promises of Jesus to St. Margaret Mary

Margaret Mary Alacoque received a private revelation from Christ in 1675 where he asked her to spread devotion to his Sacred Heart. Anyone who participated in this devotion, according to the message she received, could count on these 12 promises from Our Lord:

1. I will give them all the graces necessary for their state of life.

2. I will establish peace in their families.

3. I will console them in all their troubles.

4. They shall find in My Heart an assured refuge during life and especially at the hour of their death.

5. I will pour abundant blessings on all their undertakings.

6. Sinners shall find in My Heart the source of an infinite ocean of mercy.

7. Tepid souls shall become fervent.

8. Fervent souls shall speedily rise to great perfection.

9. I will bless the homes where an image of My Heart shall be exposed and honored.

10. I will give to priests the power of touching the most hardened hearts.

11. Those who propagate this devotion shall have their names written in My Heart, never to be effaced.

12. The all-powerful love of My Heart will grant to all those who shall receive Communion on the First Friday of nine consecutive months the grace of final repentance; they shall not die under My displeasure, nor without receiving their Sacraments; My heart shall be their assured refuge at that last hour.

St. Mary Magdalene de Pazzi

Florence, Italy (1566–1607)

Beatified: 1626

Canonized: 1669

Patroness: Naples

Feast day: May 25

Mary Magdalene de Pazzi was admitted into the Carmelite Order of Nuns in 1582 and became horribly ill very early in her vocation. During her illness, she experienced religious ecstasies, supernatural phenomena in which the person feels immense joy and happiness because of the union she (or he) has with Jesus.

Mary was also blessed with the gift of prophesy and could read souls, so when people came to visit her, she immediately knew what spiritual state they were in and what advice she should give.

St. Mary had such a personal relationship with Christ that she often spoke to him as one would a longtime or childhood friend, often with a teasing note. For example, as she aged, other nuns occasionally heard her whispering to Our Lord that he needed to speak louder to her as her hearing was beginning to fade.

St. Rose of Lima

Lima, Peru (1586–1617)

Beatified: 1667

Canonized: 1671

Patroness: the Americas

Feast day: August 30

Rose (see Figure 7-1 for her portrait) took on personal penances for the spiritual welfare of others, such as fasting outside of Lent and sleeping on the floor. At the age of 20, she became a Dominican nun and spent the rest of her days caring for the poor and destitute. She was so popular among the people for her sanctity and holiness that the pope named her patroness of the Americas.

Figure 7-1:
St. Rose of Lima, wearing a crown of roses symbolizing her purity and devotion to Christ.

*Scala/Ministero per i Beni e le Attività culturali /
Art Resource, NY*

Part III
Living the Faith

The 5th Wave — By Rich Tennant

"I'm pretty sure the Holy Father plans to reach out to other faiths. He said failing to do that just wouldn't be kosher."

In this part . . .

In this part, we look at the early days of the religious communities. The founding mothers and fathers of these groups established orders and congregations often named after them — like St. Clare and her Poor Clares, St. Dominic and the Dominicans, St. Francis and the Franciscans, St. Benedict and the Benedictines, and so on.

We also look down the halls of the aristocracy at saints who were noble if not actual royalty, such as St. Louis of France, St. Margaret of Scotland, and St. Edward the Confessor. We introduce pioneer saints who brought the Catholic faith to the New World, and we discuss those holy men who rose to the highest level of Church leadership — the saintly popes. Though Church history admits the existence of at least a dozen bad (if not rotten) popes who brought great scandal, three times as many good and holy popes surpassed their colleagues in sanctity.

Finally, we look at the saints of the Orthodox Church in America. Catholicism isn't the only religion that honors saints; so do our Eastern brethren.

Chapter 8

Leading the Faithful: Saintly Popes

In This Chapter

▶ Getting to know the popes great enough to be deemed saints

▶ Finding out about saintly popes of the early Catholic Church

*T*he supreme head of the Catholic Church is the pope, from the Italian "papa," or "father." Every Bishop of Rome has been the pope, and every pope has been the Bishop of Rome. Most popes lived in Rome; those who didn't physically live there still served as Bishop of Rome, even if by long distance.

In this chapter, we introduce those popes who've been canonized as saints and briefly describe what's known of their earthly service. We've listed the popes in chronological order for easier reference and provided the dates of their pontificate (papacy) but not their birth, because ancient records didn't keep birth information as accurately as ordination information. We don't supply patronage information either, as none of these popes are listed as patron saints.

Pope St. Peter

Pontificate: AD 33–AD 64

Feast days: SS. Peter & Paul, June 29; Chair of St. Peter, February 22

Peter became head of the Church and leader of the Christians following Christ's Resurrection and Ascension. As the premier pope of the Catholic Church, St. Peter set the stage for those to follow; every pope to serve after his reign is considered a successor to St. Peter and the Bishop of Rome (see the nearby sidebar, "Early Church hierarchy"). He established the first Christian community in the empire's capital just before being martyred in AD 64 (see Chapter 3 for more on Peter's life and martyrdom).

Early Church hierarchy

The early Church's leadership was a pyramid with bishops at the top. Bishops were successors to the 12 Apostles. Priests were successors to the 72 disciples. Deacons were the junior end of the clergy, ordained specifically for service to God's people and to assist the local bishop. Today, the deacon serves in the local parish helping the priests.

Although Rome is the center of ecclesiastical authority, other prominent centers of Christendom include Jerusalem, Alexandria, Antioch (modern-day Antakya, Turkey), and Constantinople (modern-day Istanbul). Each has its own bishop who's considered a direct successor to one of the original Apostles. Where Rome has the successor to St. Peter, Constantinople has the successor to his brother, St. Andrew. The Bishop of Alexandria is the successor to St. Mark, and the Bishop of Jerusalem is the successor to St. James.

Pope St. Linus

Pontificate: AD 64–AD 76

Feast day: September 23

Not much is known about Linus, but he is mentioned in the New Testament in St. Paul's Epistle, 2 Timothy 4:21. He was likely made a bishop by Paul.

Linus, who was probably from Tuscany, was the second pope of the Church and the first successor to St. Peter. His name appears in the Roman Canon, the part of the Catholic Mass where the Last Supper is reenacted and the priest speaks the words of Christ over the bread and wine, changing them into the body and blood of Jesus. One authoritative source *(Liber Pontificalis)* states that Linus was buried next to his predecessor, St. Peter, the first pope, on Vatican Hill. Recent archeological research has cast some doubts on the remains currently identified as Linus, but his existence is not disputed.

Pope St. Clement 1

Pontificate: AD 88–AD 97

Feast day: November 23

Clement, the fourth pope, is believed to have known Peter and Paul; his writings are a great resource for their preaching and teaching. Scholars also believe that Paul refers to Clement in Philippians 4:3. Clement was an educated man who wrote numerous letters that still survive today — many of which were responses to requests to settle disputes. His decisions were sought because he was the successor to St. Peter, and as the Bishop of Rome, he was considered to have universal primacy.

Clement is venerated as a martyr, though no historical data can back this view. Like St. Linus, Clement's name appears in the Canon of the Mass. He died in Crimea, but his remains were brought back to Rome and are enshrined at the minor basilica of St. Clement (*Basilica di San Clemente al Laterano*).

Pope St. Alexander 1

Pontificate: AD 105–AD 115

Feast day: May 3

As with many of the early popes, we don't know much about Alexander except for some minor liturgical additions he made, such as the blessing of holy water mixed with salt. He also encouraged the use of holy water in private homes.

Some historians believe that Alexander was a martyr and died under Emperor Hadrian or even Trajan, but no documented record indicates this. He was martyred by decapitation and is buried on the Via Nomentana in Rome.

Pope St. Telesphorus

Pontificate: AD 125–AD 136

Feast day: January 5

St. Telesphorus instituted a 7-week fast to prepare for the solemnity of Easter, thereby laying the foundation for the modern-day season of Lent (although Lent today lasts only 40 days). He also established the practice of celebrating Easter only on a Sunday so as to commemorate the actual day of the week that Jesus rose from the dead. Previously, people had celebrated Easter three days after Passover, and so it didn't always fall on a Sunday. Telesphorus was also the first pope to establish the Christmas midnight Mass. He was martyred for his faith and is buried near St. Peter in the Vatican.

Pope St. Hyginus

Pontificate: AD 136–AD 140

Feast day: January 11

St. Hyginus had talents in theology that were put to use against the heresy of Gnosticism during his reign. *Gnosticism* was the idea that salvation could be achieved only through secret knowledge. Followers also believed that human souls are prisoners in physical bodies. Only the invisible, spiritual realities are considered good, while anything visible and material is evil.

Gnosticism originated in Egypt, and some of its proponents came to Rome in the hopes of winning over converts. Hyginus successfully eliminated the threat from Rome, but Gnosticism wasn't completely eradicated until the fifth century. Hyginus is buried near the tomb of St. Peter at the Vatican.

Pope St. Zephyrinus

Pontificate: AD 199–AD 217

Feast day: August 26

Zephyrinus, a Roman of modest means and humble beginnings, faced several heresies during his reign, including two that created a heavy burden for this pope: adoptionism (the idea that Christ only became divine upon his baptism) and modalism (the idea that the Holy Father, the Resurrected Son, and the Holy Spirit are one entity rather than the Holy Trinity).

Zephyrinus is considered a *dry martyr* because, though he certainly suffered persecution, he may not have died a martyr's death. He's buried in a cemetery near the Catacombs of St. Callixtus in Rome.

Pope St. Callixtus 1

Pontificate: AD 217–AD 222

Feast day: October 14

Callixtus I reigned much the same way he lived — surrounded by struggles and misfortune. He was a Roman from Trastevere, the son of Domitius. While a slave of Carpophorus, Callixtus was given care of a bank, but he lost the money and ran away. Historians believe that customers took advantage of his inexperience and good nature.

Callixtus was caught and sentenced to hard labor. He was released early for good behavior, only to be jailed again for fighting in a synagogue (most likely trying to recover the money he lost). He was sent to work in the mines of Sardinia but was again released at the request of the emperor's mistress.

All we know of his papacy comes from his most vocal opponents and enemies. Tertullian and Hippolytus vigorously disagreed with Callixtus's decision to allow former adulterers, and even murderers, to receive Holy Communion after performing some tough penance and showing full contrition. They preferred the more strict response of total and perpetual excommunication for very grave sins. Callixtus's view on the mercy of God and the use of the Sacrament of Penance (confession) prevailed, and his enemies are now remembered as heretics.

His relics are buried in the Church of Santa Maria in Trastevere.

Pope St. Pontian

Pontificate: AD 230–AD 235

Feast day: August 13

Pontian, a Roman by birth, held a *synod* (a meeting of clergy) in Rome in AD 230 to condemn the heresy of *origenism* — the loose interpretation of scripture and subordination of the doctrine of the Trinity. He was exiled to Sardinia during the reign of Emperor Maximinus Thrax, who eagerly persecuted the Church. In most cases, being exiled was considered a death sentence.

Popular belief holds that Pontian abdicated his office so his nephew could be chosen as his successor. Buried in Sardinia, Pontian's remains were later moved to a papal cemetery on the Appian Way known as the Catacombs of St. Callixtus. Later, his bones were moved again to the Vatican, with other popes.

Pope St. Fabian

Pontificate: AD 236–250

Feast day: January 20

Fabian was one of the few laymen to be elected pope. After his selection, he was ordained a deacon, and then a priest, and finally, Bishop of Rome. When Pope Anterus died, many notable candidates were considered to succeed him. The crowd saw a white dove alight upon Fabian's head, almost like the scene from the Gospel when the Holy Spirit descends in the form of a dove.

The crowd interpreted this as a sign from heaven and unanimously chose Fabian as the next Bishop of Rome and Pope of the Church.

Fabian ruled during the reign of Emperor Gordian III, a time of peace in which the Church was able to expand. He divided the diocese of Rome into seven sections, built churches, and expanded cemeteries. He was responsible for the return of the remains of both Pope Pontian and the reconciled anti-pope Hippolytus.

After Emperor Gordian's rule, persecution once again threatened the Christian Church in Rome. Emperor Decius had Fabian imprisoned, and he died there in AD 250. Originally buried in the Catacombs of St. Callixtus, he was later moved to the Basilica of St. Sebastian.

Pope St. Cornelius

Pontificate: AD 251–AD 253

Feast day: September 16

Cornelius was a Roman priest when he was chosen to succeed Pope Fabian. He was displeased with *confessors* (priests and bishops who absolved the sins of contrite sinners via the sacrament of *penance,* also known as *confession*), whom he considered lax with allegedly repentant Christians — those who sought reconciliation with the Church after having denounced their faith during the Roman persecutions. At the same time, he rebuked the harshness of those who maintained that the *lapsi* (lapsed Christians) were unforgivable.

Cornelius believed that the mercy of God allowed the Church to forgive repentant sinners but that divine justice demanded a proper penance.

The persecution of Christians was renewed and Cornelius was exiled; he died pending his trial and is therefore considered a martyr. He's buried in the Catacombs of St. Callixtus.

Pope St. Lucius 1

Pontificate: AD 253–AD 254

Feast day: March 4

Lucius was born in Rome and served just 18 months as pope. Like Cornelius, he condemned those who refused reconciliation with repentant lapsi, because he believed any sin was forgivable as long as the person had true contrition and a sincere desire to avoid sin in the future.

Lucius and other Christians were exiled by Emperor Gallus, but after Gallus's death, his successor, Valerian, allowed Pope Lucius and other Christians to return to Rome after previously being exiled. Lucius died a natural death in AD 254 and is buried in the papal chambers of the Catacombs of St. Callixtus.

Pope St. Stephen I

Pontificate: AD 254–AD 257

Feast day: August 2

Stephen was a priest in Rome when he was elected pope and faced the issue of heretics conducting baptisms. Some claimed that heretics' baptisms were invalid, while others maintained that the grace of the sacrament worked regardless of the spiritual state of the minister. Pope Stephen agreed with the latter position, and thus it became doctrine for the entire Church, angering some of his opponents.

St. Stephen is buried in the papal chapel of the Catacombs of St. Callixtus.

Pope St. Sixtus II

Pontificate: AD 257–AD 258

Feast day: August 6

Sixtus (also Xystus) was a Greek philosopher before he became pope in Rome. At the time, Emperor Valerian was vehemently anti-Christian and prohibited worship, instead requiring Christians to participate in state religious ceremonies. In defiance, Sixtus II gathered the faithful in a cemetery for a mass of commemoration, for which he was arrested and beheaded.

Sixtus is buried in the papal section of the Catacombs of St. Callixtus, and his name appears in the Canon of the Mass.

Pope St. Dionysius

Pontificate: AD 259–AD 268

Feast day: December 26

Dionysius was elected Pope at a time when many priests were martyred and church property was confiscated. Dionysius exercised his papal authority in many different ways, first by settling disputes in theology over the Blessed Trinity, and then by reaffirming the Church's teaching that the Sacrament of Baptism is received only once.

In areas of government, Dionysius was left with the restructuring of the Church in Rome after Emperor Valerian's campaign of persecution. After the emperor's son ascended the throne, church land and property were returned. Dionysius reorganized the property and revitalized the decimated clergy. He's buried in the papal section of the Catacombs of St. Callixtus.

Pope St. Caius

Pontificate: AD 283–AD 296

Feast day: April 22

Caius insisted on maintaining the mandate that bishops first be ordained priests before being consecrated to the episcopacy, which some had tried to make optional. Although he was likely a relative of the Emperor Diocletian, Caius had to escape to caves and catacombs when the Diocletian persecution of Christians went into full swing. He's buried in the new part of the papal cemetery in the Catacombs of St. Callixtus.

Pope St. Marcellinus

Pontificate: AD 296–AD 304

Feast day: June 2

Marcellinus is remembered along with St. Peter as an exorcist of Rome. Both men were beheaded under the particularly vicious reign of Emperor Diocletian and are remembered in the Roman Canon of the Mass. Marcellinus guided the church for eight years, between AD 296 and AD 304.

Marcellinus was originally buried in a private cemetery, but the Christian Emperor Constantine later translated his relics, built a church over them, and buried his own mother, St. Helena, in it as well. In the ninth century, portions of the relics of both saints were gifted by the Holy See to monasteries in Germany. Miracles were attributed to the intercession of these saints during this last transfer.

Pope St. Melchiades

Pontificate: AD 311–AD 314

Feast day: December 10

Melchiades was the first pope to see the end of Roman persecution of Christians. Constantine defeated Maxentius in AD 312, and the new emperor issued his famous Edict of Milan the following year, legalizing Christianity.

At the urging of his mother, St. Helena (a devout Christian), Constantine gave Melchiades and the Church many imperial estates, like the Lateran Palace (which became the Basilica of St. John Lateran, the pope's actual cathedral) and Vatican Hill (where St. Peter's Basilica is located and where the pope now lives and works every day).

Melchiades is buried in the papal chapel of the Catacombs of St. Callixtus.

Pope St. Sylvester 1

Pontificate: AD 314–AD 355

Feast day: December 31

According to pious tradition, Emperor Constantine was miraculously cured of leprosy when he was baptized by Pope Sylvester after he had issued the Edict of Milan.

Two significant meetings took place during Sylvester's reign: the Synod of Arles, which condemned the heresy of Donatism, and the Ecumenical Council of Nicea, which condemned the heresy of Arianism. The latter council also developed the formula creed recited in the Catholic Church, based on an earlier creed of the Apostles.

On the Via Salaria he built a cemeterial church over the Catacomb of Priscilla. He is buried in this church.

Pope St. Julius 1

Pontificate: AD 337–AD 352

Feast day: April 12

Julius had to deal with the problem of the Arian heresy (Arianism denies the divinity of Christ). So much of the Christian world came under the influence of this heresy that Catholic bishops were deposed from their dioceses. Julius convened a synod, which resulted in reaffirming the pope's authority over questions of theology or governance in the Church.

Julius also built two churches in Rome that still stand today: St. Mary Trastevere and The Church of the Holy Apostles.

Pope St. Damasus

Pontificate: AD 366–AD 384

Feast day: December 11

Damasus's papacy was filled with heresies and political strife. He worked with St. Basil in the Eastern Church to enforce the documents of the Council of Nicea in Antioch, which at the time was divided between two bishops. He was also a productive laborer, working alongside St. Jerome in the Latin Vulgate translation of the Gospels, building a number of churches in Rome, restoring the catacombs, and refurbishing older places of worship. He wrote a treatise on virginity and poems on the Roman martyrs and popes. He's buried in one of the churches he built in Rome, St. Lorenzo in Damaso.

Pope St. Siricius

Pontificate: AD 384–AD 399

Feast day: November 26

Siricius was the first pope to mandate celibacy in the Latin Church. (Eastern Catholic clergy were always given the option of marriage or celibacy before ordination). Even where married clergy were permitted, only celibates could be promoted. Siricius also condemned a heresy that attacked the veracity and necessity of the perpetual virginity of Mary. He's buried in the Catacomb of Priscilla.

Pope St. Innocent 1

Pontificate: AD 401–AD 417

Feast day: July 28

Innocent stressed that dioceses should refer all major problems to the Bishop of Rome, as the pope is the supreme pastor of the universal church. A common expression was coined in this era: *Roma locuta est, causa finita est* (Rome has spoken, and the case is closed).

Innocent is buried next to his father, Pope Anastasius I, whose papacy ended prior to the celibacy mandate.

Pope St. Boniface 1

Pontificate: AD 418–AD 422

Feast day: September 4

Boniface has earned much recognition for his efforts to strengthen the papacy. He was an old man when elected pope, and some of his dissidents seized the Lateran Palace and elected their own anti-pope, Eulalius. Emperor Honorius initially tried to sort out the situation, and for a while, he asked both men to suspend their rule. Boniface complied; Eulalius did not. The emperor and those in government were angered by Eulalius's disobedience and unanimously recognized Boniface I as the authentic pope.

Boniface I also battled heresy and, along with St. Augustine of North Africa, was a champion supporter of orthodoxy. He is buried in the cemetery of Maximus on the Via Salaria, Rome.

Pope St. Celestine 1

Pontificate: AD 422–AD 432

Feast day: April 6

Much controversy existed in the Church at the time Celestine reigned, especially from North Africa. Two heresies, Pelagianism and Nestorianism, plagued orthodox theology. Pelagius denied the necessity of grace and held that human works alone could earn your way into heaven; Nestorius denied the divinity of Christ and the title of Mary the Mother of God.

With St. Augustine, Bishop of Hippo in North Africa, Celestine dealt with the heresies by convening a council in Rome that laid the groundwork for the great Ecumenical Council in Ephesus, which dealt with these heresies on an authoritative basis. At this council in Rome, Celestine asserted the primacy of Peter and his successors in the Church and in matters of faith and morals. He is buried in the Catacombs of Priscilla.

Pope St. Sixtus III

Pontificate: AD 432–AD 440

Feast day: March 28

Sixtus continued the condemnation of the heresies of Pelagianism and Nestorianism during his papacy, although his pastoral demeanor and patience led some to conclude erroneously that he had heretical sympathies with these two. In reality, he was just a kinder, gentler pope than his predecessors.

He enlarged the Basilica of St. Mary Major on Esquiline Hill in Rome, dedicated St. Peter in Chains, and built a beautiful baptistery at the Basilica of St. John Lateran.

Pope St. Leo I

Pontificate: AD 440–AD 461

Feast day: April 11

Leo was a deacon under Pope Celestine I and Pope Sixtus III. Along with Pope Gregory and Pope Nicholas, he's one of only three popes to be given the title "the Great."

A learned, erudite, and accomplished orator, Leo dealt with heresies head-on. Ninety-six of his sermons and 143 letters survive today that concern the major theological errors of Leo's time.

Although he couldn't attend the Ecumenical Council of Chalcedon (AD 451), he wrote a letter known as the "Tome of Pope St. Leo" that was so clear and well received that the council fathers said, "God has spoken to us through Peter and in the person of Leo, his successor."

Historically, Leo is remembered as the one man in all of human history who was able to dissuade Attila the Hun from sacking Rome. As Attila prepared for war in his camp outside of Rome, Leo rode up on his horse, not in armor but wearing the ecclesiastical vestments of a bishop. Attila had great awe and respect for Leo after seeing such faith and courage in an old man.

Leo is buried in St. Peter's Basilica.

Pope St. Hilarius

Pontificate: AD 461–AD 468

Feast day: February 28

Hilarius narrowly escaped death at the "Robber Council" of Ephesus (AD 449), and, when he was elected pope, he showed his gratitude by building a chapel of St. John the Apostle in the baptistery of the Basilica of St. John Lateran. Centralizing the papacy's authority in France and Spain proved to be a hallmark in his reign. He is buried at St. Lorenzo Fuori le Mura.

Pope St. Gelasius 1

Pontificate: AD 492–AD 496

Feast day: November 21

Gelasius was the first pope to use the title "Vicar of Christ." He also created a fourfold division of church donations and offerings. One part went to the poor, another to upkeep of the local parish, one portion to the bishop, and the fourth to the minor clergy.

Gelasius was an educated man and left a great depository of writings, ranging from theological letters and treatises to additions to the Roman Missal. He is buried in St. Peter's Basilica.

Pope St. John 1

Pontificate: AD 523–AD 526

Feast day: May 27

John was used as a pawn of sorts by Theodoric, the king of Italy, in an effort to mitigate the persecution and exile of Arian heretics. Emperor Justin I, a champion of orthodoxy, sought to root out the last vestiges of Arianism, but Theodoric, an Arian sympathizer, wanted John to intervene. One thing the pope didn't agree to was a concession to allow once-converted Arian heretics to return to their old ways.

That concession aside, the pope did go to Constantinople to temper the passion of the emperor. This was the first trip that any pope commenced to the capital of Byzantium. The results were bittersweet — the trip was quite successful in that the emperor received the pope with great joy and enthusiasm; on the other hand, when Pope John returned to Italy he was imprisoned by the mad king. He died in prison in AD 526.

Pope St. Felix III (IV)

Pontificate: AD 526–AD 530

Feast day: September 22

This Felix was concerned with heresies, particularly in France, where practitioners were following teachings that denied the workings of grace and free will. The pope reaffirmed the teachings of St. Augustine, who had dealt with this issue in North Africa a century earlier.

Felix was a good steward of the Church: He increased its funds and church property, converted pagan temples back into churches (including pagan temples in the Roman Forum, two of which he converted into Christian basilicas of SS. Cosmas and Damian), presided over numerous ordinations to the priesthood, and performed many charitable works. Known as a man of simplicity, humility, and charity, he was also a staunch defender of the faith.

He decreed that clerics were under ecclesiastical jurisdiction, not civil, and that only Church courts could try accused clergy and impose sentencing.

Pope St. Agapetus I

Pontificate: AD 535–AD 536

Feast day: April 22

Agapetus was an archdeacon and somewhat elderly when chosen to be pope. He was a cultured and well-learned man who owned a vast library and who hoped to establish a university in Rome with the books he collected.

Although unsuccessful, the pope traveled from Rome to Constantinople to meet with Emperor Justinian in an effort to dissuade him from invading Italy. He died in Constantinople.

Pope St. Gregory 1

Pontificate: AD 590–AD 604

Feast day: September 3

Gregory was quite literally born into a saintly heritage. He was the grandson of Pope St. Felix III and the son of Gordianus, a wealthy patrician, and Silvia, who was also a saint. Gregory started his religious life as a monk and converted the family villa in Rome to a monastery. His piety and monastic discipline marked his spiritual life as pope.

When he assumed the papacy, Rome was in shambles from wars, invasions, earthquakes, fires, and abandonment by the empire. Rome went into a steady decline as power shifted to Constantinople. Pope Gregory served to help the material needs of the people he also led spiritually in the Eternal City.

He reorganized all the patrimony due to the Holy See from estates throughout Italy; created the Gregory Missal, a compilation of changes in the traditional liturgy; and established the Gregorian chant musical style. He was a great supporter of missionary activity to England, where he sent St. Augustine of Canterbury and 49 missionaries. He is buried in St. Peter's.

Pope St. Boniface 1V

Pontificate: AD 608–AD 615

Feast day: May 8

Historians believe Pope Boniface worked closely with the great reforming pope Gregory I and was a champion of monasticism in the West. He was a member of the Benedictine Order.

He appointed the first Bishop of London and assembled a synod concerning monasticism, reforms that the bishop took back to England. The saintly pope was buried in the portico of St. Peter's, and his relics were later translated into the interior of the church.

Pope St. Martin 1

Pontificate: AD 649–AD 655

Feast day: November 12

Martin was a nuncio (papal ambassador) to Constantinople for Pope Theodore I before succeeding him in the papacy.

During his reign, Martin dealt with the heresy of *Monothelitism* — which denied that Christ had both a divine and a human will — and in so doing found himself in conflict with Emperor Constans II, who favored the Monothelists and silenced any opposition. Martin convened a council at the Lateran Palace, the official residence of the pope, in which Monothelitism was condemned, and appointed a vicar in the East to carry out his dictates, infuriating the emperor.

In retribution, the emperor sent a special dignitary to arrest the pope for high treason, but the representative converted upon seeing the pope's popularity and the doctrine's reasonableness. The emperor had to send another representative to arrest Martin and bring him to Constantinople. The arduous journey to the seat of the Byzantine Empire was difficult for Martin, who was already in failing health. He was found guilty in a mock trial and sentenced to death, but later his sentence was commuted to banishment.

It wasn't the humiliation or the terrible conditions of ill health that created Pope Martin I's suffering; rather, it was that the people of Rome had forgotten him. Nobody attempted to help or rescue him, and the Romans had in fact elected another pope.

Martin died in exile in AD 655. In AD 680, the sixth general council ratified his teachings, and Martin was venerated as the last papal martyr. He is buried at St. Martin di Monti.

Pope St. Vitalian

Pontificate: AD 657–AD 672

Feast day: January 27

Like many of his predecessors, Vitalian was forced to confront Monothelitism, the denial of the two wills of Christ. Both the emperor and the Constantinople patriarch supported this denial.

The pope maintained the Roman position but let the argument remain idle for a time. The emperor bestowed gifts upon him, and the patriarch included his name in the Constantinople diptych. When the emperor visited Rome, Vitalian received him warmly and, in another diplomatic decision, passed over the emperor's terrible treatment of his predecessor, Pope St. Martin I.

When the emperor was murdered in Sicily, Pope Vitalian backed the emperor's son, the logical successor to the empire. The son wasn't interested in doctrine, providing Vitalian an opportunity to come out with strong teachings against

Monothelitism. The Constantinople patriarch wasn't amused and tried to remove his name diptych, but the new emperor, remembering Vitalian's support, wouldn't allow it.

Vitalian is buried in St. Peter's Basilica.

Pope St. Agatho

Pontificate: AD 678–AD 681

Feast day: January 10

A Sicilian monk from Palermo, Agatho was married for 24 years before going into the monastery. He was instrumental in developing a friendly relationship between the Catholic Church and the Byzantine Empire. He convened a council in Rome, attended by more than 150 bishops, that not only condemned the Monothelitism heresy but also reaffirmed the pope's role as the custodian of the true faith.

Another great filial concern was the church in England. He sent a special envoy from Rome to look after the emerging church in this area and to teach Roman liturgical norms and chants, at the same time keeping a closer eye on the emerging church. Agatho was a well-loved pope; he gave what little money he had to his clergy in Rome and endowed St. Mary Major, one of the four major basilicas.

Pope St. Sergius 1

Pontificate: AD 687–AD 701

Feast day: September 8

Sergius, the son of a Syrian merchant, became pope under enormous controversy as anti-pope Paschal attempted to buy his way to the papacy through bribes. The influence of Constantinople and the Byzantine Empire were on the decline during Sergius's papacy. The emperor called a council, to which the pope wasn't invited, yet the emperor required him to sign the rules from the proceedings. Sergius refused, so the emperor sent troops to force the pope's signature; the troops, however, supported the pope. The emperor was eventually deposed in Constantinople and sent into exile.

Sergius turned his attention toward the new church in England and tried to reinforce Roman Christianity's foothold. He baptized the king of the Saxons, granting a *pallium* — sign of an archbishop — and thereby creating Canterbury and an archdiocese. In Rome, he restored, rebuilt, and enriched the basilicas of St. Peter, St. Paul, and St. Susana. He also established four feasts for the Blessed Virgin Mary: Annunciation, Assumption, Nativity, and Presentation. He is buried in St. Peter's.

Pope St. Gregory II

Pontificate: AD 715–AD 731

Feast day: February 11

Gregory was born in Rome. He was a librarian for four popes and was known as a brilliant scholar, but he was perhaps best known for his defense of doctrine. Emperor Leo wanted church icons destroyed, making the Church appear more accessible to Jews and Muslims, who banned such images. When the decree reached Italy, Gregory immediately rejected it, reaffirming Catholic teaching that only idols (objects or images for worship of false gods) were prohibited. Sacred art depicting Jesus and the saints was a good thing. Most illiterate people learned the faith by looking at icons and stained glass windows, often called the poor man's catechism.

Gregory also repaired the city walls and churches and opened institutions for the care of the elderly. He was a great supporter of monasticism: He turned his family estate into a monastery, restored the famous monastery of Monte Casino, and encouraged monastic vocations.

Pope St. Zacharias

Pontificate: AD 741–AD 752

Feast day: March 15

Zacharias, an Italian, was a learned man who knew how to read and write in Greek, skills that proved useful in dealing with the Byzantine emperor. At the time of his reign, the dispute over uses of sacred art and images still plagued the Church in the East; Zacharias, wise and diplomatic, cast the issue aside in favor of a better relationship with Constantinople.

Emperor Constantine V also put aside his religious differences and didn't persecute the pope and the West for retaining sacred images in worship. The emperor needed the support of the pope in dealing with the Lombards, who wanted to invade Ravenna, the last Byzantine stronghold in Italy.

Zacharias visited the king of the Lombards in a gesture of peace, forming a truce that resulted in the papal estates and political prisoners being returned to Rome. To the north, in the area of the Holy Roman Empire, the pope had excellent relations with the emperor and supported Boniface in his reign.

Pope St. Paul 1

Pontificate: AD 757–AD 767

Feast day: June 28

Paul was the brother of Pope Stephen III and became his immediate successor in AD 757. He met the challenges of his time with diplomacy, fortitude, and at times clemency, granting his allegiance to the Holy Roman emperor upon coronation. King Pepin and the pope shared a favorable relationship in which recognition of the newly formed Papal States was solidified.

Unfortunately, his relationships with the Lombard king and the emperor of Constantinople were clouded by controversy over sacred images in churches and their use in worship. Paul I died at St. Paul's Outside the Walls Basilica.

Pope St. Leo III

Pontificate: AD 795–AD 816

Feast day: June 12

Leo's papacy was one of intrigue and slander, as a splinter group begrudged his election and sought to overturn it. First, they kidnapped and beat the pope to near death. When he recovered, the group brought false charges against him — charges serious enough that Charlemagne, king of the Franks, came to Rome to help defend Leo. The pope was cleared of all charges, and, on Christmas Day, Pope Leo III crowned Charlemagne as the peace-loving emperor of the Romans, commencing the Holy Roman Empire of the West.

Pope St. Paschal 1

Pontificate: AD 817–AD 824

Feast day: February 12

Paschal's papacy was plagued by intrigue, calumny, and disobedience. He was elected and consecrated pope immediately, not waiting for the approval of the Holy Roman emperor. The emperor was such a good friend of Paschal's that he enacted a series of laws protecting the rights of the pope, the Papal States, and elections of future popes. The emperor's son visited Rome after being granted co-rule of the empire and was crowned co-emperor by the pope. From that time on, Holy Roman emperors traveled to Rome for their coronation by the pope.

Calumny inundated the pope when his papal household was involved in foul play and the pope was accused of being involved in the plot. He took a pledge of innocence before bishops to prove his innocence; however, upon his death the old lies resurfaced, and the Romans barred his burial at St. Peter's. Instead, he's buried in one of the churches he built, St. Praxedis.

Pope St. Leo IV

Pontificate: AD 847–AD 855

Feast day: July 17

The major threat during Leo's reign came from the Muslims, known as the Saracens, who attacked and destroyed cities up and down Italy's coast. Pope Leo IV rebuilt the walls of Rome and added new walls around the Vatican. He aided the reconstruction of many destroyed churches and took care of those displaced by the Saracen invasions. Internally, he worked to improve his clergy's moral status by adding several canons to Church law, reforming their education and discipline.

Pope St. Nicholas 1

Pontificate: AD 858–AD 867

Feast day: November 13

When Nicholas assumed the papacy, the church was faced with many challenges, not the least of which was the fall of Charlemagne and the resulting division of the Holy Roman Empire. No central political power existed — bishops were appointed and deposed at the whim of local nobility.

Nicholas was a champion for the sacrament of marriage, making many decisions regarding royal weddings that were being called into question. He also favored the freedom to marry over the veto powers of kings and fathers.

He ensured that food was prepared and delivered to poor invalids every day, setting aside substantial funds for their care and working to end their personal suffering. All these qualities made him one of the finest popes of his age and a true leader in the temporal and spiritual aspects of the Church — which the Church has recognized by designating him "Nicholas the Great," one of only three popes to earn the title.

Pope St. Gregory VII

Pontificate: 1073–1085

Feast day: May 25

Gregory VII was one of the most powerful popes in history, remembered for vigorously defending the independence and autonomy of the Church from the secular authority of the kings and the Holy Roman emperor.

This period was a truly trying time for the Church. Of the secular rulers — William the Conqueror of England, Philip I of France, and Henry IV of Germany — Henry IV was the most tiresome. Gregory excommunicated him twice for his infidelity; Henry IV is believed to have supported an anti-pope, or illegal rival pope.

Things inside the Church weren't much better. Gregory VII was confronted with a range of problems, including clerical laxity and a decline of moral leadership. He ordered archbishops throughout the empire to come to Rome to receive the sign of their office, the pallium, in an effort to consolidate the authority of the Holy See. He died at the monastery in Monte Casino.

Pope St. Celestine V

Pontificate: 1294

Feast day: May 19

Born Pietro di Murrone, Celestine was a hermit, from the Abruzzi section of Italy. He was not well-schooled in theology, Latin, or diplomacy; and was an unlikely choice to become a successor of St. Peter. The fact that he was made pope is testament to the terrible state of the Church in the 13th century. The throne of St. Peter had been vacant for more than two years when Pietro di Morone exhorted the cardinals to put their differences aside and elect a pope.

The five months of his papacy proved difficult for the 85-year-old Celestine. The king of the Two Sicilies, Charles II, saw an opportunity to make poor Celestine a puppet to his wishes. Charles had the pope create 13 cardinals, many of whom were French, in a bid to secure the next election of the pope.

Devastated by these machinations, Celestine wanted to abdicate the throne of Peter, which was unprecedented. With the help of Cardinal Gaetani, who eventually succeeded him as Boniface VIII, Celestine laid aside his papal robes, begged the cardinals' forgiveness, and returned to life as a hermit. Boniface VIII, worried that Celestine might be kidnapped and used to create a schism, kept Celestine a benign prisoner until the elderly hermit's death. Boniface canonized him a saint in 1313.

Pope St. Pius V

Pontificate: 1566–1572

Feast day: April 30

Michele Ghisleri, who became Pius when elected pope, was a great reformer. He accepted the "shoes of the fisherman" at a time when the Church was suffering from the Protestant revolt in most of Northern Europe. The Council of Trent had been convened before his papacy, and he implemented many of its reforms. He issued a new Roman Missal for Mass, the Roman Breviary — a scriptural prayer book for priests, and catechism — as the basis for other catechisms from children to adults, and a vernacular translation of the Bible. In addition, he enforced reform among bishops and priests, demanding that they live in the diocese and parish to which they were assigned; and he fought against *simony* (the buying and selling of ecclesiastical favors) and nepotism. These moves ushered in the age of the Counter-Reformation. Many new religious communities were formed, which helped create the armies of reform and bring back those souls lost to Catholicism.

As a politician, however, Pius V received mixed reviews. When monarchs, such as Queen Elizabeth I, left the Church and followed a new brand of religion, Pius excommunicated them. But the monarchs themselves were hardly affected. To the Catholics who remained in England, however, the excommunication proved disastrous. Those who remained in the faith were persecuted; many were sentenced to death for "high treason."

When it came to dealing with the Turks and the Muslim Ottoman Empire, however, the pope was more successful. The West united in the famous Battle of Lepanto, in which Christianity was victorious. Pius V saw the victory on October 7, 1571, as a gift from God through the intercession of the Blessed Virgin. He proclaimed a celebration known to this day as the Feast of Our Lady of the Most Holy Rosary. Originally, Pius V's feast was observed on May 5. In the new Roman calendar of 1969, it was moved to April 30.

Pope St. Pius X

Pontificate: 1903–1914

Feast day: August 21

Another great reformer of the Church, Giuseppe Melchiorre Sarto, also took the name Pius at the start of his papacy.

Among his many reforms were his attempts to address the heresy of modernism. In an encyclical 1907 letter, "Lamentabili," he condemned 65 modernist propositions. He sought to renew Bible study and liturgical music, reform the Roman Missal, and renew the Code of Canon Law — the laws that govern Church practice. He renewed and revised seminary life and training, encouraged children to receive Holy Communion at the age of reason, and championed daily Communion for all.

St. Pius X condemned the secular French states for breaking with an earlier agreement in matters of property. He defended the rights of the downtrodden in Peru, Ireland, Poland, and Portugal. He sent many missionaries to the United States to help the newly established immigrant church. Some received miracles from God through the prayers of this kind, religiously devout, and charitable pope while he was alive.

Pope Pius XII canonized him a saint in 1954.

Other Saintly Popes of the Early Catholic Church

Details about many popes who served in the earliest days of the Catholic Church have been lost to the mists of time, yet they're still considered saints. Here's a brief recap of what we know about these holy men.

Pope St. Cletus (AD 76–AD 88): Born a Roman as Cletus, he was also known by his name in Greek, Anacletus. He's listed in the Roman Canon of the Mass. His feast day is April 26.

Pope St. Evaristus (AD 97–AD 105): Evaristus, of Greek origin, was the fifth pope. He's buried next to St. Peter in the Christian cemetery on Vatican Hill, the site of the 16th-century basilica. His feast day is October 26.

Pope St. Sixtus I (AD 115–AD 125): St. Sixtus reigned for ten years before meeting a martyr's death. He's believed to be buried near the site of the first-century cemetery on Vatican Hill. He is remembered on April 3.

Pope St. Pius I (AD 140–AD 155): St. Pius I battled heretics that threatened the faith. So clear were Pope Pius I's teaching and preaching that he won over converts, including St. Justin Martyr. His feast is celebrated on July 11.

Pope St. Anicetus (AD 155–AD 166): St. Anicetus hung out with some notable theologians, such as St. Polycarp of Smyrna and St. Justin Martyr. He's most likely a martyr as well, even though no official details are known. His feast is on April 16.

Pope St. Soter (AD 166–AD 175): St. Soter introduced the solemnity of Easter as an annual celebration. Though no conclusive proof is available, he is traditionally considered a martyr and is remembered on April 22, along with another pope, St. Caius.

Pope St. Eleutherius (AD 175–AD 189): Eleutherius was a deacon in Rome before becoming a priest and then a bishop. He's remembered for his declaration that anything suitable for human consumption is suitable for Christians to eat. His feast is on May 26.

Pope St. Victor (AD 189–AD 199): Victor so strongly believed that the Church should observe a uniform date for the solemnity of Easter that he excommunicated certain churches in the East who preferred their own calendar and calculations. His feast is celebrated on July 28.

Pope St. Urban I (AD 222–AD 230): Urban reigned during the rule of Emperor Alexander Severus. Not much is known about him, other than the fact that he was a charitable and kind leader. He's buried in the papal chapel of the Catacombs of St. Callixtus, and his feast is noted on May 25.

Pope St. Anterus (AD 235–AD 236): Anterus, a Greek, was responsible for creating the Acts of the Martyrs, a collection of biographies on the early Christian martyrs documenting when, where, and how they died. He was only pope for 43 days before being martyred himself by order of Emperor Maximinus Thrax; he was buried in the newly built papal chamber of the Catacombs of St. Callixtus. His feast is celebrated on January 3.

Pope St. Felix I (AD 268–AD 274): Felix ordered the celebration of Mass over the tombs of martyred Christians in the catacombs. His feast is May 30.

Pope St. Eutychian (AD 275–AD 283): Eutychian wasn't martyred but has been considered a saint since antiquity. He reigned during a very peaceful respite between persecutions. He was the last pope to be buried in the papal chamber of the Catacombs of St. Callixtus. His feast day is December 7.

Pope St. Marcellus I (AD 308–AD 309): Marcellus wanted repentant *lapsi* to perform appropriate penances, an unpopular position that led to riots. Emperor Maxentius exiled Marcellus in an effort to calm down the populace. He died in AD 309 and is buried in the church named after him in Rome. His feast is memorialized on January 16.

Pope St. Eusebius (AD 309): Eusebius sought substantial penances from repentant *lapsi,* leading Emperor Maxentius to exile him to Sicily, where he died. Eusebius's body was transferred to Rome and buried in the Catacombs of St. Callixtus. His feast is celebrated on August 17.

Pope St. Mark (AD 336): Mark's pontificate only lasted eight months, but he established two churches in Rome: one named after the evangelist Mark, currently incorporated in Palazzo di Venezia, and the second in the cemetery of St. Balbina, which has since been destroyed. Two important documents also came out of his pontificate: the Episcopal and Martyr Deposits, both of great historical value for the Church. His feast is recalled on October 7.

Pope St. Anastasius I (AD 399–AD 401): Anastasius settled theological controversies concerning an early Church father of theology, Origen. Origen had many good theological points but had confusing ones as well. Anastasius had to clarify matters and condemn those parts that were heretical, which earned him praise from St. Jerome. Anastasius's feast day is celebrated on December 19.

Pope St. Zosimus (AD 417–AD 418): In his short time as pope, Zosimus dealt with heresy and battled against episcopal intrigue and skulduggery surrounding imperial politics. Though not the most astute in areas of Church politics, he was a holy, kind, and charitable man. His feast is December 26.

Pope St. Simplicius (AD 468–AD 483): Simplicius saw the western Roman Emperor, Romulus Augustus, defeated by barbarian invaders, thus causing the city and empire to fall once and for all in AD 476. Pope Simplicius also had to deal with the usual heresies of the times. His feast is March 10.

Pope St. Felix II (III) (AD 483–AD 492): Some historians, to separate him from the anti-pope Felix II, list this pope as Felix III. He worked with the emperor to fight heresy throughout the empire. He's buried at the Basilica of St. Paul Outside the Walls; his feast is March 1.

Pope St. Symmachus (AD 498–AD 514): Symmachus was archdeacon of the Eternal City (another name for Rome); his election to the papacy, however, was fraught with controversy as he faced struggles with the anti-pope Laurence. Symmachus embellished many churches throughout Rome and helped refugees in exile from heretical tyrants. He died on July 19 and is buried at St. Peter's Basilica.

Pope St. Hormisdas (AD 514–AD 523): Not much is known about Hormisdas, who, like the first pope, St. Peter, had a wife. She died and left him a son, who later became Pope Silverius. Hormisdas compiled a confession of faith, *Hormisdas Formula,* allowing heretics to reenter the Church. His feast day is August 6.

Pope St. Silverius (AD 536–AD 537): Silverius was a subdeacon in Rome when elected pope. He was forced to abdicate his papacy in AD 537, falling victim to scheming by Empress Theodora, who wanted the pope to restore heretical leaders to their respective dioceses. When Silverius refused, the enraged empress plotted his downfall. He was reinstated to the throne of St. Peter by the emperor, who wasn't aware of his wife's skullduggery. Pope St. Silverius's feast day is June 20.

Pope St. Adeodatus I (AD 615–AD 618): After more than 40 years as a priest, Adeodatus was elected to the papacy at a late age. He was the first pope to use lead seals on papal decrees (called *bulls*). In his will, he left a year's salary to local clergy. His feast is November 8.

Pope St. Eugene I (AD 654–AD 657): Eugene was a priest in Rome when chosen pope and struggled with the emperor over Monothelitism. Unlike his predecessor, Pope Martin I, who openly condemned the Patriarch of Constantinople for his Monothelite opinions, Eugene chose to be more diplomatic and tone down the rhetoric without denying the faith. He did refuse to sign a document that the patriarch sent to the pope, further confusing the issue of how many wills Christ had. The advancing Muslim troops against the Eastern Empire preoccupied the emperor and the patriarch, and Eugene was spared the humiliation and imprisonment suffered by his predecessor, Martin. He died in AD 657; his feast is June 2.

Pope St. Leo II (AD 682–AD 683): Leo II was an outstanding preacher who loved music but cared for the poor even more. The emperor often interfered with Church policies, and this was the case in Leo's election. It took 18 months before the emperor gave his approval and Leo could go through the coronation ceremonies. The controversy centered on the sixth ecumenical council of Constantinople III (AD 680), which condemned both the heresy of Monothelitism and Pope Honorius I (accusing him of having heretical opinions). Leo confirmed the condemnation of the heresy itself and of his predecessor's (Honorius) private opinions while making it clear that these theories never enjoyed formal approval. His feast is celebrated on July 3.

Pope St. Benedict II (AD 684–AD 685): When it came time for Benedict, proficient in both sacred music and Scripture, to be considered for the papacy, the Church of Rome still elected the popes, and they had to wait for imperial recognition before they could actually ascend the throne. Benedict got the emperor to agree to cede his approval authority to the local ruler in Italy, thus saving time between election and papal coronation. His feast is May 8.

Chapter 9

Founding Fathers and Mothers

In This Chapter

▶ Looking at the founders of the Franciscans and Dominicans

▶ Checking out some other Church Fathers and Mothers

*J*ust as a country honors its founding fathers and mothers, the Church honors the holy men and women who helped establish religious communities that have served the needs of many throughout the centuries. In this chapter, we look at the men and women who are considered the founders of various religious orders.

These founding fathers and mothers determined the name of the society they established as well as the *charism,* or spirit of the group. Even though a more formal name may have been used when these religious communities were created by their founders, many times the nickname of the organization comes from the personal name of the founding mother or father (Dominicans for the Order of Preachers; Franciscans for the Order of Friars Minor; Vincentians for the Congregation of the Mission; and so on).

St. Alphonsus Ligouri

Campania, Kingdom of Naples (current Italy) (1696–1787)

Beatified: 1816

Canonized: 1839

Patron: moral theologians, ethicists, arthritis sufferers

Feast day: August 1

Alphonsus was something of a child prodigy, earning his doctorate in law by the age of 16 and having his own legal practice at age 21. Despite his legal prowess, however, just one significant loss forced Alphonsus to reassess his life choices and realize his true calling was the priesthood.

With his legal background and thinking style, Alphonsus was able to teach moral theology in a manner that was neither too lax nor too rigorous. His manuals in ethics have been considered classics for centuries, although he was met with some early opposition from those who considered him either too progressive or too reactionary.

Alphonsus was ordained in 1726, and in less than six years, he inaugurated a new religious community for men known as the Redemptorists after Our Lord and Savior, Jesus Christ the Redeemer. The Congregation of the Most Holy Redeemer (CSsR from the Latin initials) was established as an order of missionary preachers who, to this day, are renowned for their eloquent homilies and sermons.

St. Augustine of Hippo

Algeria (AD 354–AD 430)

Patron: theology and philosophy professors, former playboys

Feast day: August 28

Augustine — the same man who would go on to establish a religious order of monks called the Augustinians — spent his early adult years in a life of debauchery and moral decadence. He immersed himself in a lifestyle filled with overindulgence and illicit pleasure, mimicking what was happening in the Roman Empire at the time. Once a stoic and respected empire, it had degenerated into rampant drunkenness, promiscuity, and hedonism.

As the empire crumbled and barbarians raided and invaded the frontier and the capital, Augustine's desire for ultimate pleasure at all costs began to wane. At the age of 18, he had already fathered a son out of wedlock, Adeodatus (meaning "gift from God"), but "the good life" took its toll, and Augustine began to yearn for something more substantial. He realized that a spiritual realm coexisted with the material world.

Unfortunately, Augustine turned from his hedonistic lifestyle to dualism, or Manichaeism — the belief that anything physical is intrinsically evil, and only the purely immaterial is good. Instead of turning to religion as his mother, St. Monica, had prayed he would, Augustine adopted a Persian philosophy that viewed the battle of good and evil as being fought between the spiritual and material.

The book of Genesis tells us that God created both the spiritual and the material and that it was "good." Christianity takes this concept a step further: The doctrine of the Incarnation teaches that God took on a human nature in Jesus Christ. In other words, the pure spirit (God) took a physical body. How could this happen if the body were evil?

St. Ambrose of Milan first broke through to Augustine, explaining that, while the world contains both good and evil, they are not equal forces. Evil is the absence of a good that ought to be present. A physical evil, for example, would be a violent hurricane that destroys a peaceful village. A moral evil is when a human being does something wrong instead of doing the right thing (like telling a lie rather than telling the truth).

Augustine pondered Ambrose's words, and after much thought and prayer — and with the help of divine grace — he accepted the faith and became a believer. He and his son were baptized in AD 384 and became ardent Christians. Augustine became a staunch defender of the faith and used the philosophy of Plato to explain and defend Catholic doctrine. After the death of his beloved mother, he sold his possessions and founded the first monastery in the West.

Augustine also fought the Pelagian heresy, a belief that any man or woman could get into heaven on his or her own merit, without the assistance of God. Augustine staunchly opposed Pelagianism and taught that any and all supernatural good works are the result of divine grace.

Augustine's religious order was named after him, the Order of St. Augustine. The abbreviation OSA comes at the end of the name of an Augustinian monk — for example, Rev. Dudley Day, OSA. Augustine initially intended to live the life of a hermit — one of solitude and little or no influence from the outside world — in an effort to escape the brutality of the Barbarians.

Augustine wrote *Confessions,* an autobiography in which he admits his wild, decadent youth and his imprudent overreaction in embracing dualism. He then explains that the Judeo-Christian religion is true because it's rooted in reality; namely, that God created both the material and the immaterial, the physical and the spiritual. Either one can be abused and misused for nefarious purposes, but good ultimately triumphs because it's inherently superior to evil.

St. Benedict of Nursia

Cassino, Italy (AD 480–AD 543)

Canonized: 1220

Patron: Europe, poison victims

Feast day: July 11

In sharp contrast to St. Augustine's early years, Benedict was turned off by the wild and rampant living taking place in Rome and fled to Subiaco, Italy, where he lived in a cave for three years. He later moved to the mountains of Monte Cassino, where he established a monastic way of life. He and his monks lived by the creed *ora et labora,* or "prayer and work," which left him to divide his days equally between spiritual reflection and manual labor. At his monastery, the chapel bells rang every three hours to call the monks to prayer.

Benedict offered stablility and guidance in the darkness of invasions and the collapse of Western civilization. His monasteries grew and spread quickly. Benedictine monasteries proliferated in Western Europe during the Middle Ages. The monks initially left the dangerous cities to live a life of simplicity, but after the Roman Empire fell (AD 476) and the barbarians became civilized, the monks' mission evolved into preserving the culture, art, literature, and education from antiquity. The monks not only preserved the Latin and Greek languages but also taught the former barbarians how to read and write. Eventually, people moved out of the old cities, and, over time, they built new ones surrounding the monks.

Benedict's twin sister, Scholastica, established the female counterpart to her brother's monastic order. Benedictine nuns operate much like their male contemporaries, also following the "*ora et labora*" way of life. Both men and women of the Benedictine order have the letters OSB after their proper names to designate that they're members of the Order of St. Benedict.

St. Clare of Assisi

Assisi, Italy (1194–1253)

Canonized: 1255

Patron: television, goldsmiths

Feast day: August 11

When she was 18 years old, Clare heard a popular preacher, St. Francis of Assisi (see his entry later in this chapter), for the first time and was so moved that she immediately decided to found her own branch of religious women to be of spiritual support to the Franciscans.

Clare established the community of the Poor Ladies (now known as the Poor Clares) to meditate day and night and offer prayers for the Church. She was joined by her sister, Agnes, as well as many other women who lived in religious poverty, much like their Franciscan counterparts. With no money or land, they begged for their daily sustenance.

The Poor Clares are still active today, with likely the most active group in Alabama at Eternal Word Television Network (EWTN) — the international Catholic media network that includes radio, Internet, shortwave radio, and satellite and cable television.

St. Dominic de Guzman

Calaruega, Province of Burgos, Kingdom of Castile (current Spain) (1170–1221)

Canonized: 1234

Patron: preachers, astonomers, the Dominican Republic

Feast day: August 8

The first vision to affect Dominic's life happened before he was even born; while she was pregnant, Dominic's mother had a vision of a dog with a torch in its mouth. The religious order Dominic would one day establish is called the Dominicans (Order of Friars Preachers) — *domini cani,* the Italian equivalent, means "hounds of the Lord," a phrase used to describe steadfast preaching.

Dominic was ordained a priest in 1194. By 1215, he formed his own religious community as a *mendicant*, or beggar, much like St. Francis of Assisi. The Dominicans, like the Franciscans, are technically not monks but friars, and they live in friaries, not monasteries.

Dominic's greatest challenge was the Albigensian heresy. Similar to the Manichaeism and dualism that St. Augustine battled centuries before, Albigensianism held that Christ didn't have a true human nature. These heretics believed that anything material or physical was intrinsically evil and that Jesus only pretended to have a real humanity along with his divinity. Creation was not good, according to the Albigensians, and Jesus was only divine and not human.

Contemplating the mysteries of Jesus

With the aid of Rosary beads, the faithful contemplate 15 mysteries of Christ by praying 10 Hail Marys (Ave Marias), followed by an Our Father (Pater Noster) and a Glory Be (Gloria). During these prayers, the worshipper ponders the Joyful Mysteries *(Annunciation, Visitation, Nativity, Presentation and Finding in the Temple),* the Sorrowful Mysteries *(Agony in the Garden, Scourging at the Pillar, Crowning of Thorns, Carrying of the Cross, Crucifixion and Death),* and the Glorious Mysteries *(Resurrection, Ascension, Pentecost, Assumption, Coronation).*

Famous Dominicans

Pope St. Pius V was a Dominican before he became Pope in 1566. Until then, popes wore the red of the cardinal's office they held before being elected Bishop of Rome and Successor of St. Peter. While some white was worn to distinguish the pope from other cardinals, it wasn't until Pius V, a Dominican whose former habit was an all-white tunic, that the popes started wearing the now-familiar all-white cassock.

St. Albert the Great, the patron saint of scientists, was another famous Dominican. He was the first to cross the bridge from alchemy to chemistry, and his thirst for scientific, philosophical, and theological knowledge motivated his greatest student, St. Thomas Aquinas. Both of these Dominican saints lived in the 13th century and left an invaluable legacy to their Order of Preachers.

Despite his eloquent preaching talent, Dominic was unable to dissuade the lay faithful in Spain and France from this growing heresy. Discouraged, he prayed for assistance, and the Virgin Mary gave him an answer. In a vision, he saw the Blessed Mother with the child Jesus, and she gave Dominic a Rosary (prayer beads). Since Hebrew times of the Old Testament, believers have used prayer beads to keep count when they pray the 150 Psalms as found in the Bible. Those same 150 beads could also be used to help defeat Albigensians, according to Dominic's vision.

Common folk used prayer beads to pray the Psalms. St. Dominic asked them to use those same beads to think about the mysteries of Christ (see the nearby sidebar, "Contemplating the mysteries of Jesus"), which reveal both His humanity and His divinity. Only a man can suffer pain and death, yet only a god can rise from the dead and ascend into heaven. The spiritual "tool" of the Rosary worked, and the Albigensian heresy was defeated. The people embraced the orthodox teaching that Christ is true God and true Man, one divine person with two complete natures, human and divine.

St. Francis de Sales

Château de Thorens, Savoy, France (1567–1622)

Beatified: 1662

Canonized: 1665

Patron: journalists

Feast day: January 24

Francis was destined by his father to study law and enter into politics, but it was his Holy Father who calmed him during a stressful and overwhelming time, causing Francis to resign himself completely to the Divine Providence. He decided to become a priest and was ordained in Geneva in 1593. He was later named Bishop of Geneva and consecrated in 1602.

Francis established the Oblates of St. Francis de Sales (*Oblati Sancti Francisci Sales*ii, O.S.F.S) to help promote the faith beyond the confines of the parish and diocese. The spirituality is based on *Introduction to a Devout Life,* a book Francis wrote for those struggling to become better Christians.

St. Francis also is one of the incorruptible saints; see his entry in Chapter 5.

St. Francis of Assisi

Assisi, Italy (1181–1226)

Canonized: 1228

Patron: animals, pet owners, veterinarians; San Francisco

Feast day: October 4

Francis — known now for his life of poverty and his work with the poor and needy — was once a spoiled young man who lived a life of ease, partying through the day and night and spending time with his friends.

Italy didn't become a unified kingdom until the 19th century, so in Francis's time, frequent battles took place between the cities and states. The people of Assisi and Perugia often were at battle; in one fight, Francis and his friends went to defend Assisi. The Perugians defeated Assisi, however, and Francis was jailed for a year.

Francis became ill with fever while in jail and spent time in the infirmary, providing him with plenty of time to think of how he had wasted his life thus far. He decided to join the military and serve with honor when he was released and went to join Count Walter of Brienne. While traveling, he had a vision of the Lord saying to him, "Go, Francis, and repair my house, which as you see is falling into ruin."

Francis misunderstood the Lord's request. He ran to his father's cloth shop and took the most expensive materials he could find. He sold the materials and his horse and took the money to the priest of a church in San Damiano that was in disrepair. Knowing that Francis had stolen the materials from his father, the priest refused the money.

Francis's father, Bernadone, was incensed when he learned what his son had done. His temper was so intense that Francis fled and hid in a cave in San Damiano for a month. He emerged dirty, unshaven, undernourished, and a general mess, making himself the subject of ridicule. His father dragged him home, beat him, and locked him in a closet. His mother helped him escape one day when his father was away on business.

Francis returned to the church in San Damiano and helped the priest there. When his father came looking for him, he told him: "Up to now I have called you my father on earth; henceforth I desire to say only 'Our Father who art in Heaven.'" He then stripped himself of his clothes and handed them to his father, donning instead the clothing of a beggar. Over time, Francis acquired some companions who sought to rebuild the Church, and he realized what the Lord had meant: The Church he wanted Francis to rebuild was not the buildings but rather the people who came to worship in them. Francis realized his mission was to preach spiritual renewal to the people of God. Pope Innocent III gave permission for him to establish a new religious community, the Order of Friars Minor (OFM), which would later be known as the Franciscans.

Francis and the others took vows of poverty, chastity, and obedience. However, unlike the monks in the monasteries who also took a vow of stability to live and die at that monastery, the Franciscans and their colleagues, the Dominicans, were mendicants; they begged for their sustenance, as they had no land and no money of their own. They literally had to live on the generosity of others.

St. Francis is known as the patron saint of animals and animal lovers because he spent time in meditation outside and was sometimes found conversing with these creatures. He even befriended a wolf in Gubbio that had been bullying the local villagers. He admonished the beast to behave, which the wolf did from then on.

Francis also traveled to the Holy Land in an attempt to convert the Muslim Saracens and thus end the Crusades peacefully. He was unsuccessful in that specific goal, but he did secure the admiration of the Caliph, who ordered that certain Christian shrines in Jerusalem be placed in the care of the Franciscans — a role the Franciscans have carried out for centuries.

Well before his life ended, Francis was blessed with the gift of the *stigmata,* the manifestation of the five wounds of Jesus on the person without any physical harm (stigmata disappears immediately at death, however). Figure 9-1 shows St. Francis with the stigmata on his hands, meditating on the Gospel while praying over a skull (a symbol of the dying self, or replacing the ego with the will of God).

Figure 9-1:
St. Francis.

Réunion des Musées Nationaux/Art Resource, NY

St. Ignatius of Loyola

Loyola, Spain (1491–1556)

Beatified: 1609

Canonized: 1622

Patron: military personnel

Feast day: July 31

Ignatius had long sought a soldier's life, and in 1517, he entered the army and served in numerous campaigns with bravery and distinction. His life took a turn, however, when his leg was shattered by a cannonball in 1521.

Recuperation was long and painful, and Ignatius had little to do but read the Bible and the *Lives of the Saints.* Ignatius plowed through both, eventually determining that he shouldn't be risking his life for an earthly king when the King of Kings promised him eternal life. Ignatius laid down his secular sword and became a "soldier for Christ," allying himself with Jesus. He established a community of men he called the Society of Jesus, later to be known as the Jesuits (see Figure 9-2).

Ignatius saw the advantage of training men in all the classics of theology and philosophy, as well as geography, science, math, languages, and other humanities. He planned to conquer error and heresy with truth and knowledge, which is why the Jesuits to this day are one of the most educated of religious communities. In addition to taking solemn vows of poverty, chastity, and obedience, Ignatius added a fourth vow, of complete service to the pope.

Popes in different times used the Jesuits and their growing influence to promote and defend the faith. Secular kings and princes, however, resented and envied the Jesuits' success and finally pressured Rome to suppress the Order in 1767. Not until the Council of Vienna in 1814 after the Napoleonic Wars was the Society of Jesus (Jesuits) restored.

Figure 9-2:
St. Ignatius contemplating the Holy Name of Jesus (*IHS*, the first three letters of Jesus's name in Greek).

*Réunion des Musées Nationaux/
Art Resource, NY*

St. Lucy Filippini

Corneto, Tuscany, Italy (1672–1732)

Beatified: 1926

Canonized: 1930

Patron: Catholic grammar schools

Feast day: March 25

After being orphaned as a young child, Lucy was taken under the wing of Cardinal Marc'Antonio Barbarigo, who inspired and protected her and encouraged her to work among the younger girls of the diocese. The Cardinal wanted Lucy to help make sure that the girls received a Christian education and upbringing.

Lucy established the Religious Teachers Filippini in 1692 to educate and train religious women, who in turn taught the young, especially young women, to prepare them for life, whether they married or entered the convent. Boys commonly received instruction to prepare them to become priests or lay Christian gentlemen, but young women seldom received such spiritual and academic guidance. The Religious Teachers Filippini was established to give these young women the tools they needed to spiritually succeed.

St. Philip Neri

Florence, Italy (1515–1595)

Beatified: 1615

Canonized: 1622

Patron: U.S. Special Forces

Feast day: May 26

Philip spent most of his life as a devout layman, only becoming ordained to the priesthood in 1551, when he was in his mid '30s. Until then, he studied and prayed and worked in the hospitals helping the sick.

He had a strong devotion to the Holy Eucharist and encouraged others to spend time in prayer before the Blessed Sacrament. After he was ordained, Philip established the Congregation of the Oratory (CO) to help priests become holier and thus help their parishioners as well.

St. Philip Neri's oratories were and remain today an innovative creation: priests living together in a quasi-community but still working as typical parish priests. The fraternity and camaraderie, as well as spiritual support, is an attempt to compensate for what's missing in most rectories (where most parish priests live). One of the most famous oratories is in London, England, where Cardinal Newman, the Anglican convert, spent his final years.

St. Vincent de Paul

France (1581–1660)

Beatified: 1729

Canonized: 1737

Patron: social workers, seminary professors

Feast day: September 27

Vincent de Paul's priesthood got off to a somewhat turbulent start. Five years after being ordained, he was captured by Turkish pirates and held hostage for two years. He eventually converted his "owner" to Christianity and was granted freedom. He returned to Rome to expand his studies and eventually ended up in a wealthy parish in Paris.

In Paris, he befriended some affluent parishioners and convinced them to use their wealth to help the poor, one of two great needs he recognized in the early 17th century. The other great need he saw was the education of the clergy; poorly educated priests helped sow the seeds of the Reformation, and ignoring the plight of the poor was equally devastating to the church and society at large.

The Black Death (bubonic plague in 1348–1350) decimated a third of the population of Western Europe and killed two-thirds of the clergy. So desperate were people for priests to administer the sacraments that sometimes uneducated and incompetent men were ordained, and their misbehavior and/or unorthodox ideas made fertile ground for religious revolution.

Vincent established the Congregation of the Mission (CM) to work on those two priorities: service to the poor and education of the clergy (seminary formation). The Council of Trent had met from 1545–1563 in response to Martin Luther and the Protestant Reformation. One of the council's decrees was the establishment of adequate seminaries to educate and supervise the formation of clergy to better serve the spiritual needs of the people in the parish.

Chapter 10

Ruling with Sanctity: Saints of Nobility

• •

In This Chapter

▶ Kings and queens who became saints

▶ Other nobles who achieved sainthood

• •

In this chapter, we look at some saintly monarchs, who were both devout Christians and virtuous rulers. We include the well known as well as the obscure to show the spectrum of holiness, even among the privileged.

St. Canute IV, King of Denmark

Denmark (1043–1086)

Canonized: 1101

Patron: Denmark

Feast day: January 19

Some historians believe that Canute was the illegitimate son of King Swein Estrithson of Denmark. He was the nephew of the king of England, and in 1081, he succeeded his brother Harold as king of Denmark. He and his wife, Adela, had a son, Charles the Good.

As a ruler, Canute was dynamic both civilly and religiously. On the civil front, he consolidated much of the power under the king through ownership of land, inheritance of possessions, and claiming booty from war and shipwrecks. In religion, he championed the rights of the poor, the vulnerable, orphans, and widows. He granted immunities and privileges to the clergy, and he commenced a rather ambitious building campaign in which many churches were built throughout the Danish kingdom.

One of his last campaigns was to reestablish his right to the throne in England. He assembled a navy and started an invasion of England, but he had to abandon the effort in Flanders. There, he sought exile with his brother Benedict in the Church of St. Alban, which he endowed with a relic of St. Alban that he had rescued from an earlier campaign in York, England. Huddled near the tabernacle in prayer, he confessed his sins, received Viaticum, and was martyred in the church sanctuary in 1086. His son Charles the Good, Count of Flanders, met a similar death in 1127 in Bruges.

Blessed Charlemagne (Charles the Great)

Germany (AD 742–AD 814)

Beatified: 1700s

Feast day: January 28

Charles was the eldest son of Pepin the Short — the king of the Franks — and Queen Bertha of Laon. His paternal grandfather was Charles Martel, who won the Battle of Tours in AD 732 and saved Europe from a Muslim invasion.

Charles saved Rome, the pope, and the Papal States when they were attacked by the Lombards. As a reward, Pope Leo III crowned Charles Holy Roman Emperor on Christmas Day, AD 800. From that point on, he was known as *Carolus Magnus* in Latin, or *Charlemagne* in French.

Under his reign, Charlemagne united Europe by supporting agricultural development and education and by codifying law. He was a devout Catholic Christian and sought to protect the unity and autonomy of the Church. During his reign, the notion of a unified Europe under one supreme secular ruler, or emperor, and one supreme spiritual ruler, or pope, first came to fruition and was called *Christendom*.

Pope Benedict XIV beatified Charlemagne in the 1700s. The anti-pope, or false pope, Paschal III, had canonized him in 1165 in an attempt to appease the Holy Roman Emperor Frederick Barbarossa and thus be recognized as pope, but to no avail. No legitimate pope has canonized Charlemagne, although he remains beatified.

St. David of Scotland

Scotland (1085–1153)

Patron: Scotland

Feast day: May 24

David was the son of St. Margaret and King Malcolm of Scotland. In 1113, he married Countess Matilda of Huntingdon and was given the title Earl of Northampton.

David was known for his piety and love of the poor and as a devoted son of the Church. At one point, he asked the pope to promote the Catholic diocese of Glasgow to an archdiocese, which would free its ties with York, England. Though the Holy See didn't grant this favor, David remained a staunch supporter of the pope.

David succeeded to the Scottish throne in 1124. He was a good civil ruler who initiated reforms among the clergy and established abbeys, churches, and dioceses throughout Scotland. Because the monasteries were centers of learning, they helped to educate the Scots. In addition, the monks introduced new agricultural methods that secured food and wealth for the people through the selling of crops to other European countries. Historians point to all these attributes as the turning point in Scottish history, when Scotland became a proper country.

St. Edward the Confessor

England (1003–1066)

Canonized: 1161

Patron: difficult marriages, monarchs of England, and separated spouses

Feast day: October 13

Edward was known to be a devoted man of God who never reproached even his enemies. On hunting trips that would take him away sometimes for days at a time, Edward took along his own chaplain and attended daily Mass.

Civil unrest in England led to Edward's exile to Normandy for a time, and he wanted to travel to the tomb of St. Peter to atone for his sins. When he was no longer exiled, Edward built and endowed a special church in London in honor of St. Peter, known as Westminster Abbey.

The abbey was built with room for 70 monks, and Pope Nicholas II bestowed special privileges. After the Protestant Reformation took hold in England with the establishment of the Anglican Church, Queen Elizabeth I dissolved the monastery and made it one of her royal chapels. However, the throne on which Edward received his crown was preserved and can still be viewed in the monastery. Every king and queen of Great Britain has been crowned on the throne of St. Edward the Confessor.

Edward is buried in his beloved abbey. When his body was exhumed nearly 100 years after his death, it was found to be incorrupt.

St. Elizabeth of Hungary

Hungary (1207–1231)

Canonized: 1235

Patron: bakers, beggars, brides, charitable societies and workers, charities, countesses, exiles, falsely accused people, homeless people, hospitals, lace makers, nursing homes, people ridiculed for their piety, and widows; invoked against death of children, in-law problems, and toothaches

Feast day: November 17

Elizabeth was the daughter of King Andrew and Queen Gertrude of Hungary. She was betrothed at the age of 4 to Hermann, the eldest son of Landgrave Hermann I of Thuringia. Her mother was murdered by Hungarian nobles in 1213, and her fiancé Hermann died unexpectedly three years later. Elizabeth was then betrothed to Ludwig, the second son.

Ludwig and Elizabeth were married in 1221, when he was 21 and she was 14. They were happily married and had three children: Hermann, Sophia, and Gertrude, who was later beatified.

Elizabeth practiced the theological virtues throughout her marriage, particularly that of charity. She was known to help alleviate the suffering of the starving by selling her royal robes and jewelry in order to buy them food. When a great famine arose in the kingdom of what's now Germany, Elizabeth felt compelled to do all she could to help.

She built and financially supported hospitals, one of which was at the foot of her residence, making it easier for her to attend to the needs of the sick on a daily basis. She cleaned, changed linens, and fed the patients.

Elizabeth joined the Third Order of St. Francis, a spirituality open to laity. Like the First and Second Orders — priests and nuns, respectively — the Third Order was designed to spread the spirituality of St. Francis of Assisi among the people.

Ludwig, answering the call to crusade against the Ottoman Turks, contracted the plague and died just six years after he and Elizabeth were married. When Elizabeth learned of her husband's death, she sank into a deep depression.

Pope Gregory IX appointed a royal defender, Father Conrad of Marburg, in the Duchy of Hesse, to oversee Elizabeth's affairs. He was an exceptionally religious and zealous man. Under his direction, Elizabeth took vows like a religious nun. In his desire to have Elizabeth grow more spiritually with the Lord, he took every form of comfort away from her, including the warmth of her children. Because of the harsh penances inflicted upon her and the rigorous life of charity she led, Elizabeth's health began to fail, and she died at the age of 24.

St. Elizabeth of Portugal

Portugal (1271–1336)

Canonized: 1625

Patron: brides, charitable societies and workers, Coimbra (a city in Portugal), difficult marriages, falsely accused people, and peace; invoked against jealousy and in time of war

Feast day: July 4

Elizabeth was the daughter of King Pedro III and Queen Constantia of Aragon, great-granddaughter of the Holy Roman Emperor Frederick II, and great-niece of St. Elizabeth of Hungary, after whom she was named. Even as a young girl, she showed concern and compassion for the poor.

At the age of 12 she married King Denis (Diniz) of Portugal. He proved to be a good ruler but a bad husband, as Elizabeth suffered his abuse and infidelity for many years. Her husband had such a jealous streak that he believed a lie that a court page told regarding an affair between Elizabeth and another page. The king ordered that the page he believed to be having the affair be killed, but through an error, the lying page was killed instead. King Denis realized God had protected the innocent page and especially his innocent wife and queen, Elizabeth. He reformed his evil ways on the spot.

The royal couple had two children: Constance, who married the king of Castile; and Affonso IV, the heir to the throne. Unfortunately, the king had sired many other illegitimate children who contended for their father's affection, if not his very throne.

The remaining years of Denis's life were filled with sickness and a slow descent to death. Elizabeth stood by his side all day in his room whenever she wasn't attending Mass. Her husband sought forgiveness for his infidelity and any cruelty imposed upon her from listening to gossip.

When Denis died, Elizabeth wanted to enter the Monastery of the Poor Clares that she founded in Coimbra, Portugal. She was dissuaded from entering strict cloister life, however, and instead took the habit of the Third Order of St. Francis and lived in a house near the monastery. In one of her last efforts at peacemaking, she went on a mission to stop a war between Portugal and Castile and was killed on July 4.

St. Helena of Constantinople

Nicomedia (in modern-day Turkey; AD 246–AD 330)

Patron: archeologists, converts, difficult marriages, divorced people, empresses, and the diocese of Helena, Montana

Feast day: August 18

Helena came from humble beginnings, but married a Roman general, Constantius I Chlorus, and they had a son, Constantine. The general was made Roman emperor in AD 293 and divorced Helena so he could marry the stepdaughter of the co-emperor, Maximian. Constantius died in AD 308, and Helena's son Constantine became the emperor.

Upon his ascension to the imperial throne, Constantine proclaimed the Edict of Milan in AD 313, which legalized Christianity after three centuries of Roman persecution. It didn't outlaw paganism, but it did remove the outlaw status Christians had been subjected to since the time of the Emperor Nero.

Although Constantine didn't fully convert to Christianity until he was on his deathbed, he dearly loved his mother and provided her with every privilege and opportunity to promote the Christian religion.

Helena traveled to Palestine at age 80 on a pilgrimage to search for the historic places in Christ's early life. She went to the place of the Crucifixion on Calvary Hill in Jerusalem and found three remnants of crosses that had been used to crucify Roman prisoners. Helena brought a sick woman to touch the three pieces of wood, and only one — the true cross of Christ — provided an immediate and complete cure.

St. Helena had a church built on the very spot where Christ died where she enshrined some of the relics of the true cross. She sent other pieces to the pope in Rome and to her son, the emperor. She also established the Church in the Garden of Olives and the Church of the Nativity in Bethlehem.

She is enshrined at St. Peter's Basilica in Rome.

St. Hedwig of Poland

Buda, Hungary (1374–1399)

Beatified: 1986

Canonized: 1997

Patron: Poland

Feast day: October 16

Hedwig was the youngest daughter of King Louis I of Hungary and Elizabeth of Bosnia and great-niece to King Casimir III of Poland. Upon Casimir's death, Louis inherited the throne of Poland. When Louis died, Hedwig's older sister, Mary, inherited the crown of Hungary while Hedwig inherited the throne of Poland. She was crowned in 1384 at the age of 10.

Hedwig was betrothed to Duke William of Austria, whom she loved, but the engagement was broken for a politically charged marriage to a pagan prince from Lithuania when she was 13. Hedwig offered up her disappointments and sufferings to Christ and was able to convert her husband, Jagiello, later known as King Landislaus II of Poland.

She was known for her charity to the sick and poor and for a revision of the laws to help the poor. She is buried at the cathedral in Kraków.

St. Kenneth

Birthplace unknown (AD 525–AD 599)

Patron: Wales

Feast day: August 1

Kenneth (also known as Canicus, Canice, and Cenydd) was a prince of Brittany, the son of King Dihoc (Deroch) of Domnonée. He was born with horrible deformities, and his pagan parents put him in a container and set him out to sea.

Kenneth washed up on the shores of Worms Head (in Wales) and survived, growing to be a Christian and a hermit. St. David of Wales met Kenneth and cured him of his birth defects. He is venerated almost exclusively in Wales.

St. Kenneth (Of Ireland)

Ireland (AD 515–AD 600)

Patron: Ireland

Feast day: October 11

A second St. Kenneth came from Ireland. Cainnech moccu Dalánn was the son of Lughadh Leithdhearg, a famous poet. He was ordained a priest and later become an abbot, or head of an abbey, in Clonard.

Kenneth didn't stay long, however, for each time he established a monastery, he went on missionary journeys seeking to bring the Catholic faith to all parts of Ireland, Scotland, and Wales. He was so successful that he is considered one of the twelve apostles of Ireland.

He also worked closely with St. Columba in Scotland and helped found many monasteries and abbeys there as well. St. Kenneth is well loved in both Scotland and Ireland to this very day.

St. Louis IX of France

Tunisia (1214–1270)

Canonized: 1297

Patron: Archdiocese of St. Louis, barbers, bridegrooms, builders, button makers, Congregation of the Sisters of St. Louis, construction workers, crusaders, distillers, French monarchs, masons, needleworkers, parenthood, prisoners, sculptors, and sick people; invoked against death of children

Feast day: August 25

Louis Capet was the son of King Louis VIII of France and Queen Blanche of Castile. His father died when he was 11, so his mother became queen-regent until Louis turned 22, at which time he became king of France and reigned for 44 years. He was 19 when he married Marguerite of Provence, with whom he had 11 children. This royal line continued until the last French monarch, Louis XVI, died during the Reign of Terror following the French Revolution.

Louis built the famous church of Sainte-Chapelle and reformed the amount that could be charged as interest on loans. He was a faithful servant of the pope, trying to stamp out religious heresy in his kingdom.

Louis organized crusades to rescue the Holy Land in 1245 and 1267. Neither was successful. In the first crusade, Louis was captured and eventually freed. During the second crusade, he became ill and died. His body was returned to Paris and interred in the Abbey of St. Denis.

Chapter 11

North American Saints

As the U.S. and Canada were being colonized and settled, European rulers and religious leaders saw the need to form religious communities to help bring in schools, hospitals, orphanages, convents, and other social institutions. European countries often sent religious men and women on missions to North America to form these new communities.

In this chapter, we profile the saints who worked and died in the New World or who were born and raised on this continent. North America may not be able to claim as many saints as Europe, but like South America, Africa, and Asia, the numbers continue to increase as the faith spreads from generation to generation.

St. Damien of Molokai

Tremelo, Belgium (1840–1889)

Beatified: 1995

Canonized: 2009

Patron: Honolulu, Hawaii; victims of AIDS; victims of leprosy

Feast day: May 10

Jozef De Veuster was a young man in Belgium when he entered religious life and joined the Missionaries of Sacred Hearts of Jesus and Mary. Taking the name of Father Peter Damien, he was sent to Hawaii in 1864 to preach the Catholic faith to the native inhabitants.

While working in the Hawaiian Islands, Father Damien learned of the leper colony on Molokai, where anyone infected with the feared disease was immediately quarantined. During the initial stages of the ailment, the victims took care of themselves, but when sores appeared and appendages began to fall off, even the government was afraid to get too close.

Six hundred people were confined to Molokai when Father Damien visited. He secured special permission from the bishop and in 1873 entered the leper colony as chaplain. He administered the sacraments, taught catechism, dressed their wounds, helped them build a place to live, made their coffins, and buried them when they died.

Father Damien was the only noninfected leper to voluntarily go and serve the spiritual and physical needs of that community. Eventually, however, he contracted the disease of leprosy himself in 1885 and died from the horrible ailment four years later.

When Pope Benedict XVI canonized Damien in 2009, a former resident of Hawaii expressed great admiration for the saint. U.S. President Barack Obama said:

> *Father Damien has also earned a special place in the hearts of Hawaiians. I recall many stories from my youth about his tireless work there to care for those suffering from leprosy who had been cast out. Following in the steps of Jesus's ministry to the lepers, Father Damien challenged the stigmatizing effects of disease, giving voice to the voiceless and ultimately sacrificing his own life to bring dignity to so many.*

St. Damien of Molokai remains a poignant example of Christian love of neighbor. His life's work exemplified the priceless value of every human being as being made in the image and likeness of God and the idea that all humans are worthy of respect and dignity. Pope Benedict reminded the crowds that saints like Damien remind us to treat the poor, the sick, the dying, the defenseless, and the oppressed with every ounce of charity and love we can muster.

St. Elizabeth Ann Seton

New York, NY (1774–1821)

Beatified: 1959

Canonized: 1975

Patron: Catholic schools

Feast day: January 4

Elizabeth Ann Seton's life was marred by tragedy, disappointment, and abandonment, but she still grew to become the founder of women's charities and a champion for poor and sick women and children.

Born Elizabeth Ann Bayley, she lived with her parents, distinguished French Huguenots of New York, and was raised in the Episcopal Church.

When Elizabeth's mother died, her father remarried, and that marriage produced seven children. Elizabeth's stepmother wasn't fond of Elizabeth or her sister, and the two were sent to live with their paternal grandparents. The separation from her father was difficult for Elizabeth, and she became depressed.

Elizabeth (see Figure 11-1) married William Magee Seton when she was 19, and the couple had five children: Anna Maria, William, Richard Bayley, Catherine Charlton, and Rebecca Mary. The family worshiped at the prestigious Trinity Episcopal Church on Wall Street. While at the church, Elizabeth established the Society for the Relief of Poor Widows and Small Children

Elizabeth's husband's business eventually went bankrupt, and the family lost its fortune. William Seton developed tuberculosis, and one of his former business acquaintances, Antonio Filicchi of Livomo, Italy, suggested the family travel to the warmth and sun of Italy to allow him to recuperate.

William was quarantined to the dark, dank ship, but Elizabeth and her eldest daughter went to stay with the Filicchi family. It was during that visit that Elizabeth was introduced to Catholicism. The Filicchi family was devout and zealous in their faith, and watching their intense piety started Elizabeth's conversion.

When William died 30 days after their arrival in Italy, Elizabeth and her daughter returned to New York. Antonio Filicchi accompanied the two and continued to lead their Catholic instruction.

Elizabeth was met with hostility and animosity when she returned to New York, because of both her interest in Catholicism and her weakened financial position. It was her Catholic faith, still in its infancy, that carried her through those times. She converted to Catholicism on March 14, 1805, and was confirmed into the faith two weeks later.

Still needing to care for and support her five children, Elizabeth tried to establish a school, and later a boarding house for an Episcopal boys' school, both of which failed because of the city's anti-Catholic sentiments.

Elizabeth was invited to establish a school in Baltimore by the Rev. John Carroll, Bishop of Baltimore. She was also involved in the early stages of the first congregation for religious women in the U.S. with hopes that this congregation would eventually merge into the French community, the Daughters of Charity.

Elizabeth took vows of chastity, poverty, and obedience at St. Mary's Seminary in Baltimore in 1809 and was given the title of Mother Seton. The habit she chose was that of a widow's outfit.

That same year, she was asked to establish a school in Emmitsburg, Maryland, and this is where her community flourished with the rules of the Daughters of Charity. She eventually saw the creation of the first Catholic school in the U.S., and she was the first native-born citizen of the U.S. to be canonized.

Figure 11-1:
Elizabeth Ann Seton was the first native-born citizen of the U.S. to be canonized.

© Bettman/CORBIS

St. Frances Xavier (Mother) Cabrini

Lombardy, Italy (1850–1917)

Beatified: 1938

Canonized: 1946

Patron: parish schools and religious education of youth

Feast day: November 13

St. Frances — born Maria Francesca in Sant'Angelo, Italy — became introduced to religious life when a priest friend asked her to help reorganize a girls' school that was being mismanaged by a woman who attempted to form a religious community. Though the original community had been suppressed, the bishop encouraged Maria to establish a missionary community with the young women she attracted.

The community flourished under Maria's tutelage, and she finally took her formal religious vows in 1877, becoming Mother Frances Xavier Cabrini (see Figure 11-2). Her new community would come to be known as the Missionary Sisters of the Sacred Heart.

Pope Leo XII directed Mother Cabrini to take her community to the West, to aid the people who had migrated from Europe.

Mother Cabrini's invitation was canceled when an original backer of a promised orphanage reneged. Not to be deterred, she pressed onward, and within 36 days of her arrival, she had repaired the broken relationship with the backer and established the orphanage.

In the next 35 years, Mother Cabrini would go on to establish 67 institutions, including convents, orphanages, hospitals, and schools in the U.S., as well as similar institutions in Central and South America. She was the first naturalized citizen to be canonized.

Figure 11-2:
Mother Cabrini established dozens of Catholic institutions in the U.S.

© Bettman/CORBIS

St. John Neumann

Prachatitz, Bohemia (1811–1860)

Beatified: 1963

Canonized: 1977

Patron: immigrants, American bishops

Feast day: January 5

John Neumann was born under Austrian-Hungarian rule in Bohemia, the third of six children. He entered the seminary in Prague and received the minor orders of the priesthood. Because early 19th-century Bohemia had so many priests, John was always interested in doing missionary work in the U.S.

Many Germans were migrating to Pennsylvania and New York, and John made the journey to the U.S., stopping with papers in hand at the Archbishop of New York's home. Within a few weeks, he was ordained to the major orders of sub-deacon, deacon, and priest.

John had a natural ability to learn language, a skill that helped him adapt to his new assignment in upstate New York: administering primarily to German and Irish immigrants. A serious illness, however, forced him to take some time to recuperate.

John eventually decided to enter the Congregation of the Most Holy Redeemer, or Redemptorists. He rose through the ranks and was named the order's superior in the U.S. At the same time, he became pastor of St. Alphonse Church in Baltimore.

His organizational skills, perseverance, linguistic talents, and determination gained him notice, and he was suggested as the next Bishop of Philadelphia. Although he turned down the offer out of humility, his obedience ultimately led him to accept the command after being asked a second and third time.

Under John's leadership, the diocese grew from having just two Catholic schools to more than a hundred. He also brought several religious communities of men and women to staff the schools, established a native order within the diocese (the Sisters of St. Francis), and administered the Oblate Sisters of St. Joseph in Baltimore for African-American women. Fifty churches were built within the diocese, which spanned from Philadelphia to New Jersey and included all of Delaware.

John also launched a devotion that remains popular in Philadelphia today, the 40 Hours Devotion, in which the Blessed Sacrament is exposed in the monstrance on the altar in the churches for all to see during that period.

John was also a prolific writer. He contributed articles to newspapers and wrote two catechisms: one for Germans and the second for the broader church. The latter catechism was suggested by the Eighth Council of Baltimore and served as the basis for the Baltimore Catechism, which was used by all parishes until the Second Vatican Council in 1965.

Bishop John Neumann was the first American bishop to be canonized a saint. The National Shrine of St. John Neumann is located in St. Peter's Church on Fifth Street and Gerard Avenue in Philadelphia.

St. Katherine Drexel

Philadelphia, PA (1858–1955)

Beatified: 1988

Canonized: 2000

Patron: philanthropists, racial justice

Feast day: March 1

Katherine was a child of privilege who learned from her family that with financial security comes responsibility to those less fortunate. The second of two girls born to a wealthy, charitable banker, Katherine learned contemplation and works of mercy from her father. Katherine's mother died five weeks after her birth, and her father, Francis Drexel, remarried and the couple had a third daughter. Katherine's stepmother, Emma Bouvier, continued the family's charitable traditions and prayer, and soon the three girls became devoted to the poor.

Throughout her adolescence and young adulthood, Katherine longed to join a contemplative religious community, but her spiritual director, Bishop O'Connor, suggested she wait and pray. She became interested in the plight of poor Native Americans and African Americans and visited many reservations and enclaves of the poor.

During a visit with Pope Leo XIII, Katherine asked if he would send missionaries to America, and he suggested that she establish her own religious community.

To create a new community, Bishop O'Connor recommended Katherine enter the Sisters of Mercy in Pittsburgh. She took the name Sister Mary Katherine, and her new religious community was called the Sisters of the Blessed Sacrament for Indians and Colored People, now simply the Sisters of the Blessed Sacrament. The community began attracting women to join and received canonical recognition during the reign of Pope St. Pius X.

With the help of her family's money, Mother Katherine was able to establish many parochial schools, missions, convents, and trade schools for Native American and African Americans, including the prestigious Xavier University in New Orleans, the only Catholic university established for African Americans.

Katherine was canonized as the first American saint to have been born after the U.S. became a nation; when Elizabeth Ann Seton was born, the U.S. was still a colony of England, and Frances Xavier Cabrini became a U.S. citizen after immigrating from Italy in the 19th century.

Also of note: Mother Cabrini and Mother Drexel had a meeting in which Mother Cabrini passed along information for Mother Drexel to see the pope for canonical recognition of her order.

Katherine's shrine is located at the motherhouse of the Sisters of the Blessed Sacrament in Bensalem, Pennsylvania.

St. Marguerite Bourgeoys

Troyes, France (1620–1700)

Beatified: 1950

Canonized: 1982

Patron: invoked against poverty and loss of parents

Feast day: January 12

Marguerite was one of 12 children born to devout Catholic parents in 17th-century France. When her mother died, Marguerite was left to raise and educate her younger siblings, all the while dreaming of following a religious vocation. She was turned down by many orders, however, because of the high number of women seeking religious life at the time.

The governor of New France came to France seeking recruits for the new settlement, Ville Marie, which is now Montreal. Marguerite was introduced to Governor Maisonneuve and accepted the invitation to be a teacher in this new territory.

Marguerite accompanied many men and their prospective brides on the arduous journey to Quebec. She became friends with Jeanne Mance, and the two worked together in Ville Marie in what would become the foundation of a new community. They became known as the Congregation of Notre Dame of Montreal. Marguerite traveled to France three times seeking new recruits and a royal charter for her order. She returned with both.

In New France, however, the Bishop didn't want this order to be on its own and preferred instead that it merge with the Ursuline Sisters in Quebec. Marguerite didn't feel the two communities could merge because of a difference in spirituality: The Ursulines were primarily a cloistered community, and Marguerite's order was to be among the people.

Marguerite's order did eventually receive approval, and she retired as Mother Superior to live out her retirement in total prayer. Her shrine is located at Notre-Dame-de-Bon-Secour Chapel in Montreal, Canada.

St. Marguerite d'Youville

Quebec, Canada (1701–1771)

Beatified: 1959

Canonized: 1990

Patron: widows and difficult marriages; invoked against the death of children

Feast day: October 16

Marguerite was left thousands of dollars in debt when she was widowed by her abusive alcoholic husband at the age of 29. She had buried four of her six children and was left to raise the two surviving boys on her own.

She opened a small shop where she made and sold clothing. Soon she had paid off all her husband's debt and had even made enough money to get her sons a good education. Both boys eventually became priests.

Charity remained an important part of Marguerite's life, and it wasn't enough for her to donate money or to help the sick in hospitals. She opened a home for the poor and underprivileged in Montreal, attracting three other women to help in the mission.

Marguerite was met with suspicion and opposition, as women of society didn't open their homes to become hostels for the poor. Already having to live with the reputation of having a drunken husband who was involved in illegal alcohol sales to the Native Americans, now Marguerite and her staff stood the ridicule of being called the "Tipsy Sisters" or *Soeurs Grises,* in Montreal's native French.

With the help of a Sulpician priest, Marguerite and the others grew into a religious community known as the "Grey Nuns." The sisters eventually adopted the rule of the Sisters of Charity and took over a failing hospital in Montreal that had tremendous debt. The sisters rebuilt the facility and paid off the debt.

Although Catholic persecution came about as part of the French and Indian War, Marguerite's religious community thrived, spreading into the U.S., Africa, South America, and China. The communities helped staff hospitals, schools, and orphanages.

St. Rose Philippine Duschene

Grenoble, France (1769–1852)

Beatified: 1940

Canonized: 1988

Feast day: November 18

Rose was educated in the Convent of the Visitation Sisters, a religious order she had hoped to join, but because of the French Revolution in 1789, all Catholic institutions and religious orders were suppressed.

She returned home and did charitable work as a layperson until 1801, when the majority of Catholic organizations were allowed to reopen. Unfortunately, the Convent of the Visitation Sisters was not among them.

Rose met Mother Borat, a woman who had recently founded a new religious community, the Society of the Sacred Heart. Heeding the call of the American bishops, Rose went to New Orleans with four sisters from the order. Rose helped to establish schools, convents, and orphanages throughout the Mississippi River Valley. She became the Mother Superior of the American branch of the Society of the Sacred Heart, and the community grew to have 64 women.

Mother Duschene eventually, at age 71, started a mission to the Native Americans, a dream she'd had since she was young. Though she was elderly and faced language barriers, Mother Duschene committed hours of her time in prayer for the Native Americans and the mission.

The North American (Canadian) Martyrs

(17th century)

Beatified: 1925

Canonized: 1930

Feast day: October 19

French settlers established a new colony in the 17th century in what is now Canada, particularly in the area of Quebec. The land was initially used for trading until French rulers decided to build permanent settlements. Religion became a major issue, and France, a Catholic country, sent missionaries from a variety of religious orders to establish schools, hospitals, orphanages, and other social services.

The native people were introduced to Christianity, and missionaries would often learn the language and translate the catechism and Bible. The natives in the vicinity of New France, however, were hostile not only to Europeans but to Christianity as well. It was under these circumstances that those now known as the North American martyrs entered New France.

Heroic figures such as Isaac Jogues, Jean de Brebeuf, and others influenced the Catholic Church in both Canada and the U.S., as part of their missionary activity and martyrdom took place in what is now upstate New York.

St. Isaac Jogues

Isaac was a Jesuit priest who worked among the Huron and Petun tribes in the Great Lakes area of New France. Living conditions weren't good and disease was rampant. Tribe members blamed Europeans for unfamiliar illnesses, and the missionaries suffered much persecution. Isaac was captured by the Mohawk Indians and held as a captive slave for 13 months, during which time he was tortured and mutilated.

Father Jogues escaped while in a camp settlement near Albany, New York, and was sent back to France to recuperate. The pope gave him special permission to celebrate Mass without the regulation fingers, as they had been amputated by the Indians. He recovered and returned to New France to continue his missionary work but was captured by the Iroquois and martyred alongside Father John de Brebeuf.

By 1650, the Iroquois exterminated the Huron tribe, which was becoming increasingly Christian. All 15 missions were consequently destroyed, yet the men and the many converts to Christianity left a lasting legacy in North America and left a mark for the future of the Catholic Church in the region. The feast day of these missionaries is observed on the Roman calendar on October 19. They are considered patron saints of the Americas and Canada.

St. John de Brebeuf

John became a member of the Jesuit order in 1617 at the age of 20. He contracted tuberculosis early in his religious formation, and while it didn't kill him, it left him incredibly weak and vulnerable to illness. He was ordained a priest in 1622 and volunteered to go to New France in 1625.

John lived among the friendly Huron Indians when he arrived in America. He mastered their language and customs and wrote a translation dictionary from French to Huron. He was expelled from the region during political battles, but he was able to return a few years later with the aid of more Jesuit men, including Father Anthony Daniels in 1632. In 1636, Fathers Isaac Jogues and Charles Garnier arrived in New France, followed by Fathers Noel Chabanel, Rene Goupil, and John de Lalande. Laymen came in 1643 and Father Gabriel Lalemant finally arrived in 1646.

The Huron and the Iroquois were often at war with each other, and working for one of the warring tribes could be fatal for the missionaries if they were captured. John composed a Huron catechism and help convert 7,000 people to the Catholic faith. He was eventually captured by the Iroquois and tortured at Sainte Marie in Canada in 1649.

Father John's companions were also subjected to Iroquois attack: Father Anthony Daniel also worked among the Huron, only to be killed by the Iroquois in 1648; Father Garnier was shot and died of a blow from a tomahawk; Father Lalemant was tortured to death; and Father Noel Chabanel was killed soon after by a member of the Huron tribe who turned against Christianity.

Companion martyrs

St. Isaac Jogues and St. John de Brebeuf were accompanied by six other Jesuit companions who were martyred during the same time frame (1642–1649): St. Antoine Daniel, St. Charles Garnier, St. Gabriel Lalemant, St. Jean de Lalande, St. Noël Chabanel, and St. René Goupil. Jogues and de Brebeuf are certainly the most famous of this group, but Pope Pius XI canonized all eight together in 1930. All went to their deaths professing their faith in Christ and the Catholic Church, and all are honored to this day, not only by the Jesuit order to which they belonged but also by the faithful in Canada and upstate New York.

The Mexican Martyrs

Besides the martyrs of Canada and the U.S., other martyrs in North America came from or died in Mexico. During the early part of the 20th century, Mexico was undergoing turbulent and violent political change. After severing ties with Spain, the newly independent Mexican government became increasingly anti-clerical and tried to control the Church, which led to a series of conflicts between the Church and the state.

Pope Pius X wrote a letter to the Mexican bishops warning of the terrible state of the Church in their country, and the bishops responded by suspending the Sacraments, including the celebration of Mass, for three years. It was their hope that the people of Mexico — the majority of whom were Catholic — would rise up against their government in support of their own rights. This act would come to be known as the Mexican Revolution of 1917.

As a result of the revolution, a severe persecution of the Church began and resulted in more than 125 martyrs, including laymen such as Manuel Morales, Salvador Puente, and David Lara. Clerical martyrs included Fathers Miguel Pro, Luis Sainz, David Bermudez, Crisobal Jara, Agustin Cortes, Jenaro Delgaldillo, Jesus Montoya, Jose Varela, Jose Hurtado, Julio Mendoza, David Velasco, Margarito Garcia, Pedro Ramirez, Rodrigo Aleman, Roman Rosales, Sabas Salazar, Toribio Gonzalez, Tranquilino Robles, Justino Madrigal, Atilono Alvarado, Miguel de la Mora, and Pedro de Jesus Lucero.

Blessed Miguel Pro

Miguel joined the Jesuits in 1911 and fled to Spain in 1914, where he continued his studies. He was ordained a priest in Belgium in 1925 and returned the following year to his native Mexico, where he had to celebrate Mass in secret because the government had closed the churches. He dressed as a layperson and worked secular jobs, using his time with the people to continue his evangelization.

The government grew weary of Father Pro's success and blamed an attempt to kill the president on Father Pro and two of his brothers. They were arrested and ordered to be executed. Father Pro's dying words were, "Long live Christ the King."

Pope John Paul II beatified Father Pro and his companions in an outdoor Mass in Mexico on September 25, 1988. Father Pro's feast is observed on November 23.

Pope John Paul II canonized an additional 25 men on May 21, 2000, including St. Jenaro Sanchez Delgadillo, a parish priest who, along with other parishioners, was imprisoned and died by hanging; and St. Cristobal Jara, a devout parish priest who was shot to death on May 25, 1927.

Other notable clerical martyrs

Many other notable clerics gave their lives for the cause. Some of them include:

- **St. Jose Maria Robles Hurtado,** who, during his brief time as a priest, founded a community of women known as the Sisters of the Sacred Heart of Jesus. He wrote many articles on the Catholic faith and promoted devotion to the Sacred Heart of Jesus. He also was involved in the Catholic action movement known as *Cristeros,* or Christ the King. Father Hurtado started to erect a cross, and thousands of pilgrims traveled to be part of the groundbreaking ceremony. The construction was in direct opposition to the government ban on all public displays of religion. He was arrested and hung on June 26, 1927, which is also his feast day.

✔ **St. Mateo Correa Magallanes** was arrested for celebrating the Sacrament of the Sick for an elderly person. In prison, he administered to the members of the Cristeros and heard confessions. Prison officials threatened to kill him unless he revealed the confessions. Father Magallanes refused and was shot to death on February 6, 1927. His feast is commemorated on May 21.

✔ **St. Toribio Romo Gonzalez** was a priest at the time parishes were being closed and he was forbidden to celebrate Mass and pray in public. Father Gonzalez set up a secret parish within a factory, but informants led government leaders to the parish, and Father Gonzalez was shot to death in bed on February 25, 1928. His feast is celebrated on May 25.

✔ **St. Rafael Guizar Valencia** became Bishop of Veracruz, Mexico, when he was in exile in Cuba. As bishop, he cared for the people during the Mexican Revolution and worked tirelessly for their cause. He was also an active member of the Knights of Columbus, a connection that enabled the American Knights of Columbus to get the American government involved in a peace treaty between the Mexican government and the Church in 1929. He returned to Veracruz and administered to his diocese until his death in 1938. Pope Benedict XVI canonized him on October 15, 2006. His feast is commemorated on June 6.

St. Juan Diego

Mexico (1474–1548)

Beatified: 1990

Canonized: 2002

Patron: Mexicans of Native Indian (Aztec) descent

Feast day: December 9

Born with the name Cuauhtlatoatzin in 1474 to Aztec Indian parents, Juan Diego lived in the area that would one day encompass present-day Mexico City. He was a simple farmworker and a married man who didn't have any children. He and his wife converted to Christianity when he was 50; he took the name Juan Diego and she became Maria Lucia. His wife died in 1529, and Juan Diego never remarried.

On a morning walk to church, he had a vision of Mary on Tepeyac Hill; she spoke to him and commanded that he ask the bishop to build a chapel in her honor on that very spot — a spot that, according to Aztec religion, was a place of worship for a pagan goddess. He believed God's intention was to replace paganism with Christianity by making a shrine to the Mother of God.

When Juan approached the bishop, the bishop demanded a sign to prove that Juan indeed saw an apparition and hadn't just imagined it.

When Juan Diego returned to his uncle's home, he found him severely ill. Instead of following the bishop's directives for a sign from the apparition, Juan searched for a priest to administer the Sacrament of the Sick to his uncle.

Mary appeared to Juan again and assured him his uncle would be fine and provided a sign for the bishop — roses, which didn't grow on the hill because of the desert-like conditions of the area. Juan gathered the roses in his cloak and returned to the bishop. As the cloak was unfolded to reveal the roses, an image of Our Lady appeared, now known as the sacred image of Our Lady of Guadalupe.

The image was a rare picture of the Virgin Mary as a pregnant mother, but also with Native Indian features like those of Juan Diego and his family. All Christian art at that time portrayed the Blessed Mother, baby Jesus, and St. Joseph as if they were Western Europeans. Our Lady of Guadalupe is one of the few sacred images showing her in the form of an indigenous native.

Tests have been performed on the image of Our Lady of Guadalupe through the second half of the 20th century. The image hasn't been painted, dyed, or sewn into the material of the cloak, and the colors have remained intact for more than 500 years. The image hangs in the basilica's shrine.

St. Philip of Jesus and the Martyrs of Japan

Died: 1597

Beatified: 1627

Canonized: 1862

Feast day: February 5

St. Philip was a 16th-century Mexican priest who had joined the Franciscan Order. He was on a ship headed to the Philippines when a storm diverted it to Japan, where the government feared a foreign invasion. Earlier in the century, St. Francis Xavier had established a successful Catholic church in Japan, and by the time of St. Philip's arrival, Japan had more than 2,000 Christians.

The emperor became hostile to people of the West and their religion, and Christians were persecuted.

Philip and the other passengers were arrested, tortured, and paraded through town on the way to a hill outside of Nagasaki, where they were killed on February 5, 1597. There were 24 martyrs of Japan, including St. Peter Baptist, St. Martin De Aguire, St. Francis Blanco, and St. Francis of St. Michael, who were all Spaniards; St. Gonsalo Garcia, St. Paul Miki, St. John Goto, and St. James Kisai, and 17 others who were native Japanese. They were fastened to crosses planted on the Hill of Martyrs in Nagasaki and speared to death. Pope Pius IX canonized St. Philip of Jesus and the 23 other men in 1862, and their feast is celebrated on February 5.

Chapter 12

American Orthodox Saints

● ●

In This Chapter

▶ Preaching and doing missionary work in the Alaska Territory

▶ Standing up to the Communist regime in Russia

● ●

Catholicism isn't the only Christian religion to officially designate certain men and women as saints. Eastern Orthodox have as strong a devotion to these heavenly friends of God as their Roman Catholic counterparts. Alaska was Russian territory before it was sold to the U.S. As such, missionaries were sent to this wilderness to spread the Orthodox faith.

Alaska became the 49th state in 1959 (first purchased for America by Secretary of State William Seward in 1867 for $7 million). The Orthodox Church in America (OCA) made great progress in this new frontier, and we highlight several of their saints in this chapter.

Understanding orthodoxy

The early church was initially set up as one Christian Church shepherded by Patriarchs from the five cities in which the Twelve Apostles had established a Christian community: Rome, Jerusalem, Antioch, Alexandria, and Constantinople. In 1054, the Patriarch of Constantinople declared his independence from the Pope and created a separate church, the Eastern Orthodox Church. The Orthodox Church in America (OCA) is part of that church.

In 1589, while maintaining informal ties with Constantinople, Moscow became the sixth Patriarchate and declared the Russian Orthodox Church *autocephalous,* or as having an independent leader. The Patriarch of Moscow declared the Orthodox Church in America autocephalous in 1970; the problem with this declaration for the OCA was that the Ecumenical Patriarch of Constantinople wasn't consulted and didn't concur. For that reason, the Greek Orthodox Church doesn't recognize the OCA as independent but rather sees it as a daughter church of Moscow.

As for the Russian Orthodox Church, it sent many missionaries to evangelize the Aleuts and Eskimo Indians in Russian North America (Alaska before it was sold to the United States in 1867).

(continued)

(continued)

Following the Bolshevik Revolution in 1917, the Patriarchate of Moscow lost much of its power and influence. The Orthodox Church in America (OCA) gained such strong independence that by 1970 Moscow and some other Eastern Churches recognized the OCA's autonomy despite the rebuff from Constantinople. And despite the disagreements regarding Church status, the different branches of Orthodoxy share cordial relations.

Unlike the Roman Catholic Church, in which canonization is a papal prerogative invoking papal infallibility, the Eastern Orthodox Churches refer to the designation of sainthood as *glorification,* and it's done by a Patriarch and/or a *synod* (a council of bishops). As such, the designation of sainthood doesn't have the same strict requirements of a certain number of miracles as are in the case for possible candidates in the Western (Latin) Church in Rome.

St. Alexander Hotovitzky

Russia (1872–1937)

Glorified: 1994

Feast day: December 4

Alexander Hotovitzky was a key figure in strengthening the Russian Orthodox Church in Russia at a time when the Bolshevik Revolution and communism fought to destroy the Christian communities in that country.

Alexander was ordained into the priesthood in 1896 at the diocesan cathedral in San Francisco. Within a week, he returned to New York to become the pastor of St. Nicholas Church and was instrumental in the establishment of many new Orthodox parishes, including those in Yonkers, New York; Passaic, New Jersey; and Philadelphia, Pennsylvania. He also edited the journal *American Orthodox Messenger.*

Father Alexander also served as a priest in Helsinki, Finland, from 1914 to 1917 — no easy task, as Finland was a primarily Protestant (Lutheran) Christian population. He was transferred to Moscow in 1917 and assigned the position of assistant pastor of Christ the Savior Cathedral.

That same year, the Bolshevik Revolution, which deposed Tsar Nicholas II and the Romanov Dynasty under the leadership of Lenin and Stalin, sought to dismantle the Russian Orthodox Church. The Communist Party was openly and publicly atheistic, and any ties between the Kremlin and the Patriarch of Moscow quickly unraveled. Religious persecution began in earnest.

Father Alexander was arrested three times between 1920 and 1937 on charges of treason and subverting the State. His only "crime" was that he refused to join the Communist Party and instead openly preached on the autonomy of the Russian Orthodox Church.

No known records detail the exact date or place of his execution, but the Orthodox Church nevertheless reveres Father Alexander Hotovitzky as a *New Martyr,* the term used for anyone executed by the Soviet Union because of allegiance to the Russian Orthodoxy.

St. Herman of Alaska

Russia (1756–1837)

Glorified: 1970

Feast day: August 9

St. Herman was the first missionary to the Alaskan territory (then called Russian North America), where he sought to preach the Orthodox faith to the Aleut and Eskimo Indians. He arrived in Kodiak with seven monks in 1794 to begin their missionary work.

Herman's mission wasn't just spiritual; besides preaching the faith, he built schools for the native children and worked to defend them from being exploited by Russian fur traders. Sometime between 1808 and 1818, Herman went to Spruce Island, which he called New Valaam; it's where he spent the rest of his life running a school, taking care of orphans, and praying.

According to pious tradition, Herman placed an icon of Theotokos (Mary, the Mother of God) on the beach before an impending tidal wave and the water never rose above the image, thus sparing the villagers.

St. Innocent of Alaska

Russia (1797–1879)

Glorified: 1977

Feast day: March 31

John (Ivan) Evseyevich Popov-Veniaminov traveled extensively through the Alaskan territory and preached wherever he went, eventually being regarded as the "Apostle of Alaska." John spoke six native dialects and preached from Sitka to Kamchatka until he was called home to Mother Russia. He was appointed the Metropolitan of Moscow (a post that ranks between the archbishop and the Patriarch) in 1867, replacing his friend and mentor, Filaret. It was at this time he took vows as a monk and assumed the name Innocent.

St. Jacob Netsvetov

Alaska (1802–1862)

Glorified: 1994

Feast day: July 26

After leaving his Alaskan home to pursue an education in Russia, Jacob was ordained a priest and sought to return home to minister to his own people. He was returned to Atka Island, Alaska, where he had been raised, and immediately took to work.

Within the first six months on the job, Father Jacob baptized 16 people, confirmed 442 people, married 53 couples, and presided over 8 funerals. He later ventured as far as the Yukon Territory of Canada, evangelizing the Orthodox faith. When he had gotten older, an ambitious assistant attempted to slander the good name of Father Jacob in the hopes of being promoted in his place. When Jacob appeared before the Archbishop, his innocence was easily established; however, the stressful situation took a toll on his health and he died at the age of 60 among his Eskimo parishioners.

St. John Kochurov

Russia (1871–1917)

Glorified: 1994

Feast day: October 31

Something of a zealot, John volunteered to leave his home in the Ryazan region of Russia to work as a missionary in Alaska (which by then was part of the United States). He arrived in New York City and found himself struggling against language and cultural barriers. Eventually John was sent to Chicago to care for Saint Vladimir's Cathedral; he secured donations from Tsar Nicholas II and from wealthy Americans and was able to renovate and restore the Cathedral to its proper glory.

Father John was elevated to Archpriest and returned to Russia in 1907 after a successful apostolate in the U.S. Unfortunately, the Russian Revolution in 1917 didn't bode well for him and other members of the clergy as the

Communists sought to eradicate the Church once and for all. Father John worked arduously in St. Petersburg, preaching to hundreds if not thousands of believers in less than ten years. He was executed by the Bolsheviks during the bloody purge of the Red Russians over the White Russians and is considered a martyr for the Orthodox religion.

St. John Maximovitch, Bishop of Shanghai and San Francisco

Russia (1896–1966)

Glorified: 1994

Feast day: July 2

John was ordained a priest in 1926, shortly after he and his family emigrated from Russia to Yugoslavia to escape the Communist purge of religion. Over the next 36 years, his career led him to bishop installments with the Russian Orthodox Church Outside of Russia (ROCOR) in Shanghai and Western Europe and eventually to the post of Archbishop of San Francisco, which he held from 1951 to 1962.

While bishop in China, Bishop John ministered to the small but growing community of believers until the Red Revolution of Mao Tse-tung persecuted Christians just as the Bolsheviks had done in Russia half a century earlier. Bishop John and 5,000 believers escaped to the Philippines. From there, Bishop John went to the U.S., where he remained for the rest of his life.

St. Juvenaly of Alaska

Russia (1761–1796)

Glorified: 1977

Feast day: September 24

In 1793, Juvenaly led a missionary journey from his home in Russia to Alaska, where he and his companions were able to convert 12,000 Alaskan natives to the Russian Orthodox faith by showing the natives' shaman that natural religion was fulfilled and perfected in the supernatural and divinely revealed Christian religion. Where others alienated the natives by denigrating their former beliefs, Juvenaly built upon them.

Juvenaly was martyred by natives in 1796, but the reason remains a mystery. One theory is that a group of local Indians resented the requirement of Orthodoxy to end polygamy. Another is that a whole tribe had second thoughts after being baptized into the faith and thought the only way to "undo" the obligation was by killing the one who baptized them. Regardless of the motive, the priest was killed in the line of duty and warranted a martyr's legacy.

St. Nikolai Velimirovic

Serbia (1880–1956)

Glorified: 2003

Feast day: March 5

During World War I, the Serbian Church sent Nikolai to England and America, where he held numerous lectures in support of fighting for the union of the Serbs and South Slavic peoples. He returned to Serbia in 1919, and in 1920, he was posted to the Ohrid archbishopric in Macedonia.

Bishop Nikolai was arrested by the Nazis in 1941 in the Žiča Monastery and was confined in the Ljubostinja Monastery. On December 14, 1944, he was sent to Dachau, a concentration camp, with Serbian Patriarch Gavrilo, where the bishop suffered brutal torture and abuse.

At the end of World War II, Bishop Nikolai fled Communist Yugoslavia and emigrated to the U.S. Some of the Orthodox Christian seminaries in which he taught include St. Sava's Serbian Orthodox Seminary in Libertyville, Illinois; St. Vladimir's Orthodox Theological Seminary, now in Crestwood, New York; and St. Tikhon's Orthodox Theological Seminary and Monastery in South Canaan, Pennsylvania. He died on March 18, 1956, while rector of St. Tikhon's.

St. Raphael of Brooklyn

Lebanon (1860–1915)

Glorified: 2000

Feast day: February 27

Rafla Hawaweeny was born of Syrian parents in Lebanon, but because of the anti-Christian efforts of radical Muslims, he was forced to flee to Russia to become ordained. He was sent to the United States to be Rector of St.

Nicholas Church in Brooklyn, and became the first Orthodox bishop to be consecrated on American soil when Bishop Tikhon and Bishop Innocent ordained him in 1904 at St. Nicholas Cathedral in Brooklyn. The new bishop's vestments were a gift from Tsar Nicholas II.

Bishop Raphael consecrated the grounds for St Tikhon's Monastery in South Canaan, Pennsylvania, in 1905 and blessed the orphanage there as well. He also founded the Antiochian Archdiocese.

Although fluent in Arabic, Bishop Raphael saw the benefit of allowing English into the Divine Liturgy because many young people were children of immigrants and therefore no longer knew the language of their ancestors.

St. Tikhon of Moscow

Russia (1865–1925)

Glorified: 1989

Feast day: September 26

Vasily Ivanovich Belavin was ordained a priest in 1891 and took the name Tikhon. He was transferred from the Pskov Seminary to the Kholm Theological Seminary in 1892 and made *archimandrite* (head of a large monastery, equivalent to an archabbot in the Roman church). Archimandrite Tikhon was consecrated Bishop of Lublin in 1897 and returned to Kholm for a year as Vicar Bishop of the Kholm Diocese.

He worked in the U.S. for several years, blessing the cornerstone for St. Nicholas Cathedral in New York in 1901 and, in 1902, consecrating the church of St. Nicholas in Brooklyn for the Syrian Orthodox immigrants. Two weeks later, he consecrated St Nicholas Cathedral in New York. In 1905, the American Mission was made an Archdiocese, and Bishop Tikhon was elevated to the rank of Archbishop.

Archbishop Tikhon returned to Russia in 1907 and was elected Patriarch of Moscow in 1917. During the Bolshevik Revolution, he condemned the execution of the Tsar and the Imperial Family. He was imprisoned in Donskoy Monastery for a year after openly opposing the government's confiscation of Church property.

Both the Russian Orthodox Church in Russia and the Orthodox Church in America owe a lot to this beloved Patriarch, who worked arduously to support his Church and who defended it to his dying day.

Part IV
Explaining the Faith

In this part . . .

In Part IV we highlight the great teachers and defenders of the faith — those educated scholars of theology who explained the doctrines of Catholic Christianity or who preached edifying and erudite sermons on religious truths. These saints aren't all men; some women saints have been named Doctors of the Church for their profound insights and influence on understanding spiritual matters.

We go from west to east, looking at the Latin Fathers of the Western Church and the Greek Fathers of the Eastern Church (before the schism of 1054), which are like two lungs of the one Church, before division disrupted that unity.

Chapter 13

Doctors of the Church

. . . .

In This Chapter

▶ Scholarly saints like Augustine, Jerome, and Thomas Aquinas

▶ Other influential Doctors of the Church

. . . .

The lives and teachings of some holy men and women were so profound and had such an impact that their titles have gone beyond the Father or Sister of the Catholic Church. These leaders are *Doctors of the Church,* a title that recognizes their works and writings as well as their lives. Final approval from the pope is required before the title may be bestowed upon a worthy recipient.

In this chapter, we introduce those doctors whose works and writings have significantly changed the world.

St. Albert the Great

Lauingen, Bavaria (1206–1280)

Beatified: 1622

Canonized: 1931

Declared a Doctor of the Church: 1931

Patron: scientists, chemists

Feast day: November 15

As a member of the Order of Preachers, also called *Dominicans,* Albert's early career included teaching assignments in Cologne, Regensburg, Strasburg, and Paris, where he earned his master's degree. His writings include a veritable library of books on philosophy, theology, and biblical studies. Thirty-eight volumes of his work are still in existence, some of which contain many of his sermons. Albert was an authority in the natural sciences — physics, geography, astronomy, mineralogy, alchemy, and biology — as well as in the branches of philosophy (logic, metaphysics, mathematics, and ethics).

Albert contributed greatly in the area of philosophy by translating works from Aristotle and incorporating them into Christian studies. Philosophy, a discipline relying on human reasoning and logic, is an indispensable tool for understanding theology, the study of divinely revealed truths.

St. Albert's greatest student, Thomas Aquinas, also became a saint and a Doctor of the Church (see his entry later in this chapter).

St. Alphonsus Liguori

Marianella, Campania, Kingdom of Naples (1696–1787)

Beatified: 1816

Canonized: 1839

Declared a Doctor of the Church: 1871

Patron: scholars

Feast day: August 1

Alphonsus left a career in law to pursue a vocation in the priesthood, eventually founding the Congregation of the Holy Redeemer, also known as *Redemptorists.* Two of his books, *The Holy Eucharist* and *Glories of Mary,* were responses to attacks on the frequency of Holy Communion and devotion to Mary.

St. Ambrose

Trier, Germany (AD 337–AD 397)

Declared a Doctor of the Church: 1298

Patron: religion teachers and students

Feast day: December 7

Ambrose was a staunch defender of the faith and the divinity of Christ, battling Arianism until eventually eliminating the heresy altogether. A collection of Ambrose's sermons formed a basis for a treatise of his theological works.

Ambrose had two significant struggles to face during his career — a clash with the Roman Emperor Theodosius and the conversion of Augustine.

Theodosius, taking revenge on those who questioned his authority, ordered the slaughter of 7,000 people just to prove a point. Ambrose commanded the emperor to do a public penance, which he did.

Ambrose delivered a sermon heard by Augustine, who was avoiding Baptism, and Augustine's mother, St. Monica. Augustine was so moved by Ambrose's sermon that he asked to be baptized immediately and went on to become one of the greatest theologians and saints of the church.

In his many writings, Ambrose dealt with issues of liturgical reformation and diocesan structure, homilies, and ascetical and poetical theology. He died on Good Friday in AD 397, but his feast is celebrated on December 7, the day he was made Bishop of Milan.

St. Anselm

Aosta, Kingdom of Burgundy (1033–1109)

Canonized: 1494

Declared a Doctor of the Church: 1720

Feast day: April 21

Anselm is considered the father of scholasticism, the medieval theological and philosophical method of learning that follows the teachings of Aristotle, St. Augustine, and other leaders of the early Christian Church. Scholasticism bridges the gap between religion and reason.

Anselm's writings contributed greatly to defining God's attributes as well as further explaining the notions of truth, free will, the origins of evil, and the art of reasoning. Two of his most notable works are *Monologium,* which provides metaphysical proofs of the existence of God, and *Proslogium,* a study of God's attributes.

He became the Archbishop of Canterbury in 1092. Though the Cathedral now belongs to the Anglican Church and suffered the ravages of the Protestant Revolt of Henry VIII, it is believed that his relics remain in a chapel dedicated to him in this edifice.

St. Anthony of Padua

Lisbon, Portugal (1195–1231)

Canonized: 1232

Declared a Doctor of the Church: 1946

Patron: finding lost items

Feast day: June 13

Saint of the "Golden Tongue"

Though his impact in the classroom and in the pulpit may have led to St. Anthony's nickname as the saint with the "Golden Tongue," the title became more significant after his death, when it was discovered that his actual tongue has remained incorrupt. So eloquently did he preach that on one occasion, when a town of heretics obstinately refused to listen to him, Anthony preached to the fish in the nearby lake. The fish in great multitude lined up in rows and columns and popped their heads out of the water, as if to listen to the great orator. When the townsfolk saw the miraculous event, they decided to listen for themselves and were soon converted back to the faith.

Anthony's remarkable speaking abilities — in the pulpit and out — earned him the title of "the Ark of the Testament" from Pope Gregory IX. His public speaking skills led to an assignment at the University of Padua, but his real talent came from the pulpit, where he won over many souls through the art of persuasion.

Anthony became a member of the Order of Friars Minor (OFM), more commonly known as the Franciscans, in 1220. He was responsible for real reform within the Church, as well as many conversions to the Church.

Anthony is the patron saint you go to whenever something (or someone) is lost. Anthony's prayer book was missing one day, and he prayed to God that he find it. Turns out that a novice stole the book and ran off, intending to leave religious life and sell the book for money. As soon as Anthony prayed, however, the novice had a change of heart, repented of his sin, and returned the book and himself to the friary. Since then, Catholics have invoked St. Anthony to find lost car keys, eyeglasses, and all kinds of items, not to mention a missing person or two.

St. Athanasius

Alexandria, Egypt (AD 296–AD 373)

Declared a Doctor of the Church: 1568

Feast day: May 2

Athanasius was a strong supporter of Christian orthodoxy and battled the philosophy and beliefs of Arian heretics. His work, *Incarnation*, speaks out in defense of Christ's divinity and humanity. He often found himself a target of attack from heretics, who were in the majority at the time, and was sent into exile many times.

Because of his works of theology (especially against Arius), his fundamental preaching and teaching, and his physical suffering because of his orthodoxy, he was made Doctor of the Church at the time of his canonization. His relics are in the city of Venice.

St. Augustine

Thagaste, Numidia (AD 354–AD 430)

Declared a Doctor of the Church: 1298

Patron: philosophers, printers

Feast day: August 28

Augustine was a champion of the Catholic faith through his writings and sermons and worked to eradicate the *Manichaeism* cult, a religious sect to which he once belonged. Followers of this religious sect believed in the separation of matter and spirit and of good and evil, leading them to indulge in immoralities.

After his conversion to the Catholic faith, Augustine wrote many spiritual and theological works, including *The Confessions of St. Augustine, Three Dialogues Against the Academicians, Of the Happy Life,* and *Of the Order.* He became the Bishop of Hippo and confronted the early stages of a new Christian heretical militant sect, the Donatists. In an act of diplomacy, Augustine met with the sect leaders, a meeting that eventually led to their decline.

Then came Pelagianism, yet another sect that denied the doctrine of original sin and taught that Baptism was merely a "golden ticket" to heaven and that grace wasn't necessary for salvation. Augustine staunchly opposed this sect through his sermons and writings.

Augustine founded a community of religious life for men and women and created a system of regulations, the Rule, to govern this community — a system that's still in use in the Order of St. Augustine.

St. Basil

Caesarea, Cappadocia (AD 329–AD 379)

Declared a Doctor of the Church: 1568

Patron: Cappadocia (a region in Turkey), hospital administrators

Feast day: January 2

Basil comes from a saintly lineage: his parents, St. Basil the Elder and St. Emmelia; some of his siblings, St. Gregory of Nyssa, St. Macrina the Younger, and St. Peter of Sebaste; and his grandmother, St. Macrina.

Basil was an eloquent orator and writer and defended the true faith in the face of opposition and slander from the Arian heretics. He died in AD 379 and is venerated in both the Eastern and Western Churches as a Doctor of the Church.

St. Bede, the Venerable

Sunderland, England (AD 672–AD 735)

Canonized: 1899

Declared a Doctor of the Church: 1879

Patron: scholars

Feast day: May 25

Bede knew at an early age that he wanted to follow the Benedictine way of life, entering a monastery for studies and eventually joining that same monastery as a monk. These monks led a life of *ora et labora* — Latin for "prayer and work" — where their entire day was divided between praying in the chapel and doing work in the monastery. The Benedictines are a highly intellectual society, as well; many monasteries had extensive libraries where theological, liturgical, and biblical scholarship were second to none.

During his life in the monastery, Bede wrote the history of England up to the eighth century and translated Scripture from Latin into Old English. One of his last works was the translation of the Gospel of John.

Venerable Bede would chant with the rest of the monks starting in the early morning and periodically throughout the day, in keeping with monastic tradition. Though unusual for a monk to be given lofty titles, Bede was called Venerable by his pupils because of his great knowledge and studious personality.

St. Bernard of Clairvaux

Fontaine-lès-Dijon, France (1090–1153)

Canonized: 1174

Declared a Doctor of the Church: 1830

Patron: beekeepers, candle makers

Feast day: August 20

Bernard, founder of the Cistercian monastery, was a valiant defender of the pope and was often called upon to preach crusades when the pope felt the Holy Land and its shrines were threatened. He did this with great zeal, believing that the sacred components of Christ's life should remain in Christian hands. During the second crusade, Bernard noticed that devotion and religious attitude among his soldiers was lacking, and they were slipping into sinful behavior, leading to the failure of the crusade.

He was a great influence on religious architecture. Most of the churches at the time were built in a Gothic style — very ornate and heavy with decoration. In contrast, Bernard's chapel and style resonated with light and simplicity, a style that became common throughout the Cistercian monastic chapel.

A vast array of his writings and sermons show a great devotion to the Blessed Virgin Mary; Bernard is credited for the composition of the famous prayer, "Memorare of Mary." He is also responsible for a series of sermons that preached against the heresy of Albigensianism. Thanks to his preaching, many people were converted, healed, and brought into line of orthodoxy.

St. Bonaventure

Bagnoregio, Province of Viterbo, Papal States (1221–1274)

Canonized: 1482

Declared a Doctor of the Church: 1588

Patron: theology professors, those suffering intestinal problems

Feast day: July 15

One of the biggest commissions of Bonaventure's life was his work seeking unification between the Eastern or Orthodox Church and the Western or Latin Church. The emperor of Constantinople asked the pope to look into the viability of unity, and Bonaventure was chosen to take on this task following the death of Thomas Aquinas. Although some progress was made, Bonaventure died before unification could take place.

Prior to this commission, Bonaventure was an excellent student at the University of Paris, proficient in philosophy and theology, especially the new scholastic mode. In his religious life, he was charitable, humble, and a hard worker. Bonaventure is considered the second founder of the Franciscan Order, following a conflict between two opposing sides: those who sought stricter enforcement of the rule and those who became lax. When he was elected superior general, Bonaventure sought out virtue, generally found in the middle of the two sides of opposition. He worked for the authentic translation of the rule of St. Francis for the order and wrote many books on mystical theology, adapting the philosophy of Plato in a Christian light.

St. Catherine of Siena

Siena, Italy (1347–1380)

Canonized: 1461

Declared a Doctor of the Church: 1970

Patron: Italy, Europe, against miscarriages

Feast day: April 29

Catherine (shown in Figure 13-1) fought for her faith early in life — first against her parents, and then against skeptics who doubted the heavenly visions she received. Some thought she was a saint, others a religious fanatic, and still others a hypocrite. She was interviewed and questioned by theologians and religious leaders, all of whom found her to be authentic.

Figure 13-1:
St. Catherine.

Alinari/Art Resource, NY

Catherine devoted her life to nursing, caring for the most seriously ill: those with cancer and leprosy. She was often able to convert sinners who would initially taunt her and gossip about her; later, she visited death-row prisoners to work for their conversion so that they could receive the Last Sacrament.

She is most famously recognized as the Patroness of Italy, a title bestowed upon her because of her industrious work in returning the pope to Italy. For more than 70 years, the popes had been in voluntary exile in Avignon, France, because of the wretched conditions in Rome and most of central Italy at the time. It had become so dangerous that, in 1305, Pope Clement V, a Frenchman, moved the Papal Curia to Avignon, to property that popes had owned for centuries.

Seven popes made Avignon home from 1305 to 1377, when Catherine traveled to the papal estates and pleaded with the Roman pontiff to return to Rome. Catherine's reputation as a respected mystic proved valuable, as her request was granted and the papal court was brought back to Rome.

St. Cyril of Alexandria

Theodosius, Egypt (AD 378–AD 444)

Declared a Doctor of the Church: 1882

Patron: Alexandria, Egypt

Feast day: June 27

Cyril worked hard defending the faith against the many heresies concerning Christ. One such heresy was expounded by Nestorius, patriarch of Constantinople, which taught that Christ is two persons — one God and the other human — instead of the orthodox teaching that Christ is one divine person with two natures: human and divine. Cyril pleaded to Pope St. Celestine I to look into Nestorianism; the pope found the teachings of Nestorius to be heretical and subsequently condemned them.

The condemnation led to the convening of the Ecumenical Council of Ephesus in AD 431, in which St. Cyril was the leading prelate. The council solemnly defined the *hypostatic union* — one divine person with two natures; human and divine. The council also affirmed the title "Mary, Mother of God." Nestorius had maintained that only the title "Mother of Christ" could be used because Mary wasn't a goddess and therefore couldn't be the mother of divinity. Cyril and the council, however, defended the use of the term "Mother of God." While remaining a human being, Mary nevertheless conceived and gave birth to the Son of God. Her Son, Jesus, is divine. Hence, by her relationship to Jesus, she can be called the "Mother of God," as her son is truly the Son of God.

Cyril was also a great advocate of Holy Communion. He staunchly believed that the bread and wine consecrated by the priest at Mass become the real, true, and substantial body and blood, soul, and divinity of Christ. He urged fellow believers to receive Holy Eucharist properly and frequently.

St. Cyril of Jerusalem

Caesarea Maritima, Palestine (AD 315–AD 386)

Declared a Doctor of the Church: 1882

Patron: Jerusalem

Feast day: March 18

Cyril of Jerusalem was an ordained priest and great philosophical instructor who so believed in the sacraments and that Jesus was the true Son of God that many of his writings set out guidelines for observing and partaking in the Sacraments of Baptism, Confirmation, and the Eucharist.

His instructions serve as the basis for the "Catechesis," one of his instructional writings. He found himself at odds with Arius, the founder of the Arianism heresy, who denied that Jesus was of the same substance as God.

The First Council of Nicea solemnly defined that the Son is indeed equal to the Father and that Christ was *consubstantial* (of the same substance, not just similar) to God the Father. The ruling was ratified again at the First Council of Constantinople in AD 381.

St. Ephraem of Syria

Nisibis, Mesopotamia (AD 306–AD 373)

Declared a Doctor of the Church: 1920

Patron: spiritual directors

Feast day: June 9

Music played a vital role in Ephraem's life, as well as in his ministry. He helped to combat the Gnostic heresy by presenting orthodox theology through hymns and music. He started using a women's choir in liturgical worship and is considered a great contributor to music in the Syriac liturgy. It is in this liturgy that Ephraem was bestowed the title, "Harp of the Holy Ghost."

The most famous collection of his writings is *Hymns against Heresies.* Among the heresies he combated with these works was docetism, which taught that Jesus's physical body was merely an illusion.

St. Francis de Sales

Château de Thorens, Savoy (1567–1622)

Canonized: 1655

Declared a Doctor of the Church: 1877

Patron: Catholic press, deaf people

Feast day: January 24

Francis was a champion of the Counter-Reformation period, using his devout faith to preach, teach, and give witness to God and winning over many converts. He was a learned man, well educated in law, philosophy, theology, and rhetoric. He founded the Oblates of St. Francis de Sales, which was a leading force during the Counter-Reformation.

With St. Jane Frances de Chantal, he cofounded the Visitation Order of Nuns, and one of his most well-known books, still in use today, is *The Introduction to the Devout Life,* which was translated into many different languages. He developed a pocket catechism based on the reforms and clear teachings of the Council of Trent; this catechism was used in his diocese when he became Bishop of Geneva. It became known as the "Bishop's Catechism" and was a bulwark in converting the area to Catholicism, especially the youth. He also created a form of sign language to help lead his instructions to the deaf.

St. Gregory Nazianzen

Arianzum, Cappadocia (AD 329–AD 390)

Declared a Doctor of the Church: 1568

Feast day: January 2

Gregory was something of a reluctant saint, fleeing his family after an ordination that was largely orchestrated by his father. His friend St. Basil convinced him to return to help his father, who was at that time bishop of their hometown diocese. St. Basil later sought to consecrate Gregory a bishop and sent him to a trouble area. Because of politics, Gregory could never take over the diocese, but he worked alongside his father as co-adjutor.

Upon the death of the Archbishop of Constantinople, Gregory was summoned to go to this see and bring the people in line with the orthodox faith. The area had suffered isolation for nearly 30 years because of the Arian heresy. Under duress but under obedience, he accepted the task to become its new archbishop.

Gregory was at first met with opposition; the Eastern Empire was expecting a more striking and majestic figure. Despite his initial reception, Gregory's sermons on the Trinity combating Arianism are most celebrated. He was attacked by the Arianists, and only after the conversion of the emperor was Gregory installed as archbishop. New enemies soon arose, however — this time with political adversaries seeking to overtake the archdiocese. Gregory asked the emperor if he could return to his native land to preserve peace, and the emperor agreed.

Pope St. Gregory the Great

Rome, Italy (AD 540–AD 604)

Canonized: AD 604

Declared a Doctor of the Church: 1298

Patron: educators, musicians, singers, popes, and those suffering from the gout

Feast day: September 3

Pope Gregory was a great reformer and skilled writer, dedicating his life as a "servant of the servants of God" in his papal role. Gregory was a magnificent evangelist, sending missionaries to the Barbarians in the north and to the pagan Anglo-Saxons of England at a time when Rome was in ruins because of the Barbarian invasions. (See Chapter 8 for more on Gregory's ascent to and actions in the papacy.)

It was his writings, however, that led to his consideration as a Doctor of the Church. During his career, Gregory wrote 40 sermons on the Gospels, as well as *The Life of St. Benedict, Commentary on the Book of Job, The Rule of Pastors,* and more than 800 letters.

St. Hilary of Poitiers

Pictavium, Gaul (France) (AD 315–AD 367)

Declared a Doctor of the Church: 1851

Patron: exiles; against snakebites

Feast day: January 13

Born of two pagan parents, Hilary used his own powers of reason and concluded that there must be a God. He was introduced to the Scriptures, which led him to convert to Christianity. He was married at the time of his episcopal consecration and, out of humility, didn't want to take a religious office — but he was unanimously nominated.

Hilary was a leader in the fight against Arianism and wrote "De fide Orientalium," a theological work addressed specifically to the followers of Arius. Other works include "De Trinitate Libri XII," a theological composition on the Blessed Trinity, and "Ad Constantium Agustum Liber Secundus," a letter presented to the emperor to defend himself against the lies of his enemies and argue for the vindication of his trinitarian treatise.

St. Isidore of Seville

Cartagena, Spain (AD 560–AD 636)

Canonized: 1598

Declared a Doctor of the Church: 1722

Patron: computers, the Internet

Feast day: April 4

Isidore is considered one of the last great early Church Fathers in the West whose textbook, *Etymologiae,* or *Origines,* was a major influence on the systemic study of classical works in the universities throughout the Middle Ages. All the classic studies — logic, theology, geography, and architecture — were covered within the pages of his textbook.

Other writings include commentaries on the Scriptures, a compendium of moral and dogmatic theology, and a book on monastic life.

St. Jerome

Stridon, Dalmatia (AD 347–AD 419)

Declared a Doctor of the Church: 1298

Patron: archeologists, Bible scholars, translators, archivists, librarians

Feast day: September 30

Using his knowledge of both Hebrew and Greek — two languages that figure heavily in both the Old and New Testaments of the Bible — Jerome translated the Bible into the Latin Vulgate, considered more authentic than prior translations because Jerome corrected prior, erroneous translations.

He also wrote vast commentaries on the Scriptures. His writings include biographies of various saints and letters, as well as a theological treatise against Arianism. His works also include many letters, including those in defense of the doctrine of the Perpetual Virginity of Mary. He is second only to St. Augustine as the most prolific writer of the early Church Fathers. He retired as a monk in Bethlehem and died there in AD 420.

St. John Chrysostom

Antioch (AD 347–AD 407)

Declared a Doctor of the Church: 1568

Patron: preachers, orators, public speaking, and those suffering from epilepsy

Feast day: September 13

St. John Chrysostom was a great orator, interpreter of sacred Scripture, and theologian who faced many assignations from other prelates who sought his position as Archbishop of Constantinople. He was one of the greatest homilists in the early Church and wrote many sermons on both the New and Old Testaments; his sermons on paganism convinced people to tear down the pagan temples. His prayers and liturgical guidelines are still in use today in the Byzantine Catholic Church.

He died in exile in AD 407 and his body was carried back with great pomp and entombed in the Church of the Apostles in Constantinople.

St. John Damascene

Damascus, Syria (AD 645–AD 749)

Canonized: 1890

Declared a Doctor of the Church: 1890

Patron: Christian artists, sick children

Feast day: December 4

Also known as St. John of Damascus, John followed in his father's footsteps working for the Muslim government until the iconoclastic heresy rocked the Church in the East; at that time, John turned his energy and focus to the defense of orthodoxy. He wrote many treatises on the orthodoxy of icons, such as spiritual paintings of the Lord, Mary, and the saints.

The emperor of Constantinople misread the Scripture concerning icons and sought to ban them, but John refused to be swayed. The emperor was infuriated and forged a letter to the caliph making false accusations, an act that led to severe punishment for John — his writing hand was severed. But through intercession from the Blessed Virgin Mary, his hand was restored.

The caliph saw his innocence and desired to reinstate his government position. However, John had another desire: to enter the monastery near Jerusalem, where he was ordained a priest and composed a plethora of writings.

Among his famous writings is the *Fountain of Knowledge,* which is divided into three sections: "Philosophical Chapters," "Concerning Heresies," and "Exact Expositions of the Orthodox Faith." In response to the Monophosyite heresy, he composed the "Trisagion" hymn, which is still used in Byzantine liturgy today.

St. John of the Cross

Fontiveros, Spain (1542–1591)

Canonized: 1726

Declared a Doctor of the Church: 1926

Patron: mystics, theologians, poets, a contemplative life

Feast day: December 14

John of the Cross was a leading reformer, both alongside St. Teresa of Avila (see her entry later in this chapter) and on his own in the Counter-Reformation. His fellow Carmelites didn't appreciate his desire to reform the order and return to the basics, for they had become accustomed to the more comfortable and worldly life they now lived. John was subsequently rejected, ignored, abused, and imprisoned. Eventually, the pope allowed him to found a branch of Carmelite priests, just as Teresa of Avila did with some Carmelite nuns. Both groups are known as *Discalced* Carmelites (meaning the absence of shoes — that is, they only wear sandals).

His writings include spiritual classics such as *The Dark Night of the Soul,* a narrative concerning the journey of the soul from earth toward heaven; *The Ascent of Mount Carmel;* and *Spiritual Canticle.* He also wrote poetry, including *O Living Flame of Love, Poems,* and *A Collection of Spiritual Maxims.* His writings (as well as St. Teresa of Avila's literary contributions) reflect the great mystical heritage that characterized the 16th-century Counter-Reformation Church in Spain.

St. Lawrence of Brindisi

Brindisi, Apulia (Italy) (1559–1619)

Canonized: 1881

Declared a Doctor of the Church: 1959

Patron: Brindisi (an ancient Italian city)

Feast day: July 21

Both a humble Franciscan friar and a great diplomat, Lawrence was sent as a *nuncio* — ambassador of the Holy See — to Bavaria, and then to Prague and Vienna to establish Franciscan friaries. The friaries became centers in which priests taught the Catholic faith.

Lawrence was also a great orator and was asked by Holy Roman Emperor Rudolf II to build an army against Ottoman threats at the Hungarian border.

His writings consisted of sermons, commentaries on the Book of Genesis, and a treatise against Martin Luther.

Pope St. Leo the Great

Tuscany, Italy (AD 400–AD 461)

Declared a Doctor of the Church: 1754

Patron: sacred music, musicians, singers

Feast day: November 10

Leo was named a Doctor of the Church because of his writings, the most prominent of which is "Tome," a letter providing a statement of faith of the Roman Catholic Church. (See Chapter 8 for more on Leo's papacy.)

St. Peter Canisius

Nijmegen, Netherlands (1521–1597)

Canonized: 1925

Declared a Doctor of the Church: 1925

Patron: catechism writers

Feast day: December 21

Peter was a leading force in the Counter-Reformation in Germany and composed the *German Catechism,* a book that taught the basic Catholic principles of faith. A member of the Society of Jesus, or Jesuits, he firmly established a Jesuit community in Germany, a community that grew and prospered into a strong conversion force.

Peter was assigned the position of papal theologian at the Council of Trent, the great reforming council. He opened several colleges, including those in Munich, Dillingen-Bavaria, and Innsbruck. He became confessor to the emperor's daughter, Queen Magdalena, and was declared Venerable by Pope Pius X in 1906.

In a text called "De Maria Virgine," he defended devotion to Mary and actively promoted the Rosary and lay associations of Mary. Other notable works by Peter are "Summa Doctrinae Christinae," "Catechismus Minimus," and "Parus Catechismus Catholicorum."

St. Peter Chyrsologus

Imola, Bologna (Italy) (AD 406–AD 450)

Declared a Doctor of the Church: 1729

Feast day: July 30

Upon the death of the Archbishop of Ravena, Peter accompanied the Bishop of Imola to Rome to deliver the people's choice of a new archbishop, the custom of the time. However, the pope, having received a vision, rejected their choice and appointed Peter archbishop instead.

After he was consecrated, Peter discovered his diocese still had links to paganism, and he used his best skills — teaching and preaching — to deliver fiery sermons to help break the stronghold of the heresy.

He is known as the "Doctor of Homilies" because of his inspirational talks. Letters still exist today that prove his theological expertise. Peter taught Holy

Communion, as well as the tenets of the Apostles' Creed, the lives of St. John the Baptist and the Blessed Virgin Mary, and the incarnation of Christ. Today, more than 176 homilies and teachings are credited to Peter.

St. Peter Damian

Ravenna, Italy (1007–1072)

Canonized: 1828

Declared a Doctor of the Church: 1828

Patron: diplomats

Feast day: February 21

Peter was a great example of clerical and monastic reform, eventually accepting the position of abbot in a monastery and founding five other monasteries.

Peter stressed proper clergy lifestyle, attacking the moral depravity among the clergy in his treatise, *Liber Gomorrhianus.*

Peter Damian also was a champion in standing up for the authentic pope. He wrote *First Crusade,* a book on personal piety; *Officium Beatae Virginis,* a book on Mary; and *De Divina Omnipotentia,* a book on the power of God. He also wrote innumerable letters, sermons, and other writings.

St. Robert Bellarmine

Montepulciano, Italy (1542–1621)

Canonized: 1930

Declared a Doctor of the Church: 1930

Patron: canon lawyers

Feast day: September 17

An ordained Jesuit priest, Robert taught himself both Greek and Hebrew, languages that would serve him well in translating the Sacred Scriptures.

He became the Archbishop of Capua in the Kingdom of Naples and rose to the rank of cardinal. He became a champion of enacting the reforms of the Council of Trent.

After the election of Pope St. Pius V, Robert returned to Rome and served the pope in various capacities. He was a special envoy to Venice when the pope placed this republic under interdict because of disobedience. Robert dealt with King James I of England and countered the sovereign's objections and false theological conclusions. He also dealt with Galileo Galilei and advised the astronomer that he should teach his scientific conclusions as hypotheses until proven as fact.

He's most noted for composing four volumes on the Christian faith, *Disputations on the Controversies,* which were used in seminaries and schools of theology for more than 300 years.

St. Teresa of Avila (Or St. Teresa of Jesus)

Avila, Spain (1515–1582)

Canonized: 1622

Declared a Doctor of the Church: 1970

Patron: lace makers, Spain, and those suffering from headaches

Feast day: October 15

Teresa, a Carmelite nun, became a great reformer and worked alongside St. John of the Cross (see his entry earlier in this chapter). Her first works of reform were within her own convent; at the time, the convent had become a social place for wealthy girls with large dowries who weren't destined to marry. Teresa emphasized that religious life is a vocation of penance, prayer, poverty, and work. Her reformed monastery became known as the Discalced Carmelites.

She's most remembered for her deeply spiritual mysticism, which she testi-fies to in the book *The Autobiography.* Other books attributed to her include *El Camino de Perfeccion, Mediation on the Song of Songs, El Castilo Interior, Relaciones, Conceptos del Amor,* and *Exclamaciones.* Not only in writing but also in practice, Teresa experienced deep mental prayer. She is usually pic-tured in ecstasy or enrapture and at times levitating, especially during Mass.

St. Thérèse of Lisieux

Alençon, France (1873–1897)

Canonized: 1925

Declared a Doctor of the Church: 1997

Patron: foreign missions; those suffering from tuberculosis

Feast day: October 1

Thérèse of Lisieux is better known as St. Thérèse of the Child Jesus. Despite her short life, she was quite a prolific writer, particularly remembered for her spiritual classic, *Story of a Soul*.

She dreamed of becoming a missionary and joining the Carmelites in Hanoi, Vietnam, but illness prevented her from ever leaving France. Thérèse was only 24 when she died from tuberculosis.

Story of a Soul is divided into three sections: childhood, a letter to Sister Marie of the Sacred Heart, and details of her religious life. She wrote this under obedience from her superiors, and it was printed after she died. In her memoirs (and in practice), she lived by a phrase she coined, "Her little way," a spiritual self-surrender to God. So many soldiers during World War I read her memoirs that she was later declared patroness of the foreign missions, even though she herself never left her monastery in France. The global impact of her life story, however, affected many around the world.

In Figure 13-2, St. Thérèse of Lisieux is shown kneeling and holding a dual picture of the child Jesus (left) and the image of the crucified face of Christ from St. Veronica's veil (right).

Figure 13-2:
St. Thérèse
of Lisieux.

Bridgeman-Giraudon/
Art Resource, NY

St. Thomas Aquinas

Roccasecca, Kingdom of Sicily (1225–1274)

Canonized: 1323

Declared a Doctor of the Church: 1567

Patron: theologians, students, academics, booksellers, Catholic schools, against thunderstorms

Feast day: January 28

Thomas Aquinas's vocation was sidelined for a time when he was kidnapped and imprisoned by his father, who didn't want his son to join the Dominican Order (founded by St. Dominic de Guzman). He preferred that Thomas enter the Benedictine Order (founded by St. Benedict), which was well established and had possibilities of promotion to abbot (the equivalent of a bishop). Thomas, however, wanted to become a Dominican, a new religious community (contemporaries of the Franciscans, founded by St. Francis of Assisi). This familial tumult did nothing to destroy his vocation, however, and he eventually took his vows as a Dominican and studied at the University of Paris. (See Chapter 9 for more on SS. Francis, Dominic, and Benedict.)

In his early days at the university, he was often misunderstood and called "dumb ox" by his classmates because they didn't recognize his real intellectual genius. Yet one of his teachers, St. Albert the Great (see the first entry in this chapter), believed that Thomas Aquinas would become one of the greatest teachers of the Church. So profound are his writings that Thomas is often called the "angelic doctor," implying the heavenly wisdom he possessed.

Thomas studied the philosophy of Aristotle and reworked it to apply to Christianity. His expression that philosophy is "the handmaiden of theology" pointed to the importance of philosophy in explaining doctrinal issues. One of his greatest collections is *Summa Theologica,* in which he uses philosophy to explain the chief tenets of the Christian faith and pose arguments. Thomas had the ability to use logic and reason to understand, explain, and defend the Catholic faith. He often exhorted his students to "never deny, seldom affirm, always distinguish." That was his way of disarming the rhetorical arguments and the irrational emotionalism often involved when people debate important issues.

He's also noted for composing prayers and music for the Mass of Corpus Christi, a feast that commemorates a eucharistic miracle in Orvieto, Italy.

His name is often invoked during thunderstorms. When Thomas was a child, his sister, who slept in the bed next to his, was struck and killed by lightning.

Thereafter, Thomas was terrified of thunderstorms, and every time a storm brewed, he went into church and prayed for God's protection.

Thomas is often shown with a sun on his chest (a symbol of sacred learning), as in Figure 13-3. The book in the figure represents his extensive writings, especially the *Summa Theologica,* and the church he holds in his right hand represents the foundation of Catholic theology he helped establish by his precise philosophical method.

Figure 13-3:
St. Thomas
Aquinas.

© National Gallery, London/
Art Resource, NY

Chapter 14

Saintly Pastors

Some saints spent their lives serving the Church as pastors — priests or bishops who cared for people's spiritual lives. *Pastor* means "shepherd," and just as the good shepherd tends to the needs and safety of his flock, so too did these men. They were exemplary in their spiritual care of those entrusted to them. This chapter discusses just some of these important men.

St. Aloysius Gonzaga

Lombardy, Italy (1568–1591)

Beatified: 1605

Canonized: 1726

Patron: young students (because of his early catechetical work with them), Jesuit novices, and people with AIDS and their caregivers

Feast day: June 21

Aloysius was the eldest son of the Marquis of Castiglione, and, as such, he was born into certain expectations and demands. His father had hopes that he would enter the military and be a strong commander, but Aloysius wanted to live a religious life.

He and his brother were sent to various royal courts, most notably to Spain as part of the child prince's retinue. That life grew tiresome for young Aloysius, and instead of taking part in the available pleasures, he continued to practice his devotions and disciplines. He fasted, rose early to pray and make a holy hour, and performed severe penances.

The death of the Spanish prince freed Aloysius from all royal duties, and he then worked toward entering a religious life. He had read journals and other material on saints and religious men and was interested in the Jesuits' account of their missionary work in India. He wanted to join the Counter-Reformation congregation.

Aloysius joined the Jesuit novitiate in Rome in 1585 as a frail young man afflicted with kidney disease and prone to chronic headaches. Schooling was in Milan, but Aloysius's health prevented him from continuing. He returned to Rome as a plague epidemic hit the city. He volunteered in the Jesuit hospital and helped care for the sick.

Aloysius contracted the plague and died in 1591. He is enshrined in Rome at the Church of St. Ignatius.

St. Ansgar

France (AD 801–AD 865)

Feast day: February 3

Ansgar was a child of nobility raised in the Abbey of Corbie near Amiens, France. He grew up in piety and devotion to the Blessed Virgin Mary and entered monastic life at the same abbey. He later transferred to Westphalia (a region in Germany), where he continued his preaching and teaching.

New opportunities for Catholicism and Christianity began to open in the northern European regions, and Ansgar stood at the forefront of those who sought to introduce Christianity to Denmark and Sweden. He was quite successful in establishing churches in these areas.

Upon being summoned by Holy Roman Emperor Louis the Pious, he returned to France and was made Archbishop of Hamburg in AD 831. He continued to promote the Church through education and the building of churches and monasteries.

When Emperor Louis died in AD 840, the empire was divided among his three sons, and new churches came under attack, including the archdiocese in Hamburg. Eventually, the new emperor, Louis II, was able to bring peace, and Ansgar rebuilt his see.

Ansgar didn't pastor to only the Church as a whole; he was also very much a pastor to the individual. Throughout his career as archbishop, he personally fed and tended to the sick and the poor, and his works of charity were known throughout the diocese. He dismissed any praise for his role of Christian service.

He is considered an apostle of northern Europe and patron saint of Denmark. He is also venerated in the Eastern Orthodox Church, as well as the Lutheran and Anglican religions.

St. Anthony, the Abbot

Egypt (AD 251–AD 356)

Patron: basket makers, butchers, victims of eczema, and hermits (a type of monk); invoked against pestilence

Feast day: January 17

Although monasticism had been in existence for some time, Anthony is considered the father of Eastern monasticism for making it known and popular in a way no other monk was able to do. As a child, he led a life of extraordinary solitude and didn't attend school outside the home. When his parents died, he inherited vast amounts of money and property and became his unmarried sister's caretaker.

While attending church services, Anthony heard a gospel passage about a wealthy young man selling all he had and giving it to the poor. He took this message as a sign that God wanted him to do the same thing, so he placed his sister in the care of consecrated virgin women — which would later become the beginning of convent life — and sold all his property.

Anthony sequestered himself in solitude and entered a period of deep prayer, fasting, reading, and manual labor, thus beginning to perfect the virtues of humility, charity, and chastity.

In AD 305, Anthony founded the first of what would be several monasteries. He is believed to have died at the age of 105 after living a life of austerity and discipline.

The city of Vienna, in Austria, has a major shrine of St. Anthony, and a monastery also exists in his honor.

St. Anthony Claret

Spain (1807–1870)

Beatified: 1934

Canonized: 1950

Patron: textile merchants, weavers, Catholic press, Claretian missionaries, and the diocese of the Canary Islands

Feast day: October 24

Anthony was born in Spain to a family involved in wool manufacturing. The family lived comfortably and stressed the importance of education. As a young adult, Anthony moved to Barcelona to continue the woolen trade but discovered he was more interested in religious life.

Anthony had hoped to enter the monastery of the strictest observance, the Carthusians, but his health wasn't strong enough to allow him to follow that austere lifestyle. Instead, he was ordained a priest for his home diocese of Vic in Catalonia, Spain. He tried missionary work by joining the Jesuits in Rome, but again, his health began to deteriorate.

Returning to Spain, he preached missions in his native diocese and the Canary Islands. He established a religious community, the Congregation of Missionary Sons of the Immaculate Heart of Mary, known as the Claretians.

Anthony's holiness, organizational skills, and missionary zeal soon caught the eye of Queen Isabella II of Spain. At her request, Pope Pius IX appointed Anthony Archbishop of Santiago in Cuba. The diocese was a physical and spiritual mess, having suffered the effects of a revolution. Archbishop Claret reorganized the diocese, established schools, emphasized clerical discipline, and restructured the seminary.

Anthony was called back to Spain to be the queen's confessor, and he worked at the military palace, Escorial, where he established a science laboratory in the monastery. In Barcelona, he established a library.

The political situation deteriorated in Italy and Spain, and Anthony went to Rome to prepare for the First Vatican Council, which would define papal infallibility. At the time, Italy was undergoing unification, the Papal States were threatened, and Anthony Claret proved to be a good support for Pope Pius IX.

St. Anthony Zaccaria

Italy (1502–1539)

Beatified: 1890

Canonized: 1897

Patron: the Barnabite community

Feast day: July 5

Anthony Zaccaria was educated in medicine and returned to his hometown to serve as a physician. It wasn't long before he felt a deep attraction to religious life, and he was ordained into the priesthood in 1527. Anthony practiced works of charity among the poor and in hospitals.

He organized three religious institutions for priests, sisters, and laypeople. The Clerks Regular of St. Paul took vows of chastity, poverty, and obedience without being monastic or mendicants. The Angelic Sisters of St. Paul was founded to help young women avoid falling into the evil ways of the world. Finally, the Laity of St. Paul was established for married couples as support in their vocation.

The Clerks Regular chose the Church of St. Barnabas in Rome as their home and thus became known as the Barnabites. Their main apostolate was to promote the sacred liturgy and the sacraments, and to that end, Anthony started a devotion of exposing the Blessed Sacrament on the altars of churches for three days, known today as the Forty Hours' Devotion. This custom was inaugurated in the United States by St. John Neumann (see Chapter 11).

Anthony practiced severe *asceticism* — rigorous self-denial and self-mortification — and it took a toll on his health. He caught a fever while preaching a mission in 1539 and died a short time later.

Pope Leo XIII canonized him, and a shrine in his honor is in the Convent of St. Paul's in Milan, Italy.

St. Augustine of Canterbury

Canterbury, England (unknown–AD 605)

Patron: Canterbury; England; Great Britain

Feast day: May 27

Augustine was a Benedictine monk and prior of a monastery near Rome. Pope Gregory the Great became aware of Augustine's gifts and talents and appointed him to missionary work in England. Because of several wars and pagan invasions, England was, at the time, divided into factions of small Christian religious communities.

Christians in England asked the pope to send more missionaries, and Augustine was chosen to lead them. The pope sent many things with Augustine to use in reestablishing the Church, including relics, sacred vessels, altar furnishings, vestments, and books. After Augustine baptized the English king, he returned to France to be ordained a bishop.

Augustine then founded a new see and built a monastery and church at the site where the Canterbury Cathedral now stands. He also established the diocese of London and Rochester and had to deal with the remnant Catholic Church that had been exiled to Cornwall and Wales by pagan invasions. Augustine's hope of reuniting this group with his reinvigorated church ultimately failed, but through his work and the missionaries that were sent by Rome, the Catholic Church now had a strong foundation in England.

St. Bernadine of Siena

Italy (1380–1444)

Canonized: 1450

Patron: advertisers, people with chest problems, gambling addicts, public relations personnel, and the diocese of San Bernardino, California

Feast day: May 20

St. Bernadine was born on September 8, the same date as the Virgin Mary, so his birth date held a special significance to him. That date served as his baptismal date, the day he was invested with the Franciscan habit, and the day of his ordination.

Information about the first 12 years of Bernadine's religious life is scarce, except that he lived the strict observance of the Franciscans, a movement within the broader order. Apparently, one of his religious brothers had a vision that Father Bernadine was to go and preach to the region of Lombardy.

Wherever he went, Bernadine preached of repentance and turning away from vices. He spread the devotion to Jesus's holy name and used the term IHS to denote his name — IHS being the first letters of Jesus's name in Greek, which was later translated to Latin. Drawn rays of sunshine emanate from the initials of this beautiful logo.

Bernadine preached throughout Italy. When he took the habit of the strict observance of St. Francis, the order had only 300 men; his preaching was so powerful and successful that at the time of his death, the order had grown to 4,000 men.

St. Bernadine was canonized by Pope Nicholas V and is buried in Aquila, Italy, the last place he preached.

St. Bruno

Germany (1030–1101)

Canonized: 1623

Patron: Ruthenia, victims of demonic possession

Feast day: October 6

As chancellor of the church in Rheims, France, Bruno witnessed many abuses and worldliness in the clergy, including those involving Archbishop Manasses of Rheims, who appointed him to his post. He reported what he saw and an investigation ensued; Archbishop Manasses was quite clever, however, and was returned to his see. Bruno and his clerical companions who challenged the archbishop were persecuted.

Bruno wanted to retire and devote himself entirely to religious life, and he went on to found the Carthusian Order in Chartreuse, France. Pope Urban II heard of Bruno's piety and called him to Rome to help him in Church government. Bruno recognized obedience to one's legitimate superior as a virtue and set out for Rome. He created a hermitage and worked on reforms in clerical life for the pope.

When Bruno was ready for a more secluded religious life, the pope granted him permission to go to Calabria, Italy. He developed two monasteries in the area and continued communication with his monastery in Chartreuse.

St. Cajetan

Italy (1480–1547)

Beatified: 1629

Canonized: 1671

Patron: the unemployed and job seekers

Feast day: August 7

Cajetan was born with the name "Gaetano" in Vicenza, Italy, and lived during a time of great political and religious upheaval. He was sent to Padua, where he received a doctorate in law and worked under Pope Julius II in the protonotary office (the church equivalent of a notary public). When Julius died, Gaetano resigned his office and studied for the priesthood. He was ordained in 1516 and took the name Cajetan.

He worked for the restoration of clergy by reviving an association of priests called Divine Love. This group worked among the poor and in hospitals.

Cajetan returned to Vicenza and, recognizing the need for reform in the Church, worked with other priests to establish the Congregation of Clerks Regular, known as the Theatines. The Theatines' mission was to revive spirit and zeal in the clergy, as Cajetan believed that no true reform could take place in the Church until the priests reformed themselves.

He died on August 7, 1547, in Naples, Italy, and was canonized in 1671 by Pope Clement X.

St. Casimir

Poland (1458–1484)

Canonized: 1522

Patron: Poland and Lithuania

Feast day: March 4

Casimir was the third eldest child of King Casimir IV and Elizabeth of Austria — daughter of Emperor Albert II — and was the grand duke of Lithuania. Very early in his life, he committed himself to chastity and celibacy and worked tirelessly for the poor. He influenced his father and older brother to distribute alms.

Casimir reluctantly obeyed his father and accepted the throne in Hungary. He was forced into politics at a time when the people of Hungary were tired of their lax king, and the Muslim Ottoman Empire was threatening to enter Christendom through Hungary. But Casimir's army was outnumbered, and he returned to Poland. His father wasn't pleased and imprisoned his son in a castle outside Kraków.

During his imprisonment, Casimir's faith, asceticism, and devotion to God blossomed. He was eventually trained in political affairs and, during his father's travels, ruled Poland in a prudent and judicious manner. He died of tuberculosis on March 4, 1484, and is buried in the cathedral Vilna in Lithuania.

St. Charles Borromeo

Italy (1538–1584)

Beatified: 1602

Canonized: 1610

Patron: catechists, catechumens, seminarians, and the diocese of Monterey, California; invoked against abdominal pain, intestinal disorders, stomach diseases, and ulcers

Feast day: November 4

Charles was named cardinal-deacon by his uncle, Pope Pius IV. Upon the death of his father, Count Gilberto Borromeo, he inherited money, land, and the title of count, all of which he renounced so he could be ordained a priest. He was soon ordained Archbishop of Milan.

Charles worked tirelessly with his uncle at the Council of Trent. When Pius IV died, the new pope, Pius V, retained Charles Borromeo. He worked on many of the deliberations of the council during the Church's Reformation, while personally working on the reformation of liturgy and sacrament as well as the establishment of the catechism of the Council of Trent.

Along with Pope St. Pius V, St. Philip Neri, and Ignatius of Loyola, the Church was armed with the renewed spirit of reform, known as the *Counter-Reformation.* Still, Charles wanted to work in his diocese; years of neglect had taken a toll on the archdiocese of Milan. He started his reforms in 1566 by implementing the deliberations of the Council of Trent, and then he regulated clerical life by establishing rectories — residences for priests. He founded seminaries for the training of priests and spent his life and fortune on the people of Milan.

St. Columban

Italy (AD 540–AD 615)

Patron: bookbinders, poets, and against floods

Feast day: November 23

Columban was born to Irish nobility in the sixth century and traveled with a small band to Iona, Scotland, and then on to France. He was ordained and founded monasteries throughout Ireland, Scotland, Italy, and France, and he adopted the rule of St. Benedict in all of them.

The rule — or *regula* in Latin — refers to the disciplines used to keep order in a religious community. The rule delineates who's in charge and of what, and it defines what the members can and can't do in everyday life. St. Benedict's rule is one of the oldest and simplest in that it centers on two aspects — prayer and work *(ora et labora).*

In addition to St. Columban's rule for monastic living, he wrote a number of letters and poetry. He died on November 23, AD 615, in Bobbio, Italy, where his monastery became a bastion of faith and learning. His body is preserved in the abbey church at Bobbio.

St. Eusebius of Vercelli

Sardinia (AD 283–AD 371)

Patron: the diocese of Vercelli, Italy

Feast day: August 2

Eusebius was instituted as a lector in Rome before eventually going to Vercelli in northern Italy to become the region's first bishop. While he was Bishop of Vercelli, the Arian heresy was infiltrating the Church. In response, Pope Liberius sent Bishop Eusebius to ask the emperor to convene a council to return the heretics to Catholicism.

The synod was held in Milan in AD 355, but Eusebius saw that the tide had turned and that reconciliation wasn't imminent. The emperor refused to accept the decrees of the Council of Nicea and condemned St. Athanasius. The emperor expected all bishops to sign this condemnation, but Eusebius refused, believing in the innocence of Athanasius and the validity of the Council of Nicea.

(Athanasius was the opponent of Arius, who denied the divinity of Christ. Nicea vindicated Athanasius and condemned Arius.)

Eusebius was then exiled to Palestine. After the ascension of the new emperor, exiled bishops were allowed to return to their sees. Eusebius met with Athanasius in Alexandria to work on clarifying other Christological doctrine.

Eusebius eventually returned to Vercelli and died there on August 1, AD 371.

St. Francis of Paola

Calabria, Italy (1416–1502)

Canonized: 1519

Patron: Calabria (a region in Italy), boatmen, mariners, and naval officers

Feast day: April 2

Francis was educated by Franciscan priests and established the Franciscan Order of Minim Friars, a type of hermit, in 1492. The strict observance of the rule of St. Francis attracted many to his new monastery in Cosenza.

Francis was known for his holiness and as a miracle worker. When King Louis XI of France became gravely ill, he summoned Francis, who initially refused. The king beseeched the pope to intercede, and Francis felt compelled to obey. He traveled to France and prepared the king for death.

Upon the king's death, Francis wanted to return to Italy, but the new king wouldn't allow him to leave, wanting Francis to stay in France because of his holiness.

Francis died at the age of 91 in France. French Protestants broke into Francis's tomb in 1562 and found his body incorrupt, or non-decayed. They burned his body, and devout Catholics retrieved fragments of his bones for veneration.

St. Jerome Emiliani

Italy (1481–1537)

Beatified: 1747

Canonized: 1767

Patron: orphans, abandoned people, and Taos Indians

Feast day: February 8

Like most men of his social status at the time, Jerome started his career in the military in the Republic of Venice. Venice's power was then being challenged, and there was a call to arms.

Jerome was captured in the northern Italian town of Treviso and jailed. While in prison, he had time to reflect on his worldly life, which was fairly devoid of God. At a church in Treviso, at the altar of Our Lady, Jerome laid down his arms and consecrated his life to the Mother of God.

Jerome was ordained a priest in 1518 and devoted himself to the sick, the poor, orphans, and victims of the plague. His apostolate attracted other men to join in his works, and he founded a new congregation of men, the Clerks Regular of Somascha, known as the Somaschi Fathers. They were dedicated to the poor and often preached in the fields where the peasants worked.

He caught a fever on one of his preaching expeditions to the fields and died in Somascha in 1537.

St. John Baptist de la Salle

France (1651–1719)

Beatified: 1888

Canonized: 1900

Patron: educators, teachers of youth, and school principals

Feast day: April 7

John was born to parents of noble origins, and upon their death, he donated his inheritance to the poor. He studied for the priesthood and was ordained in 1678. John became interested in the education of poor children early on in his priestly life and established a new religious community, the Brothers of Christian Schools, which was devoted to teaching.

John's new community soon became the largest teaching order in the post-Reformation Church. Schools sprouted up throughout France, all dedicated to the education of poor boys. The brothers used the native language of the countries they were living in rather than teach the courses in Latin.

Secular schools felt threatened, and John Baptist and his community faced great opposition. The perseverance of the community grew, and so did the construction of its schools.

One major change to the apostolate happened when King James II of England, exiled in France, wanted a school built for his sons and gentry alike. John drew up a manual for his school that set the standard for all Christian Brothers schools in terms of following a certain curriculum and code of conduct.

John's principal shrine is located in Rome at the de la Salle Generalate.

St. John Cantius (Kanty)

Poland (1390–1473)

Beatified: 1676

Canonized: 1767

Patron: Lithuania and Poland

Feast day: December 23

John taught Scripture at the University of Kraków and was a noted professor, which caused jealousy among the other professors. Already an ordained priest, he was reassigned to a parish. He was nervous about the administrative tasks of the pastor, and at first, the people in his parish didn't like him. John persevered, however, and his solemn celebration of the Mass and excellent preaching and teaching changed the parishioners' attitudes. When he was sent back to the university to teach Scripture, his parishioners didn't want him to go.

John was a great friend of the poor, often distributing his own food, materials, and money to them. So humble was he that, when traveling on pilgrimage to Rome, he walked all the way, carrying his few possessions on his back.

He died at the age of 83. A religious community founded in Chicago, the St. John Cantius Society, is named after him. This society is devoted to the restoration of the Latin liturgy, and its members celebrate the extraordinary form of the Mass — the Mass that was used before the Second Vatican Council.

St. John of Capistrano

Italy (1386–1456)

Beatified: 1650

Canonized: 1690

Patron: judges, jurists, military chaplains, and the Spanish-American Catholic Mission in San Juan Capistrano, California

Feast day: October 23

As a young man, John studied law at the University of Perugia and was eventually elected governor of the region. All of Italy was undergoing political and economic change and hardship; one city-state was at war with another.

John was captured and imprisoned, giving him time to reflect on his life. His marriage was dissolved because it had never been consummated, and he decided to enter the Franciscan Order.

John was ordained into the priesthood in 1420 and became known as a powerful orator. Emperor Frederick III called upon his talents to preach against a heretic religious group, the Hussites, that was flourishing in central Europe. The group originated in Prague and was led by reformer John Huss. Although Huss was condemned and put to death as a heretic, his movement lived on, but John of Capistrano's powerful preaching brought people back to the Church.

Catholic Europe was under great threat with the fall of Constantinople at the hands of the Muslim Turks. Pope Nicholas V called upon John to lead a crusade against the Turks, and he preached to the people of Austria and Hungary, exhorting them to come to arms. The Turks were deterred, at least for a time.

John became ill on the battlefields where he was administering the sacraments, celebrating Holy Mass, and preaching. He died on October 23, 1456.

St. Josemaria Escriva

Rome, Italy (1902–1975)

Beatified: 1992

Canonized: 2002

Patron: lay workers

Feast day: June 26

By the time he was 15, Josemaria had seen three of his sisters die as children and his father go through bankruptcy. Feeling called to the priesthood, he went to the seminary, earned degrees in theology and civil law, and was ordained in 1925.

While a parish priest, Josemaria discerned the Lord calling him further, and he founded Opus Dei, Latin for *work of God.* Nearly 35 years before the Second Vatican Council would even use the phrase "universal call to holiness," Josemaria conceptualized it and founded Opus Dei as a means by which ordinary Catholic Christians could sanctify their entire lives by sanctifying their daily work.

During the Middle Ages, the peasants thought that only the monks and nuns were capable of holiness, whereas the common folk (non-nobility) had to settle for a watered-down version of monastic spirituality. Monastic life centered on work and prayer, while secular life had lots of work but little time for prayer.

Instead of going to the chapel whenever the bell rang (as the monks and nuns had to do each day), Josemaria meditated on the lives of St. Joseph and the Virgin Mary, the two holiest people next to Jesus Christ himself. Joseph and his wife were humble, simple folk. They spent most of their day doing manual labor. As faithful Jews, Joseph and Mary did go to synagogue or temple, but not daily. It just wasn't practical to do so.

Opus Dei: Secret society?

Today, 97 percent of Opus Dei is laymen and women who work in ordinary careers doing ordinary things. While all devout Catholic Christians, their sole mission is to sanctify the world, as Christ commanded, by doing their daily work well and doing it for the Lord. The 3 percent who are clergy are ordained priests who came from the ranks of the laity as members of Opus Dei.

Of the 97 percent lay members of Opus Dei, 80 percent are *supernumeraries* — married men and women who have secular careers and live ordinary lives at home with their families. *Numeraries,* who make up the other 20 percent, are laymen and women who live celibate lives together (non-coed) and who donate most of their secular income to sustain the apostolates of Opus Dei.

The 1983 Code of Canon Law (the body of ecclesiastical laws that govern the internal operations of the Catholic Church) created an entity called a *personal prelature,* and Opus Dei was the first such organization. It merely means that the members follow an Opus Dei bishop in the same way that most lay Catholics are under the leadership of the local diocesan bishop.

Unlike the caricature of Opus Dei found in some recent movies, it's not a secret organization of the Catholic Church, and it doesn't contain albino monks, assassins, or spies. However, it does have lots of moms and dads, lawyers, doctors, plumbers, cops, firefighters, and teachers. The so-called secrecy of the prelature is nothing more than humble discretion and prudence. Unlike the clergy (bishops, priests, and deacons) and the consecrated religious (nuns, sisters, brothers, monks, friars, and so on) who work for the Church and must be accountable to it, laymen and women live private lives. They don't wear their religion or their membership in Opus Dei on their sleeve; they merely do their ordinary work at their secular jobs. They don't hide their religion or spirituality, but neither do they advertise or proselytize it. Evangelization occurs by example and witness rather than by debate.

Likewise, Josemaria thought, one's personal holiness isn't solely contingent on how much time one spends in holy places, but rather on how much of the daily work is consecrated to God. While daily prayer is absolutely essential, so is making your daily work a "prayer." Josemaria discovered that if you do your best at whatever your regular job entails and dedicate your best effort to God, then that work is made holy.

St. Martin of Tours

Upper Pannonia, Hungary (AD 316–AD 397)

Patron: beggars, equestrians, and the Pontifical Swiss Guard; invoked against alcoholism, impoverishment, and poverty

Feast day: November 11

Born to pagan parents in what is now Hungary, Martin studied and converted to Christianity at the age of 10. He became a soldier and served in the emperor's army.

When Martin was a soldier, he visited Amiens in present-day France. It was a cold morning, and at the city gate stood a beggar — cold, hungry, and with very few clothes. Martin didn't have much to offer, because soldiers were poorly paid. He got off his horse and offered what he had: half his cape.

Observing the tearing of his cloak in half, some made fun of him, while others felt guilty that they didn't do their part in helping a poor old man. As the story continued that night, Martin had a dream in which Christ the Lord came to him dressed in the remnants of his cloak. The story reflects the ways in which Christians are known for their good actions.

Martin continued as a soldier, and after a successful campaign, the emperor was ready to pay him fairly well, but Martin refused and wanted to be released from the army. This angered the emperor, because Martin was a good soldier, and he imprisoned Martin on charges of treason with hopes that he would change his mind. He was eventually released to St. Hilary of Poitiers, France.

Martin wanted to live a quiet life as a hermit and began the first monastery in this area. Upon the death of the Bishop of Tours, the people wanted him to become their new bishop. He preferred to remain a quiet monk, but he accepted the call to become their bishop. Through his preaching, teaching, and fine holy example, he won over many from paganism. Idols and temples were soon destroyed, and Catholic churches were built.

At the same time, many heretical groups began to form over confusion in doctrine. One such group was the Priscillianists — a Gnostic, Manichean religious sect. Martin successfully preached against this heresy, but when the emperor condemned members to death, Martin pleaded for leniency.

St. Nicholas of Bari

Turkey (AD 270–AD 346)

Patron: sailors, children in the West, fishermen, merchants, the falsely accused, prostitutes, repentant thieves, and pawnbrokers

Feast day: December 6

Nicholas was Bishop of Myra in Asia Minor. In his time, girls couldn't marry unless they had a proper endowment. One man, the father of three girls, lost all his money and was going to sell his daughters into prostitution. Nicholas heard this, and in the middle of the night, he took a sack of gold, enough for the eldest daughter to marry, and threw it through the open window of the man's house. He also did this for the other two daughters, and the father made it a point to see who this generous benefactor was.

As the legend grew, St. Nicholas became Sinter Klaas in Dutch and Santa Claus in English. The jolly old St. Nicholas mentioned in many Christmas carols is actually St. Nicholas of Bari. However, the present-day secular representation has little to do with the real St. Nicholas. He didn't wear a red-and-white suit, nor did he have a sleigh and eight reindeer. These were elements of the mythical "Father Christmas" that became identified with St. Nicholas after European immigrants came to the New World. The real St. Nick did dress as a bishop of his time, did many good deeds, and performed many miracles for children, whom he loved and cherished dearly.

He is revered among the Orthodox and Byzantine Catholic churches for his defense of the Christian faith against the many heresies plaguing the Church in the third and fourth centuries, especially Arianism. He is patron of sailors because, according to legend, sailors in the Mediterranean Sea invoked his name during storms, and the saint guided them safely to port. His feast is kept with great solemnity and festivity in Nordic countries.

During the Muslim takeover of many Christian cities and sites in the eastern Mediterranean, the relics of St. Nicholas were successfully moved in the 11th century to Bari, Italy, where they are today. A magnificent basilica was built in his honor in this port city. He was greatly revered among the Russians as the defender of orthodoxy, so much so that, until the Communist Revolution, Russians would travel to Bari on pilgrimage.

St. Patrick

Britain (AD 387–AD 461)

Patron: Ireland, many dioceses throughout the English-speaking world, and engineers; invoked against the fear of snakes and snakebites

Feast day: March 17

Patrick was born just south of Hadrian's Wall in Britain, which was part of the Roman Empire. He was captured by Irish pagans in his early teens and taken to Ireland, where he was enslaved for six years. During that time, he grew to like the spirit of the Irish. When he escaped and returned to his family, he vowed to one day return to Ireland.

He studied at monasteries on the continent and was eventually ordained a priest and then a bishop. Pope Celestine I commissioned Patrick to be an apostle to Ireland.

Patrick initially encountered many hardships among the pagans, particularly the druids. They weren't willing to give up their power over the old religion and feared Patrick and Christianity. Although the ruling monarch, King Laoghaire, didn't convert to Christianity, many of his family members did, and little by little, the old religion began to fade. Patrick traveled from town to town, tearing down idols and temples and establishing the Catholic Church. By AD 444, the primatial see and first cathedral of Ireland were built in Armagh.

He baptized, confirmed, and ordained priests, and he erected schools and monasteries. Thousands came into the Church under his direction. He accomplished all these activities in less than 30 years, during which time the whole island nation of Ireland was converted. Toward the end of his life, he wrote *Confessions,* in which he gives a record of his life and mission. He died on March 17, AD 461, of natural causes. He is buried in Downpatrick in present-day Northern Ireland.

Many stories are told in connection with St. Patrick. The three-leaf clover was said to be used by the saintly bishop to explain the Blessed Trinity to the pagans. Another legend has Patrick driving all the snakes out of Ireland; snakes were a popular symbol among the Irish pagans. He is certainly one of the most revered saints in the Catholic Church. The famous prayer, "St. Patrick's Breastplate," is attributed to him.

St. Paul of the Cross

Italy (1694–1775)

Beatified: 1853

Canonized: 1867

Patron: Ovada, Italy

Feast day: October 19

Paul developed a devotion to the sacred passion of Christ very early on in his life, instilled first by his mother, who taught him to spiritualize pain and inconveniences he encountered.

Paul received a vision when he was a young man that inspired him to establish a new congregation of priests, the Congregation of the Passion of Jesus Christ, commonly known as the Passionists, in 1720. The new community devoted itself to preaching missions in parishes and giving retreats in seminaries, houses of formation, and monasteries. Toward the end of his life, Paul also founded a cloistered, contemplative community of religious women, known as the Passionist Nuns.

Today, many shrines throughout Europe and in America are staffed by Passionists, including the famous shrine of St. Gabriel of the Passion in the Abruzzi Mountains in Italy and, in the U.S., the Shrine of St. Ann in Scranton, Pennsylvania. In addition, these priests work in various monasteries and retreat centers.

Paul's major shrine, which contains his relics, is the Church of St. John and Paul in Rome.

St. Vincent Ferrer

Spain (1350–1419)

Canonized: 1455

Patron: builders, construction workers, plumbers, brick makers, and tile makers

Feast day: April 5

Vincent had a great love for the poor and often shared what little he had with them. He entered the Order of Preachers, also known as the Dominicans, and was ordained a priest. Soon he became a scholarly man and received a doctorate. He was well versed in philosophy, theology, and Sacred Scripture. It is said that he had a vision of St. Dominic and St. Francis early in his priesthood and from that time on had many mystical experiences.

His great knowledge would soon be put to good use. During the Western (Papal) Schism of 1378–1417, three men claimed at the same time to be pope. Vincent began to preach the unity of the Church throughout Europe. He begged the anti-popes to resign in order to preserve this unity. This was no easy task. Anti-Pope Benedict XIII, who held court in Avignon, France, was counseled by Vincent to end the schism.

Vincent advised King Castile of Spain to withdraw his support of the Avignon anti-pope, which ended the usurped reign of Benedict. The resignation of the authentic pope and the deposing of the two anti-popes paved the way for the election of the true successor to St. Peter, which would be Vincent's greatest legacy.

Several miracles were attributed to the saint before and after his death. The major shrine is in the city of Vannes (in France) in the Vannes Cathedral, where his remains are buried.

Chapter 15

Latin Fathers of the Church

· ·

· ·

This chapter focuses on those saints who are designated Latin Fathers of the Church. These scholars helped mold and shape the early Christian Church, and because of their theological influence and their historical place in antiquity, they've earned the title *Church Father*.

The Church Fathers in this chapter are called *Latin* to differentiate them from their contemporary Eastern or Byzantine Church Fathers. Constantine established the imperial city Constantinople (formerly Byzantium) when he became Roman Emperor in the fourth century. He created the city to serve as a second Rome of sorts, giving the Roman Empire and the Catholic Church two regions — east and west. The eastern provinces were governed by Constantinople, while Rome remained in charge of the western area. The pope was the head of the Church, assisted by patriarchs of Jerusalem, Alexandria, Antioch, and Constantinople.

The Latin writings from the early Church are from the western Church Fathers; the eastern Church Fathers were more comfortable using Greek, the language of the eastern empire. (We discuss the Greek Fathers in Chapter 16.)

St. Ambrose, Bishop of Milan

Trier (Germany) (AD 340–AD 397)

Patron: beekeepers, candle makers

Feast day: December 7

What does it take to be named a Church Father?

One isn't named a Church Father simply by participating in the formation of the Christian Church, though that's certainly among the list of qualifications. In fact, there are four requisites to earning the title *Church Father.* To be considered, one must have

✔ Lived when the Church was in its youth, in the first through sixth centuries

✔ Led a saintly life not tainted by scandal or secrets

✔ Had writings free from heresies while excelling in the explanation and defense of Catholic doctrine

✔ Had writings that bore the seal of the Church, indicating approval

---

Ambrose was named Bishop of Milan out of a violent controversy following the death of Auxentius. Having not yet been baptized, Ambrose worked unsuccessfully to decline the bishopric; the emperor insisted that Ambrose be baptized and ordained on the same day, December 7, AD 347.

During his reign as bishop, Ambrose vigorously fought for the independence of the Church and defended it against imperial control and influence. He's best known for the quote *ubi petrus ibi ecclesia,* which is Latin for "where Peter is, there is the Church." In other words, wherever the pope, the successor of St. Peter, is teaching or speaking authoritatively, he is speaking for the entire Catholic Church.

Ambrose struggled against Arianism, a heresy that maintained that although Christ is similar to God the Father, he's not God's equal. Arianism further held that God adopted Jesus as his son and gave him divine-like abilities. In its early days, Christianity condemned those beliefs as heretical. The teaching now is that Christ is the second person of the Holy Trinity (God the Father, God the Son, and God the Holy Spirit). Therefore, Jesus is both God and man; divine and human. He is one divine person but has both a full and complete divine nature and a full and complete human nature.

St. Augustine, Bishop of Hippo

Thagaste, Numidia (Algeria) (AD 354–AD 430)

Patron: philosophers, printers

Feast day: August 28

Augustine is also one of the Doctors of the Church (see Chapter 13) in addition to being a Latin Father. The playboy son of a pagan father and a devout Christian mother, Augustine first lived a decadent life of hedonism where he sought to satiate every whim and craving. Much like the ancient sect of Epicureans from Roman antiquity, young Augustine lived life in the fast lane.

Fortunately, in early middle age, after having a son out of wedlock, he realized how transitory earthly life and pleasures actually are. He went from one extreme to the other, going from playboy to puritan. Augustine embraced a rigorous life and philosophy of Manichaeism, which saw the material world as evil and only the spiritual as good. That meant that the body and all physical pleasures were sinful.

With the help of the constant prayers of his mother, St. Monica (see Chapter 4), and the tutelage of St. Ambrose (see Chapter 13), Augustine cleaned up his act and was baptized a Christian. Due to his intellectual abilities and education, he soon got ordained a priest and then a bishop. His command of language and philosophy was so great that the medieval genius, St. Thomas Aquinas (see Chapter 13), admired him with awe and great respect.

His writings repudiating the heresy of Pelagianism are still studied today. Pelagius maintained that a human soul could earn or merit its way into heaven all by itself. Augustine taught that man can do nothing on his own but sin. Every good work must be animated and inspired by divine grace. When a soul accepts and cooperates with God's grace, then all things are possible.

St. Cyprian, Bishop of Carthage

Carthage (North Africa) (AD 200–AD 258)

Feast day: September 16

Cyprian, a pagan lawyer, teacher, and rhetorician, was converted to Christianity in AD 246 and became well versed in the Bible as well as the writings of Tertullian (a Church Father who started out as the shining star of Christian faith, only to later fall into heresy). His theology of the supremacy of papal teaching authority (on matters of faith and morals) would be further refined by St. Ambrose after him. Cyprian also believed in *papal primacy* — the concept that the pope has supreme jurisdiction in all Church matters. Under Cyprian's defense of papal primacy, he believed that each parish would still have the pastor as its spiritual leader, and a geographical area of parishes would be under the care of the bishop as spiritual shepherd. The role of the pope would be supervisory as well as symbolic — that is, one leader representing a universal church, making decisions regarding doctrine or discipline to be followed by believers around the world.

St. Cyprian also rebuked the priest Novatus for his leniency on those who had renounced their religion during the Roman persecutions and then returned seeking reconciliation. Although he believed in God's mercy in allowing reconciliation, Cyprian didn't want to trivialize the offense, instead seeing the rejection of Christ and the Church as a serious sin and advocating an appropriate penance. Cyprian stood in the middle of two extreme positions: those in favor of leniency who required the former apostates to go to confession, and those who believed that after one left the Church, forgiveness required a renewed baptism. Cyprian's position held that the *lapsi,* those who left the Church, would be readmitted after some public profession of faith and a public penance.

Pope St. Gregory the Great

Rome, Italy (AD 540–AD 604)

Canonized: AD 604

Declared a Doctor of the Church: 1298

Patron: educators, musicians, singers, popes, and those suffering from the gout

Feast day: September 3

Gregory's dad was a wealthy patrician (Gordianus) who owned large estates in Sicily and a mansion in Rome. His mom (Silvia) is recognized as a saint, and her feast day is November 3. Two of his aunts (his father's sisters, Tarsilla and Aemiliana) are also canonized saints.

After a short career in politics serving the empire, Gregory became a monk at the age of 34. Four years later, he was called out of the monastery and was ordained one of the seven deacons of Rome by the Pope and sent to Byzantium (Constantinople) to seek the aid of the Eastern Emperor in defending Rome from the Lombards.

Returning to Rome in 586, he was made Abbot of St. Andrew's Monastery. He happily enjoyed monastic life, but only for four years. Pope Pelagius II died in 590, and the clergy and citizenry of Rome unanimously elected Gregory the next pope. He tried to escape, feeling himself unworthy of this honor. The people found him trying to leave Rome dressed as a poor pilgrim. Confronted with his destiny and divine providence, Gregory agreed and reigned until his death in AD 604.

As pope, Gregory reformed the sacred liturgy and standardized parts of the Mass and promoted the use of sacred music in divine worship. He also wrote extensively on the faith and was very interested in missionary work. Gregory sent St. Augustine of Canterbury to establish the Catholic faith in Britain.

He was the first pope to use the title "Servant of the Servants of God," seeing the papacy as a ministry and not just a position of honor and power. Gregory did much to improve the office of pope by getting involved in spiritual, liturgical (Gregorian chant is named after him), as well as political and secular issues. He is also known for his repudiation of Patriarch Eutyches of Constantinople who denied the palpability of the resurrected body. Gregory retorted that the body of the Risen Christ was not ethereal but had substance as proved when Jesus asked Thomas to touch his hands and feet, and the times when the Resurrected Lord ate with his disciples.

St. Irenaeus, Bishop of Lyons

Smyrna, Asia Minor (AD 130–AD 200)

Feast day: June 28

During his reign as Bishop of Lyons, Irenaeus fought against Gnosticism, a heresy based on the belief that a secret to salvation exists that only the seeker — the Gnostic — can discover. Gnosticism contradicts the Judeo-Christian belief in public revelation, where God reveals the truth to everyone. It also denies the necessity of a divine grace for salvation. Gnosticism holds that only knowledge can bring true happiness, and it has no place for a personal relationship with God.

Irenaeus countered that revelation is meant for everyone and that truth doesn't belong just with the educated elite. Jesus sent the Apostles to travel the world over to spread the Good News; according to Gnosticism, its followers hide in secret locations vowing to keep new information to themselves. Irenaeus preached often on exposing the philosophical and theological inadequacies and inconsistencies of Gnosticism so his people would be open to the liberating message of the Christian Gospel.

St. Jerome

Stridon, Dalmatia (AD 343–AD 420)

Patron: librarians, bible scholars, translators

Feast day: September 30

More or less

Take a comparative look at the Catholic and typical Protestant Bibles and one notable difference appears: The Catholic Bible has seven more books in its Old Testament than its Protestant counterpart. The Catholic Old Testament has 46 books, and the Protestant version has just 39; both contain the same 27 books in the New Testament.

Why the difference?

St. Jerome, who translated the first complete Bible into one language in AD 400, used a Greek translation of the Hebrew Scriptures called the *Septuagint.* He translated all 27 of the original Christian Scriptures from Greek into his native Latin, and then he worked on one translation of the Old Testament.

During the Babylonian Exile, 7 Old Testament books — Baruch, Ecclesiasticus (or Sirach), Judith, Maccabees 1 and 2, Tobit, and Wisdom — and a few sections of Daniel and Esther were written only in Greek, the language used by exiled Jews, whereas the other 39 Old Testament books were written in pre-exile times and in Hebrew.

Eusebius Hieronymous Sophronius was baptized "Jerome" in AD 360 by Pope Liberius and was taught by Donatus, a famous pagan grammarian, and Victorinus, a Christian rhetorician.

Jerome sought to live a life of prayer as a hermit, partially because he knew living with others would be difficult. As a pagan, he could be a formidable and aggressive opponent in verbal arguments, both intellectually and emotionally. Because he could also get too intense, Jerome left the temptations of the community and lived a life free from annoyance. Pope Damasus refused to leave this brilliant scholar to his solitude, instead commissioning Jerome to translate the first volume of the Christian Bible. Before then, each book of the Old Testament and the New Testament had been written as a separate piece in either Hebrew, Aramaic, or Greek. Jerome was the first person to incorporate all 46 books of the Jewish *Septuagint* (Greek translation of the Old Testament) and all 27 books of the Christian Scriptures into one whole collection.

It took Jerome almost 18 years to fully translate all the books of the Bible into one language and volume, using Latin, the official language of the Roman Empire and the language used by the masses. St. Jerome's Latin translation of the Old and New Testament is called the *Vulgate* because it was done in the common tongue *(vulgata)* of his time. It's considered the first complete Bible, bringing all the parts of previous translations into one volume. Jerome was also the first to use the word *bible* to describe the complete collection of both the Old and New Testaments in one volume. *Biblia* in Latin comes from the

Greek *Byblos,* meaning "books." The Bible is in reality a collection of books, from Genesis to Revelation.

St. Paulinus, Bishop of Nola

Bordeaux, Gaul (France) (AD 353–AD 431)

Feast day: June 22

Paulinus was the son of Pontius Meropius Anicius Paulinus, a Roman prefect in Gaul. He became a successful lawyer and held public office like his father before him. While in Spain he met and married Therasia. Their only child died a week after birth. Paulinus was ordained a priest in AD 393 by the Bishop of Barcelona.

Paulinus corresponded frequently with St. Augustine and St. Jerome, as well as St. Ambrose and St. Martin of Tours. Fifty-one of his letters and thirty-two of his poems are still around today. Paulinus wrote on the dignity and sanctity of Christian marriage and promoted veneration (honor) of the saints, especially the martyrs and their relics to show appreciation for their sacrifice of dying for the faith. He also encouraged others to be as courageous as the martyrs were in defending their religion.

St. Peter Chrysologus

Imola, Bologna (Italy) (AD 406–AD 450)

Feast day: July 3

Peter was given the nickname *Chrysologus* — golden-worded — after preaching an eloquent sermon to Empress Galla Placidia. Bishop Felix of Ravenna saved 176 of Peter's preached sermons in the eighth century.

Peter wrote to Eutyches urging him to abandon his heresy: "We exhort you in every respect, honorable brother, to heed obediently what has been written by the most blessed pope of the city of Rome; for Blessed Peter, who lives and presides in his own see, provides the truth of faith to those who seek it." Eutyches had previously opposed the heresy of Nestorianism but had gone to the opposite extreme of Monophysitism, claiming Jesus had only one nature (divine) and not two (human and divine).

St. Vincent of Lérins

Southern Gaul (France) (unknown–AD 450)

Feast day: May 24

Vincent left the life of a soldier to become a monk in Lérins. Little else is known of his life, other than a phrase he coined that's extremely helpful in evaluating the authenticity of most things in the Catholic Church: *quod ubique, quod semper, quod ab omnibus credituni est* (that which has been taught everywhere, at all times, in all places, by all authorized teachers).

That phrase has become known as the *Vincent canon* and is considered a litmus test for orthodoxy. It can be found in his famous work, the *Commontorium*.

Chapter 16

Greek Fathers of the Church

● ●

In This Chapter

▶ Fighting against Arianism and other heresies

▶ Building the foundation of the Eastern Church

● ●

After the Roman Emperor Constantine (fourth century AD) established the imperial city of Constantinople (formerly Byzantium, currently Istanbul), he divided the empire into two parts, East and West. The Western half used the Latin language and the Eastern half used Greek. The Catholic Church was unofficially but culturally partitioned between East and West. There was one emperor and one pope but two flavors, so to speak.

So for several hundred years, Christianity was united under one roof, albeit with two traditions (Western-Latin and Eastern-Greek). By the 11th century (1054), though, the Great Schism had divided East and West into two separate churches — Catholic and Orthodox. Later, in the 17th century, several Eastern Orthodox communities came back into full communion with the pope in Rome, and they're called Byzantine Catholics or Greek Catholics to distinguish them from the Latin Roman Catholics who lived in the West.

Just as learned men from the Western Church became known as the Latin Fathers of the Church (see Chapter 15), some equally brilliant scholars from the Eastern part of the Church became known as the Greek Fathers. In this chapter, we introduce you to these Greek Fathers of the Church, men who helped in the formation of the Eastern Catholic Church.

St. Athanasius of Alexandria

Alexandria, Egypt (AD 297–AD 373)

Feast day: May 2

As an early disciple of St. Alexander, Bishop of Alexandria, Athanasius learned right away how to defend the Orthodox teachings of the Catholic Church. Alexander was a primary adversary of the Arian heretics at the Council of Nicea in AD 325, and Athanasius, an ordained deacon, assisted Alexander there. Athanasius followed the lead of St. Alexander and vigorously denounced Arianism (heresy that denied the divinity of Christ) whenever he could. He was elected Patriarch of Alexandria in AD 326 following St. Alexander's death.

Athanasius was the first to use the word "catholic" prolifically. In Greek, *katholikos* means "universal"; Athanasius injected it into the Christian vocabulary to establish a unified religion. (Today, "catholic" with a lowercase "c" still means "universal." When it's capitalized, it usually refers to the Catholic Church or faith.)

Athanasius also wrote a lengthy creed, *Quicumque vult* (whosoever wishes to be saved), to formally address Church doctrine regarding the Holy Trinity and the errors of Arianism. The creed endorses the theology of a *triune monotheism* (one God in three persons); Trinitarianism is the foundation of Christianity, and anything less — Unitarianism or dualism, for instance — is not acceptable.

St. Basil the Great, Archbishop of Caesarea

Caesarea, Cappadocia (AD 329–AD 379)

Feast day: January 2

Basil grew up surrounded by strong faith: He was the son of St. Basil the Elder and St. Emmelia; the grandson of St. Macrina the Elder; and brother to SS. Gregory of Nyssa, Macrina the Younger, and Peter of Sebastea.

With such a family lineage, Basil showed holiness at an early age, cooking meals for the poor and raising money for them. Though members of nobility typically helped the needy indirectly through their servants, Basil preferred to "get his hands dirty" and practice his faith. He eventually became a monk and is considered the father of Eastern monasticism, just as St. Benedict was for the Latin, or Western, Church (see Chapter 15).

Basil was a champion of the teachings of Nicea (AD 325) and Constantinople I (AD 360), and as such, he boldly fought the heresy of Arianism. He was also a reformer when he became Bishop of Caesarea in AD 370 in that he punished anyone found guilty of *simony* — trying to buy or sell spiritual favors — and he demanded honesty and integrity from all his clergy. Basil's followers were so fond of his service as bishop, preacher, and teacher that he was known as Basil the Great even before he died.

St. Clement of Alexandria

Athens, Greece (AD 150–AD 215)

Feast day: December 4

Clement was Origen's teacher at the Catechetical School of Alexandria. He made a great contribution in applying Greek philosophical thought to the study, defense, and understanding of Christian theology.

Clement's three great works are *Protrepticus* (exhortation to the Greeks on Christian morality); *Paedagogus* (instruction on ethical conduct); and *Stromata* (moral miscellanies). His work initiated a breakthrough by which logic and philosophy were used to explain and comprehend ideas that flowed from what had already been revealed in Scripture.

SS. Cyril and Methodius

Cyril (Constantine): Thessalonica Greece (AD 827–AD 869)

Methodius: Thessalonica, Greece (AD 826–AD 885)

Feast day: February 14

Cyril (also called Constantine) and his brother Methodius were Greeks from Thessalonica. Pope John Paul the Great proclaimed them to be "Apostles to the Slavs" and copatrons of Europe — along with St. Benedict of Nursia — for their missionary work among the Slavic peoples of Eastern Europe.

Methodius chose to embrace a monastic life, while Cyril, adept in languages and with a keen mind for theology, wanted to be a scholar. Cyril corresponded frequently with Jewish and Muslim scholars, trying to bridge the gaps among the three great monotheistic religions (Judaism, Islam, and Christianity).

The Emperor sent Cyril to convert the seminomadic Russian Khazars, and Methodius accompanied him. Cyril developed an alphabet called the Cyrillic for the Slavonic language, which is still used today in Russia and former Soviet nations.

Cyril's and Methodius's work with language and religion became well known; the two were sent to Moravia to unify those people under one language, alphabet, and religion. The Germans had been teaching the Moravians Latin, but Prince Rastislay (ruler of Moravia) sought independence from German influence.

The brothers firmly believed in using the vernacular of the local people, a belief that was in sharp contrast to the customs of the day. In the Western empire, Latin was the standard language of law, academics, and church; in the Eastern empire, it was Greek across the board. The brothers trained men for the priesthood and sent their trainees to Rome to be ordained. The German bishops contested their ordination, complaining that the new priests didn't speak Latin. The Pope rejected those arguments, allowed the men to be ordained, and gave them permission to use Slavonic in their home parishes as an approved liturgical language.

Cyril died on February 14, AD 869, and that's the date used for the brothers' feast day, although Methodius outlived his brother by 16 years.

St. Dionysius the Great

Alexandria, Egypt (AD 190–AD 264)

Feast day: November 17

Dionysius, a disciple of Origen, was born and raised in a pagan family, but as a young man, he became very well read and learned. His studies sparked a love and curiosity for truth and wisdom, which eventually led to his conversion to Christianity. After he was baptized, he used his intellectual abilities to refute heresies and to explain and defend the newfound faith he enjoyed.

He became Bishop and Patriarch of Alexandria and vigorously defended the doctrine of the Trinity. Dionysius also battled the heretical Novatians, who maintained that the *lapsi* (Christians who had renounced their faith during the Roman persecutions) could never be reconciled back into the Church. He believed the mercy of God extended to the lapsi if they repented, made a good confession, and did proper penance.

St. Gregory of Nazianzus

Arianzus, near Nazianzus, in Cappadocia, Asia Minor (AD 329–AD 390)

Feast day: January 2

Like his friend St. Basil, Gregory was raised in a family that would become quite holy: The son of St. Gregory of Nazianzus the Elder and St. Nonna, he was also a brother to St. Caesar Nazianzen and St. Gorgonia. Gregory's father was a former pagan who went on to become Bishop of Nazianzus. When Gregory the Elder was 94, he made his son his co-adjutor bishop — the person who automatically ascends to the bishopric at his predecessor's death, resignation, or retirement.

The younger Gregory was a reluctant cleric at first. He didn't feel worthy of the priesthood, let alone the possibility of becoming bishop. His father convinced him, however, what a great asset he would be to both the Church and to his father if he were to accept the position. Together they battled the Arians, and the younger Gregory was named bishop in AD 370.

Gregory reluctantly accepted the position of Archbishop of Constantinople in AD 381, in the reign of the Emperor Valens, who was a staunch Arian. Valens was succeeded two years later by Emperor Theodosius, who was a vigorous opponent of Arianism. Gregory became the subject of slander, persecution, and physical abuse for his efforts to reunite former Arians with the Church. He longed for solitude, away from the politics of the imperial city, and resigned his office seven years before he died in his hometown.

St. Gregory of Nyssa

Caesarea in Cappadocia (AD 330–AD 395)

Feast day: March 9

Gregory was the brother of St. Basil and a friend of St. Gregory Nazianzus (see Basil's and Gregory's entries earlier in this chapter). A rhetorician by trade, he was so disgusted by his students' apathy that he left teaching to become a monk and enjoy the quiet of the monastery.

When Basil became Bishop of Caesarea, he persuaded Gregory to take the assignment of Bishop of Nyssa in AD 372. Nyssa was filled with Arians, and Gregory attempted to restore the teachings of the Church. Arian Governor Demosthenes falsely accused Gregory of mismanaging church property and had the bishop imprisoned. Gregory escaped but was deposed, only to be reinstated when Emperor Gratian intervened.

Gregory attended the Second Ecumenical Council of Constantinople I (AD 381), which reaffirmed the condemnation of Arianism from the First Ecumenical Council of Nicea (AD 325). So eloquent was Gregory at this gathering of the bishops that he was called the "Father of the Fathers" for being a pillar of orthodoxy and staunch defender of the faith.

St. Gregory Thaumaturgus

Neocæsarea, Asia Minor (AD 213–AD 270)

Feast day: November 17

Born to wealthy pagans, Gregory and his brother chose to be lawyers, but on their way to the academy, the two met Origen and entered his theology school in Caesarea. (Origen was one of the most influential, prestigious, and premier Greek theologians and philosophers of his day at the turn of the third century. His teachings impacted many generations.) There they converted to Christianity.

Gregory still wanted to be a lawyer, and he returned to Neocæsarea in AD 238. The 17 Christians of his hometown learned of his conversion and elected him their bishop. His preaching was only outdone by his miraculous cures (healing the blind, deaf, lame, and so on), and he was given the name *Thaumaturgus,* which is Greek for "wonder worker." When the Decian persecutions arose in AD 250, he urged his people to go into hiding, and he and a deacon fled to the desert for two years. On his return, Gregory had to contend with plague and the barbarian invasion of the Goths. Still, he and his diocese persevered and survived.

St. Ignatius of Antioch

Rome (AD 35–AD 107)

Feast day: October 17

Ignatius was a friend of St. John the Evangelist and the third Bishop of Antioch. Some say Ignatius was the young boy Jesus took into his arms in the Gospel of Mark 9:35, although no evidence exists to substantiate this claim.

Having survived the persecution of the Roman Emperor Domitian, Ignatius was martyred by the Emperor Trajan in AD 107 by being mauled by wild animals. The journey to Rome — and his death — took several months, and Ignatius used the time to write letters that early Christians used as words of encouragement.

In his letter to the Romans, Ignatius wrote:

> *I am God's wheat and shall be ground by the teeth of wild animals . . . Let me be food for the wild beasts, for they are my way to God. I am God's wheat and shall be ground by their teeth so that I may become Christ's pure bread. Pray to Christ for me that the animals will be the means of making me a sacrificial victim for God.*

St. John Chrysostom of Constantinople

Comana, Asia Minor (AD 347–AD 407)

Feast day: September 13

John's eloquent preaching style earned him the name *Chrysostom*, which is Greek for "golden mouth." He was ordained to the minor order of Lector (Reader), which enabled him to read the Sacred Scriptures aloud at Mass. Bishop Meletius saw promise in John and ordained him a deacon in AD 381; Bishop Flavian, who succeeded Bishop Meletius, ordained John a priest in AD 386. John became renowned for the power and instruction in his sermons, and word of his spiritual wisdom got back to the emperor.

Emperor Areadius wanted John to replace Bishop Nectarius of Constantinople when he died in AD 397. John was the presumed replacement for Flavian at Antioch, but the imperial influence was such that even the Patriarch Theophilus of Alexandria consented to John being sent to Constantinople. John was ordained bishop in February of AD 398.

John was a reformer of the human heart, seeking to eliminate scandal by removing temptation altogether, ordering clergy not to have vowed religious virgins living with them as housekeepers. He cut his own living expenses in half and ordered the monks to stay in their monasteries.

Despite his friendships with Pope Innocent I and Emperor Honorius, John's enemies in Constantinople, Antioch, and Alexandria made life a living hell for him. He was constantly persecuted and subjected to lies, slander, and attempts on his life. He was eventually exiled to Pythius but died on his way there.

John Chrysostom (see Figure 16-1) structured the Divine Liturgy (Mass) that's still used today and is named in his honor. The Byzantine Catholic and Eastern Orthodox Churches sometimes use the Liturgy of St. Basil (also shown in Figure 16-1), but the Liturgy of St. John Chrysostom is more common.

HIP / Art Resource, NY

Figure 16-1:
An icon of the female martyr St. Paraskeve with SS. Gregory Nazianzus, John Chrysostom, and Basil the Great.

St. John Damascene

Jerusalem (AD 676–AD 749)

Feast day: December 3

John was also known as *Chrysorrhoas* (golden stream) and is considered the last Church Father, chronologically speaking. After Charlemagne was crowned Holy Roman Emperor on Christmas Day in the year AD 800 by Pope Leo III, the Middle Ages were fully under way, and the days of the Fathers of the Church, both East and West, were considered a closed chapter.

John's father, Mansur, was a wealthy financier who was allowed to remain a Christian and keep his wealth, which he used to buy the freedom of Christian slaves.

Mansur hired a monk to tutor John in philosophy and theology — a job the monk did so well that John fell in love with both subjects. Devouring everything he could read, John showed an almost unprecedented intellectual capacity. He applied his learning to defending the faith, especially against the heretical iconoclasts.

The iconoclasts saw images of God, the Virgin Mary, and the saints as idols, and they destroyed whatever they could get their hands on. John Damascene disproved and rebutted their arguments, creating some powerful enemies for himself. Some believe that Germanus, Patriarch of Constantinople, schemed against him and forged a letter implying that John betrayed the *caliph*

(Muslim secular ruler). The caliph then ordered John's hand chopped off; when the Blessed Virgin Mary miraculously appeared and reattached John's hand, the caliph's trust in John was restored.

St. Justin Martyr

Rome (AD 100–AD 164)

Feast day: June 1

Justin was a pagan philosopher who converted to Christianity at the age of 30. At first, he thought the wisdom of the Roman Stoics or the Greek Platonists would satisfy his intellectual hunger. He later realized that there was something beyond human knowledge, a divine wisdom, that could only be obtained by faith. As a Christian, he cherished divine revelation, not as something in competition with human philosophy but as an improvement and perfection of it.

Justin became a well-known defender of Christianity and showed the divine revelation for Gentiles to be compatible with that given the Jews in the Old Testament.

Justin was killed during a trip to Rome. He went to establish a school of Christian philosophy but was confronted by pagan philosopher Crescens, who denounced him to Roman officials as a Christian. When Justin and six of his companions failed to worship the Romans' pagan deities, they were tried and convicted. Justin was beheaded at the empire's order. His writings survived, however, and they had a pronounced influence on winning more converts from Roman and Greek paganism over to Christianity.

St. Polycarp of Smyrna

Smyrna (Turkey) (AD 69–AD 155)

Feast day: February 23

Polycarp was a disciple of the Apostle St. John the Evangelist and was a friend of St. Ignatius of Antioch. His letter to the Philippians, one of the few nonbiblical religious documents still intact, shows the existence and usage of New Testament literature during the beginning days of the ancient Christian Church.

The Romans considered the Christians to be atheists because they refused to embrace the polytheist pagan religion of the empire. The hatred for Polycarp was intense, as he was seen as a leader of this countercultural sect. Wanting to feed him to the wild animals and watch him be torn to shreds, the mobs urged the Roman officials to kill Polycarp in a horrible manner. Polycarp's enemies first attempted to burn him at the stake, but his body miraculously would not ignite. Angered, they then stabbed him to death (his blood put out the fire) and thus gave him a martyr's death. Polycarp's writings, verified by Irenaeus, give witness to the direct connection between the Apostles and the continuity of teaching and doctrine.

Part V
Living with the Saints

The 5th Wave   By Rich Tennant

"I always take St. Genesius and St. Rodney with me on stage. Genesius is the patron saint of comedians, and Rodney is the saint of crushing humiliation in case Genesius isn't working."

In this part . . .

Here we look at potential saints in the pipeline — that is, those holy people already beatified and waiting for canonization. We examine saintly things like their earthly remains, especially relics, which are either bodily leftovers of the saints (their own bones, hair, or what have you) or things they wore or used (religious garb, religious items like a cross or crucifix, and so on).

We also take a look at various shrines — those places where the saints lived, worked, died, and are buried and that have since become memorials.

Chapter 17

Saintly Shrines, Relics, and Pilgrimages

*V*eneration of the saints isn't idolatry, or false worship. According to the Christian faith, the Ten Commandments clearly condemn the worship of anyone or anything other than the Lord God.

Those same Ten Commandments also mandate that we honor our father and mother, but honoring someone isn't the same as worshipping him. Honoring the saints isn't any different. Erecting monuments and memorials to honor or remember people like George Washington, Abraham Lincoln, or Winston Churchill isn't considered idolatry, and neither is erecting similar monuments to honor and remember St. Francis of Assisi or the Blessed Virgin Mary.

Christianity is centered on the doctrine that Jesus Christ is the Son of God. He is considered both human and divine, yet one person. This mystery of his dual nature (humanity and divinity) being united in his divine personhood is called the Incarnation. Because Jesus had a real human body, lived and walked on the earth, and visited actual places, the persons, places, and things associated with him have great importance and meaning to Christians.

In this chapter, we explore some of the shrines, relics, and pilgrimages that people of faith visit or undertake as part of their spiritual journey.

Shrines

Bethlehem, Nazareth, and Calvary — Jesus's birthplace, hometown, and site of death, respectively — are considered holy places. They also are home to *shrines,* particular locations in those towns at which the faithful can pray and meditate on the life of Christ.

Places where the holy saints lived, worked, and died are also revered as holy. Usually, the town where the saint died and is buried has a shrine, and in most cases, the actual body of the holy man or woman is there as well. St. Elizabeth Ann Seton, the first native-born American to be canonized, is buried at her national shrine in Emmitsburg, Maryland. St. John Neumann is buried at his shrine in Philadelphia, Pennsylvania.

Some shrines mark the location of an extraordinary event rather than the saint's burial site. The shrine in Lourdes, France, for example, is where the Blessed Virgin Mary appeared to St. Bernadette in 1858; a spring of miraculous healing water has been there ever since. Thousands of pilgrims visit the shrine in Lourdes every year, some actually bathing in the waters of the grotto. St. Bernadette herself, however, is buried at the convent where she died in Nevers, France.

In this section, we look at popular shrines and shrines of popular saints. Some are in the place where the saint lived or is buried, while others are in local areas to make the pilgrimage more accessible to more people.

St. Maria Goretti Shrine

Located in Nettuno, just 37 miles (60 kilometers) south of Rome, this shrine honors one of Italy's most popular saints. Maria Goretti was an 11-year-old girl who forgave her attacker just before she died in 1902. Alessandro Serenelli (age 19) stabbed her 14 times when she resisted his attempts to seduce and then rape her. Pope Pius XII beatified her in 1947 and canonized her in 1950.

The shrine, built in 1969, contains her mortal remains where pilgrims make visits and offer prayers, especially for the safety of young girls and women and for the promotion of purity and chastity of all adolescents and young adults. The town of Nettuno is on the west coast of Italy between Rome and Naples, where many people vacation. The shrine also has a priceless, polychromed, wooden statue of Our Lady of Grace, which the town honors with a procession every year on the first Saturday of May.

St. Anne-de-Beaupré Shrine

Located in Quebec, Canada, this shrine is dedicated to the mother of the Virgin Mary and therefore the maternal grandmother of Jesus Christ. French settlers built it in 1658. A second (1661) and a third (1676) church were built as the previous ones became too small and insufficient. The first basilica was begun in 1876 and was large enough to accommodate all the pilgrims from Canada and the U.S., but a fire completely destroyed it in 1922. One year later, the present basilica was built at the current location.

Neo-Romanesque in architecture, the shrine to St. Anne receives hundreds of thousands of pilgrims each year. French- and English-speaking Canadians, U.S. citizens, and Europeans alike visit this holy memorial to the mother of the Mother of God. Often called the Lourdes of North America, St. Anne's shrine gets thousands of visitors who are sick and infirm.

St. Jean-Marie Vianney Shrine

Located in Ars, France, the shrine to St. John Vianney (called *Sanctuaire d'Ars* in French) is dedicated to the patron saint of all priests throughout the world. The shrine is part of the diocese of Belley Ars, of the ecclesiastical province of Lyon, France. It's a diocesan church, unlike many shrines, which are owned and operated by a religious community of men or women.

The church of St. Sixtus, a 12th-century monument, rebuilt by the efforts of St. John (Jean) Vianney, is now a gateway into the 19th-century St. Sixtus Basilica, which the priest had commissioned by the architect Pierre-Marie Bossan. The transept of the basilica contains a reliquary containing the incorrupt body of the holy pastor of Ars. An underground church was built in 1961 to handle the overflow number of pilgrims.

St. (Padre) Pio of Pietrelcina Shrine

Although Padre Pio was born in the town of Pietrelcina, he died and is buried in San Giovanni Rotondo (province of Foggia) in southern Italy, where his remains are entombed at the shrine in his honor. A church (San Maria delle Grazie) was built in 1950 because the original friary where St. Pio celebrated daily Mass was becoming too crowded. That became the shrine when he died in 1968. A new shrine was built in 2004 that can accommodate 6,500 people. It's run by the Capuchin Franciscans, the religious order to which Padre Pio belonged.

Pilgrims can visit the shrine museum in San Giovanni Rotondo, which contains the vestments the saint wore when he celebrated Mass, his religious habit, personal artifacts, and the famous gloves he wore in humility to hide the stigmata. The *stigmata* are a supernatural appearance of one or more of the five wounds of Christ on a person. Padre Pio would get the wounds in his hands and bleed every time he celebrated Holy Mass. He eventually wore the gloves to prevent people from being distracted from the divine worship.

Near the shrine of Padre Pio is the *Casa Sollievo della Sofferenza* (House to Relieve Suffering), which is the hospital the saint founded through donations of patrons. No fee or charge is assessed to any patient who comes to this medical treatment center. Built in 1956, it has state-of-the-art technology and is one of the most hygienic hospitals in Europe.

St. (Mother) Francis Xavier Cabrini

Located in northern Manhattan in New York City, less than a mile from the George Washington Bridge, the Mother Cabrini Shrine overlooks the Hudson River and the state of New Jersey. The 19th-century Italian immigrant from Lombardy came to America to help those who were being neglected in the New World because of prejudice toward Catholics and Italians alike. She founded the Missionary Sisters of the Sacred Heart of Jesus and built schools and orphanages in Chicago, Illinois; Golden, Colorado; New Orleans, Louisiana; Scranton, Pennsylvania; and Seattle, Washington, in addition to the one in New York.

When Mother Cabrini was beatified in 1938, her remains were placed in a glass-enclosed coffin to rest beneath the altar at the shrine. Pope Pius XII canonized her in 1946, and in 1957, a new shrine of St. Frances Xavier Cabrini was begun and completed in 1960. Mother Cabrini's earthly remains are now kept in an urn and were transferred to the new shrine. A wax effigy of her is displayed in the altar for veneration. Surrounding the altar are mosaics depicting her life, and a two-story stained glass window of her is at the west entrance. The shrine is part of the nearby parish of St. Elizabeth Church, at 187th Street and Wadsworth Avenue.

Many pilgrims of Italian descent visit her shrine in appreciation for the love and work she gave to the Church and her fellow *paesans* ("countrymen" in Italian).

St. Faustina Shrine

Located in Kraków, Poland, the shrine to St. Faustina Kowalska was built on the same grounds of the convent of the Congregation of Sisters of Our Lady of Mercy. That's the religious community Sister Faustina entered as a nun. She had a vision of Jesus in 1931 where he appeared with white and red rays emanating from his Sacred Heart. The white represented the grace of Baptism (because water is used) and the red represented the grace of the Holy Eucharist (because of the precious blood). Both come from the same source, both wash away sin, and both are sources of divine mercy.

Pilgrims from around the world come to visit this shrine. It was painted by the artist Adolf Hyła, who presented it to the convent chapel in Kraków-Łagiewniki as a votive offering for the miraculous saving of his family from the war. Every year on the Feast of Divine Mercy (first Sunday after Easter), large numbers of pilgrims come to the shrine to honor the request made by Jesus to St. Faustina to pray for mercy, especially for the conversion of sinners.

Relics

Things or artifacts that once belonged to the saints are also considered holy and are called *relics*. Relics are separated into three categories — first-class, second-class, and third-class.

Almost every Catholic church has some relics of the saints. These things have special meaning for those who honor and venerate the memory of their original owner.

Just as there is nothing magical about the holy places where shrines are erected, neither is there anything magical about relics. They don't bring you good luck or protect you from harm, but they are mementos of these spiritual heroes. St. Jerome stated, "We do not worship, we do not adore, for fear that we should bow down to the creature rather than to the Creator, but we venerate the relics of the martyrs in order the better to adore him whose martyrs they are."

Canon law forbids the sale of relics in any shape or form. During the Middle Ages, a few unscrupulous and wicked men sought to take advantage of the growing popularity of relics, so they took animal bones and promoted them as first-class relics of popular saints. Not only were these relics fakes, but the men were also trafficking in what was claimed to be authentic relics, which would have been a sin in itself.

Today, strict rules of documentation must accompany any relic of any class. Without the paperwork, these items can't be displayed for public veneration. Only one or two places in Rome now provide relics for Catholic churches around the world, to maintain the integrity and authenticity of the relic and prevent any fraud or abuse.

The following sections discuss each of these classes of relics.

First-class relics

First-class relics are any part of the saint's body. While hair would be considered a relic, most often a first-class relic is a piece of bone that's contained in a *reliquary* (a special container for displaying relics of the saints).

These small fragments are contained in either elaborate reliquaries or placed inside *altar stones* — a square piece of marble with a small hole containing the first-class relics of one or more saints, which is laid into the top of an altar.

When the Romans persecuted the Christians for the first 300 years after Christ's birth, Mass was celebrated secretly in the catacombs and usually over the graves of the holy martyrs. After Christianity was legalized, the practice of celebrating Mass over the relics of martyrs was maintained by placing a relic inside the altar to be used for Mass.

While most first-class relics are bones, there are others. For example:

- A relic of St. Anthony's incorrupt (non-decayed) tongue is in a reliquary at his shrine in Padua, Portugal.

- A vial of St. Januarius's blood is at his shrine in Naples, Italy, and the faithful come every year on his feast day (September 19) to witness the annual de-coagulation of his blood.

- The right forearm of St. Stephen of Hungary is in a reliquary at his shrine in Budapest.

Second-class relics

Second-class relics are things the saint personally owned, wore, or used. Clothing, writing instruments, and personal items such as a private Bible, Rosary, crucifix, ring, or religious garb, for example, are the usual things classified as second-class relics.

The gloves worn by St. Padre Pio of Pietrelcina are considered second-class relics, as they touched his body but weren't part of it. The eyeglasses worn by St. Elizabeth Ann Seton would be a second-class relic, but usually something of that size and caliber are kept in a religious museum. Pieces of the religious habit that a saint wore, or the person's vestments (if the saint was a cleric), would be more available to the common folk.

The size is inconsequential, so even a small fragment or swatch of material is all that's needed. Often, the relic itself is so small as to make it unrecognizable, but the paperwork of authenticity that accompanies every legitimate relic tells you what it is.

Third-class relics

Third-class relics are usually pieces of cloth that are touched to a first- or second-class relic. These are the most common because they don't involve the distribution or disintegration of a first- or second-class relic.

Often, you can find third-class relics attached to a holy card made soon after the canonization of a saint. The piece of cloth is usually no larger than ⅛ inch. The relic is inserted into a holy card with a prayer inscribed that's addressed to the saint for intercession before God.

Pilgrimages

Sometimes, there's more to a holy visit than the destination; often, the journey itself is worthy of note and reflection. This journey, called a *pilgrimage,* is the trip one takes from a home location to a spiritual destination, and the travel is part of the symbolism. Just as the Hebrews journeyed for 40 years in the desert before reaching the Promised Land after their Exodus from Egyptian slavery, Christians have for centuries made pilgrimages to the places where Jesus lived, walked, performed miracles, died, and was resurrected.

Hebrews, in fact, made pilgrimages every year to the Temple in Jerusalem before it was destroyed in AD 70. The last remnant of that is the Wailing Wall, where Jewish pilgrims continue to visit two millennia later. Muslims are encouraged to make at least one pilgrimage (called the *Hajj*) to Mecca in their lifetime. Likewise, Catholic Christians are exhorted to visit those places considered holy by their religion.

Pilgrimages were never meant to be easy, cheap, or comfortable. People go on pilgrimages less frequently than pleasure trips but do so with great devotion and prayer. Often, people go on pilgrimages in groups rather than individually. Traveling with others isn't always fun; some people don't like to fly, or they get seasick or carsick, for instance. Putting up with your fellow pilgrims is part of the process. The spiritual nature of the journey and the destination, however, gives pilgrims the motivation to endure more and put up with more inconvenience and even occasional hardship.

Every inconvenience and unexpected problem is seen as a spiritual challenge when on pilgrimage. These snags are meant to toughen up the traveler and be used as penance for past sins or mortification to be stronger in resisting future temptations. That's why first-class accommodations aren't promoted: The purpose of the pilgrimage is to symbolize the real-life pilgrimage when a believer travels from this world into the next.

The following sections discuss some of the earliest pilgrimages, as well as more modern-day ones.

The early pilgrimages

The first Christian pilgrimages didn't take place until the fourth century because of 300 years of Roman persecution. After the Emperor Constantine issued the Edict of Milan in AD 313 officially legalizing Christianity, the faithful could openly practice their religion. His mother, Empress St. Helena, made the first public pilgrimage to the Holy Land and went to Jerusalem to find the place where Jesus died on the cross. A church was built on the site, beginning the practice of an active church being located where a holy person lived, worked, and/or died.

Though the Romans built many roads and aqueducts throughout the empire, the popularity of pilgrimages during the Middle Ages prompted the building of more roads to help the travelers get to their destination. Hospitals, hostels, and inns were needed along the difficult routes to take care of the basic material needs (food, medicine, shelter) of the many pilgrims journeying throughout Europe. As the Crusades tried to free up the pilgrimage sites in the Holy Land, more local places were sought by those not "with sword," as they were called. Hence, the faithful journeyed to shrines in France, Germany, Italy, Portugal, Spain, and other lands. Though not places where Jesus actually walked, these shrines marked places where the saints had lived and/ or died and were often buried: Santiago de Compostela, Czestochowa, Walsingham, Fulda, Aachen, Mariazell, Monte Sant'Angelo, Rome, and so on.

American pilgrimages

Thousands of Americans make pilgrimages to the Basilica of the National Shrine of the Immaculate Conception in Washington, D.C. Dedicated to the Virgin Mary, this shrine has within it many mini-shrines to the saints and to Mary and her apparitions, such as in Lourdes, Fatima, Knock, and Guadalupe.

Many Catholic dioceses across the U.S. have pilgrimages to the National Shrine to mark anniversaries, like the founding of the diocese, or to celebrate a holy year in honor of the Blessed Virgin Mary, as the diocese of Harrisburg, Pennsylvania, did in October 2009. Parish pilgrimages also take place, where the pastor, parochial vicar, and deacon lead a group from their congregation to the shrine. Mass is celebrated in one of the many smaller chapels, and visits to the gift shop and bookstore are always popular afterwards.

When you can't afford to travel overseas, try making a local pilgrimage. Besides the Basilica of the National Shrine of the Immaculate Conception, this side of the Atlantic has many other national shrines, including

- Any of the 21 missions in California
- Basilica of the National Shrine of St. Ann in Scranton, Pennsylvania
- Blue Army Shrine in Washington, New Jersey
- Mother Cabrini Shrine in Golden, Colorado
- National Shrine of North American Martyrs in Auriesville, New York
- National Shrine of Our Lady of Czestochowa in Doylestown, Pennsylvania
- National Shrine of St. Gerard in Newark, New Jersey
- Shrine of Divine Mercy in Stockton, Massachusetts
- Shrine of Our Lady of the Snows in Belleville, Illinois
- Shrine of St. Elizabeth Ann Seton in Emmitsburg, Maryland
- Shrine of the Most Blessed Sacrament in Hanceville, Alabama
- Shrine to Our Lady of Guadalupe in La Crosse, Wisconsin

A pilgrimage for priests

Pope Benedict declared June 19, 2009, to June 19, 2010, as the "Year for Priests." Consequently, many priests, deacons, and lay faithful have made or are making pilgrimages to the shrine of St. John Vianney, the patron saint of all priests. He worked and died in Ars, France, where there's a shrine to this holy man of God (see the "St. Jean-Marie Vianney Shrine" section earlier in the chapter). Making a pilgrimage to his shrine is similar to the journey that thousands made in 2008 to commemorate the 150th anniversary of the Virgin Mary appearing to St. Bernadette in Lourdes, France.

Chapter 18

Waiting for Their Halos: Saints in the Pipeline

In This Chapter

▶ Discovering some miraculous youngsters

▶ Getting to know Mother Teresa, the people's pope, and others

As we discuss in Chapter 1, before one is formally canonized a saint, he or she is first named a *servant of God*. After one proven miracle (post-mortem), the person is *beatified* and called *blessed*. If a second miracle can be established, the pope can declare the person an official saint of the Church, who is venerated as being with the Lord in heaven.

Not everyone who is beatified is automatically canonized; that is, not all blesseds become saints. Only those beatified men and women whose inter-cession can be proven by an additional indisputable miracle are eligible for *canonization* (sainthood). In this chapter, we introduce you to some notable beatified persons whose causes for canonization are moving along as more evidence is discovered.

Blessed Francisco and Blessed Jacinta

Fatima, Portugal (1909–1919 [Francisco]; 1910–1920 [Jacinta])

Beatified: 2000

Feast day: February 20

Francisco and Jacinta Marto, along with their cousin Lucia Santos, would have been ordinary children in the obscure town of Fatima, Portugal, were it not for six monthly visits from the Mother of God.

The Fatima pope

Because the attempted assassination in 1981 of Pope John Paul II occurred on the anniversary of the first apparition of Fatima, he attributed his survival to the prayers of the Virgin Mary. He subsequently visited Fatima and had the bullet that nearly killed him encased inside the crown that adorns a statue of Our Lady of Fatima, which resides to this day at the Basilica Shrine in Fatima, Portugal.

Francisco and Jacinta, ages 8 and 7, respectively, accompanied Lucia, age 10, as she tended sheep on May 13, 1917. On that day, the three experienced the first of six apparitions of the Virgin Mary; the other five occurred on the 13th day of each of the ensuing months.

The children received three prophecies from the Virgin Mary, as well as a vision of hell, where damned souls endure eternal punishment for their unrepentant sins. The Virgin Mary warned the children in the first prophecy of the spread of Communism and its attendant abandonment of faith, six months before the Russian Revolution deposed Tsar Nicholas II. The second prophecy was of another and deadlier war to follow World War I if people didn't stop offending God by engaging in sinful behavior. Finally, the Virgin Mary presented in the third prophecy a vision of a bishop "dressed in white" (an allusion to the Bishop of Rome, the pope, who wears white) who would be attacked and shot. (Pope John Paul II was shot by would-be assassin Mehmet Ali Aca on May 13, 1981.)

The deep faith of the children following the apparitions was apparent in ways as different as the children themselves. Francisco, a quiet boy, preferred to pray alone, while Jacinta became deeply convinced that suffering through penance and sacrifice was the best way to save sinners. She believed so deeply, in fact, that while lying in a hospital bed dying of influenza, she refused to be anesthetized for surgery. Her pain, she believed, would help convert sinners.

Miracle of the sun

After the first apparition on May 13, word spread and crowds grew month after month, despite attempts by the local government to discourage such activity. On the morning of the Virgin Mary's final visit (October 13, 1917), more than 70,000 bystanders came to see what was bringing the children each month to a seemingly abandoned place.

Shortly after noon, the sun appeared in the sky after being obscured by clouds all morning. It then looked like a disc, dancing and spinning in the heavens, ebbing and growing as if the earth had been plunged toward the sun. People were able to look directly at the sight without any harm or irritation to their eyes. Despite standing in a torrential downpour before the event, everyone's clothing was dry when it ended.

Francisco and Jacinta were both victims of the influenza epidemic that swept through Europe in 1918. Francisco died peacefully at home in 1919, and less than a year later, after countless trips to the hospital, Jacinta died alone in a hospital room. Their cousin, Lucia, became a Carmelite nun and died in 2005.

A 69-year-old Portuguese woman, Maria Emilia Santos, was totally paralyzed for 22 years until February 20, 1989, when she had an instant and complete cure through the intercession of Francisco and Jacinta. This was the first miracle needed to beatify the two children.

The process for canonization for the siblings began in 1945, and their case was officially opened in 1952. They were declared venerable in 1989, and Pope John Paul II beatified Francisco and Jacinta on May 13, 2000, 83 years to the day after the first visit from the Virgin Mary.

In 2005, just a week after Sister Lucia Santos died, the canonization petition for Francisco and Jacinta was sent to the cardinal prefect of the Congregation for Sainthood Causes. The final decision is up to the pope.

In February 2008, Pope Benedict XVI announced he would waive the five-year waiting period and that the beatification process for Sister Lucia Santos could begin.

What canonization will mean

Because they were brother and sister, canonizing Jacinta and Francisco will have a great impact on family life in general and in each individual family as well. It will encourage siblings to work together and to pray together. Not only will Catholics and all Portuguese citizens be proud of these two holy children (three, if and when Lucia is canonized), but families and children around the world will find an example and beacon of hope to live as real children of God.

Pope Blessed John XXIII

Sotto il Monte, Italy (1881–1963)

Beatified: 2000

Feast day: October 11 (opening day of Vatican II in 1962)

Often called the "smiling pope" or "good Pope John" because of his conge-
nial manner and constant smile, Pope John XXIII was known for his desire
to extend an olive branch of peace to promote ecumenical dialogue. His
work wasn't an attempt to dilute Catholic teaching or alter Catholic worship;
rather, he sincerely wanted to build bridges among all the Christian churches
and other religions to work together for the peace of mankind.

Life of service

Angelo Giuseppe Roncalli was born on November 25, 1881, in Sotto il Monte,
near Bergamo, in northern Italy. He was the firstborn son of peasant parents
and 4th in a family of 14. Financially poor but spiritually rich, Angelo had a
burning desire to study for the priesthood and was supported financially by
an uncle.

The discovery of his own intellectual and cultural awkwardness in comparison to that of his seminary classmates sowed the seeds for Christian humility, which became his hallmark in life.

After his ordination as a priest in 1904, Angelo served as secretary to his
bishop, Giacomo Maria Radini-Tedeschi, and taught in the seminary of the
Diocese of Bergamo until the outbreak of World War I. He was drafted into
the Italian Army Medical Corps and served as a stretcher-bearer.

After the war ended, Angelo returned to his diocese until 1921, when Pope
Benedict XV named him Italy's director of the Society for the Propagation of
the Faith, the official organization that promotes evangelization and provides
for the social welfare of the sick, the injured, the unemployed, and the homeless. Angelo was so successful in restructuring the old organization to meet
the needs of the postwar world that Pope Pius XI promoted him to bishop in
1925. He joined the Vatican Diplomatic Corps, and his first assignment was as
Apostolic Visitor to Bulgaria.

In 1935, he was named Apostolic Delegate to Greece and Turkey. In 1944, at
the height of World War II, he became Apostolic Nuncio to France for Pope
Pius XII. He worked with a German ambassador and saved the lives of more
than 24,000 European Jews who were condemned to a horrible death in
the Nazi concentration camps. For this, many survivors in Israel consider
Roncalli a *Righteous Gentile*. (Only those non-Jews who worked to help the
persecuted escape imprisonment or death, especially during World War II,
are given this title of appreciation and affection.)

Following the end of the war in 1945, Bishop Roncalli hoped to return to
some quiet obscurity, but Pope Pius XII elevated him to cardinal and made
him Patriarch of Venice in 1953. This enabled him to participate in the papal
conclave of 1958 after the death of Pius. After four days of balloting, the elec-
tors chose him to succeed Pius XII.

Vatican II

The Second Vatican Council, commonly known as Vatican II, was the 21st such meeting of bishops in the Catholic Church. The first took place in Nicea, AD 325, and the most recent (before Vatican II) was held in the Vatican (called Vatican I) in 1869–1870.

Pope John XXIII opened Vatican II in October 1962; Pope Paul VI concluded the Council in December 1965. The Council issued 16 documents that have become blueprints for teaching, explaining, and living the Catholic faith in the modern era. None of these documents issued any new dogmas or defined any new doctrines. None changed, amended, or dissolved any previously defined teachings or traditions. Some would say that the modifications of Vatican II were simply cosmetic, adapting what was adaptable while preserving what was substantial and necessary.

The most influential innovations of the Second Vatican Council were the changes made to the Sacred Liturgy. While the essentials remained unchanged, the vernacular language was given more prominence (whereas Latin had been the norm for more than 15 centuries). Byzantine and Eastern Catholic Rites were encouraged to go back to their original customs, especially in the Sacraments.

Contrary to popular belief, Latin was never abolished and was in fact meant to remain in common parts of the Mass (although some used Vatican II to eliminate any or most traditional piety from Catholic worship). The bishops had no intention of altering moral law; claims that contraception and abortion were up for discussion at Vatican II are simply false. Neither were any defined dogmas in jeopardy. The divinity of Christ, the virginity of Mary, the inerrancy of Scripture, the infallibility of the pope, and the indefectibility of the Church were never disputed at Vatican II.

The new pope chose John XXIII as his papal name. Just shy of his 77th birthday, John XXIII was considered a "transition" pope, expected to serve for a short time. He surprised everyone when he announced three months after his coronation that he intended to convene an Ecumenical Council (see the nearby sidebar on Vatican II).

Pope John XXIII opened the Second Vatican Council, initiated the long-needed revision of the 1917 Code of Canon Law (which would finally be completed by John Paul II in 1983), and convened a diocesan Synod for the Diocese of Rome, all before his death on June 3, 1963. His aim was to open the windows of the Vatican and let in some fresh air, as he called it. Though he staunchly defended all defined dogmas and doctrines and was faithful to *authentic discipline* (priestly celibacy), John XXIII wanted the Catholic Church to be part of — and not necessarily contend with — the modern world, as long as the revealed laws of God weren't compromised.

In 1966, Sister Caterina Capitani (Daughter of Charity from Sicily) suffered from a tumor, severe gastric bleeding, and infection. Other nuns put an image of John XXIII on her stomach. The nun immediately rose from her bed and began eating. Her total and complete miraculous cure was used to promote the beatification of John XXIII.

Pope John XXIII was beatified by Pope John Paul II on September 3, 2000, before a huge crowd. His *papal encyclicals* (authoritative letters from a pope explaining the teachings of the Church as applied to modern times), "Pacem in Terris" (Latin for "Peace on Earth") and "Mater et Magistra" (Latin for "Mother and Teacher"), are still revered for their profound insight into Catholic social teaching on justice and morality. The first document dealt with a nonmilitary and nonconfrontational approach to resolving disputes among nations, employing realistic diplomacy whenever possible. It also strongly promoted international recognition and defense of human rights for all human beings, regardless of nationality. The second document concerned the moral responsibility of the state (secular government) to provide help for basic human needs (food, shelter, employment, and education) for citizens who are unable to secure these for themselves. While not advocating a socialist type of government (Pope John XXIII remained politically neutral), John XXIII did underscore the moral imperative for all people to help each other, not just individually but communally as well. He defended the intrinsic right of ownership of private property and repudiated forced nationalization of business while advocating social responsibility to care for the poor and disadvantaged.

What canonization will mean

Canonizing a modern pope will encourage the faithful that even their leaders can and ought to seek holiness — saintly pastors have saintly parishioners and vice versa. It would also dispel the urban legend that only monks and nuns can become Saints. John XXIII is considered the Father of the Second Vatican Council, so his canonization would be seen by some as a vindication of Vatican II across the board.

Blessed Kateri Tekakwitha

Ossernenon, New York (1656–1680)

Beatified: 1980

Feast day: July 14 (USA); April 17 (Canada)

Kateri Tekakwitha was a young Native American woman who followed her devout faith despite knowing she would become estranged from her family and friends.

Following her faith

Kateri was born in 1656 in a village called Ossernenon, near Aurielsville, New York, the daughter of a Mohawk warrior chief and a Christian Algonquin who had been captured by the Iroquois. Kateri's parents and her brother died from a smallpox epidemic when she was only 4 years old; though she survived, her eyesight was impaired and her face slightly disfigured from the disease.

A turning point came in 1667, when Kateri met some French Jesuit missionaries who preached to her about Jesus Christ and the Catholic Church. It took her nine years, however, to ask for Baptism, because she knew she would incur the disapproval — and even wrath — of many of her tribe.

Eventually, Kateri left her village, as they refused to accept her conversion to Christianity. She ended up in Caughnawaga on the St. Lawrence River, where some Christian Native Americans found a refuge and home. There, she cared for the sick and elderly of the village and spent time in prayer before the Blessed Sacrament in the *Tabernacle* (the large metal container, often fashioned to look like the Hebrew Ark of the Covenant, that contains the consecrated hosts of bread that Catholics believe have become the Body of Christ).

Kateri died at the age of 24 on April 17, 1680. Her devout faith inspired many Native Americans to embrace Christianity and Catholicism. She was declared venerable by the Catholic Church in 1943 and beatified in 1980. Paul Vezina, a 32-year-old Canadian, was miraculously healed of pulmonary tuberculosis in 1939 after praying a novena (nine-day prayer) to Kateri Tekakwitha. This was the needed miracle for her beatification.

What canonization will mean

Blessed Kateri Tekakwitha is the first Native American to be beatified and would be the first to be canonized, as well. She has therefore been declared the patroness for all Native Americans.

Canonizing Kateri Tekakwitha will be a huge source of pride and joy for Native Americans and for all women, too. Having a Native American saint will help evangelization (spreading the faith) and sustain those already baptized and confirmed as Catholic Christians who have similar ancestry as Kateri. Sadly, there were instances where Native Americans were physically forced to convert and abandon their natural religions, but they weren't the majority, and many more like Kateri freely, willingly, and happily embraced Catholic Christianity. While not abandoning all her traditions and heritage, canonizing a Native American like her will show that Christianity is compatible with the Native American people and that those who accept it do so because they see it as a natural completion and fulfillment of the faith given them by their forefathers and foremothers.

Blessed Marie Rose Durocher

Quebec, Canada (1811–1849)

Beatified: 1982

Feast day: October 6

Sister Marie Rose Durocher's life was dedicated to caring for the poor and the sick and to educating young children. She created the Sisters of the Holy Names of Jesus and Mary just two years after a government action established legal protection for Catholics in Canada.

A life of work, sacrifice, and love

Eulalie Durocher was born on October 6, 1811, at St. Antoine in Quebec, Canada, the 10th of 11 children. When Eulalie turned 16, like most girls her age, she fell in love, but not with any earthly boy. She fell in love with Christ and desperately wanted to become a *Bride of Christ* (the metaphorical term for religious sisters and nuns) by entering the convent. Her poor health initially kept her from being admitted into the religious order.

In 1931, two years after her mother died, she and her father moved in with her brother, Theophile, a priest. She became his housekeeper and cook. Bishop Ignace Bourget asked Eulalie to form a religious community of women in 1843. She took the name Marie Rose and called the group the Sisters of the Holy Names of Jesus and Mary.

Sister Marie Rose, along with companions Mélodie Dufresne and Henriette Céré, dedicated herself to the teaching and welfare of children. Despite poor health, she wasn't averse to hard work and often labored long into the night, only getting minimal sleep. Still, she saw her work as a labor of love and did everything joyfully and enthusiastically. Personal comfort and convenience were alien concepts to Marie Rose Durocher, while Christian charity and patience were her life mottos. Her legacy was a life dedicated and devoted to serving the poor and the sick and educating children.

What canonization will mean

Declaring Marie Rose Durocher a saint will be an important milestone for Catholic Canadians and for religious women as well. Europe has had the most saints, only because the Church has been there for two millennia. Catholicism wasn't brought to the New World of North and South America until 15 centuries after the time of Christ. So countries like Canada, Mexico, and the U.S. are much younger than their elder European brethren. Having homegrown saints inspires a nation and encourages vocations to serve the Church.

Marie Rose's canonization will boost Canadian pride and bear witness to the personal piety and shared faith of millions of citizens who practice the same religion as this holy woman. St. Marie Rose would also inspire other women to be pioneers in working for the Church and serving the poor.

Blessed Miguel Agustin Pro Juarez, S.J.

Zacatecas, Mexico (1891–1988)

Beatified: 1988

Feast day: November 23

Father Miguel Agustin Pro Juarez spent his life caring for abused and exploited workers, despite his own illness, and boldly shared his faith at a time when his native Mexico banned the exhibition of religious garb and the government persecuted the Catholic Church.

Fighting persecution

Miguel Agustin Pro Juarez was born January 13, 1891, at Zacatecas, Mexico, the son of a mining engineer. The 3rd of 11 children, Miguel entered the Society of Jesus (the Jesuits) in 1911. He was soon exiled because of the Mexican Revolution and traveled to the U.S., Spain, Nicaragua, and Belgium, where he was ordained in 1925.

Father Miguel suffered from stomach ulcers but remained vigilant in his mission to work among his own people in Mexico, especially among the mineworkers who were being brutally exploited and abused. By the time he returned to his homeland, the new Mexican constitution had banned all Catholic schools and the wearing of any religious garb whatsoever. The Church was violently persecuted, and many priests, bishops, and nuns were deported, arrested, tortured, and killed as a result of the government's promotion of virulent anti-Catholicism.

Father Miguel was arrested and charged with a failed assassination attempt on the president; his only true crime was clandestinely celebrating Mass for his people. Politicians made him a scapegoat, however, and he was condemned to death by firing squad on November 23, 1927. As he stood before the firing squad, he held his Rosary and crucifix and declared, "Viva Cristo Rey" ("Long live Christ the King").

Pope John Paul II beatified Miguel Pro on September 25, 1988, in an open-air public Mass before thousands in Mexico — which, ironically, was still an illegal activity even six decades after Miguel's death.

What canonization will mean

Canonizing Miguel Pro will be an enormous shot in the arm to the Catholic Church in Mexico, as he was one of the most beloved martyrs to die for the faith at the hands of an aggressively antireligious government. Despite improvements in church-state relations, Mexico still evinces a noticeable tension and residual anticlericalism. Recognizing a national and religious hero will be of mutual benefit, because many laity also fought an unjust administration for the sake of the common good of all Mexicans.

Blessed Teresa of Calcutta (Also Known As Mother Teresa)

Macedonia (1910–1997)

Beatified: 2003

Feast day: September 5

Mother Teresa worked among the poorest of the poor — lepers and untouchables, those very often shunned in Hindu culture. Literally picking these abandoned men, women, and children from the gutters and ghettos of

Calcutta, India, this little nun and her companions rescued many from an ignoble death.

A life of empathy

Mother Teresa was born Agnes Gonxha Bojaxhiu on August 26, 1910, in Macedonia. Her father died when she was 8, and her mother supported the family with her embroidery. When she was 18, Agnes joined the Sisters of Loreto convent (formally called the Institute of the Blessed Virgin Mary) in Dublin. There she took the name of her beloved heroine, Saint Thérèse of Lisieux (also known as St. Thérèse of the Child Jesus). In 1929, Sister Mary Teresa (this was her complete and formal religious name) was sent to teach at St. Mary's School for Girls, Loreto, in Calcutta. After she took her final solemn profession of vows (poverty, chastity, and obedience), committing herself to this life in 1937, she became known as Mother Teresa to her sisters and eventually to the world.

While riding the train from Calcutta to Darjeeling on September 10, 1946, for her annual retreat, Mother Teresa felt a "call within a call." She described it as an awareness of the presence of God and a deep conviction that the Lord was calling her to branch out of her current apostolate. She was made aware of the thirst that Jesus had for the poorest of the poor, for in their suffering, he, too, shared their pain and misery.

After two years of prayer and discernment, Mother Teresa got ecclesiastical permission to establish her own religious community, the Missionaries of Charity. Over time, the Missionaries of Charity would grow into a community of 4,000 sisters in 123 countries around the world.

Mother Teresa was awarded the Nobel Peace Prize in 1979. She addressed the United Nations in 1985 and that same year opened the first house to care for AIDS patients in New York City. She was given honorary U.S. citizenship in 1991 and the U.S. Congressional Gold Medal just a few months before her death on September 5, 1997.

Normally, no one can be considered for beatification (and, their supporters hope, eventual sainthood) until five years after death. This waiting period provides time for emotions to return to normal so the process can be guided not by sentimentality but by facts. In the case of Mother Teresa, though, Pope John Paul II allowed the process to begin in 1999 because a verified miracle had occurred soon after Mother Teresa's death. A 30-year-old Indian woman, Monica Besra, was apparently cured of stomach cancer after praying to Mother Teresa.

Pope John Paul II officially beatified Mother Teresa on October 19, 2003, with more than 300,000 pilgrims in attendance at St. Peter's Square, Rome.

What canonization will mean

Mother Teresa's canonization as a saint will have great influence not only to promote work for the poor but also for perseverance in times of adversity. Despite opposition and suspicion, she held her ground and kept doing what she knew she had to do. Even recent disclosures of her "dark night of the soul" reveal a very human phenomenon. Many people of faith feel abandoned at some time, even though they know that the Lord is always there. But feeling this way doesn't indicate lack or weakness of faith. Faith is an act of the intellect where one assents to the existence and presence of God. You can believe in God and not always feel his affection. Theologians say this is to entice us to want heaven all the more, where there is both knowledge of God and the enjoyment of his love. Anyone who has ever felt dryness in his spiritual life will be encouraged to know that Mother Teresa went down that same road. Her canonization as a saint will prove that this is not an impediment but merely a necessary trial to achieve holiness.

Part VI
The Part of Tens

The 5th Wave   By Rich Tennant

In this part . . .

We use the familiar *For Dummies* feature of the Part of Tens to focus on some interesting esoterica of the saints.

We give you ten popular litanies of saints, ten famous novenas (nine days of prayer), and the top ten saint shrines. We also include a list of ten saintly families to show you that the apple doesn't fall far from the tree in many cases where a husband and wife or parents and children have been declared saints.

Chapter 19

Ten Favorite Litanies of the Saints

In This Chapter

▶ A litany for all the saints

▶ Popular litanies for specific saints

*L*itanies are invocations that one makes to a saint asking for spiritual intercession before Jesus. This chapter introduces some of the favorite litanies people use in seeking intercession.

Catholicism firmly believes that only one mediator lies between God and man: Jesus Christ. An intercessor, on the other hand, merely asks a favor for someone else. Each litany, whether recited, chanted, or sung, begins with an address to the Holy Trinity (Father, Son, and Holy Spirit).

Litany of the Saints

The most ancient litany of the Church is one directed to all the saints. It's used every year at the Easter vigil, the night before Easter Sunday, when Baptisms are celebrated. It's also used during the Sacrament of Holy Orders, when a man is ordained a deacon, priest, or bishop.

The traditional litany follows, with the congregation's responses in italics. Brackets indicate saints who've been added to the traditional litany.

> Lord, have mercy on us. *Christ, have mercy on us.*
> Lord, have mercy on us. Christ, hear us. *Christ, graciously hear us.*
> God, the Father of heaven, *have mercy on us.*
> God the Son, Redeemer of the world, *have mercy on us.*
> God the Holy Spirit, *have mercy on us.*
> Holy Trinity, one God, *have mercy on us.*
> Holy Mary, *pray for us.*
> Holy Mother of God,
> Holy Virgin of virgins,
> St. Michael,
> St. Gabriel,

St. Raphael,
All you holy angels and archangels,
All you holy orders of blessed spirits,
[Holy Abraham],
[Holy Moses],
[Holy Elijah],
St. John the Baptist,
St. Joseph,
All you holy patriarchs and prophets,
St. Peter,
St. Paul,
St. Andrew,
St. James (the Greater),
St. John,
St. Thomas,
St. James (the Lesser),
St. Phillip,
St. Bartholomew,
St. Matthew,
St. Simon,
St. Thaddeus,
St. Matthias,
St. Barnabas,
St. Luke,
St. Mark,
All you holy apostles and evangelists,
All you holy disciples of the Lord,
All you Holy Innocents,
St. Stephen,
[St. Ignatius of Antioch],
[St. Polycarp],
[St. Justin],
St. Lawrence,
St. Vincent,
SS. Fabian and Sebastian,
SS. John and Paul,
SS. Cosmas and Damian,
SS. Gervase and Protase,
[St. Cyprian],
[St. Boniface],
[St. Stanislaus],
[St. Thomas Becket],
[SS. John Fisher and Thomas More],
[St. Paul Miki],
[SS. John Brebeuf and Isaac Jogues],
[St. Peter Chanel],

[St. Charles Lwanga],
[SS. Perpetua and Felicity],
[St. Maria Goretti],
All you holy martyrs,
St. Sylvester,
[St. Leo the Great],
St. Gregory,
St. Ambrose,
St. Augustine,
St. Jerome,
[St. Athanasius],
[SS. Basil and Gregory Nazianus],
[St. John Chrysostom],
St. Martin,
St. Nicholas,
[St. Patrick],
[SS. Cyril and Methodius]
[St. Charles Borromeo],
[St. Francis de Sales],
[Pope St. Pius X],
All you holy popes and confessors,
All you holy doctors,
St. Anthony,
St. Benedict,
St. Bernard,
St. Dominic,
St. Francis of Assisi,
[St. Thomas Aquinas],
[St. Ignatius Loyola],
[St. Francis Xavier],
[St. Vincent de Paul],
[St. John Mary Vianney],
[St. John Bosco],
All you holy priests and Levites,
All you holy monks and hermits,
St. Ann,
St. Mary Magdalene,
St. Agatha,
St. Lucy,
St. Agnes,
St. Cecilia,
St. Catherine,
St. Anastasia,
[St. Catherine of Siena],
[St. Theresa of Avila],
[St. Rose of Lima],

All you holy virgins and widows,
[St. Louis],
[St. Monica],
[St. Elizabeth of Hungary],
[St. Frances Cabrini],
[St. John Neumann],
[St. Elizabeth Ann Seton],
[St. Katherine Drexel],
[St. Juan Diego],
All you holy men and women, Saints of God, *pray for us.*
Be merciful, *spare us, O Lord.*
Be merciful, *graciously hear us, O Lord.*
From all evil, *O Lord deliver us.*
From all sin,
From thy wrath,
From sudden and unprovided death,
From the snares of the devil,
From anger, and hatred, and all ill will,
From the spirit of fornication,
From the scourge of earthquake,
From plague, famine, and war,
From lightning and tempest,
From everlasting death,
Through the mystery of thy holy Incarnation,
Through thy coming,
Through thy birth,
Through thy Baptism and holy fasting,
Through the institution of the Most Blessed Sacrament,
Through thy cross and passion,
Through thy death and burial,
Through thy holy Resurrection,
Through thine admirable Ascension,
Through the coming of the Holy Ghost the Paraclete,
In the day of judgment, *O Lord deliver us.*
Lamb of God, who takes away the sins of the world, *spare us, O Lord.*
Lamb of God, who takes away the sins of the world, *graciously hear us, O Lord.*
Lamb of God, who takes away the sins of the world, *have mercy on us.*

Let us pray. Almighty, everlasting God, who hast dominion over both the living and the dead and art merciful to all who, as thou foreknowest, will be thine by faith and works; we humbly beseech thee that they for whom we intend to pour forth our prayers, whether this present world still doth detain them in the flesh or the world to come hath already received them stripped of their mortal bodies, may, by the grace of thy fatherly love and through the intercession of all the saints, obtain the remission of all their sins. Through our Lord Jesus Christ, thy Son, who with thee in the unity of the Holy Spirit liveth and reigneth God, world without end. *Amen.*

Litany of the Blessed Virgin Mary

The second most familiar and ancient litany is that of the Blessed Virgin Mary. Many forms have developed from ancient to medieval times. The version that follows has been in use since Pope Sixtus V issued it in 1587, replacing all earlier versions.

Lord, have mercy on us. *Christ have mercy on us.*
Lord, have mercy on us. Christ, hear us. *Christ graciously hear us.*
God, the Father of heaven, *have mercy on us.*
God the Son, Redeemer of the world, *have mercy on us.*
God the Holy Spirit, *have mercy on us.*
Holy Trinity, one God, *have mercy on us.*
Holy Mary, *pray for us.*
Holy Mother of God,
Holy Virgin of virgins,
Mother of Christ,
Mother of divine grace,
Mother most pure,
Mother most chaste,
Mother inviolate,
Mother undefiled,
Mother most amiable,
Mother most admirable,
Mother of good counsel,
Mother of our Creator,
Mother of our Savior,
Virgin most prudent,
Virgin most venerable,
Virgin most renowned,
Virgin most powerful,
Virgin most merciful,
Virgin most faithful,
Mirror of justice,
Seat of wisdom,
Cause of our joy,
Spiritual vessel,
Vessel of honor,
Singular vessel of devotion,
Mystical rose,
Tower of David,
Tower of ivory,
House of gold,
Ark of the Covenant,
Gate of heaven,
Morning star,
Health of the sick,

Refuge of sinners,
Comforter of the afflicted,
Help of Christians,
Queen of angels,
Queen of patriarchs,
Queen of prophets,
Queen of apostles,
Queen of martyrs,
Queen of confessors,
Queen of virgins,
Queen of all saints,
Queen conceived without original sin,
Queen assumed into heaven,
Queen of the most holy Rosary,
Queen of peace,
Queen of the family, *pray for us.*
Lamb of God, who takes away the sins of the world, *spare us, O Lord.*
Lamb of God, who takes away the sins of the world, *graciously hear us, O Lord.*
Lamb of God, who takes away the sins of the world, *have mercy on us.*
Pray for us, O holy Mother of God.
That we may be made worthy of the promises of Christ.

Let us pray. Grant, we beseech thee, O Lord God, unto us thy servants, that we may rejoice in continual health of mind and body and, by the glorious intercession of Blessed Mary ever Virgin, may be delivered from present sorrows, and enter into that joy which has no end. Through Christ our Lord. *Amen.*

When the litany is prayed after the Rosary, the following ending replaces the one above:

O God, whose only begotten Son, by his life, death, and Resurrection has purchased for us the rewards of eternal life, grant, we beseech you, that while meditating of the mysteries of the most holy Rosary of the Blessed Virgin Mary, we may imitate what they contain and obtain what they promise, through Christ our Lord. Amen.

Litany of St. Joseph

As patron of the universal Church, St. Joseph is second only to his wife, the Virgin Mary, in terms of honor and respect. Head of the Holy Family (Jesus, Mary, and Joseph), he was the beloved spouse of the Mother of God and the guardian of the Christ child.

Lord, have mercy. *Christ, have mercy.*
Lord, have mercy. Christ, hear us. *Christ, graciously hear us.*
God, the Father of heaven, *have mercy on us.*
God the Son, Redeemer of the world, *have mercy on us.*
God the Holy Spirit, *have mercy on us.*
Holy Trinity, one God, *have mercy on us.*
Holy Mary, *pray for us.*
St. Joseph, *pray for us.*
Renowned offspring of David,
Light of patriarchs,
Spouse of the Mother of God,
Chaste guardian of the Virgin,
Foster father of the Son of God,
Diligent protector of Christ,
Head of the Holy Family,
Joseph most just,
Joseph most chaste,
Joseph most prudent,
Joseph most strong,
Joseph most obedient,
Joseph most faithful,
Mirror of patience,
Lover of poverty,
Model of artisans,
Glory of home life,
Guardian of virgins,
Pillar of families,
Solace of the wretched,
Hope of the sick,
Patron of the dying,
Terror of demons,
Protector of the Holy Church, *pray for us.*
Lamb of God, who takes away the sins of the world, *spare us, O Lord.*
Lamb of God, who takes away the sins of the world, *graciously hear us, O Lord.*
Lamb of God, who takes away the sins of the world, *have mercy on us.*
He made him the lord of his household.
And prince over all his possessions.

Let us pray. O God, in your ineffable providence you were pleased to choose Blessed Joseph to be the spouse of your most Holy Mother; grant, we beg you, that we may be worthy to have him for our intercessor in heaven whom on earth we venerate as our protector: You who live and reign forever and ever. *Amen.*

Litany of St. Dominic

St. Dominic is a popular saint of the 13th century. He's famous for spreading devotion to the Blessed Virgin Mary via the Rosary (prayer beads). Although the religious community he founded is called the Order of Preachers, the members are more commonly known as the Dominicans. The titles used in this litany mainly come from lofty descriptions the general populace ascribed to this saint.

God the Father of heaven, *have mercy on us.*
God the Son, Redeemer of the world, *have mercy on us.*
God the Holy Spirit, *have mercy on us.*
Holy Trinity, one God, *have mercy on us.*
Holy Mary, *pray for us.*
Holy Mother of God, *pray for us.*
Holy Virgin of virgins, *pray for us.*
Holy Father St. Dominic,
Light of the Church,
Day star of the world,
Preacher of grace,
Rose of patience,
Most zealous for the salvation of souls,
Most desirous of martyrdom,
Evangelical man,
Lover of the Word,
Ivory of chastity,
Man of an apostolic heart, doctor of truth,
Model of poverty,
Rich in purity of life,
Burning as a torch for the salvation of sinners, herald of the Gospel,
Rule of obedience,
Shining as the sun in the temple of God,
Enriched with the grace of Christ,
Clothed in heavenly virtue,
Lamb of God, who takes away the sins of the world, *spare us, O Lord.*
Lamb of God, who takes away the sins of the world, *graciously hear us,*
O Lord.
Lamb of God, who takes away the sins of the world, *have mercy on us,*
O Lord.
Pray for us, O holy Father St. Dominic,
That we may be worthy of the promises of Christ.

Let us pray. Lord, let the holiness and teaching of our Father Dominic come to the aid of your Church. May he help us now with his prayers as he once inspired people by his preaching. We ask this through our Lord Jesus Christ, your Son, who lives and reigns with you and the Holy Spirit, one God, forever and ever. *Amen.*

Litany of St. Francis of Assisi

St. Francis was a contemporary and friend of St. Dominic. His followers devised this litany as means of promoting devotion and respect for this hero of the poor. Though not as old as the religious community (Order of Friars Minor) itself, the litany may have originated in the 15th century.

Lord, have mercy on us. *Christ, have mercy on us.*
Lord, have mercy on us. Christ, hear us. *Christ, graciously hear us.*
God the Father of heaven, *have mercy on us.*
God the Son, Redeemer of the world, *have mercy on us.*
God the Holy Spirit, *have mercy on us.*
Holy Trinity, one God, *have mercy on us.*
Holy Mary, conceived without sin, *pray for us.*
Holy Mary, special patroness of the three Orders of St. Francis, *pray for us.*
St. Francis, seraphic patriarch,
St. Francis, most prudent father,
St. Francis, despiser of the world,
St. Francis, model of penance,
St. Francis, conqueror of vices,
St. Francis, imitator of the Savior,
St. Francis, bearer of the marks of Christ,
St. Francis, sealed with the character of Jesus,
St. Francis, example of purity,
St. Francis, image of humility,
St. Francis, abounding in grace,
St. Francis, reformer of the erring,
St. Francis, healer of the sick,
St. Francis, pillar of the Church,
St. Francis, defender of the faith,
St. Francis, champion of Christ,
St. Francis, defender of thy children,
St. Francis, invulnerable shield,
St. Francis, confounder of the heretics,
St. Francis, converter of the pagans,
St. Francis, supporter of the lame,
St. Francis, raiser of the dead,
St. Francis, healer of the lepers,
St. Francis, our advocate,
Lamb of God, who takes away the sins of the world, *spare us, O Lord.*
Lamb of God, who takes away the sins of the world, *graciously hear us, O Lord.*
Lamb of God, who takes away the sins of the world, *have mercy on us.*
Christ, hear us. *Christ, graciously hear us.*
Pray for us, O Blessed Father Francis,
That we may be made worthy of the promises of Christ.

Let us pray. O Lord Jesus Christ, who, when the world was growing cold, in order to renew in our hearts the flame of love, imprinted the sacred marks of thy passion on the body of our Blessed Father Francis, mercifully grant that by his merits and prayers we may persevere in bearing the cross and may bring forth fruits worthy of penance, thou who livest and reignest, world without end. *Amen.*

Litany of St. Gerard Majella

St. Gerard is the patron saint of pregnant women and difficult pregnancies and the special patron to overcome infertility. This litany shows the religious community to which he belonged, the Redemptorists, also called the Congregation of the Most Holy Redeemer (CSSR).

Lord, have mercy on us. Christ, *have mercy on us.*
Lord, have mercy on us. Christ, hear us. *Christ, graciously hear us.*
God the Father of heaven, *have mercy on us.*
God the Son, Redeemer of the world, *have mercy on us.*
God the Holy Spirit, *have mercy on us.*
Holy Trinity, one God, *have mercy on us.*
Holy Mary, Mother of perpetual help, *pray for us.*
St. Joseph, foster father of Christ, *pray for us.*
St. Alphonsus, founder of the Congregation of the Most Holy Redeemer, *pray for us.*
St. Gerard Majella,
St. Gerard, enriched with extraordinary graces from early youth,
St. Gerard, perfect model of a faithful servant,
St. Gerard, bright pattern of the working classes,
St. Gerard, great lover of prayer and work,
St. Gerard, seraph of love toward the Blessed Sacrament,
St. Gerard, living image of the crucified Savior,
St. Gerard, zealous client of the Immaculate Virgin Mary,
St. Gerard, bright mirror of innocence and penance,
St. Gerard, admirable model of heroic obedience,
St. Gerard, silent victim of ignominious calumny,
St. Gerard, great before God by thy deep humility,
St. Gerard, truly wise by thy childlike simplicity,
St. Gerard, supernaturally enlightened in divine mysteries,
St. Gerard, solely desirous of pleasing God,
St. Gerard, zealous promoter of the conversion of sinners,
St. Gerard, wise counselor in the choice of vocation,
St. Gerard, enlightened guide in the direction of souls,
St. Gerard, loving friend of the poor and afflicted,
St. Gerard, safe refuge in sickness and sorrow,
St. Gerard, wonderful protector of unbaptized children,
St. Gerard, compassionate intercessor in every necessity,
St. Gerard, honor and glory of the Redemptorist Order,

Lamb of God, who takes away the sins of the world, *spare us, O Lord.*
Lamb of God, who takes away the sins of the world, *graciously hear us, O Lord.*
Lamb of God, who takes away the sins of the world, *have mercy on us.*
Pray for us, St. Gerard,
That we may be made worthy of the promises of Christ.

Let us pray. O God, who was pleased to draw Blessed Gerard to thyself from his youth, and to render him conformable to the image of thy crucified Son, grant, we beseech thee, that following his example, we may be transformed into the selfsame image, through the same Christ Our Lord. *Amen.*

Litany of St. Philomena

St. Philomena was a fourth-century virgin martyr whose admirers included SS. John Vianney, Madeleine Sophic Barat, Peter Eymard, and Peter Chanel. Her litany is difficult to date, but it's popular and considered quite old.

Lord have mercy. *Lord have mercy.*
Christ have mercy. *Christ have mercy.*
Lord have mercy. *Lord have mercy.*
God the Father of heaven, *have mercy on us.*
God the Son, Redeemer of the world, *have mercy on us.*
God the Holy Ghost, *have mercy on us.*
Holy Trinity, one God, *have mercy on us.*
Holy Mary, Queen of Virgins, *pray for us.*
St. Philomena, *pray for us.*
St. Philomena, filled with the most abundant graces from your very birth,
St. Philomena, faithful imitator of Mary,
St. Philomena, model of virgins,
St. Philomena, temple of the most perfect humility,
St. Philomena, inflamed with zeal for the glory of God,
St. Philomena, victim of the love of Jesus,
St. Philomena, example of strength and perseverance,
St. Philomena, invincible champion of chastity,
St. Philomena, mirror of the most heroic virtues,
St. Philomena, firm and intrepid in the face of torments,
St. Philomena, scourged like your divine spouse,
St. Philomena, pierced by a shower of arrows,
St. Philomena, consoled by the Mother of God when in chains,
St. Philomena, cured miraculously in prison,
St. Philomena, comforted by angels in your torments,
St. Philomena, who preferred torments and death to the splendors of a throne,
St. Philomena, who converted the witnesses of your martyrdom,
St. Philomena, who wore out the fury of your executioners,

St. Philomena, protectress of the innocent,
St. Philomena, patron of youth,
St. Philomena, refuge of the unfortunate,
St. Philomena, health of the sick and the weak,
St. Philomena, new light of the church militant,
St. Philomena, who confounds the impiety of the world,
St. Philomena, who stimulates the faith and courage of the faithful,
St. Philomena, whose name is glorified in heaven and feared in hell,
St. Philomena, made illustrious by the most striking miracles,
Lamb of God, who takes away the sins of the world, *spare us, O Lord.*
Lamb of God, who takes away the sins of the world, *graciously hear us, O Lord.*
Lamb of God, who takes away the sins of the world, *have mercy on us.*
Pray for us, great St. Philomena,
That we may be made worthy of the promises of Christ.

Let us pray. We implore thee, O Lord, by the intercession of St. Philomena, virgin and martyr, who was ever most pleasing to thine eyes by reason of her eminent purity and the practice of all the virtues, pardon us our sins and grant us all the graces we need. *Amen.*

Litany to Old Testament Saints

This litany is relatively new in the sense that most litanies are directed to canonized saints of the Christian era. This is one of the few litanies exclusively about pre-Christian holy men and women, still considered saints in heaven but from Old Testament times and references in the Bible.

Lord, have mercy on us. *Christ, have mercy on us.*
Lord, have mercy on us. Christ, hear us. *Christ, graciously hear us.*
God the Father of heaven, *have mercy on us.*
God the Son, Redeemer of the world, *have mercy on us.*
God the Holy Spirit, *have mercy on us.*
Holy Trinity, one God, *have mercy on us.*
God of Abraham, *have mercy on us.*
God of Bethel, *have mercy on us.*
Mighty one of Jacob, *have mercy on us.*
God of Abraham, Isaac, and Jacob, *have mercy on us.*
God Almighty (El Shaddai), *have mercy on us.*
God the most high, *have mercy on us.*
Archangel Michael, *pray for us.*
Archangel Gabriel,
Archangel Raphael,
All you holy angels and archangels,
Noah,
All you holy people before the flood,
Abraham,

Isaac,
Jacob,
Joseph,
All you holy patriarchs,
Aaron,
All you holy priests,
Moses,
Joshua,
All you holy leaders,
David,
All you holy kings,
Job,
Tobit,
All you holy men,
Sarah,
Rebecca,
Rachel, pray for us.
Miriam
Deborah,
Ruth,
Hannah,
Judith,
Esther,
All you holy women,
Samuel,
Jeremiah,
Ezekiel,
Daniel,
Malachy,
Elijah,
Elisha,
Isaiah,
All you holy prophets,
Abel,
Eleazar,
Ananias,
Azariah,
Mishael,
All you holy martyrs and heroic witnesses,
All you holy men and women, Old Testament saints of God,
Be merciful, *spare us, O Lord.*
Be merciful, *graciously hear us, O Lord.*
From all evil, *O Lord, deliver us.*
From all sin,
From breaking your commandments,
From falling away from the faith,
From doubting your word,
From denying your name,
From fear of profaning your name,

From lack of sincere repentance,
From losing hope,
From fear of fraternal correction,
From doubt of your power,
From all false desires,
From lack of zeal in your service,
Lamb of God, who takes away the sins of the world, *spare us, O Lord.*
Lamb of God, who takes away the sins of the world, *graciously hear us, O Lord.*
Lamb of God, who takes away the sins of the world, *have mercy on us. Amen.*

Litany of St. Thérèse of Lisieux (Or St. Thérèse of the Little Flower)

St. Thérèse is one of most popular saints, second only to St. Francis of Assisi. Her simple way of life and her successful path to holiness is expressed in the verses of this litany.

Lord have mercy. *Lord have mercy.*
Christ have mercy. *Christ have mercy.*
Lord have mercy. *Lord have mercy.*
God, the Father in heaven, *have mercy on us.*
God the Son, Redeemer of the world,
God the Holy Spirit,
Holy Trinity, one God,
Holy Mary, Mother of God, *pray for us.*
St. Joseph,
St. Teresa of Jesus,
St. John of the Cross,
St. Thérèse of the child Jesus and the holy face, *pray for us.*
St. Thérèse, gift of God to Carmel,
St. Thérèse, gift of God to the Church,
St. Thérèse, patroness of the missions,
St. Thérèse, Doctor of the Church,
St. Thérèse, beloved child of the Heavenly Father,
St. Thérèse, passionately in love with Jesus,
St. Thérèse, who so wanted to resemble the child Jesus,
St. Thérèse, who so wanted to resemble the suffering Jesus,
St. Thérèse, on fire with love through the Holy Spirit,
St. Thérèse, who gave us the little way of spiritual childhood,
St. Thérèse, who sought only the truth,
St. Thérèse, who chose all that God wanted,
St. Thérèse, who understood and practiced humility of heart,

St. Thérèse, who forgot yourself to make others happy,
St. Thérèse, who fought with the weapons of prayer and sacrifice,
St. Thérèse, who wanted to love like Jesus himself,
St. Thérèse, who understood and lived charity,
St. Thérèse, who praised the work of the Creator,
St. Thérèse, who praised the mercies of the Lord,
St. Thérèse, poor, chaste and obedient,
St. Thérèse, faithful in the little things,
St. Thérèse, free and joyful,
St. Thérèse, patient and courageous,
St. Thérèse, simple in joy and suffering,
St. Thérèse, tried in our faith,
St. Thérèse, who hoped against all hope,
St. Thérèse, who refused God nothing,
St. Thérèse, rapidly consumed by love,
St. Thérèse, martyr of love,
St. Thérèse, nourished by the Word of God,
St. Thérèse, burning with desire to the Eucharist,
St. Thérèse, love in the heart of the Church,
St. Thérèse, Word of God for the world,
St. Thérèse, teacher of the spiritual life,
St. Thérèse, apostle of mercy,
St. Thérèse, offered to merciful love,
St. Thérèse, who came before God with empty hands,
St. Thérèse, happy in your weakness,
St. Thérèse, trusting in spite of everything,
St. Thérèse, who found in abandonment to the Father an ocean of peace,
St. Thérèse, consumed with zeal for the salvation of souls,
St. Thérèse, sister and friend of all,
St. Thérèse, support of your missionaries,
St. Thérèse, mother of a multitude,
St. Thérèse, seated at the table of the sinners,
St. Thérèse, who made a condemned criminal your first child,
St. Thérèse, close to prisoners, sister of the wounded in life,
St. Thérèse, friend of unbelievers,
St. Thérèse, close to those who are tempted and who doubt,
St. Thérèse, close to those who despair,
St. Thérèse, presence of pardon and peace,
St. Thérèse, witness of God, our merciful Father,
St. Thérèse, witness of Christ, Servant and Savior,
St. Thérèse, witness of the spirit of love and holiness,
Lamb of God, who takes away the sins of the world, *spare us, O Lord.*
Lamb of God, who takes away the sins of the world, *graciously hear us, O Lord.*
Lamb of God, who takes away the sins of the world, *have mercy on us, O Lord.*
Pray for us, St. Thérèse,
That we may be made worthy of the promises of Christ.

Let us pray. God our Father, you have promised your kingdom to those who are willing to become like little children. Help us to follow the way of St. Thérèse with confidence, so that by her prayers, we may come to know your eternal glory. Grant this through our Lord Jesus Christ, your Son, who lives and reigns with you and the Holy Spirit, one God forever and ever. Amen.

Litany of St. Thomas Aquinas

The "angelic doctor" of the 13th century is the most famous Dominican saint and is the patron saint of all theologians and scholars of philosophy. He's also the patron saint of Catholic education. This litany was developed in the Thomistic renewal of the 17th century.

Lord, have mercy on us. *Christ, have mercy on us.*
Lord, have mercy on us. Christ, hear us. *Christ, graciously hear us.*
God the Father of heaven, *have mercy on us.*
God the Son, Redeemer of the world, *have mercy on us.*
God the Holy Spirit, *have mercy on us.*
Holy Trinity, one God, *have mercy on us.*
Holy Mary, Glorious Mother of the King of Kings, *pray for us.*
St. Thomas of Aquinas, *pray for us.*
St. Thomas most chaste,
St. Thomas most patient,
Prodigy of science,
Silently eloquent,
Reproach of the ambitious,
Lover of that life which is hidden with Christ in God,
Fragrant flower in the garden of St. Dominic, *pray for us.*
Glory of the Friars preachers,
Illumined from on high,
Angel of the schools,
Oracle of the Church,
Incomparable scribe of the man-God,
Satiated with the odor of his perfumes,
Perfect in the school of his cross,
Intoxicated with the strong wine of his charity,
Glittering gem in the cabinet of the Lord,
Model of perfect obedience,
Endowed with the true spirit of holy poverty,
Lamb of God, who takes away the sins of the world, *spare us, O Lord.*
Lamb of God, who takes away the sins of the world, *graciously hear us, O Lord.*
Lamb of God, who takes away the sins of the world, *have mercy on us.*

Chapter 20

Ten Famous Novenas to the Saints

A novena is a nine-day prayer. Christians began the practice of nine days of prayer at the time of Jesus. The period between the Ascension and Pentecost was nine days, and the Blessed Virgin Mary and the Apostles met in the Upper Room and prayed for nine days following Christ's Ascension. Since that time, any group of nine days of prayer is called a novena. Novenas are directed to a particular saint and are usually arranged so that the end of the novena occurs on the eve or actual liturgical feast day of that saint.

This chapter includes the most well-known novenas still being used today.

Novena of the Miraculous Medal

The Virgin Mary appeared to St. Catherine Laboure in 1830 in Paris and asked that she get a medal made which would eventually become known as the Miraculous Medal. It has an image of Mary on one side and the letter M on the back. Inscribed on the front is the phrase, "O, Mary, conceived without sin, pray for us who have recourse to thee."

In addition to promoting the wearing of the Miraculous Medal, St. Catherine Laboure also promoted the praying of this novena for nine consecutive days, or on the same day for nine consecutive months:

O Immaculate Virgin Mary, Mother of our Lord Jesus and our Mother, penetrated with the most lively confidence in your all-powerful and never-failing intercession, manifested so often through the Miraculous Medal, we your loving and trustful children implore you to obtain for us the graces and favors we ask during this novena, if they be beneficial to our immortal souls, and the souls for whom we pray.

(Insert personal petition here.)

You know, O Mary, how often our souls have been the sanctuaries of your Son who hates iniquity.

Obtain for us then a deep hatred of sin and that purity of heart which will attach us to God alone so that our every thought, word, and deed may tend to his greater glory.

Obtain for us also a spirit of prayer and self-denial that we may recover by penance what we have lost by sin and at length attain to that blessed abode where you are the Queen of angels and of men. Amen.

Novena to St. Joseph

St. Joseph was the Virgin Mary's husband and Jesus's adopted or foster father. He is invoked as the patron saint of workers, husbands, and a happy death. This novena is used to pray for his intercession to obtain a job, find or sell a home, or for a dying person to have a peaceful departure. The first part of the prayer is said every day, followed by the appropriate prayer for each of the nine novena days:

O glorious St. Joseph, faithful follower of Jesus Christ, to you we raise our hearts and hands to implore your powerful intercession in obtaining from the benign heart of Jesus all the helps and graces necessary for our spiritual and temporal welfare, particularly for the grace of a happy death and the special favor we now request.

(Insert personal request here.)

O guardian of the Word Incarnate, we feel animated with confidence that your prayers in our behalf will be graciously heard before the throne of God.

O glorious St. Joseph, through the love you bear to Jesus Christ and for the glory of his name, hear our prayers and obtain our petitions. Amen.

First day

O great St. Joseph, with feelings of unlimited confidence, we beg you to bless this novena that we begin in your honor. "You are never invoked in vain," says the seraphic St. Theresa of Jesus.

Be you then to me what you have been to that spouse of the Sacred Heart of Jesus and graciously hear me as you did her. Amen.

St. Joseph, pray for us!

Second day

O Blessed St. Joseph, tenderhearted father, faithful guardian of Jesus, chaste spouse of the Mother of God, we pray and beseech you to offer to God the Father, his divine Son, bathed in blood on the cross for sinners, and through the thrice holy name of Jesus obtain for us of the eternal Father the favor for which we implore your intercession.

(Insert personal request here.)

Amid the splendors of eternity, forget not the sorrows of those who pray, those who weep; stay the almighty arm which chastises us, that by your prayers and those of your most holy spouse, the heart of Jesus may be moved to pity and to pardon. Amen.

St. Joseph, pray for us!

Third day

Blessed St. Joseph, enkindle in our cold hearts a spark of your charity. May God be always the first and only object of our affections. Keep our souls always in sanctifying grace and, if we should be so unhappy as to lose it, give us the strength to recover it immediately by a sincere repentance. Help us to such a love of our God as will always keep us united to him.

Amen.

O glorious St. Joseph, through the love you bear to Jesus Christ and for the glory of his name, hear our prayers and obtain our petitions.

(Insert personal request here.)

Fourth day

St. Joseph, pride of heaven, unfailing hope for our lives, and support of those on earth, graciously accept our prayer of praise. You were appointed spouse of the chaste Virgin by the Creator of the world. He willed that you be called Father of the Word and serve as agent of our salvation. May the triune God who bestowed upon you heavenly honors, be praised forever. And may he grant us through your merits the joy of a blessed life and a favorable answer to our petition.

(Insert personal request here.)

Amen.

St. Joseph, pray for us!

Fifth day

O holy St. Joseph, what a lesson your life is for us, ever so eager to appear, so anxious to display, before the eyes of men, the graces that we owe entirely to the generosity of God, which we plead in this novena.

(Insert personal request here.)

Grant that we may attribute to God the glory of all things, that we may love the humble and hidden life, that we may not desire any other position than the one given us by Providence, and that we may always be a docile instrument in the hands of God. Amen.

St. Joseph, pray for us!

Sixth day

O glorious St. Joseph, appointed by the eternal Father as the guardian and protector of the life of Jesus Christ, the comfort and support of his Holy Mother, and the instrument in his great design for the redemption of mankind; you who had the happiness of living with Jesus and Mary, and of dying in their arms, be moved with confidence we place in you, and procure for us from the Almighty, the particular favor which we humbly ask through your intercession.

(Insert personal request here.)

Amen.

St. Joseph, pray for us!

Seventh day

O faithful and prudent St. Joseph, watch over our weakness and our inexperience; obtain for us that prudence which reminds us of our end, which directs our paths and which protects us from every danger. Pray for us, then, O great saint, and by your love for Jesus and Mary, and by their love for you, obtain for us the favor we ask in this novena.

(Insert personal request here.)

Amen.

St. Joseph, pray for us!

Eighth day

O blessed Joseph, to whom it was given not only to see and to hear that God whom many kings longed to see and saw not; to hear and heard not; but also to carry him in your arms, to embrace him, to clothe him, and to guard and defend him, come to our assistance and intercede with him to look favorably on our present petition.

(Insert personal request here.)

Amen.

St. Joseph, pray for us!

Ninth day

O good St. Joseph, help us to be like you, gentle to those whose weakness leans on us; help us to give to those who seek our aid, succor that they may journey unafraid. Give us your faith, that we may see the right shining above the victories of might. Give us your hope that we may stand secure, untouched by doubting, steadfast to endure, an understanding heart may bring us peace. Give us your purity that the hour of death finds us untouched by evil's breath. Give us your love of labor that we shirk no lot in life that calls us for honest work. Give us your love of poverty so that we live contented, let wealth come or go. Give us your courage that we may be strong; give us your meekness to confess our sins. Give us your patience that we may possess the kingdom of our souls without distress. Help us, dear saint, to so live that when life ends we pass with you to Jesus and his friends.

O glorious St. Joseph, hear our prayers and obtain our petitions. Amen.

St. Joseph, pray for us!

Our Lady of Good Remedy

St. John of Matha founded a religious order called the Trinitarians in 1198 to ransom Christian slaves and set them free. Trinitarians needed large amounts of money and placed their fundraising efforts under the patronage of Mary. They were so successful that they were able to free thousands of people. In gratitude for her miraculous assistance, St. John of Matha honored Mary with the title of Our Lady of Good Remedy. The Church celebrates her feast day on October 8. Our Lady of Good Remedy is often depicted as the Virgin Mary handing a bag of money to St. John of Matha. This novena is prayed to ask Our Lady of Ransom for deliverance from present tribulations:

O Queen of heaven and earth, most Holy Virgin, we venerate thee. Thou art the beloved daughter of the most high God, the chosen Mother of the Incarnate Word, the Immaculate Spouse of the Holy Spirit, the Sacred Vessel of the most Holy Trinity.

O Mother of the Divine Redeemer, who under the title of Our Lady of Good Remedy comes to the aid of all who call upon thee, extend thy maternal protection to us. We depend on thee, dear Mother, as helpless and needy children depend on a tender and caring mother.

Hail, Mary, full of grace, the Lord is with thee; blessed are thou among women and blessed is the fruit of thy womb, Jesus. Holy Mary, Mother of God, pray for us sinners, now and at the hour of our death. Amen.

O Lady of Good Remedy, source of unfailing help, grant that we may draw from thy treasury of graces in our time of need.

Touch the hearts of sinners, that they may seek reconciliation and forgiveness. Bring comfort to the afflicted and the lonely; help the poor and the hopeless; aid the sick and the suffering. May they be healed in body and strengthened in spirit to endure their sufferings with patient resignation and Christian fortitude.

Hail, Mary, full of grace, the Lord is with thee; blessed are you among women and blessed is the fruit of your womb, Jesus. Holy Mary, Mother of God, pray for us sinners, now and at the hour of our death. Amen.

Dear Lady of Good Remedy, source of unfailing help, thy compassionate heart knows a remedy for every affliction and misery we encounter in life. Help me with thy prayers and intercession to find a remedy for my problems and needs, especially for

(Insert special intentions here.)

On my part, O loving Mother, I pledge myself to a more intensely Christian lifestyle, to a more careful observance of the laws of God, to be more conscientious in fulfilling the obligations of my state in life, and to strive to be a source of healing in this broken world of ours.

Dear Lady of Good Remedy, be ever present to me, and through thy intercession, may I enjoy health of body and peace of mind, and grow stronger in the faith and in the love of thy Son, Jesus.

Hail, Mary, full of grace, the Lord is with thee; blessed are you among women and blessed is the fruit of your womb, Jesus. Holy Mary, Mother of God, pray for us sinners, now and at the hour of our death. Amen.

Verse: *Pray for us, O Holy Mother of Good Remedy.*
Response: *That we may deepen our dedication to thy Son, and make the world alive with his spirit.*

Novena to St. Dominic

St. Dominic de Guzman founded the Order of Preachers, more commonly known as the Dominicans, in the 13th century. The Virgin Mary appeared to him one day and gave him the Rosary to help battle the Albigensian heresy that denied the humanity of Christ. This novena is said before his feast day (August 8) to ask his intercession for a particular spiritual assistance:

O renowned champion of the faith of Christ, most holy St. Dominic, who didst renounce the honor and dignity of an earthly principality to embrace the poor, laborious, and mortified life which should distinguish a disciple of him who has said: "If any man will come after me, let him take up his cross and follow me."

O burning torch, who being thyself consumed with the fire of divine love, didst incessantly labor to enkindle that sacred flame in the hearts of others, look down upon me from that throne of glory where thou enjoyest the reward of all thy labors, and obtain that some sparks of that blessed fire may be lighted in my soul, to animate and encourage me under any crosses or trials with which it shall please the divine goodness to visit me.

Thou, O great saint, regardest as nothing all the afflictions thou didst endure, and all the toils thou didst undergo for the promotion of God's holy cause; obtain, I beseech thee, that the same ardent love which strengthened thee, may make sweet to me labors, humiliations, disgraces, or whatever other mortifications I may have to suffer for the name of Jesus. May I ever bear in mind that nothing can happen to me but by the particular dispensation of a God who is infinitely wise, and therefore knows what is best for my welfare; infinitely powerful, and consequently able to effect it; and above all, infinitely merciful and loving, who has laid down his life for my redemption, and continues daily to give new proofs of his love and bounty.

O tender Father of the poor who, when all other resources were exhausted, didst offer thyself for their relief, obtain for me that true spirit of compassion for the suffering members of Jesus Christ, which shone forth so conspicuously in thy holy life. May I, by charity to those whom Jesus so dearly loves, lay up for myself treasures in heaven, where thou now enjoyest that which the eye hath not seen, nor the ear heard, nor the heart of man conceived, but which God has prepared for those who love him, and who prove themselves his disciples by the observance of his divine precept "love one another."

I praise and thank God for the high degree of sanctity to which he has raised thee, and the special privileges by which he has distinguished thee. I conjure thee, by that gratitude with which thou shalt for all eternity be penetrated for thy divine benefactor, implore for me the grace to root out of my heart whatever is not agreeable in his sight, especially that evil habit by which I most frequently offend him. Obtain likewise the favors I request in this novena, through thy powerful intercession.

(Insert intentions here.)

O glorious Mother of God, Queen of the most sacred Rosary, thou who didst love Dominic with the affection of a mother, and were most tenderly loved and honored by him, look upon me, for his sake, with an eye of pity, deign to join with him in presenting these petitions to thy most Blessed Jesus. I sincerely desire from this moment to love him with all my heart, and serve him with all my strength, and now place myself under thy powerful protection, as a sure means of obtaining all the graces necessary to serve him faithfully here, that I may eternally rejoice with him hereafter. Amen.

Novena to St. Jude Thaddeus

St. Jude Thaddeus was one of the original 12 Apostles. He wrote an epistle in the New Testament and is considered a relative, possibly a cousin, of Jesus. He is known as the patron saint of hopeless cases or difficult situations. This novena asks his intercession and, in return, persons who have their prayers answered typically promote devotion to St. Jude:

Most holy apostle, St. Jude, faithful servant and friend of Jesus, the Church honors and invokes you universally, as the patron of difficult cases, of things almost despaired of, pray for me, I am so helpless and alone.

Intercede with God for me that he bring visible and speedy help where help is almost despaired of. Come to my assistance in this great need that I may receive the consolation and help of heaven in all my necessities, tribulations, and sufferings, particularly

(Insert request here.)

and that I may praise God with you and all the saints forever. I promise, O Blessed St. Jude, to be ever mindful of this great favor granted me by God and to always honor you as my special and powerful patron, and to gratefully encourage devotion to you. Amen.

May the heart of Jesus in the most blessed sacrament be praised, adored, and loved with grateful affection, at every moment, in all the tabernacles of the world, unto the very end of time! Amen.

May the most Sacred Heart of Jesus be praised and glorified now and forever. Amen.

St. Jude pray for us and hear our prayers. Amen.

Blessed be the Sacred Heart of Jesus.
Blessed be the Immaculate Heart of Mary.
Blessed be St. Jude Thaddeus, in all the world and for all eternity.

Follow this prayer with the Our Father and the Hail Mary.

Novena to St. Gerard

St. Gerard Majella is the patron saint of expectant mothers, mothers with difficult pregnancies, and those women who hope to conceive and give birth to healthy children. Say once a day for nine days, especially beginning on October 7 and ending on October 15, the eve of the Feast of St. Gerard:

First day

St. Gerard, ever full of faith, obtain for me that, believing firmly all that the Church of God proposes to my belief, I may strive to secure through a holy life the joys of eternal happiness.

Say nine Hail Marys.

Verse: *Pray for us, O St. Gerard.*
Response: *That we may be made worthy of the promises of Christ.*

Let us pray. O Almighty and everlasting God, who didst draw to thyself St. Gerard, even from his tenderest years, making him conformable to the image of thy crucified Son, grant we beseech thee, that imitating his example, we may be made like unto the same divine image through Jesus Christ our Lord. Amen.

Second day

St. Gerard, most generous saint, who from thy tenderest years didst care so little for the goods of earth, grant that I may place all my confidence in Jesus Christ alone, my true treasure, who alone can make me happy in time and in eternity.

Say nine Hail Marys.

Verse: *Pray for us, O St. Gerard.*
Response: *That we may be made worthy of the promises of Christ.*

Third day

St. Gerard, bright seraph of love, who despising all earthly love, didst consecrate thy life to the service of God and thy neighbor, promoting God's glory in thy lowly state, and ever ready to assist the distressed and console the sorrowful, obtain for me, I beseech thee, that loving God the only God and my neighbor for his sake, I may be hereafter united to him forever in glory.

Say nine Hail Marys.

Verse: *Pray for us, O St. Gerard.*
Response: *That we may be made worthy of the promises of Christ.*

Fourth day

St. Gerard, spotless lily of purity, by the angelic virtue and thy wonderful innocence of life thou didst receive from the infant Jesus and his Immaculate Mother, sweet pledges of tenderest love, grant, I beseech thee, that I may ever strive in my lifelong fight, and thus win the crown that awaits the brave and the true.

Say nine Hail Marys.

Verse: *Pray for us, O St. Gerard.*
Response: *That we may be made worthy of the promises of Christ.*

Fifth day

St. Gerard, model of holy obedience, who through thy life didst heroically submit to the judgment of those who represent Jesus Christ to thee, thus sanctifying thy lowliest actions, obtain for me from God cheerful admission to his holy will and the virtue of perfect obedience, that I may be made conformable to Jesus, my model, who was obedient even to death.

Say nine Hail Marys.

Verse: *Pray for us, O St. Gerard.*
Response: *That we may be made worthy of the promises of Christ.*

Sixth day

St. Gerard, most perfect imitator of Jesus Christ our Redeemer, do thou whose greatest glory was to be humble and lowly, obtain that I too, knowing my little-ness in God's sight, may be found worthy to enter the kingdom that is promised to the humble and lowly of heart.

Say nine Hail Marys.

Verse: *Pray for us, O St. Gerard.*
Response: *That we may be made worthy of the promises of Christ.*

Seventh Day

St. Gerard, unconquered hero, most patient in suffering, do thou who didst glory in infirmity, and under slander and most cruel ignominy didst rejoice to suffer with Christ, obtain for me patience and resignation in my sorrows, that I may bravely bear the cross and gain the crown of everlasting glory.

Say nine Hail Marys.

Verse: *Pray for us, O St. Gerard.*
Response: *That we may be made worthy of the promises of Christ.*

Eighth day

St. Gerard, true lover of Jesus in the Blessed Sacrament of the Altar, do thou who didst kneel long hours before the tabernacle, and there didst taste the joys of the Paradise. Obtain for me, I beseech thee, the spirit of prayer and an undying love for the most holy sacrament, that thus receiving frequently the body and blood of Jesus, I may daily grow in his holy love and merit the priceless grace of loving him even to the end.

Say nine Hail Marys.

Verse: *Pray for us, O St. Gerard.*
Response: *That we may be made worthy of the promises of Christ.*

Ninth day

St. Gerard, most favorite child of heaven, to whom Mary gave the infant Jesus in the day of thy childhood, to whom she sweetly came before thou didst close thine eyes in death, obtain for me I beseech thee, so to seek and love my Blessed Mother during life, that she may be my joy and consolation in this valley of tears, until with thee, before the throne of God, I may praise her goodness for all eternity. Amen.

Say nine Hail Marys.

Verse: *Pray for us, O St. Gerard.*
Response: *That we may be made worthy of the promises of Christ.*

Novena to St. Philomena

St. Philomena is the patron saint of babies, infants, children, and adults who seek to live a life of purity and chastity. Say once a day for nine days, especially beginning on August 31 and ending on September 8, the eve of the Feast of St. Philomena:

We beseech thee, O Lord, to grant us the pardon of our sins by the intercession of saint, virgin, and martyr, who was always pleasing in thy sight by her eminent chastity and by the profession of every virtue. Amen.

Illustrious virgin and martyr, St. Philomena, behold me prostrate before the throne whereupon it has pleased the most Holy Trinity to place thee. Full of confidence in thy protection, I entreat thee to intercede for me with God, from the heights of heaven deign to cast a glance upon thy humble client! Spouse of Christ, sustain me in suffering, fortify me in temptation, protect me in the dangers surrounding me, obtain for me the graces necessary to me, and in particular

(Insert personal petition here.)

Above all, assist me at the hour of my death. St. Philomena, powerful with God, pray for us. Amen.

O God, most Holy Trinity, we thank thee for the graces thou didst bestow upon the Blessed Virgin Mary, and upon thy handmaid Philomena, through whose intercession we implore thy mercy. Amen.

Novena to St. Peregrine

St. Peregrine is the patron saint of those afflicted with any type of cancer. This novena is prayed from April 25 to May 3, the eve of his feast day:

Glorious wonder worker, St. Peregrine, you answered the divine call with a ready spirit, and forsook all the comforts of a life of ease and all the empty honors of the world to dedicate yourself to God in the order of his holy Mother.

You labored manfully for the salvation of souls. In union with Jesus crucified, you endured painful sufferings with such patience as to deserve to be healed miraculously of an incurable cancer in your leg by a touch of his divine hand.

Obtain for me the grace to answer every call of God and to fulfill his will in all the events of life. Enkindle in my heart a consuming zeal for the salvation of all.

Deliver me from the infirmities that afflict my body.

(Insert personal request here.)

Obtain for me also a perfect resignation to the sufferings it may please God to send me, so that, imitating our crucified Savior and his sorrowful Mother, I may merit eternal glory in heaven.

St. Peregrine, pray for me and for all who invoke your aid.

Novena to St. Ann

St. Ann is the mother of the Virgin Mary and hence the maternal grandmother of Jesus. She is the patroness of women seeking a good, loving, and faithful husband, as well as of many other spiritual and temporal requests. Say once a day for nine days, especially beginning on July 17 and ending on July 25, the eve of the Feast of St. Anne:

O glorious St. Anne, filled with compassion for those who invoke thee and with love for those who suffer, heavily laden with the weight of my troubles, I cast myself at thy feet and humbly beg of thee to take under thy special protection the present affair which I commend to thee.

(Insert personal request here.)

Be pleased to commend it to thy daughter, the Blessed Virgin Mary, and lay it before the throne of Jesus, so that he may bring it to a happy outcome. Cease not to intercede for me until my request is granted. Above all, obtain for me the grace of one day beholding my God face to face, and, with thee and Mary and all the saints, of praising and blessing him for all eternity. Amen.

Good St. Anne, mother of her who is our life, our sweetness, and our hope, pray to her for us and obtain our request.

Good St. Anne, mother of her who is our life, our sweetness, and our hope, pray to her for us and obtain our request.

Good St. Anne, mother of her who is our life, our sweetness, and our hope, pray to her for us and obtain our request.

Good St. Anne, pray for us. Jesus, Mary, Anne.

Novena to St. Michael the Archangel

St. Michael is the archangel of the Bible who fought Lucifer (now known as Satan, or the devil), the bad angel that rebelled against God along with one-third of the angelic community. Michael and the other two-thirds of the angels defeated the evil ones. The good went into heaven, and the bad were cast into hell. This novena to him goes back many centuries, as does devotion to all angels as messengers of God and agents of divine protection.

Glorious St. Michael, guardian and defender of the Church of Jesus Christ, come to the assistance of his followers, against whom the powers of hell are unchained. Guard with special care our Holy Father, the Pope, and our bishops, priests, all our religious and lay people, and especially the children.

St. Michael, watch over us during life, defend us against the assaults of the demon, and assist us especially at the hour of death. Help us achieve the happiness of beholding God face to face for all eternity. Amen.

St. Michael, intercede for me with God in all my necessities, especially

(Insert personal intention here.)

Obtain for me a favorable outcome in the matter I recommend to you. Mighty prince of the heavenly host, and victor over rebellious spirits, remember me for I am weak and sinful and so prone to pride and ambition. Be for me, I pray, my powerful aid in temptation and difficulty, and above all do not forsake me in my last struggle with the powers of evil. Amen.

Chapter 21

Ten Popular Shrines of the Saints

● ●

In This Chapter

▶ Shrines in Europe

▶ Shrines in the United States

● ●

A popular form of piety in the Middle Ages involved making a *pilgrimage* — a journey to a religious place. Aside from obvious locations like the Holy Land where Jesus was born, lived, died, and rose from the dead, the traveling faithful often visit shrines of the saints. This chapter highlights ten such shrines, whether they be the actual burial site for an individual saint or a spot dedicated in his or her honor.

Basilica of St. Francis of Assisi

The basilica of St. Francis is in the medieval Italian town of Assisi, 90 miles north of Rome. The basilica is dedicated to the saint who, along with St. Dominic in the 13th century, established the mendicant orders of the Franciscans and Dominicans, respectively.

Construction of the church began two years after Francis's death in 1226; it wasn't completed until 1253. It was built on land donated by Francis's friend, Simone di Pucciarello. St. Francis's remains are interred in the lower church. Southwest of the basilica is the *Sacro Convento* (Sacred Convent), which includes papal apartments for visiting popes and is not open to the public.

The basilica was damaged in an earthquake in 1997 in which four people died. The lower level was undamaged, and the upper level has been repaired.

Catedral de Santiago de Compostela

This Spanish cathedral in the northwest town of Santiago de Compostela was built over the grave of St. James the Greater after the earlier church was destroyed by the Moors. Construction of the structure, with its Baroque facade, started in 1060 and was completed in 1211. St. James's remains were discovered in AD 819, and the earlier church was built over his grave.

The 12th-century *Portico da Gloria,* behind the western facade, is a central highlight of the cathedral. It follows the style of the Romanesque period and was built by Master Mateo between 1168 and 1188. Other features include the famous Botafumeiro, or incense burner; a pulley mechanism used to swing the burner is located in a dome above the crossing. The Botafumeiro, built by Jose Losada in 1851, is the largest censer in the world — it's 5 feet, 3 inches tall and weighs 176 pounds.

One of the largest Romanesque churches of Spain (if not all of Europe), the Catedral de Santiago de Compostela is third only to Lourdes and Fatima in the number of pilgrims that visit each year and in popularity among the faithful. Before the Marian apparitions in those other locations, this was the premier pilgrimage site, second only to Rome itself.

Cologne Cathedral

The Cologne Cathedral in Cologne, Germany (the *Kölner Dom*), is dedicated to both St. Peter and the Virgin Mary. It's believed that the church possesses the relics of the Magi who visited the Christ child, as recounted in the second chapter of the Gospel According to St. Matthew.

Construction of the cathedral was started in the 13th century on the ruins of a 4th-century Roman temple and took more than 600 years to complete. The cornerstone was laid on August 15, 1248, and the work was finally finished in 1880 in the presence of King of Prussia and first German Emperor Wilhelm I.

World War II aerial bombs hit the church 14 times, but the building survived.

Besides housing the relics of the Magi, the Cologne Cathedral also has the Gero Cross *(Gero-Kreuz),* carved in AD 976, the oldest surviving monumental crucifix north of the Alps. In the Blessed Sacrament Chapel, inside the cathedral, is the *Madonna of Milan (Mailänder Madonna),* an exquisite wooden sculpture depicting Mary and the child Jesus from the year 1290. Another jewel of the cathedral is the Chapel of the Virgin *(Marienkapelle),* where the painting of the *Patron Saints of Köln* by Stefan Lochner (1442) is displayed.

House of the Virgin Mary

According to pious tradition, the Virgin Mary lived under the care of St. John the Beloved (also known as John the Evangelist) in Ephesus (on the western coast of modern-day Turkey) until her Assumption into heaven sometime before the end of the first century. The Gospel of John tells of Jesus giving his mother to the care of the Beloved Disciple just before his death on the cross (John 19:26 27), and history records that John lived in Ephesus both before and after his exile to the island of Patmos.

Often confused with the Cathedral *Meryem Kilisesi* (Turkish for "Mary's Church"), where the Ecumenical Council of Ephesus convened in AD 431, the House of the Virgin Mary (called *Meryem Ana Evi* in Turkish) in Ephesus is the home where believers contend the Virgin Mary lived in her later years. Now a shrine, it has an altar where Mass is celebrated in addition to a place of prayer and reflection for other religions.

Pope Paul VI visited the House of the Virgin Mary in 1967, Pope John Paul II came in 1979, and Pope Benedict XVI visited in 2006. Every year, pilgrims flock to this shrine, especially on the Feast of the Assumption, August 15, which commemorates Mary's body and soul being taken up to heaven by her Divine Son, Jesus. The Eastern Orthodox and Byzantine Catholics call this the Feast of the Holy *Dormition* (or falling asleep) of the Blessed Virgin Mary.

La Madeleine

La Madeleine is a church dedicated to St. Mary Magdalene in Paris, France. Construction started during the reign of King Louis XV in 1764, and the church was first designed by Constant d'Ivry. A second architect who favored a design imitating the Roman Pantheon wasn't well received, and work came to a halt from 1790 to 1806.

Emperor Napoleon decided to erect a "temple of glory" to his Grand Army, and he commissioned Pierre-Alexandre Vignon as imperial architect. Workers leveled what remained from the first efforts on the church and started building what was to be a Greek-like temple. King Louis XVIII ordered in 1814 that the Madeleine should be a church, but in 1837 it was almost designated the first railway station of Paris. The Madeleine was finally consecrated a church in 1842. The exterior is surrounded by large Corinthian columns and a frieze of the Last Judgment above the portico. A painting by Ziegler in the chancel depicts the history of Christianity, with the Emperor Napoleon conspicuously in the forefront.

St. Peter's Basilica

Most of the liturgical celebrations in Rome take place in St. Peter's Basilica, the residence of the Holy Father.

The Circus of Nero, the site of St. Peter's death in AD 64, was held on the site where St. Peter's Basilica now stands. St. Helena, the mother of the Emperor Constantine, convinced her son to build a church in AD 324 over the tomb of this special saint.

Pope Nicholas V decided in the mid-15th century that the old basilica should be rebuilt and hired architect Bernardo Rossellino to start renovating the old church. Both died before completion, and Pope Sixtus IV had the Sistine Chapel built instead.

Pope Julius II commissioned construction on the existing basilica in 1506, and it was completed in 1626 under Pope Paul V. The first chief architect was Donato Bramante, followed by Raphael. Michelangelo then served as main architect and designed the famous dome, while Bernini designed the great colonnade, with 140 statues atop, circling the piazza of St. Peter's Square.

A crypt containing the remains of St. Peter and other popes — including Pope John Paul the Great — is located under the main church. Over the actual tomb is a 927-ton bronze baldacchino (canopy) reaching 90 feet tall; under this canopy is the altar at which the pope celebrates Holy Mass.

St. Peter's is the largest church in the world, covering 5.7 acres and capable of holding 60,000 people inside. The basilica welcomes the greatest number of visitors each year and hosted the largest number of heads of state, presidents, prime ministers, and monarchs gathered together during the funeral of Pope John Paul II in 2005.

The pope has general audiences with the public outside in the piazza in front of the basilica when the weather allows. When the weather is bad, audiences are held inside the Pope Paul VI hall, adjacent to the Vatican.

St. Peter's Basilica lies inside the independent nation of Vatican City, the smallest sovereign nation on earth (100 acres and 900 citizens).

St. Stephen's Basilica

This church honoring St. Stephen, king and now patron saint of Hungary, is the largest in the nation. Construction of the church, which holds the incorrupt right hand of the saintly monarch, was started in 1855 and completed 50 years later, in 1905. The basilica is said to hold 8,500 people and is second in size only to St. Peter's Basilica in Rome.

Visitors can see the city of Budapest from the top of the basilica. A statue of St. Stephen, made of white Carrara marble by Alajos Strobl, stands in the middle of the high altar. The church is also home to the largest bell in the country, weighing in at 9 tons.

Sanctuaire d'Ars

Pope Benedict XVI declared St. John Vianney patron of all priests in his "Year for Priests" letter in June 2009; prior to that time, he had been the patron saint of diocesan parish priests. His final resting place in a small town in France has become a popular shrine for millions of pilgrims.

Ars, a small community northwest of Lyons and 250 miles south of Paris, was a spiritually desolate place at the time of St. John Vianney (see Chapter 5). The would-be saint was unsure of his direction when travelling to Ars and stopped to ask a young boy for help. When the boy told him the proper road to follow, John thanked the boy and said, "You have shown me the way to Ars; now I will show you the way to heaven."

The original church John served now stands as the nave of the basilica built after his death. His incorrupt body is located in the shrine in his honor. Several side chapels John had built onto the church still remain, and a separate chapel — the Chapel of the Heart — houses the relic of John's heart, which was removed from his body.

St. Patrick's Cathedral

The building that now stands as St. Patrick's Cathedral in New York City replaced an earlier and smaller church. Old St. Patrick's, the earlier church, is the oldest Catholic building in New York and remains a functioning parish. The new St. Patrick's Cathedral was designed by American architect James Renwick. Construction started in 1858 but was interrupted by the Civil War. It was finally opened and consecrated in 1879.

The original proposed site for the cathedral was a countryside area thought to be too far from the inner city. Then-Archbishop Hughes persevered in his vision of building the most beautiful Gothic cathedral in the New World, in what eventually would become the heart of the city.

The cathedral is dedicated to the patron saint of the Roman Catholic archdiocese of New York and the patron saint of Ireland, St. Patrick. Many Irish immigrants helped fund and build the current church, and most of the archbishops who served as spiritual shepherds of the archdiocese were of Irish ancestry. More than 100 parishioners pledged $1,000 each, and thousands of Irish Americans donated their pennies, nickels, dimes, and quarters to pay for this elegant house of worship.

St. Patrick's Cathedral is a Gothic building made of white marble and stone that seats approximately 2,400 people. The St. Michael and St. Louis altar was designed by Tiffany's, and the St. Elizabeth altar was designed by Paolo Medici of Rome. The cathedral also contains a statue of St. Elizabeth Ann Seton, the first American-born saint.

The stained-glass windows came from Chartres, France; Birmingham, England; and Boston, Massachusetts. The cathedral's replica of Michelangelo's *Pieta* statue is three times larger than the original in Rome.

More than 3 million people visit St. Patrick's Cathedral every year. Pope Paul VI visited in 1964, Pope John Paul II visited in 1979, and Pope Benedict XVI visited in 2008. St. Patrick's hosted the most funerals of the firefighters who died during the aftermath of the terrorist attack on the World Trade Center on September 11, 2001. Wakes and/or funeral masses were also held there for Senator Robert F. Kennedy, Governor Alfred E. Smith, and Prime Minister Jan Ignace Paderewski of Poland, as well as for Babe Ruth, Vince Lombardi, and Joe DiMaggio.

St. Spiridon Orthodox Cathedral

St. Spiridon was an Eastern Orthodox Christian saint who lived in the fourth century. This cathedral dedicated in his honor is in Seattle, Washington, and was built by the Orthodox Church in America (OCA) in 1895 to minister to the needs of Greek, Russian, and Serbian immigrants of the Orthodox faith.

The Greeks formed their own church in 1918 and built St. Demetrios Greek Orthodox Church in 1921. An estimated 6,000 Russian refugees fled Communist persecution and traveled to Seattle in the aftermath of the Bolshevik Revolution in Russia in 1917. The current cathedral was built in 1941 and resembles the famous onion-domed Russian churches, whereas the old St. Spiridon looked more like the typical New England Puritan-style meetinghouses.

Chapter 22

Ten Saintly Families

*T*his chapter introduces the ten most famous saintly families, from the Holy Family of Jesus, Mary, and Joseph to St. Cyril and St. Methodius.

There's no such thing as a "holiness gene," so when more than one member of a family becomes a saint, it's likely because of good examples rather than good ancestry. One saintly member of a family has a profound influence on his relatives, particularly his siblings.

Jesus, Mary, and Joseph

The most obvious family of saints is the Holy Family: Jesus, Mary, and Joseph. Though Joseph wasn't the biological father of Jesus, his marriage to Mary created a legal paternal bond, according to both the ancient world and Hebrew culture.

Saints Matthew and Luke give detailed genealogies for Jesus through his adopted father, showing that Joseph is a descendant of both King Solomon and King David, as well as Abraham, Isaac, and Jacob. St. Luke's list takes the genealogy back to Adam.

Joseph is noted in the Bible when Jesus was 12 years old and went missing. Mary and Joseph find him three days later in the Temple of Jerusalem, teaching the teachers. Little else is said about Joseph in the Bible except that he's the husband of Mary and the father of Jesus.

Some Eastern Orthodox churches believe Joseph may have had other children from a previous marriage in which his wife died, but the Catholic Church believes he had no other children. Rather, Joseph may have inherited nieces and nephews from a deceased brother or sister.

We detail the Holy Family's story in Chapter 2, beginning with Mary learning that she, a virgin betrothed to the carpenter Joseph, would give birth to the Christ child, and running through Jesus's life, death, and resurrection.

St. Joachim and St. Ann (Grandparents)

Mary's parents, Joachim and Ann, are named in the apocryphal Gospel of James, a writing that's considered not to have been divinely inspired and is therefore not included in the Catholic Bible. The two aren't named at all in the Gospels of Matthew, Mark, Luke, or John, but they're mentioned in several non-canonical, or unofficial, Scripture sources. Joachim and Ann are believed to be Jesus's maternal grandparents and are the patron saints of all grandparents. Because Mary was probably in her late teens when she married Joseph, it's entirely possible that Joachim and Ann were not only still alive for the birth of their grandson but also may have visited on occasion.

St. Elizabeth, St. Zachariah, and St. John the Baptist (Cousins of the Lord)

The Gospel of Luke identifies Elizabeth as Mary's cousin and Zachariah as Elizabeth's husband. The couple is childless and elderly when Gabriel visits Zachariah and tells him his barren wife will give birth to a son. Zachariah, in his shock and disbelief, is speechless until the child, John the Baptist, is born. Mary visits Elizabeth during her sixth month of pregnancy, when Mary herself is just a few days into her own pregnancy. The meeting of the two women is called the Visitation and is one of the Joyful Mysteries of the Rosary (see Chapter 2).

When Mary enters Elizabeth's room, Elizabeth's unborn child leaps for joy inside his mother as he miraculously recognizes the presence of the Savior. Still inside his mother's womb, John the Baptist starts his mission to announce the arrival of the Messiah. John is not mentioned again until the two young cousins have grown to adulthood.

John the Baptist was so named not because he belonged to the Baptist Church (which was established by John Smyth in 1608) but because he baptized people at the Jordan River. The Greek word *baptizein* means to wash; John was symbolically washing the faithful in preparation for the Savior and Redeemer (Jesus), so he was given the title "the Baptist."

John baptized Jesus at the Jordan. The two aren't mentioned together again until Jesus learns of his cousin's death three years later (see Chapter 6).

St. Martha, St. Mary, and St. Lazarus

Martha, Mary, and Lazarus were siblings with whom Jesus established a close friendship as an adult. Scholars believe that the four were very close, and Jesus spent time relaxing with this family during his three-year mission.

The Gospel of John states that Jesus wept at Lazarus's tomb, only the second time the Bible mentions him crying. (The first is when Jesus weeps over the city of Jerusalem as he prophesies its destruction, later done by the Romans.) Jesus's tears show the crowd the depth of the men's friendship, and the Gospel of John tells how Jesus raises Lazarus from the dead after he's in the tomb for four days.

St. Peter and St. Andrew

Peter and his brother Andrew were fishermen and some of the first men whom Jesus chose to be his apostles. Andrew was first a disciple of John the Baptist when he encountered Jesus; upon realizing that Jesus was the Messiah, he went to his brother Peter and introduced him to Christ. Jesus invited both brothers to join him to become "fishers of men," meaning that they would catch souls by preaching the Gospel.

Jesus gives Peter charge of the Church in Matthew 16:18, and Peter is therefore considered the first Bishop of Rome and the first pope; he was martyred in the capital of the empire around AD 64.

Peter's brother Andrew got as far as Greece before his martyrdom and is the patron saint of Scotland and Russia. Peter was crucified upside down, as he felt unworthy to die exactly like Jesus did on Good Friday (he denied knowing Christ three times the day Jesus died). Andrew was crucified on a cross that resembled the letter X.

St. James and St. John

James and John were brothers and were fishermen like Peter and Andrew. Their mother asked Jesus if her sons could sit to the right and left of him, securing a good assignment. The other apostles were jealous, but Jesus did often call on the two siblings, along with Peter. One such example is the Transfiguration, when Jesus took just Peter, James, and John up Mount Tabor, where Moses and Elijah appeared out of nowhere and stood side by side next to Jesus. Peter, James, and John also accompanied Jesus to the Garden of Gethsemane to pray before his Crucifixion, only to be found asleep three times by Christ.

John is the author of one of the four Gospels, an epistle, and the last book of the Bible, the Book of Revelation (also known as the Apocalypse). He is called the Beloved Disciple because, among the 12 Apostles, he was conspicuously the best friend to Jesus. James is called the Greater to distinguish him from the other St. James the Apostle, known as the Less, so named only because of the chronological meetings of the two men and Jesus.

According to pious tradition, James preached all the way to Spain before his death by Herod's sword, whereas John died a natural death of old age, probably around age 100. One attempt was made to boil John alive in hot oil, but he didn't die (see Chapter 3). Exiled to the island of Patmos, St. John ended up in Ephesus, where he had previously spent many years taking care of the Virgin Mary.

St. Macrina the Elder, Grandmother of St. Macrina the Younger, Basil the Great, St. Gregory of Nyssa, and St. Peter of Sebaste

Macrina the Elder lived in the last half of the third century AD and the first half of the fourth. She was the mother of St. Basil the Elder and had a great influence on her family, as evidenced by the numerous saints who came from that same gene pool. Basil the Elder and his wife Emmelia had several children who became saints, including Basil the Great, Gregory, Peter, and Macrina the Younger.

The family lived during the Roman persecution of Diocletian and never abandoned the faith, as did some of their contemporaries. Basil the Great is known as the father of Eastern monasticism, and he and Gregory are also recognized as Eastern Fathers of the Church (see Chapter 16).

St. Felicity and Her Sons: St. Januarius, St. Felix, St. Philip, St. Silvanus, St. Alexander, St. Vitalis, and St. Martial

Felicity of Rome lived in the second century AD and was devoted to the poor. She was arrested for her faith and ordered to worship pagan gods. Her seven sons — Januarius, Felix, Philip, Silvanus, Alexander, Vitalis, and Martial — were arrested when she refused. They were ordered to worship the Roman deities, and they followed their mother's example and refused to commit idolatry.

After they made several appeals to judges, all of which were rejected, Emperor Antonius ordered the mother and her sons executed. Felicity was forced to watch her children murdered one by one, yet none of them flinched and none denied the Christian faith.

St. Benedict and St. Scholastica

Benedict and Scholastica (see Chapter 9) were sixth-century twins and co-founders of Western monasticism. St. Benedict started many monasteries of men, later to be known as Benedictines, while his sister Scholastica established monasteries for women. Monastic life involves a commitment to one place (monastery) and daily prayer and work (*ora et labora* in Latin).

St. Benedict established the monasteries of Subiaco and Monte Cassino, both famous sites in Italy and still fully functioning monasteries to this day. St. Scholastica set up a monastery of Benedictine nuns 5 miles from Monte Cassino in a town called Plombariola.

The two met once a year and conferred on spiritual matters, as they regarded the residents of their monasteries as their spiritual brothers and sisters.

St. Boris and St. Gleb

Boris and Gleb were brothers, sons of St. Vladimir I of Kiev and grandchildren of St. Olga, the first Christian queen of Ukraine. They lived in tenth-century Ukraine. Vladimir continued his mother's work of promoting the Christian religion in the realm.

After Vladimir's death, the kingdom was supposed to be divided among his sons, but Boris and Gleb's eldest half-brother Svyatopolk, who denied the faith and despised his brothers' religiosity, greedily sought to rule alone. Boris was supported by an army but he called them off, explaining that he couldn't raise a hand against his own brother, no matter how badly his brother treated him. Boris was later martyred by Svyatopolk's henchmen. Svyatopolk invited Gleb to Kiev, but Gleb was martyred on the journey.

St. Cosmas and St. Damian

Cosmas and Damian were twin brothers who lived near the seaport of Aegea (modern-day Ayas in Turkey) in the Gulf of Issus in the third century AD. They were both physicians, and neither charged anyone for medical services. Patrons of pharmacists, these two were martyred under the Roman persecution of Diocletian.

Their most famous miraculous cure was the grafting of a leg from a recently deceased Ethiopian to replace a patient's ulcerated leg. According to pious tradition, they were hung on a cross and subsequently stoned, shot with arrows, and finally beheaded.

St. Cyril and St. Methodius

Cyril and Methodius were brothers who lived in the eighth century AD. Born in Thessalonica, Greece, they became missionaries to Eastern Europe and spread the Christian faith to the Slavic peoples. Their message got as far as Russia.

Their feast day is February 14, also known as St. Valentine's Day. Pope John Paul II named them copatrons of Europe (along with St. Benedict of Nursia) in 1980 because of their mutual influence on the spread of the faith. Cyril is given credit for devising the Cyrillic alphabet, which the Russians still use today.

Part VII
Appendixes

The 5th Wave   By Rich Tennant

"I used to celebrate all the saints' feast days until my bathroom scale told me I was becoming a little too saintly."

In this part . . .

No book on saints would be complete without giving you the information you really need: who to call on when you need assistance with a particular circumstance or issue. For example, if you're missing something, you can look up the patron saint of lost items (St. Anthony) and ask for his help. If you have eyesight troubles, you can look up the patron saint of that malady (St. Lucy) and seek her intercession. We also give you a long list of patron saints for places (like St. Patrick and Ireland) and for occupations (like St. Joseph Cupertino and airline pilots).

While we're at it, we provide a comprehensive listing of feast days for the saints, starting with the Solemnity of Mary on January 1 and going clear through to the Feast of Pope Sylvester on December 31.

Helping Hands: A Listing of Patron Saints

From accountants to writers, there's a patron saint for just about everyone. This listing of patron saints for occupations, hobbies, illnesses, and other characterizations is a helpful reference tool, particularly as you read the chapters on the saints and the lives they lived. Think of this appendix as the Yellow Pages for heaven, listing the various holy men and women and their respective areas of spiritual intercession.

Accountants: St. Matthew

Actors: St. Genesius of Rome

Adopted children: St. Thomas More

Advertising: St. Bernadine of Siena

Air travelers: St. Joseph Cupertino

Amputees: St. Anthony

Animals: St. Francis of Assisi

Architects: SS. Barbara and Thomas the Apostle

Arthritis: St. James

Artillery: St. Barbara

Artists: St. Luke

Astronomers: St. Dominic

Athletes: St. Sebastian

Aviators: St. Joseph Cupertino

Bachelors: St. Christopher

Bakers: St. Honoratus

Bankers: St. Matthew

Barren women: St. Anthony

Basket makers: St. Hilarion

Birds: St. Francis of Assisi

Blacksmiths: St. Dunstan

Blindness: St. Lucy, Archangel Raphael

Bodily ills: Our Lady of Lourdes

Bookkeepers: St. Matthew

Boy scouts: St. George

Breast cancer: St. Agatha

Brewers: SS. Luke and Nicholas

Bricklayers: St. Stephen

Brides: St. Nicholas

Builders: St. Barbara

Cab drivers: St. Fiacre

Cabinetmakers: St. Anne

Cancer patients: St. Peregrine

Candle makers: St. Ambrose

Carpenters: St. Joseph

Cavalry: St. George

Charitable societies: St. Vincent de Paul

Chemists: St. Albert the Great

Childbirth: SS. Anne and Gerard

Children: St. Nicholas, Infant of Prague

Chivalry: St. George

Churches: St. Joseph

Civil servants: St. Thomas More

Clergy: St. Charles

Comedians: St. Maturinus

Common cold: St. Quentin

Composers: St. Cecilia

Computer science: St. Isidore of Seville

Conception: Archangel Gabriel

Cooks: SS. Lawrence and Martha

Court workers: St. Thomas More

Cramps: St. Maurice

Cranky children: St. Sebastian

Dancers: St. Vitus

Deacons: SS. Stephen and Lawrence

Dentists: St. Apollonia

Desperation: SS. Jude and Rita

Diabetes: St. Paulina

Dieticians: St. Martha

Difficult marriages: St. Thomas More

Diplomats: Archangel Gabriel

Doctors: St. Luke

Dog bites: St. Hubert

Dog lovers: St. Roch (St. Rocco)

Domestic workers: St. Martha

Doubters: St. Joseph

Druggists: Archangel Raphael

Dying: SS. Barbara and Joseph

Editors: St. John Bosco

EMTs: St. Luke

Engineers: St. Joseph

Environmentalists: St. Francis of Assisi

Epilepsy: St. Vitus

Eye diseases: Archangel Raphael, St. Lucy

Faith: St. Anthony

Falsely accused: SS. Gerard and Padre Pio

Families: Jesus, Mary, and St. Joseph

Family harmony: St. Dymphna

Farmers: SS. Isidore of Seville and George

Fathers: St. Joseph

Fever: SS. Peter and Hugh of Cluny

Fire: St. Lawrence

Firefighters: St. Florian

Fireworks: St. Barbara

Fishermen: SS. Andrew and Peter

Florists: St. Theresa

Foot trouble: St. Peter

Gardeners: SS. Fiacre and Rose of Lima

Geologists: St. Eligius

Glass industry: St. Luke

Glaziers: St. Mark

Goldsmiths: St. Luke

Gout sufferers: St. Andrew

Grandmothers: St. Anne

Gravediggers: St. Anthony

Greetings: St. Valentine

Grocers: Archangel Michael

Hairdressers: St. Martin de Porres

Happy death: St. Joseph

Hardware: St. Sebastian

Headaches: St. Denis

Hermits: St. Hilarion

Hernias: St. Conrad of Piacenza

Hesitation: St. Joseph

HIV-AIDS patients: St. Lazarus of Dives

Home sellers/buyers: St. Joseph

Horsemen: St. Anne

Hospital administrators: St. Basil the Great

Hospital staff: St. Martin de Porres

Housekeepers: St. Anne

Housewives: St. Anne

Hunters: St. Hubert

Immigrants: St. Francis Xavier (Mother) Cabrini

Impossible causes: SS. Jude and Rita

Incest victims: St. Dymphna

Infertility: St. Anthony

Insanity: St. Dymphna

Invalids: St. Roch (St. Rocco)

Jewelers: St. Luke

Jurists: St. Juan Capistrano

Laborers: SS. Joseph and James

Lawyers: SS. Genesius and Thomas More

Leather workers: St. Crispin

Librarians: St. Jerome

Lightning: St. Barbara

Locksmiths: St. Dunstan

Loneliness: St. Rita

Long life: St. Peter

Lost articles: St. Anthony

Lovers: St. Valentine, Archangel Raphael

Lumbago: St. Lawrence

Machinists: St. Hubert

Marital fidelity: St. Monica

Mental illness: St. Dymphna

Merchants: St. Francis of Assisi

Messengers: Archangel Gabriel

Midwives: St. Raymond

Milliners: St. Catherine

Miners: St. Barbara

Missing persons: St. Anthony

Missions: SS. Theresa and Paul

Monks: St. Benedict

Motorcyclists: Our Lady of the Miraculous Medal

Musicians: St. Cecilia

Navigators: O.L. Star of the Sea

Needleworkers: St. Francis of Assisi

Nerves: St. Dymphna

Notaries: SS. Luke and Mark

Nurses: SS. Agatha and Camillus

Organ makers: St. Genesius

Orphans: St. Louise

Painters: St. Luke

Paramedics: St. Luke

Paratroopers: Archangel Michael

Pawnbrokers: St. Nicholas

Peddlers: St. Lucy

Peril at sea: Archangel Michael

Pharmacists: SS. Cosmas and Damian

Philosophers: SS. Catherine Alexandria and Thomas Aquinas

Physicians: St. Luke

Physicists: St. Albert the Great

Pioneers: St. Joseph

Plague victims: St. Roch (St. Rocco)

Plasterers: St. Bartholomew

Poets: St. David

Poison sufferers: St. Benedict

Police officers: Archangel Michael

Polio: St. Margaret Mary

Porters: St. Christopher

Postal workers: Archangel Gabriel

Potters: St. Sebastian

Preachers: St. Dominic de Guzman

Pregnant women: St. Gerard

Priests: St. John Vianney

Printers: St. Augustine

Prisoners: St. Barbara

Prisoners of war: St. Leonard

Public relations: St. Paul

Publishing: St. John Bosco

Race relations: St. Martin de Porres

Radio: Archangel Gabriel

Radiologists: Archangel Michael

Realtors: St. Joseph

Rheumatism: St. James

Sailors: SS. Brendan and Elmo

Salesmen: St. Lucy

Scholars and schools: St. Thomas Aquinas

Scientists: St. Albertus Magnus

Sculptors: St. Claude

Secretaries: St. Genesius

Seminarians: St. Charles

Servants: St. Martha

Service women: St. Joan of Arc

Shipbuilders: St. Peter

Shoemakers: SS. Crispin and Crispinian

Sick people: St. Camillus

Singers: SS. Gregory and Cecilia

Skaters: St. Lidwina

Skin disease: St. Peregrine

Snake bites: St. Patrick

Social justice: St. Joseph

Soldiers: SS. George, Joan of Arc, and Martin of Tours

Steelworkers: St. Sebastian

Stenographers: St. Cassian of Tangiers

Stockbrokers: St. Matthew

Stomach trouble: St. Charles Borromeo

Stone carvers: St. Peter

Storms: St. Barbara

Stress: St. (Padre) Pio of Pietrelcina

Students: St. Thomas Aquinas

Surgeons: SS. Cosmas and Damian

Tanners: St. James

Tax collectors: St. Matthew

Teachers: St. Gregory

Television: St. Clare, Archangel Gabriel

Temptation: Archangel Michael

Theologians: St. Thomas Aquinas

Throat trouble: SS. Cecilia and Blaise

Tongue trouble: St. Catherine

Toothaches: St. Patrick

Travel safety: St. Christopher

Truck drivers: St. Christopher

Tuberculosis: St. Theresa

Tumors: St. Rita

Ulcers: St. Charles

Undertakers: St. Dismas

Universal Church: St. Joseph

Veterinarians: SS. James and Francis of Assisi

Victims of poverty: St. Martin de Porres

Victims of religious persecution: St. Sebastian

Vocalists: St. Cecilia

Waiters/waitresses: St. Zita

Watchmakers: SS. Joseph and Peter

Widows: St. Paula

Workingmen: St. Joseph

Writers: SS. Lucy, Catherine Sienna, and Jerome

Appendix B

Patron Saints of Countries and Places

• •

*J*ust as there are patron saints for people and occupations, so are there saints for places. Some saints are patrons of their homeland, while others are patrons of the country where they worked and died. Here's a quick reference, matching locations with their patron saints.

Africa

St. Moses the Black

Algeria

Our Lady of Africa

St. Cyprian of Carthage

Americas; New World

Our Lady of Guadalupe

St. Isaac Jogues and companions

St. Joseph

St. Mary Ann de Paredes

St. Rose of Lima

Angola

Immaculate Heart of Mary

Argentina

Immaculate Conception of Mary

Our Lady of Lujan

St. Francis Solano

St. Laura Vicuna

Armenia

St. Bartholomew the Apostle

St. Gregory the Illuminator

Australia

Our Lady Help of Christians

St. Francis Xavier

Austria

Our Lady of Mariazell

St. Colman of Stockerau

St. Florian

St. Joseph

St. Leopold the Good

St. Maurice

St. Severinus of Noricum

Belgium

Our Lady of Baeuraing

Our Lady of Banneux

St. Joseph

Bolivia

Our Lady of Capucdana

Our Lady of Mount Carmel

St. Francis Solano

Virgin de la Candelaria

Virgin of Copacabana

Borneo

St. Francis Xavier

Brazil

Our Lady of Nazareth

Our Lady of the Immaculate Conception

Our Lady Who Appeared

St. Anthony of Padua

St. Peter of Alcantara

Bulgaria

SS. Cyril and Methodius

Canada

Mary of the Hurons

Our Lady of the Cape

St. Anne

St. George

St. Isaac Jogues

St. John de Brébeuf

St. Joseph

Central America

Our Lady of Guadalupe

St. Rose of Lima

Chile

Our Lady of Mount Carmel

St. Francis Solano

St. James the Greater

China

St. Francis Xavier

St. Joseph

Colombia

Our Lady of Chiquinquira

Our Lady of the Rosary

St. Louis Bertran

St. Peter Claver

Congo; Zaire; Belgian Congo

Immaculate Conception of Mary

Our Lady, Queen of Nations

Costa Rica

Our Lady of the Angels

Crete

St. Titus

Croatia

St. Joseph

Cuba

Our Lady of Charity of El Cobre

Virgin de Regla

Cyprus

St. Barnabas

Czechoslovakia; Czech Republic

St. Adalbert

SS. Cyril and Methodius

St. John Nepomucene

St. Ludmila

St. Procopius

St. Sigismund

St. Vitus

St. Wenceslaus

Denmark

St. Anskar

St. Canute

Dominican Republic

Our Lady of High Grace

St. Dominic de Guzman

East Indies

St. Francis Xavier

Thomas the Apostle

Ecuador

Most Pure Heart of Mary

Our Lady of Quinche

Sacred Heart of Jesus

Egypt

St. Mark the Evangelist

El Salvador

Our Lady of Peace

England

Our Lady of Mount Carmel at Aylesford

Our Lady of Walsingham

St. Augustine of Canterbury

St. Cuthbert

St. George

St. Gregory the Great

Equatorial Guinea

Our Lady of the Immaculate Conception

Ethiopia

St. Frumentius

Europe

St. Benedict

St. Bridget of Sweden

St. Catherine of Siena

SS. Cyril and Methodius

St. Teresa Benedicta of the Cross

Finland

St. Henry of Uppsala

France

Our Lady of LaSallette

Our Lady of Lourdes

Our Lady of Pontmain

Our Lady of the Assumption

Our Lady of the Miraculous Medal

St. Denis

St. Joan of Arc

St. Martin of Tours

St. Remigius

St. Thérèse of Liseux

Georgia, former USSR

St. George

St. Nino

Germany

Archangel Michael

Our Lady of Altotting

Our Lady of Kevelaer

St. Boniface

St. George

St. Peter Canisius

St. Swithbert

Gibraltar

Our Lady of Europe

St. Bernard of Clairvaux

Gozo

St. George

Greece

The Holy Mountain of
Our Lady

St. Andrew the Apostle

St. George

St. Nicholas of Myra

Guatemala

Our Lady of the Rosary

St. James the Greater

Haiti

Our Lady of Perpetual Help

Honduras

Our Lady of Suyapa

Hungary

Our Lady of Hungary

St. Astricus

St. Gerard Sagredo

St. Stephen of Hungary

Iceland

St. Thorlac Thorhallsson

India

Our Lady of Bandel

Our Lady of Bandra

Our Lady of the Assumption

St. Rose of Lima

St. Thomas the Apostle

Iran; Persia

St. Maruthas

Ireland

Our Lady of Knock

Our Lady of Limerick

St. Brigid of Ireland

St. Columba

St. Kevin

St. Patrick

Isle of Man

St. Maughold

Italy

Our Lady of Loreto

Our Lady of Perpetual Help

Our Lady of Pompeii

Our Lady of Tears

Our Lady of the Snow

St. Bernadine of Siena

St. Catherine of Siena

St. Francis of Assisi

Jamaica

Mary of the Assumption

Japan

Our Lady of Japan

St. Francis Xavier

St. Peter Baptist

Korea

Mary the Blessed Virgin

St. Joseph

Latin America

St. Rose of Lima

Lithuania

St. Casimir of Poland

St. Cunegundes

St. George

St. John of Dukla

St. John of Kanty

Luxembourg

St. Cunegundes

St. Philip the Apostle

St. Willibrord

Macedonia

St. Clement of Ohrid

Madagascar

St. Vincent de Paul

Malta

St. George

St. Paul the Apostle

Mexico

Our Lady of Guadalupe

St. Elias Nieves

St. Joseph

Monaco

St. Devota

Moravia

SS. Cyril and Methodius

St. Wenceslaus

Netherlands; Holland

St. Bavo

St. Plechelm

St. Willibrord

New Zealand

St. Francis Xavier

St. Our Lady Help of Christians

Nicaragua

Our Lady of the Immaculate Conception of El Viejo

St. James the Greater

Nigeria

Our Lady Queen of Nigeria

St. Patrick

North Africa

St. Cyprian of Carthage

Norway

St. Olaf II

Oceania

Mary, Queen of Peace

St. Peter Chanel

Pakistan

St. Thomas the Apostle

Palestine

St. George

Panama

Immaculate Conception

Immaculate Heart of Mary

St. Mary of La Antigua

Paraguay

Our Lady of Lujan

Our Lady of the Assumption

Our Lady of the Miracles of Caacupé

St. Francis Solano

Peru

Our Lady of Mercy

St. Francis Solano

St. Joseph

St. Martin de Porres

St. Rose of Lima

St. Turibius of Mogroveio

Philippines

Immaculate Heart of Mary

Our Lady of the Turumba

St. Rose of Lima

Poland

Our Lady of Czestochowa

St. Adalbert of Prague

St. Casimir of Poland

St. Cunegundes

St. Florian

St. Hyacinth

St. John of Kanty

St. Stanislaus of Cracow

Portugal

Archangel Gabriel

Our Lady of Fatima

Our Lady of the Immaculate Conception

St. Anthony of Padua

St. Francis Borgia

St. George

St. John de Brito

St. Vincent of Saragossa

Puerto Rico

Mary, Our Lady of Providence

Romania

St. Nicetas

Russia

St. Andrew the Apostle

St. Basil the Great

SS. Boris and Gleb

St. Nicholas of Myra

St. Thérèse of Lisieux

St. Vladimir I of Kiev

San Marino

St. Marinus

Scandinavia

St. Anskar

Scotland

St. Andrew the Apostle

St. Columba

St. Margaret of Scotland

St. Palladius

Serbia

St. Sava

Sicily

Andrew Avellino

St. Agatha

St. Ciro

St. Lucy

St. Nicholas of Myra

St. Rosalia

Slovakia

Our Lady of the Assumption

South Africa

Our Lady of Shongweni

Our Lady of the Assumption

South America

St. Rose of Lima

Spain

Our Lady of Guadalupe of Estremadura

Our Lady of Montserrat

Our Lady of Ransom

Our Lady of the Pillar of Saragossa

St. James the Greater

St. John of Avila

St. Teresa of Avila

Sri Lanka (formerly Ceylon)

Our Lady of Madhu

St. Lawrence

St. Thomas the Apostle

Sudan

St. Josephine Bakhita

Sweden

St. Anskar

St. Bridget of Sweden

St. Eric of Sweden

St. Gall

St. Sigfrid

Switzerland

Our Lady of the Hermits

St. Gall

St. Nicholas of Flue

Syria

St. Barbara

Tanzania

Our Lady of the Immaculate Conception

Tunisia

Immaculate Conception of Mary

Uganda

Mary, Queen of Africa

Ukraine

St. Josaphat

United States

Immaculate Conception of Mary

Our Lady of Victory

Uruguay

Blessed Virgin Mary

Our Lady of Lujan

Our Lady of the Thirty-Three

St. James the Lesser

St. Philip the Apostle

Venezuela

Our Lady of Coromoto

Vietnam

Our Lady of La Vang

St. Joseph

Wales

St. David of Wales

West Indies

St. Gertrude the Great

St. Gregory the Great

St. Rose of Lima

Yugoslavia (former; now patron of Dubrovnik, Croatia)

St. Blaise

SS. Cyril and Methodius

Appendix C

Calendar of Feast Days for the Saints

• •

*E*ach day of the calendar year is a day of celebration in the Catholic Church. Jesus, Mary, and the saints are honored on various days, either with solemnity days or feast days. *Solemnities* are the highest ranking days and are usually holy days of obligation, while *feast days* generally include specific Scripture readings and prayers.

The feast days listed in bold in this appendix are obligatory observances for the Catholic Church in the United States. The others are either optional or are observed in other countries. Feasts of Our Lord Jesus Christ or the Blessed Virgin Mary are listed in bold italics.

January

1 — ***Solemnity of Mary, Mother of God;*** St. Clarus; Blessed Berka Zdislava; St. William of Dijon; St. Telemachus; St. Odilo; St. Almachius; St. Basil; St. Concordius; St. Connat; St. Cuan; SS. Elvan and Mydwyn; St. Eugendus; St. Euphrosyne; St. Fulgentius; St. Fanchea; St. Joseph Mary Tommasi; St. Justin of Chieti; St. Maelrhys; St. Magnus.

2 — **SS. Basil the Great & Gregory Nazianzen;** St. Adelard; St. Caspar del Bufalo; St. Gaspar; St. Adalard; St. Argeus; St. Aspasius; St. Blidulf; St. Seraphim of Sarov; St. Artaxus; St. Martinian; St. Munchin.

3 — St. Genevieve; St. Bertilia; St. Blitmund; SS. Zosimus and Athanasius; St. Wenog; SS. Theopemptus and Theonas; St. Cyrinus; St. Daniel; St. Finlugh; St. Fintan; St. Florentius of Vienne; St. Narses.

4 — **St. Elizabeth Ann Seton;** Blessed Angela of Foligno; St. Aquilinus; Blessed Thomas Plumtree; St. Dafrosa; St. Ferreolus; St. Hermes; St. Libentius; St. Rigobert; St. Mavilus; St. Pharaildis; St. Abraham.

5 — St. John Neumann; St. Charles of Sezze; St. Rogers; St. Syncletica; St. Apollinaris Syncletica; St. Talida; St. Cera; St. Convoyon; St. Emiliana; St. Gaudentius; St. Gerlac; St. John Nepomucene Neumann; St. Lomer; Martyrs of Egypt; St. Paula.

6 — Epiphany; Blessed Andre Bessette; St. Melanie; St. Anastasius VIII; St. Wiltrudis; St. Schotin; St. Diman; St. Edeym; St. Eigrad; St. Erminold; St. Hywyn; St. John de Ribera; St. Macra; St. Melanius; St. Merinus; St. Peter of Canterbury.

7 — St. Raymond Pennafort; St. Aidric; St. Anastasius XVIII; St. Brannock; St. Valentine; St. Theodore of Egypt; St. Tillo; St. Canute Lavard; St. Clerus; St. Crispin; St. Cronan Beg; Blessed Edward Waterson; St. Emilian; SS. Felix and Januarius; St. Julian of Cagliari; St. Kentigema; St. Lucian of Antioch; St. Reinold; St. Nicetas of Remesiana.

8 — St. Thorfinn; St. Apollinaris; St. Albert of Cashel; St. Athelm; St. Atticus; St. Wulsin; SS. Theophilus and Helladius; St. Severinus; St. Carteris; St. Ergnad; St. Arhard; St. Eugenian; St. Frodobert; St. Garibaldus; St. Gudula; St. Lucian; St. Maximus.

9 — St. Adrian, abbot; St. Brithwald; St. Vatalicus; St. Waningus; St. Epicharis; St. Foellan; St. Julian and companions; St. Marciana; St. Maurontus; St. Paschasia; St. Abhor (Amba Hor).

10 — St. William of Bourges; St. Thomian; St. Saethryth; St. Dermot; St. John Camillus the Good; St. Marcian; St. Nicanor; St. Peter Urseolus; St. Petronius.

11 — St. Alex; St. Anastasius X; St. Boadin; St. Brandan; St. Vitalis of Gaza; St. Theodosius; St. Theodosius of Antioch; St. Theodosius the Cenobiarch; St. Salvius; SS. Ethenea and Fidelmia; St. Honorata; St. Hyginus, pope; St. Leucius of Brindisi; St. Palaemon; SS. Paldo, Tato, and Taso; SS. Peter, Severus, and Leucius.

12 — St. Tatiana; St. Arcadius; St. Caesaria; St. Martina; St. Anthony Mary Pucci; St. Bartholomew Alvarez; St. Victorian of Asan; Blessed Vincent de Cunha; St. Zoticus; SS. Tigrius and Eutropius; St. Salvius; St. Satyrus; Ephesus Martyrs; Blessed John Gaspard Cratz; St. John of Ravenna; St. Martin of Leon.

13 — St. Hilary of Poitiers; Blessed Yvette; St. Elian; St. Agrecius; St. Andrew of Trier; St. Viventius; St. Enogatus; St. Erbin; St. Glaphyra; St. Gumesindus; St. Hermylus; St. Kentigen Mungo; St. Leontius of Cuesaren.

14 — St. Felix of Nola; St. Sava; St. Barbasymas; St. Datius; St. Deusdedit; St. Euphrasius; St. Felix; St. Macrina the Elder; Martyrs of Mount Sinai; Martyrs of Raithu.

15 — St. Bonitus; St. Ita; St. Arnold Jansen; St. Blaithmaic; St. Tarsicia; St. Teath; St. Sawl; St. Secundina; St. Ceolwulf; St. Emebert; St. Ephysius; St. Eugyppius; Blessed Frances de Capillas; St. John Calabytes; SS. Liewellyn and Gwmerth; St. Lleudadd; St. Macarius the Great; St. Malard; SS. Maura and Britta; St. Maximus of Nola; St. Paul the Hermit; Blessed Peter of Castelnau; St. Abeluzius.

16 — St. Valerius; St. Titian; St. Triverius; St. Dunchaid O'Braoin; St. Fulgentius; St. Fursey; SS. Fusca and Marura; St. Henry of Cockct; St. Honoratus; St. James of Tarentaise; St. Liberata; St. Melas.

17 — St. Anthony the Abbot; Blessed Gonzalo de Amarante; St. Sulpicius; St. Achillas; St. Julian Sabas the Elder; St. Mildgytha; St. Pior.

18 — St. Ammonius; St. Archelais and companions; St. Volusian; St. Ulfrid; St. Vincenza Mary Lopez y Vicuna; St. Day; St. Deicola; St. Fazzio; St. Leobard; St. Liberata; SS. Moseus and Ammonius.

19 — St. Pontianus; St. Fillan; St. Henry of Sweden; St. Henry of Uppsala; St. Arcontius; St. Arsenius; St. Bassian; St. Branwallader; St. Wulfstan; St. Canute IV; St. Catellus; St. Contentius; St. Firminus; St. Germanicus; St. Remigus; Blessed Nathalan; St. Messalina; SS. Paul, Gerontius, and companions; St. Pontian; St. Absadah.

20 — Pope St. Fabian; St. Sebastian; St. Euthymius; St. Fechin; St. Maurus; St. Eustochium Calafato; St. Neophytus; St. Molagga; St. Abadios.

21 — St. Agnes; Blessed Inez; St. Meinrad; St. Alban Bartholomew Roe; St. Brigid; St. Vimin; Blessed Thomas Reynolds; Blessed Edward Stransham; St. Epiphanius; St. Fructuosus; St. Lawdog; St. Maccalin; St. Patroclus.

22 — St. Vincent the Deacon; St. Vincent Pallotti; St. Anastasius XIV; St. Blaesilla; St. Brithwald; St. Vincent of Digne; SS. Vincent, Orontius, and Victor; Blessed William Patenson; St. Dominic of Sora; St. Francis Gil de Frederich; St. Matthew Alonso Leziniana; St. Paschasius.

23 — St. Ildephonsus; St. Agathangelus; St. Amasius; St. Asclas; St. Barnard; SS. Severian and Aquila; St. Colman of Lismore; St. Emerentiana; St. Eusebius; St. Henry Suso; St. John the almonter; St. Luthfild; St. Maimbod; St. Ormond; St. Parmenas; St. Abakuh.

24 — St. Francis de Sales; St. Artemius; St. Barbylas; St. Bertre; St. Zama; Blessed William Irel; St. Thyrsus anjd Projectus; St. Cadoc; St. Exuperantius; St. Guasacht; Blessed John Grove; St. Macedonius; St. Mardoinus.

25 — Conversion of St. Paul the Apostle; St. Amarinus; St. Apollo; St. Artemas; St. Bretannion; St. Donatus; St. Dwynwen; St. Eochod; SS. Juventius and Maximus; St. Racho; St. Maurus; St. Peter Thomas.

26 — SS. Timothy and Titus; St. Paula; St. Margaret of Hungary; St. Alberic; St. Ansurius; St. Athanasius; St. Theofrid; St. Thordgith; St. Conan; St. Robert of Newmister.

27 — St. Angela Merici; St. Marius; St. Avitus; St. Theodoric of Orleans; St. Candida; St. Datius; St. Devota; St. Emerius; St. Gamo; St. Gamelbert; St. Gilduin; St. Julian of Le Mans; St. Julian of Sora; St. Lupus of Chalons; St. Natalis; St. Maurus.

28 — St. Thomas Aquinas; Blessed Amadeus of Lausanne; St. Antilnus; St. Valerius; SS. Thyrsus, Leucius, and Callinicus; St. Cannera; St. Flavian; St. Glastian; St. James the Hermit; St. Jerome Lu, Blessed; St. John of Reomay; St. Julian of Cuenca; Blessed Lawrence Wang; Blessed Roger of Todi; St. Richard of Vaucelles; St. Odo of Beauvais; St. Palladius; St. Paulinus of Aquileia; St. Petere Nolasco.

29 — St. Aquilinus; St. Blath; St. Voloc; St. Valerius; St. Sabinian; SS. Sarbelius and Barbea; St. Caesarius; SS. Papias and Maurinus.

30 — St. Hippolytus; St. Aldegunais; St. Aleaunie; St. Alexander; St. Armentarius; St. Barsimaeus; St. Bathildis; St. Tudy; St. Savina; St. Felician; St. Hyacinth; St. Martina; St. Matthias; St. Mutien-Marie Wiaux.

31 — St. John Bosco; St. Aidan; St. Syrus; St. Marcella; St. Adamnan of Coldingham; St. Aidan of Ferns; St. Athanasius; St. Bobinus; St. Ulphia; St. Tarskius; St. Trypbaena; SS. Saturninus, Thrysus, and Victor; St. Eusebius; St. Francis Xavier Bianchi; St. Geminian; St. Julius of Novara; St. Madoes; SS. Marana and Cyra; St. Martin Manuel; St. Nicetas; St. Metranus.

February

1 — St. Bridig of Irel and Blessed Andrew of Segni; Blessed Anthony Manzi; St. Brigid; St. Veridiana; St. Seiriol; St. Cinnia; St. Crewanna; St. Darulagdach; St. John of the Grating; St. Kinnia; St. Paul of Trois Chateaux; St. Pionius.

2 — Presentation of the Lord; St. Joanm de Lestonnac; St. Adalbald of Ostrevant; St. Adeloga; St. Apronian; St. Theodoric; St. Cornelius; Ebsdorf Martyrs; St. Feock; St. Flosculus; St. Fortunatus; St. Lawrence of Canterbury.

3 — St. Blaise; St. Ansgar; St. Laurentinus; St. Anatolius; St. Berlinda; St. Werburg; SS. Tigides and Remedius; St. Celerinus; St. Deodatus; St. Caellainn; St. Hadelin; Blessed John Nelson; St. Lawrence of Spoleto; St. Liafdag; SS. Lupicinus and Felix; St. Margaret; Blessed Rabanus Maurus; Blessed Odoric of Pordenone; St. Oliver; St. Philip of Vienne.

4 — St. Joan of Valois; St. Aldate; St. Andrew Corsini; St. Aventinus of Chartres; St. Vulgis; St. Vincent of Troyes; St. Theophilus the Penitent; St. John de Britto; Blessed John Speed; St. John Stone; St. Joseph of Leonissa; St. Liephard; St. Rembert; St. Nicholas Studites; St. Nithard; St. Obitius; St. Modan.

5 — St. Agatha; St. Abraham; St. Adelaide of Bellich; St. Avitus of Vienne; St. Vodoaldus; St. Leo Karasuma; St. Louis Ibachi; St. Modestus; St. Philip of Jesus.

6 — St. Paul Miki and companions; St. Mel; St. Dorothy; St. Am; Blessed Diego de Avezedo; St. Francis Nagasaki; St. Antholian; St. Anthony Dainan; St. Bonaventure of Miako; St. Tanco; St. Theophilus the Lawyer; St. Thomas Danki; St. Thomas Kozaki; SS. Saturninus, Theophilus, and Revocata; St. Cosmas; St. Francis of St. Michael; St. James Kisai; St. John Soan de Goto; St. Relindis; St. Mun; St. Martin de Aguirre; St. Martin Loynaz of the Ascension; St. Matthias of Meako; St. Michael Kozaki; St. Peter Shukeshiko.

7 — St. Richard; St. Adaucus; St. Amulwinus; St. Anatolius; St. Augulus; Blessed William Richardson; St. Theodore Stratelates; St. Tressan; St. Chrysolius; St. Fidelis; St. Julian of Bologna; St. Lawrence of Siponto; St. Luke the Younger; Blessed Rizzerio; St. Meldon; St. Moses.

8 — St. Jerome Emiliani; St. Josephone Bakhita; St. Cointha; St. Cuthman; St. Dionysius; St. Elfleda; St. Honoratus; St. Kigwe; St. Llibio; St. Nicetius of Besancon; St. Oncho; St. Meingold; SS. Paul Lucius and Cyriacus; St. Paul of Verdun; St. Peter Igneus.

9 — St. Apollonia; St. Alex; St. Alto; Blessed Alvarez of Cordoba; St. Ammon; St. Ansbert; St. Teilo; St. Cronan the Wise; St. Cuaran; St. Eingan; St. Raynald of Nocera; St. Nebridius; St. Nicephorus; St. Michael Febres Cordero.

10 — St. Scholastica; Blessed Alexander of Lugo; St. Andrew; St. Aponius; St. Austreberta; St. Baldegundis; St. William of Maleval; St. Trumwin; St. Paganus; St. Paul and ninety companions.

11 — Our Lady of Lourdes; St. Severinus; St. Paschal; St. Adolf of Osnabruck; St. Ardanus; St. Calocerus; St. Desiderius; St. Jonas; St. Lucius.

12 — St. Buonfiglio Monaldo; St. Febronia; St. Julian; St. Anthony Kauleas; St. Anthony of Saxony; St. Benedict Revelli; Blessed Thomas Hemerford; St. Damian; St. James Feun, Blessed; St. John of Nicomedia; St. Julian the Hospitaler; St. Juventius of Pavia; St. Ludan; St. Meletius of Antioch; St. Modestus; SS. Modestus and Ammonius; SS. Modestus and Julian.

13 — St. Catherine de Ricci; St. Agabus; Blessed Archangela Girlani; St. Benignus; St. Dyfnog; St. Ermengild; St. Gosbert; St. Huno; Blessed John Lantrua of Triora; St. Julian of Lyons; St. Lezin; St. Martinian; St. Modomnoc; St. Polyeuctus.

14 — SS. Cyril and Methodius; St. Valentine; St. Maro; St. Abraham of Carrhae; St. Antoninus of Sorrento; St. Auxentius; St. Theodosius; St. Contran; St. Dionysius; St. Eleuchadius; St. Nostrianus.

15 — St. Jordan; St. Walfrid; St. Faustinus; St. Agape; St. Berach; St. Winaman; St. Saturninus; St. Craton; St. Decorosus; St. Dochow; St. Druthmar; St. Jovita; St. Georgia; St. Farannan; St. Faustus; St. Joseph of Antioch; St. Quinidius.

16 — St. Daniel; St. Gilbert of Sempringham; St. Jeremy; St. Aganus; St. Elias and companions; St. Honestrus; St. Julian of Egypt; St. Juliana of Cumae; St. Onesimus.

17 — Seven Founders of the Servite Order; St. Alexis Falconieri; St. Benedict of Cagliari; St. Theodulus; St. Constabilis; St. Donatus; St. Fintan; St. Fortchem; St. Faustinus and companions; St. Habet Deus; St. Hugh dei Lippi Uggucioni; St. Julian of Caesarea; St. Loman; St. Manettus; St. Polychronius.

18 — St. Simon; St. Agatha Lin; St. Angilbert; Blessed William Harrington; St. Theotonius; St. Charalampias; St. Colman of Lindisfame; St. Flavian of Constantinople; Blessed John Pibush; SS. Leo and Paregorius; St. Lucius; Blessed Martin; St. Maximus.

19 — St. Alvarez; St. Alvarez of Corova; St. Auxibius; St. Barbatus; St. Beatus; St. Boniface of Lausanne; St. Valerius; St. Zambdas; St. Belina; Blessed Lucy; St. Odran.

20 — St. Amata; St. Bolcan; St. Valerius; St. Wulfric; SS. Tyrannio and Silvanus; St. Sadoth; St. Colgan; St. Eleutherius of Tournai; St. Leo of Catania; Martyrs of Tyre.

21 — St. Peter Damian; St. Avitus II of Clermont; St. Valerius; St. Verulus and companions; St. Severian; St. Felix of Metz; St. Gundebert; St. Paterius; Blessed Pepin; St. Peter of the Scribe.

22 — Chair of St. Peter; St. Margaret of Cortona; St. Aristion; St. Athanasius; St. Baradates; SS. Thalassius and Limuneus; St. Elwin; Blessed John the Saxon; St. Raynerius; Martyrs of Arabia; St. Maximian of Ravenna; St. Papias.

23 — St. Polycarp; St. Peter Damian; St. Cemeuf; St. Alexander Akimetes; St. Boswell; St. Zebinus; St. Willigis; St. Serenus the Gardener; St. Dositheus; St. Felix of Brescia; St. Florentius; St. Jurmin; St. Lazarus Zographos; St. Romana; St. Martha; St. Ordonius; St. Medrald; St. Milburga; St. Polycarp of Smyrna.

24 — St. Adela; St. Betto; St. Sergius; St. John Theristus; St. Modestus; St. Montanus; St. Primitiva.

25 — St. Tarasius; St. Walburga; Blessed Constantius; St. Ananias II; St. Aventanus; St. Victorinus; St. Saesarius of Nazianzus; Blessed Didacus Carvalho; St. Donatus; Blessed Dominic Lentini.

26 — St. Isabel of France; St. Alexander; St. Alexander of Alexandria; St. Victor; St. Dionysius of Augsburg; St. Fortunatus; St. Faustinian; St. Nestor; St. Papias.

27 — St. Leander of Seville; St. Alexander; St. Anne Line; St. Augustus Chapdelaine; St. Baldomerus; St. Thalelaeus; St. John of Gorze; Blessed Mark Barkworth.

28 — Blessed Villana; St. Cacrcalis; St. Hedwig, Blessed; St. Hillary, pope; St. Macarius; St. Romanus of Condat; St. Ruellinus.

March

1 — St. David; St. Aubin; St. Albinus; St. Monan; St. Herculaflus; SS. Hermes and Adrian; St. Leo Luke; St. Leo of Rouen; St. Lupercus; St. Rudsind; Adrianus.

2 — Blessed Charles the Good; St. Agnes of Boheinia; St. Willeic; St. Chad; St. Cynibild; St. Fergna; St. Gilstlian; SS. Jovinus and Basileus; Martyrs of Campania; St. Paul, Heraclius, and companions.

3 — St. Katharine Drexel; St. Cunegundes; St. Anselm of Nonantola; St. Arthelais; St. Winwaloc; St. Titian; St. Sacer; Blessed Mary Angela Truskowska; St. Calupan; St. Camilla; St. Cele-Christ; St. Cleonicus; St. Foila; St. Felix; SS. Hemiterius and Cheledonius; St. Lamalisse; St. Non; SS. Marinus and Asterius.

4 — St. Casimir; Blessed Humbert; St. Lucius I; St. Adrian; St. Appian; St. Basil and companions; St. Basinus; St. Casimir of Poland; St. Felix of Rhys; St. Owen; St. Peter of Pappacarbone; St. Placide Viel.

5 — St. John Joseph of the Cross; St. Piran; St. Virgilius of Arles; St. Theophilus; St. Caron; St. Carthach; St. Colman of Armagh; Blessed Dionysius Fugishima; St. Gerasimus; St. Kiernan; St. Olivia; SS. Phocas and Antioch.

6 — St. Colette; St. Baldred; St. Balther; St. Basil; St. Bilfrid; Sind Cadroe; St. Conon; Saont Fridolin; SS. Kyneburga, Kyneswide, and Tibba; St. Marcian; St. Ollegarius.

7 — SS. Perpetua and Felicity; St. Ardo; St. Theophylact; St. Deifer; St. Drausinus; St. Enodoch; Blessed John Ireland; Blessed John Larke; St. Paul of Prusa; St. Paul the Simple.

8 — St. John of God; St. Senan; St. Arian and companions; St. Beoadh; St. Veremundus; St. Vincent Kadlubek; St. Duthac; St. Julian of Toledo; St. Rhian; St. Quintilis; St. Ogmund; St. Philemon.

9 — St. Frances of Rome; St. Catherine of Bologna; St. Anthony; St. Bosa; St. Pacian.

10 — St. Anastasia Patricia; St. Marcarius of Jerusalem; St. John Ogilvie; St. Alexander; St. Attalas; St. Victor; St. Sedna; St. Codratus of Corinth; St. Droctoveus; St. Emilian; St. Himelin; St. Kessag; Martyrs of Armenia.

11 — St. Aurea; St. Constantine; St. Aengus; St. Armunia; St. Benedict Crispus; St. Vigilius; St. Teresa Margaret Redi; SS. Trophimus and Thalus; St. Candidus; St. Firmian; SS. Heraclis and Zosimus; St. Peter the Spaniard.

12 — St. Fina; St. Seraphina; St. Theophanes; St. Alphege; St. Bernard of Carinola; St. Vindician; St. Egdunus; Blessed Joseph Tshang-ta-Pong; Blessed Luigi Orine, Blessed; St. Mamilian; St. Maximilian; St. Mura McFeredach; St. Paul Aurelian; St. Nicomedia; St. Peter the Deacon.

13 — Bl Agnello of Pisa; St. Roderic; St. Agnellus of Pisa; St. Ansovinus; St. Urpasian; St. Theusetas; St. Sabinus; St. Heldrad; St. Kevoca; St. Macedonius; St. Ramirus and companions; SS. Roderic and Salomon; St. Nicephorus; St. Mochoemoc.

14 — St. Matilda; St. Mathilda; Blessed Ambrose Fernandez; St. Boniface Curitan; St. Diaconus; Blessed Dominic Jorjes; Martyrs of Valeria.

15 — St. Louise de Marillac; St. Matrona; St. Aristobulus; Blessed William Hart; St. Clement Maria Hofbauer; St. Leocrita; St. Mancius; St. Raymond of Fitero; St. Nicander; St. Menignus; St. Monaldus of Ancona.

16 — St. Abban; St. Hilary; St. Aninus; St. Abraham Kidunaja; St. Dentlin; St. Eusebia; St. Finian Lobhar; St. Finian Munnu; Blessed John Amias; Blessed John Cacciafronte; St. Julian Anazarbus; Blessed Robert Dalby; St. Megingaud.

17 — **St. Patrick;** St. Gertrude of Nivelles; St. Jan Sarkander; St. Joseph of Arimathea; St. Paul of Cyprus; Blessed Peter Lieuo.

18 — **St. Cyril of Jerusalem;** St. Alexander; Blessed Christian; St. Salvatore; St. Edward the Martyr; St. Ansellm of Lucca; SS. Trophimus and Eucarpius; St. Salvator of Horta; St. Frediano; SS. Narcissus and Felix.

19 — ***St. Joseph, Husband of Mary;*** St. Adrian; St. Gemus; St. John the Syrian of Pinna; St. Lactali; St. Landoald; St. Leontius; St. Quintius; St. Pancharius.

20 — Blessed John of Parma; St. Cuthbert; St. Alexandra and companions; St. Anastasius XVI; St. Archippus; St. Benignus; St. Urbitius; St. Wulfram; St. William of Penacorada; St. Tetricus; St. Herbert; SS. John, Sergius, and companions; St. Martin of Braga; St. Nicetas; St. Paul and companions; St. Photina.

21 — St. Enda; St. Birillus; St. Serapion the Scholastic; St. Lupicinus; St. Nicholas von Flue.

22 — St. Lea; St. Nicholas Owen; St. Basil of Ancyra; St. Benvenutus Scotivoli; St. Trien; St. Saturninus; SS. Callinica and Basilissa; St. Darerca; St. Deogratius; St. Epaphroditus; St. Octavian; St. Paul of Narbonne.

23 — **St. Turibius of Mongrovejo;** St. Fidelis; St. Benedict of Campania; St. Victorian; St. Theodulus; St. Toribio Alfonso de Mogrovejo; St. Domitius; St. Felix; St. Joseph Oriol; St. Julian; St. Nicon.

24 — St. Aldemar; St. Timolaus and companions; St. Seleucus; St. Caimin; St. Cairlon; St. Domangard; St. Epicharis; St. Hildelitba; St. Latinus; St. Macartan; SS. Romulus and Secundus; SS. Mark and Timothy; St. Pigmenius.

25 — ***Annunciation of the Lord;*** St. Dismas; St. Dula; St. Harold; St. Hermenland; St. James Bird, Blessed; St. Kennocha; St. Lucy Filippini; St. Robert of Bury; St. Edmunds; St. Quirinus; St. Pelagius of Laodicea.

26 — St. Margaret Clitherow; St. Braulio; St. Castulus; St. Alfwold; St. Basil the Younger; St. Bathus and companions; St. Theodore; St. Garbhan; St. Ludger; St. Quadratus; St. Mochelloc; SS. Montanus and Maxima; St. Peter.

27 — St. Alexander; St. Alkeld; St. Amator; St. Augusta; St. John of Egypt; St. Rupert; St. Matthew of Beauvais.

28 — St. Alexander; St. Venturino of Bergamo; St. Tutilo; SS. Castor and Dorotheus; St. Conon; St. Gundelindis; St. James Claxton, Blessed; St. Rogatus; St. Stephen Harding.

29 — St. Armogastes and companions; St. Berthold; St. Secundus; St. Firminus; St. Gladys; St. Gwynllyw; St. Lasar; St. Ludolph; St. Mark; St. Pastor.

30 — Blessed Amadeus IX of Savoy; St. Zosimus; St. Tola; St. Clinius; St. Domninus; St. Fergus; St. John Climacus; St. Leonard Muraildo; St. Mamertinus; St. Regulus; St. Quirinus; St. Osburga; St. Pastor; St. Peter Regulatus.

31 — St. Benjamin; St. Guy of Pomposa; St. Achatius; St. Balbina; St. Theodulus; St. Daniel; St. Machabeo; St. Renovatus; St. Abda.

April

1 — St. Venantius; SS. Victor and Stephen; St. Walericus; St. Theodora; SS. Caidoc and Fricor; St. Cellach; St. Dodolinus; St. Hugh of Grenoble; St. Macarius, the Wonder-Worker; SS. Quintian and Irenaeus; St. Melitina.

2 — **St. Francis of Paola;** St. Mary of Egypt; St. Abundius; St. Amphianus; St. Appian; St. Bronach; St. Urban of Langres; St. Theodosia; St. Dominic Tuoc; SS. Longis and Agnofleda; St. Nicetius; St. Musa; St. Polycarp of Alexandria.

3 — St. Richard of Wyche; St. Fara; St. Agape; St. Attala; St. Vulpian; SS. Evagrius and Benignus; St. Richard of Chichester; St. Nicetas.

4 — **St. Isidore of Seville;** St. Tigernach; St. Benedict the Black; St. Benedict the Moor; St. Agathopus; St. Ageranus; St. Zosimus; St. Theonas of Egypt; St. Guier; St. Gwerir; St. Hildebart; Blessed Peter of Poitiers; St. Plato.

5 — **St. Vincent Ferrer;** St. Albert of Montecorvino; St. Becan; St. Zeno; SS. Theodore and Pausilippus; St. Derferl-Gadam; St. Ethelburga; Martyrs of London.

6 — St. Berthane; St. Brychan; St. Ulehad; St. Winebald; St. William of Eskilsoe; SS. Timothy and Diogenes; St. Elstan; St. Florentius; St. Rufina; St. Paul Tinh; St. Platonides.

7 — **St. John Baptist de la Salle;** St. Herman Joseph; St. Celsus; St. Aibert; Blessed Alexander Rawlins; St. Aphraates; St. Brynach; Blessed Ursulina; St. Saturninus; St. Calliopus; St. Cyriaca and companions; Blessed Edward Oldcome; St. Epiphanius; St. Finan; St. Gibardus; St. Goran; St. Hegesippus; St. Henry Walpole; St. Pelagius; St. Peleusius.

8 — St. Julie Billiart; St. Walter of Pontoise; St. Aedesius; St. Amantius; St. Concessa; St. Dionysius of Corinth; St. Julia of Billiart; St. Redemptus; St. Perpetuus.

9 — St. Acacius; St. Waldetrudis; Blessed Thomas of Tolentino; St. Casilda; St. Demetrius; St. Dotto; St. Gaucherius; St. Hedda; St. Hugh of Rouen; St. Madrun; Martyrs of Croyl; Martyrs of Pannonia; St. Mary Cleophas.

10 — St. Michael de Sanctis; Blessed Anthony Neyrot; St. Apollonius; St. Beocca; St. Terence; St. Fulbert; St. Macarius the Ghent; St. Malchus; St. Michael of the St.s; St. Palladius; St. Paternus.

11 — **St. Stanislaus;** St. Marguerite d'Youville; St. Gemma Galgani; St. Antipas; St. Barsanuphius; St. Domnio; St. DGdebertha; St. Machai; St. Maedhog; St. Philip of Gortyna.

12 — St. Julius; St. Allerius; St. Vissia; St. Victor; St. Zeno; St. Wigbert; St. Tetricus; St. Sabas; St. Damian.

13 — **Pope St. Martin I;** St. Caradoc; St. Carpus; Blessed Edward Catheriek; St. Gunioc; St. Hermengild; Blessed John Lockwood; St. Martius; St. Maximus.

14 — St. Lydwine; St. Peter Gonzales; St. Abundius; St. Ardalion; St. Tassach; St. Thomais; St. Tiburtius; St. Domnina; St. Lambert of Lyon; St. Peter Gonzalez.

15 — St. Paternus; St. Hunna; St. Ruadan; St. Maro; SS. Maximus and Olympiades; St. Mundus.

16 — St. Bernadette; St. Benedict Joseph Labre; St. Bernadette Soubirous; St. Turibius of Astorga; SS. Callistus and Charisius; St. Contardo; St. Drogo; St. Encratia; St. Herve; St. Lambert of Saragossa; St. Paternus.

17 — St. Anicetus; St. Villicus; Blessed Wando; St. Elias; SS. Fortunatus and Marcian; St. Landericus; St. Mappalicus; St. Robert of Chaise Dieu; SS. Peter and Hermogenes.

18 — St. Agia; St. Apollonius the Apologist; St. Wicterp; St. Calocerus; St. Cogitosus; St. Corebus; SS. Eleutherius and Anthia; St. Galdinus; St. Gebuinus; St. Laserian; St. Perfectus.

19 — St. Alphege; St. Ursmar; St. Vincent of Collioure; St. Timon; St. Crescentius; St. Gerold; St. Hermogenes; St. James Duckett, Blessed; St. Paphnutius; St. Pavoni; St. Anthony.

20 — St. Marian; St. Agnes of Montepulciano; St. Victor; St. Theodore Trichinas; St. Theotimus; St. Francis Page; St. Hugh of Anzy le Duc; Blessed John Finch; St. Marcian of Auxerre; Blessed Robert Watkinson.

21 — **St. Anselm;** St. Beuno; St. Anastasius XI; St. Anastasius the Sinaite; St. Apollo and companions; St. Arator; St. Conrad of Parzham; St. Froduiphus; St. Maximian of Constantinople.

22 — St. Abdiesus; St. Acepsimas; St. Apelles; St. Arwald; St. Authaire; St. Bicor; St. Tarbula; St. Theodore of Sykeon; St. Senorina; SS. Epiphanius and Alexander; St. Joseph of Persia; St. Leo of Sens; St. Leonides of Alexandria; St. Mareas; St. Opportuna; St. Milles; SS. Parmernius, Chrysoteins, and Helimenas.

23 — **St. George;** SS. Felix, Fortunatus, and Achilleus.

24 — St. Fidelis of Sigmaringen; St. Egbert; St. Alexander; St. William Firmatus; St. Sabus; SSt. Deodatus; St. Diarmaid; St. Dyfnan; St. Mellitus of Canterbury.

25 — **St. Mark;** St. Anianus; Blessed William Marsden; St. Macaille; St. Macedonius; Blessed Robert Anderton; St. Robert of Syracuse; St. Mella; St. Phaebadius; SS. Philo and Agathopodes.

26 — St. Aldo; St. Cletus; St. Basileus; St. Trudpert; St. Franca Visalta; St. Lucidius; St. Riquier; St. Pasdhasius Radbertus; St. Peter of Braga.

27 — Blessed Peter Armengol; St. Zita; St. Adelelmus; St. Asicus; St. Winewald; St. Tertullian; St. Theophilus; SS. Castor and Stephen; St. Enoder; St. Floribert; St. John of Constantinople; St. Lawrence Huong; St. Liberalis.

28 — St. Theodora; St. Peter Chanel; St. Louis Mary Grignion; St. Vito; St. Luchesio; St. Valerie; St. Aphrodisius; St. Artemius; St. Valeria; SS. Theodora and Didymus; St. Cronan of Roscrea; St. John Baptist Thanh; St. Louis de Montfort; St. Mark of Galilee; St. Pamphilus; St. Patrick of Prusa; St. Peter Hieu; St. Pollio; St. Gianna Beretta Molla.

29 — **St. Catherine of Siena;** St. Peter of Verona; St. Ava; St. Agapius; St. Wilfrid the Younger; St. Torpes; St. Tychicus; St. Senan; St. Daniel; St. Dichu; St. Endellion; St. Fiachan; St. Hugh the Great; St. Robert of Molesmes; Blessed Robert Bruges; Martyrs of Corfu; St. Paulinus of Brescia.

30 — Pope St. Pius V; St. Adjutor; St. Joseph Cottolengo; St. Ajuture; St. Aimo; St. Aphrodisius; St. Cynwl; St. Desideratus; St. Donatus; St. Forannan; Blessed Francis Dickenson; St. Lawrence of Novara; St. Louis von Bruck; St. Marianus; St. Maximus; Blessed Miles Gerard; St. Pomponius.

May

1 — St. Joseph the Worker; St. Marculf; St. Andeolus; St. Aceolus; St. Acius; St. Aldebrandus; St. Amator; St. Arigius; St. Asaph; St. Benedict of Szkalka; St. Bertha; St. Brieuc; St. Theodard; St. Ceallach; St. Cominus; St. Grata; St. John-Louis Bonnard; SS. Orentius and Patientia; St. Panacea.

2 — St. Athanasius; St. Zoe; St. Ultan; SS. Vindemialis, Eugene, and Longinus; St. Waldebert; St. Wiborada; St. Valentine; St. Saturninus; St. Felix of Seville; St. Joseph Luu; St. Neachtian.

3 — St. Philip; St. James the Less; St. Adalsindis; St. Alexander; St. Ansfrid; SS. Timothy and Martha; St. Scannal; St. Diodorus; St. Gluvias; St. Juvenal of Narni; St. Philip of Zell.

4 — St. Florian; St. Judas Cyriacus; St. Venerius; St. Augustine Webster; St. Sacerdos; Blessed Carthusian Martyrs; St. Conleth; St. Cyriacus; St. John Houghton; St. John Payne; St. Richard Reynolds; St. Robert Lawrence; Blessed Martyrs of the Carthusian Order; Martyrs of England; Forty Martyrs of England and Wales; St. Nepotian; St. Paulinus of Sinigaglia St. Pelagia of Tarsus.

5 — St. Angelo; St. Aventinus; St. Brito; St. Theodore of Bologna; St. Sacerdos; St. Crescentiana; St. Echa; Blessed Edmund Ignatius Rice; St. Hilary; St. Hydroc; Blessed John Haile; St. Jovinian; St. Jutta; St. Nectarius; St. Nicetius; St. Maurontus; St. Maximus of Jerusalem.

6 — Blessed Edward Jones; Blessed Anthony Middleton; St. Benedicta; St. Theodotus; St. Eadbert; St. Heliodorus; St. Lucius of Cyrene; St. Petronax.

7 — Blessed Rose; St. John of Beverly; St. Villanus; SS. Serenidus and Serenus; St. Domitian; St. Flavius; St. Juvenal of Benevento; St. Liudhard; St. Quadratus; Blessed Michael Ulumbijski; St. Peter of Pavia; St. Placid.

8 — St. Victor Maurus; St. Desideratus; St. Abran; St. Wiro; St. Acacius; St. Victor the Moor; St. Dionysius; St. Helladius of Auxerre; St. Maria Magdalen of Canossa; St. Odrian; St. Peter of Tarantaise.

9 — St. Pachomius; St. Beatus; St. Beatus of Vendome; St. Brynoth; St. Vincent; Blessed Thomas Pickering; St. Sanctan; St. Gerontius; St. Gorfor; St. Hermas; St. John of Chalons.

10 — St. Solange; St. Alphius; St. Aurelian; St. William of Pontoise; St. Calepodius; St. Cataldus; St. Comgall; Blessed Damien de Veuster; St. Dioscorides; St. Epimachus; SS. Gordian and Epimachus; St. John of Avila; SS. Quaratus and Quintus; St. Peter Van.

11 — Blessed Albert of Bergamo; St. Anastasius VI; St. Anastasius VII; St. Anthimus; St. Walbert; St. Walter; St. Tudy; St. Francis Jerome; St. Gangulphus; Blessed John of Rochester; St. Majolus; St. Mamertius; St. Odilo of Cluny; Blessed Matthew Gam; St. Maximus; Blessed Peter the Venerable; St. Ignatius of Laconi.

12 — SS. Nereus and Achilleus; St. Pancras; St. Flavia Domitilla; St. Diomma; St. Dionysius; St. Dominic de la Calzada; St. Epiphanius of Salamis; Blessed Francis Patrizzi; St. Richrudis; St. Philip of Agirone.

13 — Our Lady of Fatima; Blessed Imelda; St. Abban; St. Agnes of Poitiers; St. Valerian; St. Servatus; St. Glyceria; St. John the Silent; St. Juliana of Norwich; St. Mael; St. Natalis; St. Onesimus; St. Merewenna; St. Mucius.

14 — St. Matthias the Apostle; St. Michael Garicoits; St. Boniface; SS. Victor and Corona; St. Vincent of Lerins; St. Carthach the Younger; St. Engelmer; St. Engelmund; St. Just; St. Maria Dominic Mazzarello.

15 — St. Isidore the Farmer; St. Dymphna; St. Bertha; St. Hallvard; St. Achillas; St. Andrew; St. Britwin; St. Waldalenus; St. Torquatus; St. Caesam; St. Cassius; St. Dionysia; St. Caesarea; St. Gerebrand; St. Hilary; St. Nicholas the Mystic; St. Peter.

16 — St. Adam; St. Brendan; St. Ubald Baldassini; St. Andrew Bobola; St. John Nepomucene; St. Simon Stock; St. Abdas; St. Annobert; St. Carantoc; St. Domnolus; SS. Felix and Gennadius; St. Fidouls; St. Forannan; St. Germerius; St. Hilary; St. Honoratus of Amiens; St. Peregrinus.

17 — St. Adrio; St. Thethmar; St. Cathan; St. Heradius; St. Madem; St. Maiduif; St. Restituta; St. Paschal Baylon.

18 — Pope St. John I; St. Felix of Cantalice; St. Venantius; St. Theodotus; St. Dioscorus; St. Elgiva; St. Felix of Spoleto; St. Feredarius; St. Merililaun.

19 — St. Celestine; St. Dunstan; Blessed Alcuin; St. Theophilus of Corte; SS. Calocerus and Parthenius; St. Cyriaca and companions; St. Hadulph; Blessed Peter de Duenas; Blessed Peter Wright; St. Philoterus.

20 — St. Bernadine of Siena; St. Theodore of Pavia; St. Basilissa; St. Anastasius XIII; St. Aquila; St. Austregisilus; St. Basilla; St. Baudelius; St. Thalelaeus; St. Hilary; St. Plautilla.

21 — St. Eugene de Mazenod; St. Ansuinus; St. Barrfoin; St. Valens; St. Theobald of Vienne; SS. Timothy, Polius, and Eutychius; St. Secundinus and companions; St. Serapion the Sindonite; St. Constantine the Great; St. Gollen; SS. Nocostratus, Antiochus, and companions; SS. Polyeuctus, Victorius, and Donatus.

22 — St. Rita; St. Quiteria; St. Aigulf; St. Atto; St. Ausonius; St. Basiliscus; St. Bobo; St. Boethian; SS. Castus and Emilius; St. Conall; St. Fulk; St. Helen; St. John Baptist Machado; Blessed John of Cetina; Blessed John Forest; St. Marcian of Ravenna; St. Romanus of Subiaco; Blessed Matthias of Arima; St. Michael Ho-Dinh-Hy; Blessed Peter of the Assumption; St. Peter Pareuzi.

23 — St. John Baptist Rossi; St. Julia; St. Didier; St. William of Rochester; St. Ivo; St. Crispin of Viterbo; St. Desiderius; SS. Epiphanius and Basileus; St. Euphrosyne of Polotsk; SS. Eutychius and Florentius; St. Goban; St. Leontius; St. Quintian; Martyrs of Cappadocia; Martyrs of Mesopotamia; St. Michael of Synnada.

24 — St. Joanna; St. Jessica; St. Afra; St. Vincent of Porto; St. Zoellus; St. David I; SS. Donatian and Rogatian; St. Gerard de Lunel; St. John del Prado; St. Manaen; St. Robustian; St. Nicetas of Pereaslay; St. Meletius.

25 — Pope St. Gregory VII; St. Mary Magdalene de Pazzi; Venerable Bede; St. Zenobius; St. Madeline Sophie Barat; St. Urban; St. Aldhelm; St. Dionysius of Milan; St. Dunchadh; St. Egilhard; St. Genistus; St. Julius of Dorostorum; St. Leo of Troyes; SS. Maximus and Victorius.

26 — St. Philip Neri; Blessed Eva of Liege; St. Alphaeus; St. Becan; St. Berencardus; St. Zachary; St. Dyfan; SS. Fugatius and Damian; St. Guinizo; St. Felicissimus; St. John Hoan; St. Marian de Paredes; St. Quadratus; St. Oduvald; St. Matthew Phuong; Blessed Peter Sanz.

27 — St. Augustine of Canterbury; St. Bruno; St. Frederick; St. Ranulphus; St. Restituta of Sora; St. Melangell; St. Acculus.

28 — St. Bernard of Montjoux; St. Mariana; St. William of Gellone; Blessed Thomas Ford; St. Senator; St. Caraunus; St. Emilius; St. Heliconis; Blessed John Shert; St. Justus of Urgel; Blessed Margaret Pole; Blessed Robert Johnson; St. Paul Hanh; St. Podius; St. Accidia.

29 — SS. Votus, Felix, and John; St. William Amaud; St. Theodosia and companions; St. Conon; St. Eleutherius; St. John de Atares; Blessed Richard Thirkeld; St. Restitutus; Blessed Martyrs of Toulouse; St. Maximus of Trier; St. Maximus.

30 — St. Ferdinand III of Castile; St. Joan of Arc; St. Hubert; St. Anastasius XV; St. Venantius; St. Walstan; Blessed Willim Filby; Blessed Thomas Cottam; Blessed Lawrence Richardson; St. Luke Kirby; St. Madelgisilus; Blessed Richard Newport; Blessed Maurus Scott.

31 — **Visitation of the Virgin Mary;** St. Vitalis; SS. Winnow, Mancus, and Mybrad; St. Thomas Du; St. Cantius; SS. Cantianus, Cantianilla, and Protus; St. Crescentian; St. Hermias; St. Mechtildis; St. Paschasius.

June

1 — **St. Justin;** St. Inigo; St. Candida; Blessed Alexius; Blessed Alphonsus de Mena; Blessed Andres Sushinda; Blessed Andrew Tokuan; Bl Anthony of Tuy; St. Atto; St. Wistan; St. Valens; St. Telga; Blessed Theobald; St. Thespesius; St. Secundus; St. Caprasius; St. Conrad of Trier; St. Crescentian; Blessed Dominic Nifaki; Blessed Dominic of Fiunga; Blessed Dominic of the Holy Rosary; Blessed Dominic Shibioge; Blessed Dominic Tomaki; St. Eneco; Blessed Ferdinand Ayala; St. Firmus; St. Fortunatus; SS. Felinus and Gratian; Blessed John Storey; St. Justin Martyr; St. Juventius; St. Leo Tanaka; St. Reverianus; St. Ronan; St. Pamphilus.

2 — **SS. Marcellinus and Peter;** St. Erasmus; St. Eugene; St. Blandina; St. Adalgis; St. Alexander; St. Bodfan; St. John de Ortega; Martyrs of Lyons; St. Nicholas Peregrinus; St. Ada.

3 — **St. Charles Lwanga and companions;** St. Kevin; St. Achilleus Kewanuka; St. Adolphys Ludigo-Mkasa; St. Albert of Como; St. Ambrose Kibuka; St. Anatole Kiriggwajjo; St. Andrew Kagwa; St. Athanasius Badzekuketta; St. Brune Seronkuma; St. Caecilius; St. Conus; St. Cronan; St. Davinus; St. Dionysius Sebuggwao; St. Glushashallaich; St. Hilary; St. James Buzabalio; St. John Maria Muzeyi; St. John Mary Mzec; St. Joseph Mukasa; Blessed Kizito; St. Liphardus; St. Lucillian; St. Luke Banabakiutu; St. Noe Mawaggali; Martyrs of Uganda; St. Mathias Mulumba; St. Matthias Murumba; St. Mbaga Tuzinde; St. Morand; St. Mugagga; St. Mukasa Kiriwawanyu; St. Paula; SS. Pergentinus and Laurentinus; St. Pontian Ngondwe; St. Abidianus.

4 — St. Petroc; St. Alexander; St. Aretius; St. Breaca; St. Buriana; St. Walter; St. Saturnina; St. Clateus; St. Cornelius; St. Croidan; St. Elsiar; St. Francis Caracciolo; St. Rutilius and companions; St. Quirinus; St. Nennoc; St. Optatus of Milevis; St. Metrophanes.

5 — St. Boniface of Mainz; St. Adalar; St. Waccar; St. Tudno; St. Sanctinus; St. Eoban; St. Felix of Fritzlar; St. Florentius; Blessed Franciscan Martyrs of China; St. Luke Loan; St. Marcian.

6 — St. Norbert; St. Agobard; St. Ceratius; St. Claud; St. Eustorgius II; St. Jarlath; St. Philip the Deacon; St. Alexander; St. Amantius; St. Bertrand; St. Vincent of Bevagna; Blessed Walter Pierson; St. Cocca; St. Gudwal; Blessed John Davy; St. John of Verona; Blessed Robert Salt; St. Nilammon; Martyrs of Tarsus.

7 — Martyrs of Gottschalk; St. Robert of Newminster; St. Anthony Mary Gianelli; St. Vulphy; St. Willibald; St. Deochar; St. Gotteschalk; St. Landulf of Yarigilia; St. Lycarion; St. Meriadoc; St. Paul of Constantinople.

8 — St. William of York; St. Medard; St. Bron; St. Sallustian; St. Severinus; St. Calliope; St. Clodulf; St. Edgar the Peaceful; St. Eustadiola; St. Gildard; St. Heraclius of Sens; St. Levan; St. Robert of Frassinoro; St. Maximinius of Aix; St. Melania the Elder; St. Muirchu; Blessed Pacificus of Cerano.

9 — St. Ephrem; Blessed Diana; St. Columba; Blessed Anne Mary Taigi; St. Baithin; St. Vincent of Agen; St. Cummian; St. Julian; St. Richard of Andria; St. Maximian of Syracuse; St. Pelagia of Antioch.

10 — Blessed Clive; St. Landericus; Blessed Olivia; St. Getullus; Blessed Amata; St. Amelberga; St. Aresius and companions; St. Astericus; St. Bardo; St. Basilides and companions; St. Bogumilus; St. Timothy; Blessed Caspar Sadamazu; St. Censurius; SS. Crispulus and Restitutus; St. Gezelin; St. Maurinus; St. Maximus.

11 — St. Barnabas; St. Blitharius; St. Tochmura; St. Herebald; St. Parisius; St. Paula Frasinetti; St. Peter Rodriguez and companions.

12 — St. John of Sahagun; St. Amphion; St. Ternan; St. Christian; Sain Cominus; St. Cunera; SS. Cuniald and Geslar; St. Ampliatus; St. Gerebald; SS. Marinus, Vimius, and Zimius; St. Odulf; St. Olympius; St. Christian; St. Peter of Mount Athos.

13 — St. Anthony of Padua; St. Aquilina; St. Augustine of Huy; St. Triphyllius; St. Damhnade; SS. Fortunatus and Lucian; St. Gyavire; St. Felicitas; St. Felicula; St. Rambert; St. Peregrinus.

14 — St. Anastasius XVII; SS. Valerius and Rufinus; St. Cearan; St. Dogmael; St. Elgar; St. Joseph the Hymnographer; St. Lotharius; St. Marcian of Syracuse; St. Quintian; St. Mark of Lucera; St. Nennus; St. Methodius I.

15 — St. Germaine Cousin; St. Vitus; St. Aleydis; St. Crescentia; St. Alice; St. Abraham; St. Adelaide; St. Benildis; St. Vouga; Blesseds Thomas Green, Thomas Scryven, and Thomas Reding; St. Trillo; SS. Domitian and Hadelin; St. Dulas; St. Edburga of Winchester; St. Hesychius; St. Landeilnus; St. Lybe; St. Orsisius; St. Melan.

16 — St. Benno; Blessed Guy Vignotelli; St. John Francis Regis; St. Aurelian; St. Aureus; St. Berthaldus; Blessed William Greenwood; St. Tychon; St. Cettin; St. Colman McRhoi; St. Curig; SS. Felix and Maurus; SS. Ferreolus and Ferrutio; St. Luthgard; SS. Quiriacus and Julitta.

17 — St. Emily de Vialar; St. Herve; St. Teresa of Portugal; St. Harvey; St. Adulf; St. Antidius; St. Avitus; St. Briavel; Blessed Emmanuel d'Abreu; St. Gundulphus; St. Himerius; St. Hypatius; St. Manuel; St. Rainbold; St. Raynerius; St. Nectan; SS. Nicander and Marcian; St. Moling; St. Montanus.

18 — St. Gregory Barbarigo; St. Marina; St. Alena; St. Amandus; St. Aquilina; St. Calogerus; St. Guy; St. Elizabeth of Schonau; St. Fortunatus; St. Leontius; SS. Mark and Marcellian; St. Osmanna.

19 — St. Romuald; St. Gervase; St. Didier; St. Ursicinus; St. Zosimus; Blessed William Exmew; Blessed Thomas Woodhouse; Blessed Sebastian Newdigate; St. Deodatus; St. Hildegrin; St. Protase.

20 — St. Albert of Magdeburg; Blessed Anthony Turner; St. Bagne; Blessed Balthasar de Torres; St. Benignus; St. Vincent Kaun; Blessed William Harcourt; Blessed Thomas Whitbread; St. Florentina; St. Francis Pacheco; St. Govan; St. Helena; Blessed John Baptist Zola; Blessed John Fenwick and John Gavan; Blessed John Kinsako; St. Novatus; Blessed Michael Tozo; SS. Paul and Cyriacus; Blessed Paul Shinsuki; Blessed Peter Rinshei.

21 — St. Aloysius Gonzaga; St. Lazarus; St. Urciscenus; St. Terence; St. Corbmac; St. Demetria; St. Agofredus; St. Alban of Mainz; St. John Rigby; St. Leutfridus; St. Maine; St. Ralph; St. Raymond of Barbastro; SS. Rufinus and Martia; St. Martin of Tongres.

22 — St. Thomas More; St. John Fisher; St. Paulinus of Nola; St. Aaron; St. Alban; St. Nicetas; St. Consortia; St. Eberbard; St. Flavius Clemens; Martyrs of Ararat.

23 — St. Ethelreda (Audrey); St. Agrippina; St. Joseph Cafasso; St. Walhere; St. Thomas Garnet; St. Etheidreda; St. Hiduiphus; St. James of Toul; St. John; St. Libert; St. Moelray; St. Peter of Juilly.

24 — Birthday of St. John the Baptist; St. Kundegunda; St. Amphibalus; St. Bartholomew of Fame; St. Theodulphus; St. Germoc; St. Faustus and companions; St. John of Tuy; Blessed Joseph Yuen; St. Rumold; St. Orentius.

25 — St. William of Vercelli; St. Prosper of Aquitaine; St. Adalbert; St. Selyf; St. Dominic Henares; St. Gallicanus; St. Gohardus; St. Maximus of Turin; St. Moloc; St. Molonachus.

26 — **St. Josemaria Escriva de Balaguer;** St. Anthelm; St. Vigilius; Blessed Teresa Fantou; St. Salvius; St. Corbican; St. David; St. Hermogius; SS. John and Paul; St. John of the Goths; St. Marie Magdalen Fontaine; St. Maxentius; St. Pelagius; St. Perseveranda.

27 — St. Cyril of Alexandria; St. Laszlo; St. Anectus; St. Arialdus; St. Zoilus; Blessed Thomas Toan; St. Samson; St. Crescens; St. Deodatus; St. Ferdinand of Aragon; St. John of Chinon; St. Joseph Hien.

28 — **St. Irenaeus;** St. Almus; St. Argymirus; St. Austell; St. Benignus; St. Vincenza Gerosa; St. Theodichildis; St. Crummine; St. Egilo; St. Heimrad; St. John Southworth St. Paul I, pope; St. Plutarch.

29 — *SS. Peter (first pope) and Paul;* SS. Salome and Judith; St. Cassius; St. Cocha; St. Mary.

30 — **First Martyrs of the See of Rome;** Blessed Raymond Lull; St. Martial; St. Airick; St. Basilides; St. Bertrand; St. Vincent Yen; St. Theobald; St. Clotsindis; St. Erentrudis; St. Lucina; St. Marcian; St. Ostianus; Martyrs of Rome; Blessed Philip Powell.

July

1 — **Blessed Junipero Serra;** St. Gall; St. Amulf; St. Veep; St. Theodoric; St. Servan; St. Carilefus; SS. Castus and Secundinus; St. Cewydd; St. Domitian; St. Eparchius; St. Felix of Como; SS. Julius and Anron; St. Juthware; St. Martin of Vienne.

2 — St. Bernadino Realino; St. Acestes; St. Ariston and companions; St. Lidanus; St. Otto of Bamberg; St. Oudaceus; St. Monegundis; St. Aberoh (Aburom, Arianus).

3 — **St. Thomas;** St. Anatolius; St. Bladus; St. Byblig; St. Tryphon and companions; St. Cillene; St. Dathus; St. Gunthiem; St. Guthagon; St. Hyacinth; St. Joseph Peter Uyen; St. Maelmuire O'Gorman; St. Mark; Blessed Raymond Lull; St. Philip Minh.

4 — **St. Elizabeth of Portugal;** St. Ulric; Blessed Anthony Fantosat; St. Aurelian; St. Bertha; Blessed William Andleby; St. Theodore of Cyrene; Blessed Thomas Bosgrave; Blessed Thomas Warcop; Blessed Edward Fulthrop; St. Henry Abbot, Blessed; Blessed John Carey; Blessed John Cornelius; St. Jucundian; St. Laurianus; St. Namphanion; St. Odo the Good; Blessed Patrick Salmon; St. Peter of Luxembourg.

5 — St. Anthony Mary Zaccaria; St. Athanasius; St. Athanasius the Athonite; St. Zoe; St. Triphina; St. Domitius; St. Edana; SS. Fragan and Gwen; St. Marinus; St. Numerian; St. Philomena.

6 — St. Maria Goretti; St. Modwenna; St. Merryn; Blessed Thomas Alfield; St. Tranquillinus; St. Dominica; St. Goar; St. Rixius Varus; St. Romulus and companions; St. Noyala; St. Monennaa.

7 — St. Pantaenus; St. Ampelius; St. Angelelmus; St. Apollonius; St. Astius; St. Bonitus; St. Ethelburga; St. Felix of Nantes; Blessed Lawrence Humphrey; St. Maolruain; Blessed Ralph Milner; St. Odo of Urgell; SS. Medran and Odran; St. Palladius.

8 — St. Adrian III; St. Kilian; St. Priscilla; St.s Abrahamites; St. Albert of Genoa; St. Apollonius; St. Arnold; St. Auspicius; St. Withburga; St. Grimbald; St. Landrada; B. Mancius Araki; St. Raymond of Toulouse; Blessed Peter the Hermit.

9 — St. Godfrey; Blessed Adrian Fortescue; St. Adrian Van Hilvarenbeek; St. Agilulfus; St. Alberic Crescitelli; St. Anatolia; St. Andrew Wouters; St. Brictus; St. Veronica Giuliani; St. Zeno; St. Willehad of Denmark; St. Cornelius; St. Francis Rod; St. Golvinus; St. James Lacop; St. John of Cologne; St. John of Osterwick; St. Justus of Poland; St. Leonard Wegel; Martyrs of Gorkum; St. Nicasius Jonson; St. Nicholas Poppel; St. Patermuthius; St. Peter of Asche.

10 — St. Alexander; St. Amalberga; St. Anthony Pechersky; St. Theodosius Pechersky; Blessed Emmanuel Ruiz; St. Etto; St. Lantfrid; St. Leontius; SS. Rufinus and Secundus; Martyrs of Damascus; St. Pascharius; St. Peter of Perugia; St. Peter Tu.

11 — St. Benedict of Nursia; St. Oliver Plunkett; St. Olga; St. Abundius; St. Amabilis; St. Turketil; St. Sabinus; SS. Sabinus and Cyprian; St. Cindeus; St. Drostan; St. Hidulphus; St. John of Bergamo; St. Leontius the Younger; St. Marcian.

12 — St. Jason; St. John Gaulbert, abbot; St. Agnes De; Blessed Andrew Oexner of Riun; St. Ansbald; St. Viventiolus; St. Veronica; Blessed David Gonson; St. Epiphania; St. John Jones; St. John the Iberian; Blessed John Naisen; Blessed John Tanaka; St. Leo of Lucca; Blessed Louis Naisen; St. Marciana; SS. Nabor and Felix; Blessed Matthias Araki; St. Menulphus; Blessed Monica Naisen; St. Paternian; Blessed Peter Araki Kobjoje; St. Paulinus of Antioch; St. Peter Khanh.

13 — St. Henry; St. Silas; St. Francis Solano; St. Teresa de los Andes; Blessed Thomas Tunstal; St. Turiaf; St. Serapion; St. Dogfan; St. Henry II; St. Myrope.

14 — **Blessed Kateri Tekakwitha;** Blessed Humbert; St. Ulrich; St. William Breteuil; St. Cyrus of Carthage; St. Heraclas; St. Justus; St. Libert; Blessed Richard Langhorne; St. Nicodemus of the Holy Mountain; St. Optatian; St. Phocas.

15 — **St. Bonaventure;** St. Swithun; St. Vladimir; St. Donald; St. Edith of Polesworth; St. Abudimus; Blessed Alphonsus de Vaena; St. Andrew Nam-Thuong; Blessed Anne Jahouvey; Blessed Anthony Francisco; St. Apronia; St. Athanasius; St. Baldwin; SS. Secundinus, Agrippinus, Maximus, Fortunatus, and Martialis; St. Seduinus; St. Catulinus; St. David of Sweden; St. Egino; St. Felix of Pavia; St. Jacob of Nisibis; Blessed Joanninus de San Juan; Blessed John Fernandez; Blessed Mark Caldeira; Blessed Nicholas Dinnis; Blessed Peter Berna; St. Peter Tuan; St. Plechelm; St. Pompeius Maria Pirotti.

16 — *Our Lady of Mount Carmel;* St. Carmen; St. Mary Magdalen Postel; St. Athenogenes; St. Vitalian; St. Valentine; St. Tenenan; St. Domnio; St. Fulrad; St. Faustus; St. Helier; St. Marie St. Henry; St. Reineldis.

17 — St. Marcellina; St. Alexis; Blessed Ceslaus; St. Andrew Zorard; St. Ansueris; Blessed Antoinette Roussel; St. Theodosius; St. Theodota; St. Turninus; Carmelite Nuns of Compiegne; St. Clement of Okhrida; St. Cynllo; St. Ennodius; Blessed Francis Brideau; St. Frances de Croissy; St. Fredegand; St. Generosus; St. Hyacinth; Blessed Juliette Verolot; St. Madeleine Brideau; St. Madeleine Lidoine; St. Marie Claude Brard; St. Marie Croissy; St. Marie Dufour; St. Marie Hanisset; St. Marie Meunier; St. Marie Trezelle; Blessed Rose Chretien; St. Nerses Lambronazi; SS. Nicholas, Alexandra, and companions; Martyrs of Scillitan; St. Acllinus.

18 — St. Amulf; St. Camillus de Lellis; St. Frederick; St. Bruno of Segni; St. Theneva; St. Dominic Nicholas Dat; St. Edburga of Bicester; St. Emilian; St. Goneri; St. Gundenis; St. Julian; St. Marina; St. Rufillus; St. Maternus; St. Minnborinus; St. Pambo; St. Philaster.

19 — SS. Justa and Rufina; St. Macrina the Younger; St. Ambrose Aut-pert; St. Arsenius the Great; St. Aurea; St. Epagaphras; St. Felix of Verona; St. John Plessington.

20 — St. Margaret of Antioch; St. Wilgefortis; St. Elias; St. Aurelius; St. Barhadbesciabas; St. Wulmar; St. Sabinus; St. Severa; St. Etheidwitha; SS. Flavian and Elias; St. John of Pulsano; St. Joseph of Barsabas; St. Margaret; St. Paul of St. Zoilus.

21 — **St. Lawrence of Brindisi;** St. Victor; St. Arbogast; St. Wastrada; St. Zoticus; SS. John and Benignus; St. John of Edessa; St. Julia of Troyes.

22 — St. Mary Magdalene; SS. Philip Evans and John Lloyd, Martyrs; St. Wandrille; St. Theophilus; St. Dabius; St. Joseph of Palestine; St. Meneleus; St. Movean; St. Pancharius; St. Plato.

23 — St. Bridget of Sweden; St. Anne; St. Apollinaris; St. Valerian; SS. Trophimus and Theophilus; St. John Cassian; St. Liborius; SS. Rasyphus and Ravennus; St. Romlua; Martyrs of Bulgaria.

24 — St. Declan; St. Ursicinus; SS. Victor, Sterentius, and Antigones; St. Vincent; SS. Wulfhade and Ruffinus; St. Dictinus; St. Godo; St. John Boste; Blessed Joseph Fernandez; St. Kinga; St. Lewina; Blessed Maria Pilar Martinez Garcia and companions; SS. Niceta and Aquilina; St. Menefrida; SS. Meneus and Capito.

25 — St. James the Greater; SS. Thea and Valentina; St. Theodemir; St. Cucuphas; St. Ebrulf; SS. Florentius and Felix; St. Glodesind; St. Magnericus; St. Nissen; St. Paul of Gaza.

26 — SS. Joachim and Anne, Jesus's grandparents; Blessed William Ward; St. Valens; St. Hyacinth; Blessed John Ingram; St. Pastor.

27 — SS. Natalie and Aurelius; St. Pantaleon; Blessed Rudolf Aquaviva; St. Malchus; St. Maximaian; St. Martinian; St. Dionysius; St. John Serapion; St. Constantine; St. Anthusa; St. Bartholomea Capitanjo; St. Theobald of Marly; Blessed Titus Brandsma; St. Ecclesius; St. Felix; St. Hermolaus; Blessed Rudolf Acquaviva; St. Maurus.

28 — St. Innocent I; Blessed Anthony della Chiesa; St. Arduinus; St. Botuid; St. Samson; St. Camelian; St. Lucidius; St. Lyutis; SS. Nazarius and Celsus; St. Peregrinus.

29 — St. Martha; St. Olaf; St. Lupus; St. William of St.-Brieuc; St. Seraphina; St. Serapia; St. Callinicus; Blessed John Baptist Lo; Blessed Joseph Tshang; St. Kilian; St. Lazarus; Blessed Louis Bertran; St. Lucilla and companions; Blessed Mancius of the Holy Cross; St. Martha Wang; St. Olaf of Norway; Blessed Paul Tcheng; Blessed Peter of the Holy Mother of God.

30 — St. Peter Chrysologus; St. Abdon; St. Ursus; St. Tatwine; Blessed Thomas Abel; Blessed Edward Powell; St. Ermengytha; St. Hatebrand; St. Julitta; Blessed Richard Featherstone; St. Rheticus; St. Rufinus; St. Olaf of Sweden; St. Maxima.

31 — St. Ignatius Loyola; St. Helen of Skoyde; St. Justin de Jacobis; St. Calimerlus; St. Democritus; St. Calimerius; St. Emmanuel Phung; St. Firmus of Tagaste; St. Neot; Martyrs of Syria; St. Peter Quy.

August

1 — St. Alphonsus Liguori; St. Hope; St. Sofia; St. Charity; St. Peter of Alcantara; St. Peter in Chains; St. Almedha; St. Arcadius; aint Bernard Due; St. Verus; Blessed Thomas Weloume; St. Secundel; St. Dominic Van Honh Dieu; St. Elined; St. Friard; St. Jonatus; St. Justin; St. Leonitis; St. Leus; St. Rioch; St. Mary the Consoler; St. Peregrinus.

2 — **St. Eusubius of Vercelli;** St. Alfreda; St. Betharius; St. Boetharius; St. Theodota; St. Thomas of Dover; St. Rutilius; St. Maximus of Padua; St. Peter of Osma; St. Plegmund.

3 — St. Peter Julian Eymard; St. Lydia Purpuraria; St. Abibas; St. Aspren; Blessed Waltheof; St. Trea; St. Senach; St. Dalmatius; St. Gamaliel; St. Faustus; St. Peter of Anagni.

4 — **St. John Marie Vianney;** St. Agabius; St. Aristarchus; Blessed William Home; St. Terullinus; St. Eleutherius; St. Epimachus; St. John Baptist Vianney; St. Lua; St. Raynerius of Spalatro; St. Peregrinus; Maceratus and Viventius.

5 — **Dedication of St. Mary Major Basilica;** St. Abel; St. Addal; St. Afra; St. Venantius; St. Theodoric; St. Cantidius; St. Cassian of Autun; St. Emygdius; St. Gormcal; St. Nouna; St. Memmius; St. Paris.

6 — *Transfiguration of the Lord;* St. Agapitus; St. Hormisdas, pope; St. James the Syrian; Martyrs of Cardena.

7 — **St. Cajetan;** St. Claudia; St. Agathangelo Noury; St. Albert of Trapani; St. Victricius; St. Carpophorus; St. Donat; St. Donatian; SS. Donatus and Hilarinus; St. Donatus of Besancon; St. Faustus; St. Hypercchios; SS. Peter, Julian, and companions; St. Acirianus.

8 — **St. Dominic de Guzman;** St. Altman; St. Ternatius; SS. Eleutherius and Leonides; St. Ellidius; St. Emilian; St. Gedeon; Blessed John Felton; St. Leobald; St. Marinus; Blessed Mary MacKillop; St. Mommulus; St. Myron.

9 — **St. Teresa Benedicta of the Cross (Edith Stein);** St. Nathy; St. Amedeus; St. Amor; St. Autor; St. Bandarius; St. Samuel of Edessa; St. Secundian; St. Serenus; St. Domitian of Chalons; SS. Fikrmus and Rusticus; St. Julian; St. Romanus Ostiarius; St. Numidicus; St. Maurilius; St. Phelim.

10 — **St. Lawrence, martyr;** St. Agilberta; St. Aredius; St. Asteria; St. Thiento and companions; St. Deusdedit; St. Acrates (Aragawi).

11 — St. Clare; St. Susanna; St. Blane; St. Lelia; St. Alexander of Comana; St. Attracta; St. Taurinus; St. Tiburtius; St. Chromatius; St. Digna; St. Francis of St. Mary; St. Gagericus; Blessed Lawrence Nerucci; St. Rufinus.

12 — St. Ja ne Francis de Chantal; St. Euplius; St. Anicetus; St. Anthony Peter Dich; St. Just; St. Cassian of Benevento; St. Hilaria; St. James Nam; SS. Macarius and Julian; St. Merewenna; St. Michael My; St. Murtagh.

13 — SS. Pontian and Hippolytus; St. Radegunde; St. Benilde; St. Benilde Romancon; St. Wigbert; St. William Freeman; St. Tikhon of Zadonsk; St. Cassian of Imola; St. Cassian of Todi; SS. Centolla and Helen; St. Francis of Pesaro; St. Herulph; St. Junian; St. Ludoiph; St. Radegund; St. Nerses Glaietsi; St. Maximus the Confessor.

14 — St. Maximilian Kolbe; St. Fachanan; St. Anastasius; St. Anthony Primaldi; St. Athanasia; St. Ursicius; St. Werenfrid; St. Demetrius.

15 — *Assumption of Mary;* St. Tarsicius; St. Alipius; St. Altfrid; St. Arduinus; St. Amulf; St. Limbania; St. Neopolus.

16 — St. Stephen of Hungary; St. Rocco; St. Armagillus; St. Arsacius; St. Beatrix da Silva; St. Uguzo; St. Titus; St. Serena; St. Diomedes; St. Eleutherius; St. Fructuosus; Blessed John of St. Martha; Blessed Mary Magdalen Kiota.

17 — St. Clare of Montefalco; Blessed Bartholomew; St. Amor of Amorbach; St. Anastasius IX; St. Theodulus; Blessed Thomas Vinyemon; Blessed Casper and Mary Vaz; St. Donatus; St. Drithelm; St. Frances Bizzocca; Blessed Francis Kuloi; Blessed Francis Kurobiove; St. Hiero; St. Hyacinth; St. James the Deacon; St. John of Monte Marano; St. Liberatus; Blessed Louis Someyon; St. Luke Kiemon; St. Mamas; Blessed Martin Gomez; Blessed Michael Kiraiemon; St. Myron; SS. Paul and Juliana.

18 — St. Helena; St. Agapitus; Blessed Thomas Guengoro; St. Daig Maccairaill; St. Firminus of Metz; SS. Florus and Laurus; St. Hugh the Little; St. James Guengoro, Blessed; SS. John and Crispus; SS. Leo and Juliana; Blessed Raynald of Ravenna; Blessed Mary Guengoro.

19 — St. John Eudes; Blessed Emily Bicchieri; St. Andrew the Tribune; Blessed Anthony; St. Baldulfus; Blessed Bartholomew Monfiore; St. Bertuolf; Blessed Thomas Koyanangi; SS. Timothy, Thecla, and Agapius; St. Sebald; St. Calminius; St. Credan; St. Donatus; St. Elaphius; St. Guenninus; St. James Denshi, Blessed; Blessed John Foyamon; Blessed John Nangata; St. John Yano; St. Julius; Blessed Lawrence Rokuyemon; Blessed Leo Suchiemon; Blessed Louis Flores; St. Louis of Toulouse; St. Magnus; St. Marianus; St. Marinus; St. Rufinus; St. Namadia; Blessed Michael Diaz; St. Mochta; Blessed Paul Sanchiki; Blessed Peter Zuniga.

20 — St. Bernard of Clairvaux; St. Amadour; St. Bernard of Valdeiglesias; St. Edbert; St. Haduin; St. Heliodorus; St. Herbert Hoscam; SS. Leovigild and Christopher; St. Lucius; St. Ronald; Martyrs of Thrace; St. Maximus.

21 — Pope St. Pius X; St. Abraham of Smolensk; St. Anastasius Cornicularius; St. Apollinaris Sidonius; St. Avitus I of Clermont; St. Bassa and companions; St. Cyriaca; St. Hardulph; St. Joseph Nien Vien; St. Leontius the Elder; St. Luxorius; St. Quadratus; St. Paternus.

22 — Queenship of Mary; St. Sigfrid; St. Andrew; St. Andrew the Scot; St. Antoninus; St. Amulf; St. Athanasius; Blessed William Lacey; St. Ethelgitha; St. Gunifort; St. Hippolytus of Porto; St. John Kemble; St. John Wall; Blessed Richard Kirkman; St. Martial; St. Maurus and companions.

23 — St. Rose of Lima; St. Apollinaris; St. Astericus and companions; St. Victor of Vita; St. Zacchaeus; St. Theonas; St. Tydfil; St. Ascelina; St. Ebba; St. Eugene; St. Flavian of Autun; St. Lupicinus; St. Lupus; St. Restitutus; St. Quiriacus; St. Minvervius; St. Philip Benizi.

24 — St. Bartholomew (St. Nathanael); St. Ouen; St. Aurea; St. Yrchard; St. Tation; St. Sandratus; St. Jane Antide Thouret; St. Romanus of Nepi; St. Massa Candida.

25 — St. Louis King of France; St. Joseph Calasanz; St. Genesius; St. Patricia; St. Maria Michaelas Desmaisieres; St. Warinus; St. Yrieix; St. Gerintius of Italica; St. Gurloes; St. Hunegund; St. Julian; Blessed Louis Baba; Blessed Louis Sasanda; Blessed Louis Sotelo; St. Maginus; St. Marcian; SS. Nemesius and Lucilla; St. Menas; Blessed Peter Vasquez.

26 — St. Bichier; St. Alexander; St. Bregwin; St. Victor; St. Zephyrinus; St. Teresa of Jesus Jomet Ibars; Blessed Thomas Percy; St. Secundus; St. Elias; St. Felix of Pistoia; St. Jane Elizabeth Bichier des Ages; St. Rufinus; St. Pandwyna; St. Pantagathus.

27 — St. Monica; St. Honoratus; St. Anthusa the Younger; St. Caesarius of Arles; St. Decuman; St. Ebbo; St. Gebhard; St. John; St. Licerius; St. Malrubius; St. Margaret the Barefooted; SS. Rufus and Carpophorus; St. Namus; St. Phanurius; St. Poemon.

28 — St. Augustine of Hippo; St. Edmund Arrowsmith; Blessed John Roche and Margaret Ward; St. Hermes; St. Moses the Ethiopian; St. Alexander of Constantinople; St. Vivian; Blessed William Dean; Blessed William Guntei; Blessed Thomas Felton; Blessed Thomas Holford; St. Fortunatus; St. Gorman; St. Hugh More, Blessed; St. Julian of Auvergne; Blessed Robert Morton; St. Rumwald; St. Pelagius.

29 — Beheading of St. John the Baptist; St. Sabina; St. Medericus; St. Adelphus; St. Basilla; St. Velleicus; St. Sebbi; St. Candida; St. Edwold; SS. Hypatius and Andrew; St. Hyperdulia; Blessed Richard Herst; SS. Nicaeas and Paul.

30 — St. Rumon; St. Pammachius; St. Agilus; St. Bononius; Blessed Edward Shelley; St. Gaudentia; SS. Felix and Adauctus; St. Loaran; Blessed Richard Leigh; St. Richard Martin; SS. Pelagius, Aresenius, and Sylvanus; St. Peter of Trevi.

31 — St. Aidan of Lindisfame; St. Raymond Nonnatus; St. Albertinus; St. Amatus; St. Aristides; SS. Theodotus, Rufina, and Ammia; St. Caesidius; St. Dominic del Val; Blessed Richard Bere; St. Paulinus of Trier.

September

1 — St. Giles, abbot; St. Fiacre; St. Beatrice da Silva Meneses; St. Agia; St. Ammon; St. Anna the Prophetess; St. Verena; St. Victorious; SS. Vincent and Laetus; St. Terentian; St. Constantius; St. Lupus of Sens; St. Lythan; St. Regulus; St. Nivard; Blessed Michael Ghebre.

2 — St. Ingrid of Sweden; St. Agricolus; St. Antoninus; St. Brocard; St. Zeno; St. William of Roeskilde; St. Valentine; St. Castor; St. Diomedes; St. Elpidius; St. Justus of Lyons; St. Nonossus; St. Maxima.

3 — Pope St. Gregory the Great; St. Phoebe; St. angus MacNisse; St. Aigulf; St. Andrew Dotti; St. Anthony Ishida; St. Auxanus; St. Balin; Blessed Bartholomew Gutierrez; SS. Zeno and Chanton; St. Sandila; St. Frugentius; St. Gabriel of St. Magdalen, Blessed; St. Hereswitha; SS. John of Perugia and Peter of Sassoferrato; St. Macanisius; St. Mansuetus; St. Regulus; St. Martin de Hinojosa; St. Natalis; St. Maurilius.

4 — St. Rosalia; St. Ultan; St. Thamel and companions; St. Theodore; St. Salvinus; St. Caletricus; St. Candida the Elder; St. Hermione; St. Magnus; St. Marinus; St. Rhuddlad; SS. Rufinus, Silvanus, and Victalicus; St. Monessa.

5 — St. Bertin; St. Alvitus; St. Bertinus; St. Victorinus; Blessed William Browne; St. Charbel; St. Herculanils; St. Joseph Canh; St. Lawrence Giustiniani; St. Romulus; St. Quintius; St. Obdulia; St. Peter Tu.

6 — St. Arator; Blessed Thomas Tsughi; St. Cagnoald; St. Chainaldus; SS. Cottidus, Eugene, and companions; St. Donatian; St. Faustus; SS. Felix and Augebert; St. Maccallin; St. Magnus; St. Onesiphorous; St. Petronius.

7 — St. Cloud; St. Regina; St. Grimonia; St. Eustace; St. Alcmund; St. Anastasius the Fuller; St. Augustalus; St. Tilbert; St. Carissima; St. Clodoald; St. Diuma; St. Graus; St. Hilduard; Blessed John Duckett; Blessed John Maid; St. John of Lodi; St. John of Nicomedia; Blessed Louis Maki; St. Madalberta; St. Marek Krizin; Blessed Ralph Corby; St. Memorius; St. Pamphilus.

8 — Birthday of Virgin Mary; St. Adrian; St. Adela; Blessed Athony of St. Bonaventure; Blessed Thomas of St. Hyacinth; Blessed Thomas Tomaki; SS. Timothy and Faustus; St. Corbinian; St. Disibod; Blessed Dominic of Nagasaki; St. James Fayashida, Blessed; Blessed John Inamura; Blessed John Tomaki; St. Kingsmark; Blessed Lawrence Jamada; Blessed Leo Kombiogi; Blessed Louis Nifaki; St. Louis of Omura; St. Romanus Aybara; St. Nestor; Blessed Matthew Alvarez; Blessed Michael Jamada; Blessed Michael Tomaki; St. Paul Aybara.

9 — St. Peter Claver; St. Kieran; St. Hyacinth; St. Isaac the Great; St. Bettelin; St. Wulfhilda; St. Wilfrida; St. Severian; SS. Felix and Constantia; St. Joseph of Volokolamsk; St. Omer; St. Osmanna.

10 — Blessed Agnes Takea; Blessed Agnes Tsao-Kouy; Blessed Angelus Oruscci; Blessed Anthony Kiun; Blessed Anthony of Korea; Blessed Anthony Sanga; Blessed Anthony Vom; St. Apollinaris Franco; St. Autbert; Blessed Bartholomew Shikiemon; St. Barypsabas; St. Veranus; Blessed Thecla Nangashi; St. Theodard; Blessed Thomas of the Holy Rosary; Blessed Thomas Sherwood; St. Salvius of Albi; Blessed Sebastian Kimura; St. Candida the Younger; St. Cosmas; Blessed Damien Yamiki; Blessed Dominic Nakano; St. Dominic Shamada; St. Finian; St. Francis de Morales; St. Frithestan; St. Gundislavus Fusai, Blessed; St. Hyacinth Orfanel, Blessed; Blessed John Kingoku; Blessed John of Korea; St. Joseph of St. Hyacinth; St. Leo Satsuma; Blessed Louis Kawara; Blessed Lucy de Freitas; Blessed Richard of St. Ann; SS. Nemesian, Felix, and companions; Blessed Mary Tokuan and Mary Choun; Blessed Mary Tanaura; St. Menodora; Blessed Michael Shumpo; Blessed Michael Yamiki; Blessed Paul Tanaka; Blessed Peter Nangashi; Blessed Peter Avila; Blessed Peter Sampo; Blessed Peter Sanga; St. Peter Martinez; St. Achilleus.

11 — St. Paphnutius; St. Adelphus; St. Almirus; St. Ambrose Edward Barlow; St. Bodo; St. Vincent of Leon; St. Theodora; Blessed Caspar Kotenda; St. Daniel; St. Deiniol; St. Diodorus; St. Emilian; SS. Felix and Regula; Blessed Francis Takea; Blessed John-Gabriel Perboyre; St. Patiens; Blessed Peter Ikiemon; St. Peter of Chavanon.

12 — St. Guy of Anderlecht; St. Ailbhe; St. Autonomous; Blessed Thomas Zumarraga; St. Sacerdos; St. Curomotus; St. Eanswida; St. Francis of St. Bonaventure; St. Hieronides; St. Macedonius; Blessed Mancius of St. Thomas; St. Peter of St. Claire.

13 — St. John Chrysostom; St. Amatus; St. Venerius; St. Columbinus; St. Ligorius; SS. Macrobius and Julian; St. Nectarius; St. Maurilius; St. Philip.

14 — *Triumph of the Cross;* SS. Caerealis and Sallustia; St. Cormac; St. Crescentian; St. Crescentius; St. Gabriel du Fresse, Blessed; St. Notburga; St. Maternus.

15 — Our Lady of Seven Sorrows; St. Valerian; St. Aichardus; St. Aprus; St. Vitus; SS. Emilias and Jeremiah; St. Hernan; St. Joseph Abibos; St. Leobinus; St. Mamilian; Blessed Roland de'Medici; St. Ribert; St. Ritbert; St. Nicomedes; St. Maximus; St. Melitina; St. Merinus.

16 — St. Cornelius; St. Cyprian; St. Ninian; St. Edith of Wilton; St. Ludmilla; St. Abundius; St. Curcodomus; St. Dulcissima; St. Eugenia; SS. Lucy and Geminian; St. Rogellus; Blessed Michael Fimonaya; Blessed Paul Fimonaya.

17 — St. Robert Bellarmine; St. Hildegarde; St. Brogan; St. Agathoclia; St. Ariadne; St. Uni; SS. Valerian, Niacrinus, and Gordian; St. Theodora; St. Satyrus; St. Columba; St. Emmanuel Trieu; St. Flocellus; St. Hildegard of Bingen; St. Justin; St. Lambert of Maastricht; St. Rodingus; SS. Narcissus and Crescentio; St. Peter Arbues.

18 — St. Dominic Trach; St. Ferreolus; St. Hygbald; St. John de Massias; St. Joseph of Cupertino; St. Richardis; St. Methodius of Olympus.

19 — St. Januarius; St. Emily de Rodat; Blessed Alphonsus de Orozco; St. Amulf; St. Theodore of Tarsus; Blessed Thomas Akafuji; St. Trophimus; St. Sequanus; St. Goeric; St. Maria de Cerevellon; St. Peleus; St. Pomposa.

20 — SS. Andrew Kim Taegon, Paul Chong Hasang, and companions; St. Agapitus; St. Vincent Madelgarus; SS. Theodore, Philippa, and companions; Blessed Thomas Johnson; St. Candida; St. Dionysius; St. Eusebia; SS. Fausta and Evilasius; St. John Charles Cornay; St. Lawrence Imbert; Martyrs of Korea.

21 — St. Matthew the Apostle; SS. Chastan and Imbert; St. Maura Troyes; St. Alexander; St. Thomas Dien; St. Francis Jaccard; St. Gerulph; St. Hieu; St. Mabyn; St. Meletius; St. Pamphilus.

22 — St. Maurice; St. Thomas of Villanueva; St. Salaberga; St. Sanctinus; SS. Digna and Emerita; St. Emmeramus; St. Florentius; St. Jonas; St. Lauto; St. Lioba; St. Lolanus; Martyrs of the Theban Legion.

23 — St. Padre Pio; St. Thecla; St. Linus; St. Adamnan; St. Andrew and companions; SS. Xantippa and Polyxena; Blessed William Way; St. Cissa; St. Constantius.

24 — St. Anathalon; St. Andochius; St. Bercthun; St. Ysam; SS. Chuniald and Gislar; St. Rusticus; Martyrs of Chalcedon; St. Paphnutius.

25 — St. Finbar; Blessed Herman the Cripple; St. Vincent Strambi; St. Albert of Jerusalem; St. Anacharius; Blessed Augustine Ota; St. Austindus; St. Sergius; St. Caian; St. Ceolfrid; St. Cleophas; St. Egelred; St. Firminus of Amiens; St. Fymbert; St. Herculafilis; St. Lupus of Lyons; Blessed Mancius Shisisoiemon; Blessed Mark Criado; St. Mewrog; St. Paphnutius; SS. Paul and Tatta; St. Abadir.

26 — **SS. Cosmas and Damian;** St. Justina of Antioch; St. Neol; St. Amantius; St. Vigilius; St. Theresa Coudere; St. Senator; St. Callistratus; St. Colman of Elo; St. John of Meda; St. Marie Teresa Couderc; St. Nilus the Younger; St. Meugant.

27 — **St. Vincent de Paul;** St. Elzear; St. Adheritus; SS. Adolphus and John; St. Barrog; St. Bonfilius; St. Ceraunus; St. Deodatus; St. Epicharis; SS. Fidentius and Terence; St. Hiltrude; St. John Mark; St. Absadi.

28 — **St. Wenceslaus;** St. Lorenzo Ruiz; St. Annemund; SS. Willigod and Martin; St. Tetta; St. Thiemo; Blessed Thomas Kufioji; St. Conwall; St. Eustochium; St. Faustus; St. John Kokumbuko; Blessed Lawrence Shizu; St. Machan; St. Mark; St. Martial; St. Maximus; Blessed Michael Kinoshi; St. Paternus; Blessed Peter Kufioji.

29 — **SS. Michael, Raphael, and Gabriel, archangels;** St. Gabriella; St. Theodota; St. Dadas; St. Fraternus; St. Garcia; St. Grimoaldus; St. Gudelia; St. Liutwin; St. Ludwin; Blessed Richard Rolle de Hampole; St. Rhipsime; St. Quiriacus.

30 — **St. Jerome;** St. Gregory the Enlightener; SS. Victor and Ursus; St. Enghenedl; St. Laurus; St. Leopardus; St. Midan.

October

1 — **St. Therese of Lisieux;** St. Remigius; St. Bavo; St. Aretas and companions; SS. Verissimus, Maximus, and Julia; St. Virila; Blessed Caspar Fisogiro; St. Dodo; Blessed Edward Campion; Blessed Edward James; St. Fidharleus; Blessed John Robinson; Blessed Robert Widmerpool; Blessed Robert Wilcox; St. Ralph Crockett; St. Romanus the Melodist; St. Melorius; St. Piaton; SS. Abreha and Atzbeha (Aizan and Sazana).

2 — **Holy Guardian Angels;** St. Leger; St. Beregisius; St. Theophilus; St. Eleutherius; Blessed Francis Chakichi; St. Gerinus; St. Leodegarius; St. Leudomer; Blessed Louis Chakichi; Blessed Lucy Chakichi.

3 — St. Adalgott; St. Widradus; St. Candidus; St. Cyprian; St. Dionysius; St. Ebontius; SS. Ewald and Ewald; St. Gerard Miles; St. Hesychius; St. Maximian; St. Menna.

4 — St. Francis of Assisi; St. Adauctus; St. Ammon; St. Aurea; SS. Crispus and Gaius; St. Domnina; St. Hierotheus; St. Mark; St. Quintius; St. Peter of Damascus; St. Petronius.

5 — St. Flora; St. Faustina; St. Flavia; St. Alexander; St. Apollinaris; St. Attilanus; St. Aymard; St. Boniface; Blessed William Hartley; St. Thraseas; Blessed Francis Xavier Seelos; St. Charitina; SS. Firmatus and Flaviana; St. Galla; St. Magdalevus; Blessed Raymond of Capua; Blessed Robert Sutton; St. Meinuph; St. Palmatius; St. Placid.

6 — St. Bruno; Blessed Marie Rose Durocher; St. Faith; Blessed Adalbero; St. Aurea; St. Sagar; St. Ceollach; St. Epiphania; St. Francis Trung; St. Magnus; St. Maria Francesca Gallo; St. Nicetas; Martyrs of Trier; St. Pardulphus.

7 — *Our Lady of the Holy Rosary;* St. Artaldus; St. Sergius; St. Justina of Padua; St. Adalgis; St. Apuleius; SS. Sergius and Bacehus; St. Canog; St. Dubtach; St. Helanus; St. Mark; St. Osyth; St. Palladius.

8 — St. Keyne; St. Pelagia; St. Amor of Aquitaine; St. Badilo; St. Benedicta; St. Ywi; St. Thais; St. Triduna; St. Demetrius; St. Reparata; St. Martin Cid; St. Nestor; Blessed Matthew de Eskandely; SS. Palatias and Laurentia; Blessed Peter of Seville.

9 — SS. Denis, Rusticus, and Eleutherius; St. John Leonardi; Blessed Gunther; St. Ghislain; St. Louis Bertrand; St. Alfanus; St. Andronicus; St. Theodoric of Emden; St. Sabinus; St. Demetrius; St. Deusdedit; St. Dionysius; St. Domninus; St. Geminus; St. Goswin; SS. Lambert and Valerius.

10 — St. Francis Borgia; St. Cerbonius; St. Aldericus; St. Tanca; St. Victor and companions; St. Cassius; St. Daniel; St. Fulk; St. Gercon; St. Maharsapor; St. Patricain; St. Paulinus of Capua; St. Paulinus of York; St. Pinytus.

11 — St. Kenneth; St. Canice; St. Gummarus; St. Alexander Sauli; St. Anastasius V; St. Ansillo; St. Tharacus; St. Sarmata; St. Ethelburga; St. Firminus of Uzes; St. John of Bridlington; St. Juliana of Pavilly; St. Nectarius; St. Peter Tuy; St. Placidia.

12 — St. Wilfrid; St. Edwin; St. Amicus; St. Salvinus; St. Seraphinus; Blessed Camillus Constanzi; St. Domnina; St. Edistius; St. Fiace; SS. Felix and Cyprian; St. Heribert; St. Maximillian of Lorch; St. Monas; St. Pantalus.

13 — St. Edward the Confessor; St. Agilbert; St. Berthoald; St. Venantius; St. Theophilus; St. Carpus; St. Chelidonia; St. Colman of Stockerau; St. Comgan; St. Fyncana; St. Faustus; St. Regimbald; St. Romulus; St. Maurice of Camoet.

14 — Pope St. Callistus I; St. Burkard; St. Calixtus; St. Angadresma; St. Bernard of Arce; St. Burchard; SS. Saturninus and Lupus; St. Carponius; St. Dominic Loricatus; St. Donatian; St. Fortunata; St. Fortunatus of Todi; St. Manakus; St. Manechildis; St. Rusticus; St. Menehould.

15 — St. Teresa of Avila; Blessed Victoria Strata; St. Severus; St. Agileus; St. Antiochus; St. Aurelia; St. Thecla of Kitzingen; St. Sabinus; St. Callistus; St. Cannatus; St. Fortunatus; St. Leonard Vandoeuvre.

16 — St. Gerard Majella; St. Hedwig; St. Margaret Mary Alacoque; St. Maxima; St. Ambrose; St. Balderic; St. Baldwin; St. Bercharius; St. Bertrand of Comminges; St. Vitalis; St. Saturninus and companions; St. Conogon; St. Dulcidius; St. Eliphius; St. Eremberta; St. Florentius of Trier; St. Junian; St. Kiara; St. Lull; St. Magnobodus; St. Mummolinus.

17 — St. Ignatius of Antioch; St. John the Dwarf; St. Anstrudis; St. Berarius; St. Victor; SS. Victor, Alexander, and Marianus; St. Colman of Kilroot; St. Florentius; St. Francis Isidore Gagelin; St. Herodion; St. Louthiem; St. Mamelta; St. Marie Magdalen Desjardin; St. Regulus; St. Richard Gwyn; St. Rudolph of Gubbio; St. Nothlem.

18 — St. Luke the Evangelist; St. Justus of Beauvais; St. Asclepiades; St. Athenodorus; St. Tryphonia; St. Gwen; St. Kevoca; St. Monon.

19 — St. Isaac Jorgues; St. John de Brebeuf; St. Paul of the Cross; St. Charles Garnier; St. Laura; St. Altinus; St. Anthony Daniel; St. Aquilinus; St. Beronicus; St. Varus; St. Veranus; St. Theofrid; St. Cleopatra; St. Desiderius; St. Eadnot; St. Frideswide; St. Lupus of Soissons; St. Philip Howard.

20 — Blessed Adeline; St. Artemius; St. Usthazanes; St. Acca; St. Adelina; St. Aderald; St. Barsabas; St. Bernard of Bagnorea; St. Bertilla Boscardin; St. Vitalis; St. Caprasius; Blessed Francis Serrano; St. Martha; St. Maximus of Aquila.

21 — St. Viator; St. Ursula; St. Hilarion; St. Condedus; St. Agatho; St. Astericus; St. Berthold; St. Tuda; St. Wendolinus; St. Cilinia; St. Dasius; St. Gebizo; St. Hugh of Ambronay; St. Maichus; St. Maurontus.

22 — Blessed Alix Le Clercq; St. Abercius Marcellus; SS. Alexander, Heraclins, and companions; St. Alodia; St. Benedict of Macerac; St. Bertharius; St. Verecundus; St. Donatus of Fiesole; St. Mark; St. Nepotian; St. Nunctus; St. Mary Salome; St. Mellon; St. Moderan; St. Philip; St. Philip of Heraclea.

23 — St. John of Capistrano; St. Allucio; St. Amo; St. Benedict of Sebaste; St. Verus; St. Theodoret of Antioch; Blessed Thomas Thwing; SS. Servandus and Cermanus; St. Severinus; St. Severinus Boethius; St. Clether; St. Domitius; St. Elfleda; St. John of Syracuse; Blessed Joseph Leroux; St. Leothade; St. Oda; St. Romanus of Rouen; St. Maroyeus; St. Paul Tong Buong.

24 — St. Anthony Mary Claret; St. Bernard of Calvo; St. Senoch; St. Cadfarch; St. Fromundus; St. Felix; St. Joseph Thi; St. Marcius; St. Martin of Vertou; Martyrs of Nagran.

25 — SS. Crispin and Crispinian; St. Chrysanthus; St. Daria; St. Fronto; St. Tabitha; St. Cyrinus; St. Dulcardus; SS. Fronto and George; St. Fructus; St. Goeznoveus; St. Guesnoveus; St. Hilary; St. Hildemarca; St. Lupus of Bayeux; St. Minias.

26 — St. Bean; St. Evaristus; St. Albinus; St. Alfred the Great; St. Cuthbert; St. Eadfrid; St. Fulk; St. Gibitrudis; St. Lucian; St. Rogatian; St. Rusticus; St. Quadragesimus.

27 — St. Abraham the Poor; St. Abban of Murnevin; St. Frumentius; SS. Vincent, Sabina, and Christeta; St. Capitolina; St. Desiderius; St. Elesbaan; St. Florentius; St. Gaudiosus; St. Namatius; St. Odhran; St. Abraham the Poor, or Abraham the Child; St. Abuna (Frumentius).

28 — **St. Jude Thaddaeus;** St. Simon the Zealot; St. Abraham; St. Anastasia II; St. Anglinus; St. Salvius; St. Eadsin; St. Ferrutius; St. Fidelis of Como; St. Godwin; St. Honoratus of Vercelli; St. John Dat; St. Remigius.

29 — St. Narcissus; St. Abraham of Rostov; St. Anne; St. Bond; St. Zenobius; St. Terence of Metz; St. Theodore; St. Colman of Kilmacduagh; St. Donatus of Corfu; Douai Martyrs; St. Elfleda; St. Eusebia; St. Hyacinth; St. John of Autun; St. Kennera; St. Maximilian.

30 — St. Herbert; Blessed Angelus of Acri; St. Alphonsus Rodriguez; St. Arilda; St. Artemas; St. Talacrian; SS. Zenobius and Zenobia; St. Theonestus; St. Saturninus; St. Serapion; St. Dorothy of Montau; Blessed John Slade; St. Macarius; St. Maximus.

31 — St. Quentin; St. Antoninus; St. Amulf; St. Bega; St. Wolfgang; St. Notburga; St. Abaidas (known as Abadias).

November

1 — *All Saints Day;* St. Amabilis; St. Austremonius; St. Valentine Berrio-Ochoa; St. Vigor; St. Salaun; St. Severinus; St. Cadfan; St. Caesarius and companions; SS. Caesarius and Julian; St. Ceitho; SS. Cyrenia and Juliana; St. Dingad; St. Floribert; SS. John and James; St. Licinius; St. Mary the Slave; St. Mathurin; St. Pabiali; Blessed Paul Navarro; Blessed Peter Onizuko; St. Acha the Confessor.

2 — *All Souls in Purgatory;* St. Maura; St. Acyndinus; St. Arnicus; St. Victorinus of Pettau; St. Theodotus; St. Carterius; Blessed John Bodey; St. Jorandus; St. Justus of Trieste; St. Marcian.

3 — St. Martin de Porres; St. Winifred; St. Acepsimas; St. Vulganius; DSaisnt Valentinian; SS. Valentine and Hilary; St. Cristiolus; St. Domnus of Vienne; St. Elerius; St. Englatius; St. Florus; St. Germanus; St. Guenhael; St. Hermengaudis; St. Hubert; St. Malachy O'More; St. Quaratus; St. Papulus; St. Peter Francis Neron; St. Pirmin.

4 — St. Charles Borromeo; St. Clarus; St. Birrstan; St. Vitalis; St. Emeric; St. Joannicus; SS. Nicander and Hermas; St. Modesta; SS. Philologus and Patrobas; St. Pierius.

5 — St. Elizabeth; St. Sylvia; St. Bertilia; St. Dominator; St. Domninus; St. Fibitius; St. Galation; SS. Felix and Eusebius; St. Laetus; St. Magnus.

6 — St. Leonard; St. Atticus; St. Barlaam; St. Winoc; St. Demetrian; St. Edwen; St. Efflam; St. Felix of Fondi; St. Felix of Thynissa; St. Joseph Khang; St. Leonard of Noblac; St. Leonard of Reresby; St. Leonianus; St. Pinnock.

7 — St. Ernest; St. Achillas; St. Amarand; St. Amaranthus; Blessed Anthony Baldinucci; St. Auctus; St. Blinlivet; St. Vincent Liem; St. Willibrord; St. Tremorus; St. Cumgar; St. Engelbert; St. Florentius of Strasbourg; St. Gebetrude; St. Hieron; St. Hyacinth Castaneda; St. Rufus of Metz; St. Melasippus; Blessed Peter Ou.

8 — St. Castorius; St. Wiomad; St.s Tysilio; St. Cybi; St. Pope Deusdedit; Four Crowned Martyrs; St. John Baptist Con; DSt. Joseph Nghi; St. Martin Tho; St. Martin Tinh; St. Moroc; St. Paul Ngan; St. Willehad.

9 — Dedication of Basilica of St. John Lateran; St. Agrippinus; St. Alexander; St. Benignus; St. Vitonus; St. Ursinus; St. Theodore Tyro; SS. Eustolia and Soprata; St. Orestes; St. Pabo.

10 — Pope St. Leo the Great; St. Aedh MacBricc; St. Theoctiste; St. Tiberius; SS. Trypbaena and Tryphosa; St. Tryphon; St. Demetrius; St. Elaeth; St. Guerembaldus; St. John of Ratzeburg; Justus of Canterbury; St. Leo of Melun; St. Monitor.

11 — St. Martin of Tours; St. Theodore; St. Athenodorus; St. Bartholomew of Rossano; St. Bertuin; St. Veranus; St. Theodore of Studites; St. Cynfran; St. Joseph Pignatelli; St. Rhediw; St. Mennas; St. Menuas; St. Aba Mina.

12 — St. Josaphat of Polotsk; St. Anastasius XIX; St. Astericus; St. Benedict and companions; St. Ymar; St. Cadwallader; St. Cummian Fada; St. Emilian Cucullatus; St. Lebuin; St. Livinus; St. Machar; St. Renatus; SS. Rufus and Avignon; DSt. Namphasius; St. Nilus the Elder; St. Paternus; St. Patiens.

13 — St. Frances Xavier (Mother) Cabrini; St. Homobonus; St. Brice; St. Didacus; St. Abbo; St. Arcadius and companions; St. Caillin; St. Chillien; St. Columba; St. Dalmatius; St. Devinicus; St. Gredifael; St. Quintian; St. Maxellendis; St. Mitrius.

14 — St. Lawrence; St. Alberic; St. Venaranda; St. Serapion; St. Clementinus; St. Dubricus; St. Hypatius; St. Jucundus of Bologna; St. Lawrence O'Toole; St. Modanic.

15 — St. Albert the Great; St. Zachary; St. Leopold; St. Abibas; St. Amulf; St. Zachariah; SS. Secundus, Fidentian, and Varicus; St. Desiderius; St. Findan; St. Gaius of Korea; St. Hugh Faringdon, Blessed; St. Hugh Green, Blessed; Blessed John Eynon; Blessed John Rugg; Blessed John Thorne; St. Luperius; St. Machudd; St. Malo; Blessed Richard Whiting; Blessed Roger James; St. Paduinus.

16 — St. Gertrude; St. Margaret of Scotland; St. Gratia; Blessed Gratia; St. Agnes of Assisi; St. Othmar; St. Afan; St. Africus; St. Agnes of Assisi; St. Alfrick; St. Elpidius; St. Fidentius; St. Gobrain; St. Joseph Moscati; St. Rufinus.

17 — St. Elizabeth of Hungary; SS. Valentine and Dubatitus; St. Hugh of Lincoln; St. Roque Gonzalez de Santa Cruz; St. Hugh; St. Gregory Thaumaturgus; St. Hilda; St. Acisclus; St. Alphaeus; St. Anianus; Blessed Salomea; St. Dionysius of Alexandria; St. Hugh of Noara; St. Namasius; Martyrs of Paraguay.

18 — Dedication of the Basilicas of SS. Peter and Paul; St. Rose Philippine Duchesne; St. Odo; St. Anselm; St. Thomas of Antioch; St. Hesychius of Antioch; Blessed John Shoun; St. Keverne; St. Leonard Kimura; SS. Romanus and Barula; St. Nazarius; St. Oriculus and companions; St. Mawes; St. Maximus; St. Mummolus.

19 — St. Atto; St. Azas and companions; St. Barlaam; SS. Severinus, Exuperius, and Felician; St. Crispin; St. Faustus; St. James of Sasseau; St. Nerses the Great; St. Maximus; St. Medana; St. Mechtildis of Helfta.

20 — St. Bernward; St. Ampelus; St. Autbodus; St. Bassus and companions; St. Benignus; St. Dasius; St. Edmund Rich; St. Edmund the Martyr; St. Felix of Valois; St. Francis Xavier Can; St. Leo of Nonantula; St. Nerses; SS. Octavius, Solutor, and Adventor; St. Maxentia of Beauvais.

21 — *Presentation of the Virgin Mary;* St. Gelasius; St. Albert of Louvain; St. Amelberga; St. Digain; St. Heliodorus; St. Hilary; St. Rufus of Rome; St. Maurus.

22 — St. Cecilia; St. Tigridia; St. Devniolin; St. Lucretia; SS. Mark and Stephen; St. Maurus.

23 — Pope St. Clement I; St. Columban; Blessed Miguel Pro; St. Amphilocus; St. Wilfretrudis; St. Trudo; St. Rachilidis; St. Paternian; St. Paulhen.

24 — St. Andrew Dun-Lac; St. Colman of Cloyne; St. Chrysogonus; St. Alexander; St. Anthony Nam-Quynh; St. Bieuzy; St. Vincent Diem; Blessed Thaddeus Lieu; St. Crescentian; Dominican Martyrs of Vietnam; St. Eanfleda; St. Firmina; SS. Flora and Mary; St. Felicissimus; St. Kenan; Blessed Lawrence PeMan; St. Leopardinus; St. Marinus; St. Romanus of Le Mans; Martyrs of the Dominican Order in Vietnam; Martyrs of Vietnam; St. Peter Domoulin Bori; Peter Khoa and Vincent Diem.

25 — St. Catherine Laboure; St. Catherine of Alexandria; St. Alnoth; St. Jucunda; St. Mercurius; St. Mesrop; St. Moses.

26 — St. Conrad; St. John Berchmans; St. Alypius; St. Amator; St. Basolus; St. Bellinus; St. Dominic Doan Xuyen; St. Faustus; St. Leonard of Port Maurice; St. Martin of Arades; St. Nicon; St. Peter of Alexandria; St. Phileas.

27 — St. James Intercisus; St. Secundis; St. Acacius; St. Acharius; Blessed Alexius Nakamura; Blessed Anthony Kimura; St. Apollinaris; Blessed Bartholomew Sheki; St. Basileus and companions; St. Bilhild; St. Valerian; St. Virgilius; Blessed Thomas Kotenda and companions; St. Seachnall; St. Severinus; St. Fergus; St. Gallgo; St. John Angeloptes; Blessed John Ivanango and John Montajana; Blessed Leo Nakanishi; Blessed Romanus; Blessed Matthias Kosaka and Matthias Nakano; St. Maximus of Reiz; Blessed Michael Takeshita.

28 — St. James of the Marches; St. Andrew Trong; St. Valerian; St. Fionnchu; St. Hippolytus; St. James Thompson, Blessed; St. Rufus and companions; St. Papinianus.

29 — St. Brendan of Birr; St. Sadwen; SS. Saturninus and Sisinius; St. Cuthbert Mayne; Blessed Dionysius; St. Egelwine; St. Gulstan; St. Hardoin; St. Radbod; St. Paramon and companions; St. Philomenus.

30 — St. Andrew the Apostle; St. Zosimus; St. Trojan; St. Tudwal; St. Constantius; St. Joseph Marchand; St. Maura.

December

1 — St. Eligius; St. Edmund Campion; St. Agericus; Blessed Alexander Briant; St. Ananias; St. Ansanus; St. Ursicinus; St. Candres; St. Castritian; St. Constantian; SS. Diodorus and Marianus; St. Grwst; Blessed John Beche; St. Leontius; Blessed Richard Langley; St. Natalia; St. Olympiades.

2 — St. Bibiana; St. Chromatius; St. Lupus of Verona; St. Pontian.

3 — **St. John Francis Xavier;** St. Abbo; St. Agricola; St. Attalia; St. Birinus; St. Cassian; Blessed Edward Coleman; St. Eloque; St. Lucius; St. Mirocles.

4 — **St. John Damascene;** St. Francis Xavier; St. Ada; St. Anno; St. Bernard degli Uberti; St. Bertoara; St. Theophane Venard; St. Theophanes and companions; St. Clement of Alexandria; St. Felix of Bologna; St. Francis Galvez; St. Osmund; St. Maruthas; St. Meletius; St. Abba Isa.

5 — St. Gerald; St. Anastasius; St. Sabas; St. Basilissa; St. Bassus; St. Cawrdaf; St. Crispina; St. Dalmatius; St. Firminus; St. Galagnus; St. Gerbold; St. John Almond; St. John the Wonder-Worker; St. Julius; St. Nicetius; St. Nicholas Tavigli; St. Pelinus.

6 — **St. Nicholas;** St. Dionysia; St. Abraham of Kratia; St. Asella; St. Majoricus; St. Peter Pascual; St. Polychronius.

7 — **St. Ambrose;** St. Victor of Piacenza; St. Servus; St. Anianas; St. Maria Giuseppe Rossello; Martyrs of Africa; SS. Polycarp and Theodore.

8 — ***Immaculate Conception of Mary;*** St. Romaric; St. Macarius; St. Patapius.

9 — **St. Juan Diego;** St. Balda; St. Budoc; St. Valeria; St. Cyprian; St. Ethelgiva; St. Francis Fasani; St. Gorgonia; St. John Roberts; St. Julian of Apamea; St. Leocadia; St. Restitutus; Martyrs of Samosata; Martyrs of Saragossa; St. Peter; St. Peter Fourier.

10 — **Pope St. Gregory III;** St. Eulalia of Merida; St. Thomas of Farfa; Blessed Thomas Somers; Blessed Sebastian Montanol; SS. Carpophorus and Abundius; St. Deusdedit; St. Edmund Genings; St. Florentius of Carracedo; St. Gemellus; St. Guitmarus; St. Hildemar; Blessed John Mason; St. Julia of Merida; St. Lucerius; St. Mennas; St. Mercurius; Blessed Peter Tecelano; St. Peter Duong; St. Polydore Plasden.

11 — **Pope St. Damasus I;** St. Daniel the Stylite; St. Damasus; St. Barsabas; St. Victoricus; Fuscian and Gentian; St. Trason; St. Sabinus; St. Cian; St. Fidweten; St. Pens; St. Acepsius.

12 — ***Our Lady of Guadalupe;*** St. Corentin; St. Abra; St. Agatha; St. Alexander; St. Ammonaria; St. Vicelin; Blessed Thomas Holland; St. Colman of Glendalough; St. Corentius; St. Edburga; St. Finian of Clonard; St. Hermogenes; St. Maxentius.

13 — **St. Lucy;** St. Jodoc; St. Autbert; St. Edburga; SS. Einhildis and Roswinda; St. Elizabeth Rose.

14 — **St. John of the Cross;** St. Jucundus; St. Agnellus; St. Bartholomew Buonpedoni; St. Venantius Fortunatus; St. Viator; St. Drusus; St. Fingar; St. Heron; SS. Justus and Abundius; St. Nicasius; St. Matronian; St. Pompeius.

15 — St. Mary Di Rosa; St. Adalbero; St. Urbitius; St. Valerian; St. Florentius; St. Nino; St. Maximus; St. Paul of Latros.

16 — St. Ado of Vienne; St. Albina; St. Beoc; St. Valentine; Blessed Raynald de Bar; St. Nicholas Chrysoberges.

17 — St. Begga; St. John of Martha; St. Olympias; St. Briarch; St. Wivina; St. Tydecho; St. Eigil; St. Florian; St. Maxentiolus.

18 — St. Flannan; St. Rufus; St. Auxentius; St. Bodagisil; St. Victurus; St. Winebald; SS. Theotimus and Basilian; St. Samthan; St. Desideratus; St. Gatian; SS. Rufus and Zosimus; St. Quintus; St. Moses; St. Paul My; St. Peter Truat; St. Adjutor.

19 — St. Augustine Moi; St. Bernard Valeara; St. Thomas De and companions; St. Darius; St. Dominich Uy; Blessed Francis Man; St. Francis Xavier Mau; St. Fausta; St. Manirus; St. Ribert; St. Nemesius; SS. Meuris and Thea.

20 — St. Ammon; St. Ursicinus; St. Dominic of Brescia; St. Dominic of Silos; St. Julius; SS. Liberatus and Bajulus; Blessed Peter de la Cadireta; St. Peter Thi; St. Philogonius.

21 — **St. Peter Canisius;** Blessed Adrian; St. Anastasius XII; St. Andrew Dung Lac; St. Themistoeles; St. Severinus; St. Glycerius; St. Honoratus of Toulouse; SS. John and Festus; St. John Vincent.

22 — St. Amaswinthus; St. Zeno; St. Chaeromon; St. Demetrius; St. Flavian; St. Hunger.

23 — **St. John of Kanty;** St. Servulus; St. Victoria; St. Vintila; St. Theodulus; St. Dagobert II; St. John Cantius; Martyrs of Crete; St. Nicholas Factor; SS. Migdonius and Mardonius.

24 — St. Adele; St. Emiliana; St. Adela; St. Tarsilla; St. Venerandus; St. Caranus; St. Delphinus; St. Lucian.

25 — *Nativity of the Lord;* St. Eugenia; St. Adalsindis; St. Anastasia III; St. Alburga; Blessed Michael Nakashima.

26 — St. Stephen Protomartyr; St. Vincentia Maria Lopez Y Vicuna; St. Neol Chabanel; St. Amaethlu; St. Archelaus; St. Zeno; St. Zosimus; St. Tatha; St. Theodore the Sacrist; St. Pope Dionysius; St. Marinus; St. Abadiu.

27 — St. John the Apostle and Evangelist; St. Fabiola; SS. Theodore and Theophanes; St. Nicarete; St. Maximus.

28 — Holy Innocents; St. Anthony the Hermit; St. Troadius; St. Caesarius; St. Castor; St. Domnio; SS. Eutychius and Domitian; SS. Romulus and Conindrus; St. Maughold.

29 — St. Thomas Becket; St. Aileran; St. Albert of Gambron; Blessed William Howard; St. Trophimus; St. Trophimus of Arles; SS. Callistus, Felix, and Boniface; St. Dominic; St. Ebrulf.

30 — St. Anysia; St. Anysius; St. Sabinus; St. Egwin; Blessed John Alcober; St. Liberius; St. Mansuetus; St. Raynerius.

31 — Pope St. Sylvester; St. Melania; St. Barbatian; St. Zoticus; SS. Sabinian and Potentian; St. Columba of Sens; St. Donata; St. Hermes; St. Offa.

Index

· ·

Notes